# THE TOLERANCE TRAP

THE TOLERANCE TRAP

SUZANNA DANUTA WALTERS

# THE

# TOLERANCE

# TRAP

*How God, Genes, and Good Intentions*
*Are Sabotaging Gay Equality*

NEW YORK UNIVERSITY PRESS
*New York and London*

NEW YORK UNIVERSITY PRESS
New York and London
www.nyupress.org

First published in paperback in 2016

References to Internet websites (URLs) were accurate at the time of writing.
Neither the author nor New York University Press is responsible for URLs
that may have expired or changed since the manuscript was prepared.

Library of Congress Cataloging-in-Publication Data
Walters, Suzanna Danuta.
The tolerance trap : how God, genes, and good intentions are sabotaging
gay equality / Suzanna Danuta Walters.
pages cm
Includes bibliographical references and index.
ISBN 978-0-8147-7057-3 (hardback)
ISBN 978-1-4798-1193-9 (paperback)
1. Gay rights. 2. Tolerance. 3. Equality. I. Title.
HQ76.5.W35 2014
323.3'264—dc23          2013045557

New York University Press books are printed on acid-free paper,
and their binding materials are chosen for strength and durability.
We strive to use environmentally responsible suppliers and materials
to the greatest extent possible in publishing our books.

Manufactured in the United States of America

10 9 8 7 6 5 4 3 2 1

Also available as an ebook

*For my fabulous daughter, Emma*
*and in memory of my equally fabulous mother, Marianne*

I'm not willing to just be tolerated. That wounds my love of love and of liberty.

—Jean Cocteau

# CONTENTS

# The B Side: Gay Rights
# after Gay Marriage

In our shape-shifty culture, where reality TV stars morph into politicians faster than you can say "You're fired!" it is hard to keep up with the warp and woof of all things gay. In the eighteen months since this book first came out, any number of significant events have stirred the rainbow waters. Olympic superathlete and Kardashian clan member Bruce Jenner transitioned to Caitlyn and became the symbol—alongside *Orange Is the New Black* breakout star Laverne Cox—of a "transgender tipping point." The Boy Scouts finally changed their policy to allow gay adult leaders (although not if the troop is church-sponsored), Amazon series *Transparent* won an Emmy, and the CEO of Silicon Valley's largest company—Apple—came out. After years of protest and lawsuits, gay groups marched for the first time in New York's St. Patrick's Day Parade, the White House introduced the first gender-neutral bathroom, pop star and erstwhile ne'er-do-well Miley Cyrus told us she's "gender fluid," and gorgeous tattooed model Ruby Rose became the cover girl that launched a thousand "girl crushes." President Obama's 2015 State of the Union address contained three references to gay rights, as did his final one in 2016, he signed into law a number of executive orders protecting LGBT federal workers and providing for equal treatment for gays seeking asylum, and he has vigorously supported a Civil Rights Act to ban discrimination against LGBT folks. Cate

Blanchett starred as a sultry lesbian seducer in the closeted but oh-so-sexy 1950s melodrama *Carol* and queer characters have populated hot TV series such as *Empire* and *How to Get Away with Murder*. *Fun Home*—quite possibly the queerest Broadway musical ever (take that *Cats!*)—swept the Tony's and garnered accolades across the board. Indeed, the increasingly complex and integrated forms of queer representation in popular culture is enough to cheer the soul of even the most cynical cultural critic, myself included. Queerness abounds: not just through the groundbreaking performances in *Transparent* or *Fun Home*, but through ordinary forms of sexual nonconformity that slip into every nook and cranny of cultural expression, from the sexually adventurous lesbian sister in *Jane the Virgin* to out referees at macho team sports events and gorgeous gay dads braiding their daughter's hair on viral YouTube videos.

On the flip side, and there is always a flip side, the story of the victorious forward march to a queer-friendly future was revealed to have more than a few twisty plot lines. While transgender media stars reveled in their newfound visibility, the homicide rate for trans folks hit a historic high, with trans women of color bearing most of the brunt of the violence. In twenty-eight states, it is still legal to discriminate against LGBT people in the areas of employment, housing, and public accommodation, same-sex adoption laws still vary by state, and the Houston Anti-Discrimination Ordinance (dubbed the "bathroom bill" by opponents) was soundly defeated.[1] Kim Davis—the Kentucky clerk who launched a thousand tweets when she refused to issue marriage licenses to same-sex couples and was found in contempt of court—is only the most dramatic character in a ramped-up backlash against the Supreme Court marriage decision. While she may be the most annoying (and bizarre), more damaging in the long run are the plethora of religious-exemption laws (known as Religious Freedom Restoration Acts, or RFRAs) working their way through state and federal branches. And of course recent anti-gay and anti-trans state laws passed in North Carolina and Mississippi have only upped the backlash ante.

But back to "our side": the biological determinism that framed contemporary gay rights discourse has become even more entrenched as the law of the land and the "rational" voice of good thinking liberal allies and savvy homosexuals. As I toured the country speaking about this book, my arguments against the "born this way" doctrine came under the most intense fire—from bookstore attendees at readings, from interviewers, and most virulently from the emails and letters I received that assured me I was "worse than Hitler" for suggesting that biological arguments for sexual desires and identities were both bad science and bad politics. Some critics were more benign, acceding to the tendentiousness of the biological arguments but arguing that their political effectiveness outweighed their potential dangers. But more were deeply committed to the idea that this "thing" called sexual identity (as if it were a "thing") was determined in ways both simple and profound by organic processes (genes, neurons, hormones) wholly detached from either individual agency or social forces. When I began my research for *The Tolerance Trap*, I had no idea how pervasive this ideology was, nor how far-reaching its implications. After decades of social constructionist arguments about sexuality, gender, race, and just about everything else, it was both shocking and disheartening to see so many (including activists and academics) come under the sway of biological determinist rhetoric. It was as if activists believed we couldn't "win" without arguing that we had no volition and theorists believed we couldn't understand deeply felt desire and identity without recourse to immutability.

If anything, I underestimated the reach of the "born this way" discourse and its tenacity even in the face of critical investigation. But the arguments I make in this book—both the larger one about the limits of "tolerance" for advancing a robust version of social belonging and the allied ones about marriage, immutability, and associated discourses that both undergirded and displayed the "tolerance trap"—are ones I stand by without hesitation. There are two, connected, questions that seem urgent to me now. The first is whether the movement, for years so focused on marriage equality, will now "pivot." And the related question concerns the content of that pivot: will "tolerance" remain the defining discourse, underwritten by claims to biological determinism and insistence that we are "just like you?" Or will that pivot reimagine queer politics, queer identity, queer belonging along lines that open up and challenge tired ways of doing intimacy, kinship, social movements?

And what of marriage? It was clear to me even as I finished writing this book that it was simply a matter of time before the Supreme Court would rule positively. Indeed, states were falling "our" way like dominos, and lower court rulings seemed to point the way to a positive SCOTUS decision. But even though many were optimistic, it did come as a welcome surprise when, on June 26, 2015, the Supreme Court ruled definitively in *Obergefell v. Hodges*, making same-sex marriage the law of the land and linking the Unites States with the twenty or so other countries in which same-sex marriage was fully legal. It would be churlish and, moreover, dishonest to say I was not moved. As a civil rights victory, it was momentous and am I decidedly *not* of the opinion that gaining access to institutions formerly segregated is simply making a (pink) silk purse out of a sow's ear. Real people will gain real benefits from this decision, and not just rich white gays but all sorts of lesbians and gays who want to be on their partner's health insurance, who want to be recognized as a legal parent without the humiliation (and cost) of "adopting" their progeny, who want to receive their partners' Social Security benefits and would face poverty if they couldn't, who want to live with their lover from another country. These are just a few of the very substantial shifts in the lives of those formerly excluded from an institution they desire to enter. They are not to be minimized.

To so many, though, the narrative was now neatly wrapped up: if Stonewall was the raucous riot that launched a robust social movement, then the SCOTUS decision was the composed acquiescence to the dreams and aspirations embodied in that movement. No surprise, I am not overly fond of such linear progress narratives: both the notion of Stonewall as originating event and

SCOTUS as logical endpoint are organization-generated and media-friendly über-stories that push aside the messy complications of a movement that has many histories, many goals, and much internal dissent. So what difference does a Supreme Court decision make? Does the decisive victory of the *Obergefell* decision in the summer of 2015 mean that the era of (real) queer integration and freedom is now at hand? Or does it mean that the era of same-sex marriage is (simply) here?

Clearly, if marriage is your cup of tea or, more to the point, your pièce de résistance, then the movement has essentially done its job. Whatever one thinks of foregrounding marriage as the ultimate gay rights issue (and my opinion on this should be clear), one has to marvel at the magisterial political organizing and strategic work done to get to the June decision. The combination of state-based campaigns with savvy legal maneuvering and a robust effort at altering public opinion is a model other issue-based campaigns would do well to follow. But single-issue-based it is, and that is precisely its success and its limitation. In a piece in the *Atlantic* covering the success of the marriage movement, these tactics are approvingly relayed, including the strategy of shifting hearts and minds by focusing on . . . hearts. Or, as journalist Molly Ball says in that piece, the organizers won over voters by redirecting the campaign "from an argument about the rights and benefits of marriage to one about the fundamental human desire for love and commitment" in order to *"make an emotional argument based on positive values."*[2]

When I wrote this book, I was worried that putting marriage front and center would not only dull our movement to the vibrancy of queer difference but would set up further hierarchies of good (married) gays deserving of social inclusion and approval and those gays further placed outside the perimeters of legitimacy. The marriage campaign's strategies—delineated in the *Atlantic* article and any number of other postmortems—may have been successful, but part of that success was dependent upon a re-framing of gay rights as a warm and fuzzy Disney romance, with that magic kiss bestowed upon loving couples because, in the flowery language of Justice Kennedy's decision for the court in *Obergefell v. Hodges*, "No union is more profound than marriage, for it embodies the highest ideals of love, fidelity, devotion, sacrifice, and family. In forming a marital union, two people become something greater than once they were."[3] And lead attorney Mary L. Bonauto opened her oral argument by claiming that,

> the intimate and committed relationships of same-sex couples, just like those of heterosexual couples, provide mutual support and are the foundation of family life in our society. If a legal commitment, responsibility and protection that is marriage is off limits to gay people as a class, the stain of unworthiness that follows on individuals and families contravenes the basic constitutional commitment to equal dignity.[4]

So we are to be compared to heterosexuals, marriage is the foundation of family life, and we carry a presumably nasty stain if we aren't allowed access to it. I'm glad we won, for sure, but the elevation of marriage to a sanctified throne of legitimate intimacy ignores not only the history of the institution (coverture, ownership of women and children, cradle of gender training, site of terrible violence and abuse) but promulgates the (falsely) transcendent over the prosaic but more ethical argument for simple equity.

It is still too early to discern the broader effects of marriage equality. While it unquestionably won't usher in some grand and complete era of queer freedom, it just may shift the ground in ways we can't know in advance. Yes, it may continue the complicated and not wholly pernicious process of normalization and assimilation. But it might also, first, allow minds and hearts and resources to shift to other pressing matters and, second, might have salutary consequences in broadening our conceptions of what counts as family, as love, as intimacy, as kinship.

It is a testament to how central marriage has been to our collective sense (however inaccurate, however flawed) of "the movement" that editorials, articles, panels (I've been on more than I care to mention) post-*Obergefell* all ask the same question, "now what?" After this victory, what remains undone? To many, including both single-issue marriage-centered groups, such as Evan Wolfson's Freedom to Marry Project, and putatively broader-based organizations, such as New York's Empire State Pride Agenda (ESPA), the answer was clear: close up shop. Indeed, ESPA's announcement that its "work was done" raised eyebrows and sparked criticism even from those resolutely committed to the group's mainstream goals.

Too often, even when a pivot seemed on offer, organizations appeared to tick off marriage and simply move down the laundry list in a hierarchy of "issues" or rights. Marriage equality? Check. Next? Perhaps passage of the Employment Non-Discrimination Act (ENDA) or statewide nondiscrimination statutes? Given the decades-old inability to pass ENDA, some are arguing for a broader tack; immediately following the June marriage decision, a coalition of gay rights groups and their allies began work on a comprehensive bill known as the Equality Act, which, if passed, would "update" the Civil Rights Act of 1964 to add sexual orientation and gender identity to the other protected categories, effectively outlawing discrimination in housing, public accommodation, employment, and so on.

While this is gathering some momentum, prospects are slim given both the bleak history of ENDA and a Republican-controlled Congress. And while this new Equality Act may gain some traction, it appears that the more fundamental repositioning of mainstream lesbian, gay, bisexual, and transgender (LGBT) groups concerns trans rights, including enhanced legal protections and more targeted anti-violence activism. Trans rights are increasingly understood—however problematically—as the "next frontier" for "gay" rights. To cite just a few examples, the National Gay and Lesbian Task Force changed its name in 2014 to the national LGBTQ Task Force, and its website and publications reveal a strong commitment to trans rights. Even the reluctant Human Rights Campaign issued some version of an "apology" for its neglect of trans issues, and most of the large organizations—not to mention our popular media culture—seem to be engaging with some (attenuated, to be sure) version of trans inclusivity as central to a broader LGBT political agenda. The Arcus Foundation—a longtime funder of LGBT causes and historically one of the more forward-thinking of the funding organizations—plans to announce a major trans initiative to complement its work in both international and local human rights, and other groups seem to be putting more emphasis on anti-violence work, bullying prevention, homeless gay youth, and the tough question of achieving "lived equality." Still others see an increasing divide between gays living in states with a range of protections and anti-discrimination statutes and those in so-called "low equality" states (often in the South), where few protections exist. These groups are therefore considering a more geographical and regional shift in resources. And some tentative steps—generally in more localized contexts, it is true—have been made in allying gay rights to the growing movement against police brutality, known as Black Lives Matter. This is all to the good, for sure. There are encouraging signs that there is a recalibration going on.

But aspects of this approach continue to plague me. First, as we go down that list we do need to note what is *not* being checked off, what doesn't even make the list as a "gay rights" issue. What, for example, of reproductive justice? The gay movement has recognized that gender self-determination and volition—embodied most explicitly in the trans movement—are part and parcel of a broader inclusive agenda of queer freedom. This would logically lead to a rigorous and substantive commitment to reproductive rights and autonomy. If marriage was heralded as the sign of full inclusion and equal treatment, then how can women's bodily autonomy (central to *our* full inclusion and equal treatment in those self-same family institutions) not be imagined as key to that equality?

In 2014, more than seventy LGBT organizations signed an open letter to the family of Michael Brown, who was gunned down by the police in Ferguson, Missouri. This is a promising sign and one hopes it blossoms into full-fledged engagement with racial justice. But where are the letters to bombed Planned Parenthood offices? Where are the LGBT signatories condemning the murder of abortion providers? As the list of issues and concerns populates organization websites, curiously absent (with a few notable exceptions, such as the Task Force's website) is reference to women's equality, gender justice, sexual violence, abortion rights, or—god forbid—feminism.

This was not always the case. While gay and queer movements have a long and complicated history with feminist activism, the combination of marriage as the focus and biological determinism as the discursive frame has given a one-two punch to gay/feminist alliances (although, it should be noted, pretty much *all* feminist organizations explicitly support gay rights). Most critics of the mainstream gay rights movement bemoan the sexual normativity, or the lack of attention to questions of economic and racial justice. But surprisingly little has been said of the (lack of) commitment of gay rights activists to explicitly feminist concerns. I am more worried—these days—about what marriage centrality will do to what should be a queer desire: constructing a more feminist world. Both the institution of marriage and the underlying discourse of biological immutability (the "born this way" mantra) have always been, to put it mildly, a dead end for women and feminists more broadly. It is, as we are wont to say, no accident that the key concern (marriage) and key overarching trope (immutability) are at best problematic in terms of gender equity and at worst central components of what we might call the reproduction of gender-normative and even anti-feminist ways of being and doing.

Indeed, a number of critics have analyzed the frustrating reality of a successful marriage-equality movement alongside a much more vulnerable reproductive-justice movement, a situation made even more vexing given that reproductive autonomy is (arguably) more vital than marriage for human flourishing. Many would point to the legal reasoning applied to each movement. While abortion rights relied largely on privacy arguments (strongly criticized by such divergent feminist figures as Catharine McKinnon and Ruth Bader

Ginsburg), *Obergefell* made a stronger equality case. As Jill Lepore points out in a wonderful *New Yorker* piece, "privacy doctrine left reproductive rights vulnerable."[5] How very vulnerable is clearly due not only to the faulty legal reasoning that got us *Roe* but also to the rise of the religious right, for whom control of women's reproductive lives was arguably more central than maintaining heterosexual hegemony. And, as Katha Pollitt insightfully argues, reproductive rights are deeply about gender equity, sexual freedom, and women's autonomy, whereas gay marriage is all about love, romance, family values, and rainbow unicorns.[6] Marriage rights ask nothing of heterosexuals. Reproductive rights cut to the heart of patriarchal control and masculinist ideologies.

So it is of some deep concern that the "pivots" of the movement don't include a feminist call to arms, especially given that we are living in a historical context in which reproductive rights are under such concerted attack and remain out of reach for so many women. Indeed, the expansion of religious-exemption laws could be a way to finally link (relink?) queer equality and women's equality; both are under threat from and have been whittled away by laws centered on religious exemptions in right-wing attempts to push back against legislative gains for women and gays. I argued in this book that tolerance is a trap and deep integration and a renewed commitment to an expansive vision of sexual and gender liberation is the way forward. But that vision must be feminist, it must recognize that marriage equality without gender equality is (to paraphrase Anita Bryant, a notorious homophobe from the past) like a day without sunshine. But unlike marriage equality, feminism (including but not limited to reproductive justice) is not an "issue" that can be checked off a list of rights acquisitions. It is a revolution.

## Notes

1 The Houston Equal Rights Ordinance—which would have banned discrimination on the basis of sexual orientation and gender identity—was passed by the city council in May 2014 and then was on the November

ballot as Proposition 1 in 2015, after a bitter and lengthy battle to put the matter to a referendum. Opponents successfully raised the (wholly unsubstantiated) fear of sexual predation in women's bathrooms, even though the ordinance said nothing whatsoever about bathroom use! It was just one example of the forms the backlash will take.

2  Molly Ball, "What Other Activists Can Learn from the Fight for Gay Marriage," *Atlantic*, July 14, 2015, www.theatlantic.com. Emphasis in the original.

3  *Obergefell et al. v. Hodges, Director, Ohio Department of Health et al.*, 576 U.S. at 28. (2015).

4  *Obergefell et al. v. Hodges, Director, Ohio Department of Health et al.*, U.S. No. 14-562 (oral argument 04/28/2015): 4.

5  Jill Lepore, "To Have and to Hold: Reproduction, Marriage, and the Constitution," *New Yorker*, May 25, 2015, www.newyorker.com.

6  Katha Pollitt, "There's a Reason Why Gay Marriage Is Winning While Abortion Rights Are Losing, *Nation*, April 22, 2015, www.thenation. com.

# Introduction

# That's So Gay! (Or Is It?)

Ain't nothin' wrong with bein' a little gay.
Everybody's a little gay.

—Honey Boo Boo

At first glance, tolerance seems like a good thing. Really, who doesn't applaud tolerance? What individual doesn't want to be seen as tolerant? It seems to herald openness to difference and a generally broad-minded disposition. Indeed, one of the primary definitions of "tolerance" concerns sympathy or indulgence for beliefs or practices differing from or conflicting with one's own. But it is a word and a practice with a more complicated history and with real limitations. The late Middle English origins of the word indicate the ability to bear pain and hardship. In fact, some of the first uses of the word can be found in medieval pharmacology and toxicology, dealing with how much poison a body can "tolerate" before it succumbs to a foreign, poisonous substance.

In more contemporary times, we speak of a tolerance to something as the capacity to endure continued subjection to it (a plant, a drug, a minority group) without adverse reactions. We speak of people who have a high tolerance for pain or worry about a generation developing a tolerance for a certain type of antibiotic because of overuse. In more scientific usages, it refers to the allowable amount of variation of a specified quantity—the amount "let in" before the thing itself alters so fundamentally that it becomes something else and the experiment fails. So tolerance almost always implies or assumes something negative or undesired or even a variation contained and circumscribed.

It doesn't make sense to say that we tolerate something unless we think that it's wrong in some way. To say you "tolerate" homosexuality is to imply that homosexuality is bad or immoral or even just benignly icky, like that exotic food you just can't bring yourself to try. You are willing to put up with (to tolerate) this nastiness, but the toleration proves the thing (the person, the sexuality, the food) to be irredeemably nasty to begin with. But here's the rub: if there is nothing problematic about something (say, homosexuality), then there is really nothing to "tolerate." We don't speak of tolerating pleasure or a good book or a sunshine-filled day. We do, however, take pains to let others know how brave we are when we tolerate the discomfort of a bad back or a nasty cold. We tolerate the agony of a frustratingly banal movie that our partner insisted on watching and are thought the better for it. We tolerate, in other words, that which we would rather avoid. Tolerance is not an embrace but a resigned shrug or, worse, that air kiss of faux familiarity that barely covers up the shiver of disgust.

This book challenges received wisdom that asserts tolerance as the path to gay[1] rights. Most gays and their allies believe that access to marriage and the military are the brass ring of gay rights and that once we have achieved these goals we will have moved into a post-gay America. Most gays and their allies believe that gays are "born that way" and that proving biological immutability is the key to winning over reluctant heterosexuals and gaining civil rights. Most gays and their allies believe that the closet is largely a thing of the past and that we have entered a new era of sexual ease and fluidity. Most gays and their allies think that we have essentially won the culture wars and that gay visibility in popular culture is a sign of substantive gay progress. Most gays and their allies believe that gay is the new black: hip, happening, embraced. Most gays and their allies believe that if those who are anti-gay just got to know us as their PTA-going neighbors, they would love us. Most gays and their allies believe that we are almost there: we can see the end of the tunnel, where a rainbow world of warm inclusion awaits us. These people are wrong.

*The Tolerance Trap* challenges this fantasy of completion and takes a hard look at the ways of thinking that allow us all to imagine that inclusion is at hand and tolerance is the way to get it. The tolerance mindset offers up a liberal, "gay-positive" version of homosexuality that lets the mainstream tolerate gayness. Its chief tactic is the plea for acceptance. Acceptance is the handmaiden of tolerance, and both are inadequate and even dangerous modes for accessing real social inclusion and change, as I hope to demonstrate in this book. The "accept us" agenda shows up both in everyday forms of popular culture and in the broader national discourse on rights and belonging. "Accept us" themes run the gamut: accept us because we're just like you; accept us because we're all God's children; accept us because we're born with it; accept us because we're brave and bereft victims and you can rescue us; accept us because we're wild and wacky drag queens with hearts of gold who can provide homespun advice to floundering heterosexuals; accept us because we can be your best girlfriend; accept us because then you can save us from our own self-hatred and vanquish homophobia in the process; accept us because we make you look hip and tolerant. The "accept us" trope pushes outside the charmed circle of acceptance those gays and other gender and sexual minorities, such as transgendered folks and gays of color, who don't fit the poster-boy image of nonstraight people and who can't be—or don't want to be—assimilated.

This book takes on the illusion of progress that is rooted in a watered-down goal of tolerance and acceptance rather than a deep claim for full civil rights. The leap to claim we are "almost there" prevents all of us (gay and straight alike) from fully including lesbians and gays into American society in a way that embraces—rather than merely tolerates—the rich traditions and differences they bring to the table. A too-soon declaration of victory hurts both gays and straights; it short-circuits the march toward full equality and deprives us all of the transformative possibilities of full integration.

———

Here is the conventional story of gay rights: We start with the Stonewall Riots. As most Americans know, and as President Obama spoke of in his inaugural address in 2013, Stonewall is a triumphant story of gay citizens—long stigmatized and unfairly persecuted—standing up for themselves and fighting back. It is now more than forty years since the hot summer night of those riots. That auspicious event—when lesbians, gays, transsexuals, and queers erupted in street protests—seems like ancient history, feels like the turbulent storm before the calm of a newly tolerant America. While at the time these Stonewall icons were pilloried in the press as pansies run amok, now they are lionized and heralded as the shot across the bow of straight America, even as their righteous anger looks as dated as the clothes they were wearing. American politics and culture were indisputably altered from that signal moment of frustration when those who were denied even the right to freely associate, much less share in the fullness of American life, engaged in open defiance, voicing the rage that became a full-throated yell of social rebellion. Now, mainstream films like *Brokeback Mountain* and *The Kids Are All Right* entertain moviegoers with their forthright gay themes and scenes. Obligatory (if still tokenized) gay characters dot the cultural landscape: the surprisingly gay character in a tedious romcom, the coyly queer older man in a star-studded indie hit, the incidentally gay sister of the lead in a serious drama. Where once a gay kiss on TV prompted religious groups to boycott and advertisers to pull out, now even the resolutely heterosexual *Desperate Housewives* indulges in an occasional Sapphic evening with barely a whisper of public opprobrium.

There are many ways to map this complicated and contradiction-filled history of gays in American society, but it wouldn't be totally inaccurate to say that there has been an enormous shift in the past fifteen years or so from a place of either invisibility or coded and brutally stereotyped images to a new place of an attenuated but nevertheless expansive new gay presence. When same-sex wedding announcements sit next to their hetero counterparts, gay *American Idols* are the toast of the town, and an openly gay TV anchor (Rachel Maddow) is the darling of the airwaves—inducing girl crushes from straight women and men alike, not to mention her adoring lesbian fans—we do get a sense that the times are a-changing. It is hard to pick up a newspaper, thumb through *People*, or click on a reality-TV spectacle without encountering some version (however limited, circumscribed, tarted up, or dumbed down) of "gayness," a minor note still within the cacophony that is heterosexuality but no longer just the sad triangle tinkling alone in the back of the high school band.

It is not just popular culture that has been touched by the fairy dust of gay inclusion. There is concrete social and policy change as well. Thousands of middle and high schools now have gay-straight alliances. Cities and states across the country prohibit discrimination on the basis of sexual orientation, and most of our major corporations and universities include gays in their anti-discrimination rules and have in-house support and outreach groups. While full-on marriage is still limited to a few states, many more allow civil unions or some version of partner protections, and the Supreme Court decisions of June 2013, forty-four years after Stonewall, look set to eventually make same-sex marriage the law of the land. There are more out gay politicians in state and local government—we even have had our first openly lesbian senator elected in 2012!—and gays are assuredly a voting bloc[2] courted by at least one of our political parties.

Truth be told, this has all happened pretty damn quickly. Some observers argue, with no small amount of evidence, that "gays may have the fastest of all civil rights movements."[3] Recent polls bolster this claim, detailing dramatic shifts in public attitudes in just twenty years, while earlier polls indicate a much longer trajectory for, say, attitudes related to racial integration. Some change has moved so quickly that folks of my generation really do experience a "before and after" of gay life. Growing up as a gay kid in Philadelphia in the 1970s, I knew not one other gay youth my age, nor did I expect to. I was terrified and isolated, and I imagined this secret to be the nuclear detonation that would evaporate my family's love. And I come from a family of progressive Jews for whom religious antagonism toward sexuality was nonexistent! I can't stress enough the enormity of the shift, a shift evidenced in popular culture and political life but also in the self-understandings of gays themselves and the perceptions of gays held by heterosexuals. For those from even earlier generations, this new reality of visibility and inclusion seems truly miraculous. These changes are just the tip of the pink iceberg.

For many social analysts, this moment is surely a harbinger of a new era when sexual orientation matters little in how one lives one's life. As longtime gay activist and sociologist Jeffrey Weeks argues, "The sharp binary schism . . . that has structured, defined and distorted our sexual regime for the past couple of centuries . . . is now profoundly undermined as millions of gays and lesbians, bisexuals and transgendered people have not so much subverted the established order as lived as if their sexual difference did not, in the end, matter." While many dismiss these changes as mere begrudging acceptance or, worse, a kind of normalizing of radical gay identity, Weeks reminds us that we should "never underestimate the importance of being ordinary."[4]

While I am perhaps more skeptical than Weeks and more ambivalent about the depth of the change, I would be the last person to see these huge shifts in American culture as "homo lite" window dressing on an essentially unchanged body politic. Changes have been real and substantial; I would, without question, have preferred to emerge as gay in this day and age rather than my own. This is dramatically evident when the gains for American gays are situated in the broader international context, where in many countries movements for sexual equality are still largely nascent, openly gay anythings (activists, mayors, artists, campaigns) are rare, out queers are the victims of vigilante violence, and homosexuals are imprisoned and brutalized by regimes that officially declare them either nonexistent or criminal.

And yet despite all the undeniable progress, the fact is it's far too early to declare the end of *American* homophobia.[5] In recent years, two thirteen-year-olds hanged themselves after anti-gay harassment at school. A college freshman jumped off the George Washington Bridge after his roommate surreptitiously filmed him making out with another man and streamed it over the Internet.[6] Three Bronx men were abducted and tortured by a youth "gang" whose only apparent motivation was "punishment" for their perceived homosexuality.[7] A man was shot to death in the heart of gay New York—Greenwich

Village—by a gunman shouting homophobic bile. A young trans woman was brutally beaten in a Maryland McDonald's as she tried to use the female restroom. This is a drop in the bucket. The stories of violence to self and others are myriad.

There may be gay-wedding announcements and the Supreme Court may have gone a long way toward marriage equality in repealing key provisions of the Defense of Marriage Act, but same-sex marriage is still illegal and unpopular in the vast majority of states. President Obama moved to repeal "Don't Ask, Don't Tell" but took it painfully slowly, commissioning studies that dragged on for a year or more, keeping discriminatory hiring in the military the law of the land. Violence continues to flourish (2011 was a record year for anti-gay hate crimes), and gay youth are still disproportionately suicidal and homeless.[8]

Even the new visibility of gays in our public square of popular culture is limited in numbers and delimited in terms of race and class. Too often, in our film and TV images, gays are narrowly depicted as either desexualized or oversexualized, making of gay sexuality either the sum total of a character's identity or, alternately, the unspoken absence. Gay characters are squeezed into these and other simple oppositions, shown as nonthreatening and campy "others" or equally comforting and familiar boys (and they usually are boys, not girls) next door. Needless to say, this new gay visibility is largely white, monied, and male.

So which is the real America? Is it *Modern Family* (beloved by both 2012 presidential candidates) and blissfully united gay couples surrounded by loving kith and kin? Or is it kids jumping off bridges, pushed to the brink by a callous culture? Or, yet again, is gayness now so "post-" that it has morphed into that ultimate sign of hipness: mockery? Now pro-gay comedians such as Jon Stewart can say "that's so gay" on *The Daily Show*, and his hip audience laughs knowingly because homophobia is seen as firmly rooted in the past, as archaic as those angry queers resisting arrest at the Stonewall bar in 1969.

The answer is all of the above. Would that it was clear-cut and simple, but the trajectory of gay visibility (and gay rights more broadly) is not a singular and linear narrative of progress and victory. Nor is it a depressing story of no movement at all. As the late British literary theorist Raymond Williams wrote, the new or the current always maintains "residual" traces of the past, not simply as "the past" but reformulated and refigured through the structures of the new.[9] In other words, it's a complicated story.

So perhaps we can broadly characterize it like this: the first stage of gay visibility (really up until the explosions of the late 1960s) was marked either by absence, coded and subterranean images, or the pathos of abject stereotypes. The second phase, in the late '80s and early '90s—spurred by social movements, Hollywood niche marketing, commodification, and disease—irrevocably brought gays out of the closet but into the problematic space of public spectacle, a space to finally be *seen* but not necessarily to be *known* in any meaningful way. And now, it might be that we are in a third phase: a phase of banal inclusion, normalization, assimilation, and everyday unremarkable queerness in which tolerance seems finally achieved. But is a tolerant America what we—that is, gay and straight alike—really want? Or, put another way, is it *all* that we want? Is mainstreaming—acceptance and tolerance—the beginning of the march toward true inclusion? Or might tolerance be its premature end? And what does tolerance mean? Does inclusion mean the end of "gay culture" itself? Is tolerance not the benign endgame of liberal societies but instead the trap that keeps those same societies from becoming more deeply liberal and more truly inclusive?

———

Americans are uniquely hasty to assert a "post-" right before we approach the finish line, effectively shutting off the real and substantive public debate needed for that final push. We did it with women's rights, declaring an era "post-feminist" while women remained lower-paid, sexually vulnerable adjuncts to a still male-dominant culture. We're doing it now with racial equality, depicting the election of our first black president as an indication that the long struggle for civil rights is essentially over (apparently over enough to nullify the need for the Voting Rights Act), even as poverty and incarceration rates disproportionately climb in African American communities. This idea of "post-" (racial, feminist, gay, whatever) depends on painting bigotry as the aberrant acts of isolated monsters. As Ta-Nehisi Coates cogently puts it, commenting on the invasive frisking of black actor Forest Whitaker in a New York deli in 2013, "In modern America we believe racism to be the property of the uniquely villainous and morally deformed, the ideology of trolls, gorgons and orcs. We believe this even when we are being racist."[10] Similarly, we increasingly paint homophobia as "external" to our everyday lives, even as it flourishes in public spaces and discreet corners alike.

Surely, one significant marker in the march toward social justice for gays has been irrevocably passed: silence and invisibility. The days of homosexuals as unspeakable and unseeable, as easy and acceptable targets for violence and denigration, are gone forever. But just because the openly gay genie is out of the bottle—and sashaying down the gay pride runway—doesn't mean that we've reached "post-gay" liberation or that real and dangerous retrenchments could not easily occur. The historical precedents for retrenchments following a period of new inclusion are legion—from the persecution of assimilated Jews in Weimar Germany to the "backlash" attacks on women throughout the '80s and '90s or the viciousness of anti-gay activism during the early days of the AIDS crisis. We have seen gains lost, communities come under stepped-up attack, identities reimagined as dangerous and evil.

We Americans tend to look at the road ahead and see not where it continues to branch off and divide but rather where it ends, where it comes to a full stop. Like a mirage of shimmering water on a hot and barren desert, we imagine we have found the source that will quench our national thirst for justice even as it continues to be just beyond our reach. We get part of the way there, and instead of doing that last hard work of pushing through to the end, we prematurely declare victory. When it comes to matters of homegrown injustice, we get to the shores of Normandy and turn around and go back, comfortable in our conviction that we already know the outcome.

By doing so, we pat ourselves on the back and avoid the deeper challenges. In declaring victory too early, we set the stage to get angry with those who still claim disenfranchisement and discrimination. We turn the tables and say we live in a "feminized" world in which boys and men are dealt a bad hand. We rail at "racial preferences" and claim minorities already have "too much" help from the government. We're doing this now with lesbians and gays, creating the fantasy that gayness isn't still an impediment to full participation and citizenship. We assert that gays already have too much political power and should back off. We claim that they want "special rights" and are pressing a "gay agenda" and that they have been tolerated just about enough. By declaring the end just in sight, we prevent ourselves from crossing the finish line and achieving real integration and inclusion. The framework of "tolerance," a framework that has come to dominate public discussion about gay and lesbian rights, enables this fantasy of completion. Because tolerance sets the bar so low (just don't hate us so much, just give us a modicum of "acceptance"), we imagine we have reached the pinnacle before we've even really started climbing the mountain.

Tolerance allows bigotry to stay in place and shores up irrational hatred even as it tries to corral it. Tolerance allows homosexuality to remain designated as "less than" heterosexuality, as a problem, as a dilemma, as a threat to the moral good. It allows the moral obfuscation "love the sinner and hate the sin" because it deliberately avoids reckoning with questions of value and belief. Part of creating a truly democratic, inclusive, and integrated society is recognizing each other as human, as amazingly different, as worthy of rights, and moving beyond mere recognition to a deeper embrace. Tolerance cannot do that work of deeper recognition because it is inevitably fixated on a (distancing) acceptance of the (intruding) other. The politics of recognition and belonging are of a different order than the politics of tolerance.

Of course, there are limits to tolerance—as there should be. Most of us are intolerant of brutal acts of random violence or equally brutal acts of state violence such as rape as a tool of war. Yet when we think of such heinous things, we don't use the language of tolerance. We *abhor* war, rape, or violence. We ethically *oppose* them (or should!). Tolerance is a language both too weak to address real evil and too vague to address real integration.

Further, tolerance finds strange common ground with the naturalization or biologization of homosexuality (discussed in more detail in part 2) and is often the default zone when inequality cannot be overcome but neither can complete exclusion be politically justified. Political philosopher Slavoj Žižek sees the move to tolerance as the aftereffect of the failures of progressive revolutions: "political differences, differences conditioned by political inequality, . . . are naturalized and neutralized into cultural differences, different ways of life, which are something given, something that cannot be overcome, but must be merely tolerated."[11] What he implies here is that tolerance is apolitical and individual, that mode a society falls back on to avoid deeper challenges to the social order. Political theorist Wendy Brown makes a similar argument in her book *Regulating Aversion*. Tolerance, in her view, signals a "retreat from more substantive visions of justice." Tolerance undercuts the potential for citizens to reckon with conflict productively and "be transformed by their participation."[12]

Tolerance allows for a temporary "multiculturalism" but also privatizes political debates by transforming social change into a tepid *personal* "acceptance" of (some) gays. If one "tolerates" homosexuality, one is not changed or challenged by its ways of life and love, ways that are sometimes quite similar to those of heterosexuals but often radically different. Tolerance is a trap precisely because it offers up a rosy *myth* in place of rough-hewn *history*. It cuts corners on liberation, producing a far shoddier and cheaper product than originally desired. And worse: we all think we got a bargain.

Tolerance is not active. Rather, most forms of tolerance are enacting what educational theorist Michalinos Zembylas calls a kind of "passive indifference," which is essentially a practice that advocates noninterference in the lives of others even though their "lifestyles" may be distasteful to those who are doing the tolerating.[13] But there can be a kind of tolerance that is deeper than mere charitable forbearance and that verges on real respect and perhaps even substantive understanding. We see this sometimes when we practice tolerance for the beliefs that form, say, religious ideologies we do not share. Surely, documents such as UNESCO's Declaration of Principles on Tolerance and projects such as the Teaching Tolerance toolkits from the Southern Poverty Law Center are genuine calls for a more just and peaceful and respectful attitude toward minorities and marginalized communities.[14]

But can we imagine a tolerance that pushes those who are doing the tolerating to be themselves transformed? That insists we truly recognize and respect others *for* their differences rather than accept them in spite of perceived or real dissimilarities? Can there be, in other words, a *robust* tolerance? I would argue that tolerance is not up to the challenge of deep respect and social recognition. It is too weak, too attenuated, too limited, too easily turned into its opposite to do the work of vigorous and inclusive integration. The very fact that both "sides" use this word with such self-righteousness (straight allies pay homage to our newly tolerant society just as conservatives inveigh against "too much" tolerance) should point to its weakness as the bearer of real social change. Tolerance, like acceptance, is transient, dependent on circumstances and whims. It can turn on a dime.

Tolerance and acceptance are inevitably linked in American discussions of rights and difference. We tend to think there is an easy transition from tolerance of the despised minority to a broader and deeper acceptance of that same group. We learn to tolerate, and then we come to accept, maybe even to love. Or so the story goes. But who is this "we" that tolerates? Who has the right to "accept" another? No civil rights movement worthy of the name has banked its future on being tolerated or accepted. Women didn't demurely request tolerance; they demanded voting rights and pay equity. African Americans continue to struggle not for some bizarre "acceptance" of their skin tone but instead for an end to discrimination in work, in schools, in housing, in the judicial system. They want, as do all these groups, full and deep integration and inclusion in the American dream. Disabled Americans don't want to be tolerated; they want streets made accessible to them and laws strong enough to protect them from discrimination.

Immigrants—Jews, Irish, Italians, Latinos—who arrived in this country by the millions and over the hundreds of years of US history—came often escaping persecution and discrimination. Many came with deep desires to be assimilated but just as often arrived with the pride of their difference worn proudly on their sleeves. My grandparents were among them, Russian and Polish Jews leaving a world of pogroms and second-class lives. They came wanting—and often demanding—not simply respite from the tyranny of the majority but an enthusiastic integration into this promising new land. Lady Liberty's message wasn't "Give me your tired, your poor, your huddled masses yearning to breathe free . . . so we can begrudgingly tolerate them." I can't imagine that the word "tolerance" was central to that early immigrant vocabulary. The active presence of immigrant Jews (and many other impoverished others) in labor movements and social justice struggles in those early days is testament to a demand for rights and redress that makes the quest for tolerance look like a meek supplication. To live freely and fully is not to be "tolerated" but to be included, even sometimes celebrated. The ethical alternative to discrimination and bigotry is not tolerance but rational thought and a commitment to equality. Respect and recognition and belonging are the gold standard, not a tepid tolerance that shuts the door on deep freedom.

This is, I think, the core of what is meant in the overused and often misunderstood concept of integration. As a nation, we tend to work with a very weak notion of integration. For many Americans, integration is almost synonymous with assimilation, in which "others" are added into the social stew without fundamentally altering its flavor. For example, we often blur the important distinction between literal desegregation (the opening up of previously barricaded pathways and social spaces, such as the military) and thoroughgoing integration in which multiple identities and cultures structurally and substantively alter institutions of civil society and even ways of life more broadly construed. Most ethnic and racial minorities have wrestled with this dilemma: to retain historically produced cultural specificities while at the same time demanding access to—and being part of—mainstream and dominant culture. Dominant cultures often resist this deeper inclusion, preferring instead to downgrade integration to simple desegregation and push an inclusion and assimilation (premised on tolerance) that is essentially a "one-way" street, leaving mainstream institutions and practices unaltered. Integration, then, has come to have a negative valence among radicals of all sorts, as "inclusion" becomes the code word for a kind of weak liberal tolerance that broaches no challenge to majority dominion even as it lets a few (even married) gays sit at the table.

I turn back to the notion of integration for a number of reasons. First, while it has often *implied* assimilation, integration in and of itself need not mean giving up unique cultural styles in the quest for equal treatment. But second, and more crucially, integration as a framework gets us away from the tired divisions that have too often torn apart social movements. Tolerance is a trap because it most assuredly comes down on one side of these divides: gays are tolerated as long as they buy into a supposedly universal idea of "rights" that takes as the default position an unquestioned heterosexual standard. Tolerance does sometimes tolerate difference, but it can never celebrate it; nor can it allow the difference of others to jolt its own certitudes.

These debates—over assimilation, over how to retain the uniqueness of a community while at the same time fully integrating, over multiculturalism and the melting pot, over the meaning of full citizenship—have been circulating for years in the gay community as in other minority communities. Earlier gay theorists and organizations (e.g., the Daughters of Bilitis, the Mattachine Society, and many others) debated these issues as they percolated in representation, culture, psychology, and the law. Radical queer movements (now and in the past) of course want full citizenship but don't really want to be "assimilated" if that means relinquishing the challenge to heterosexual rule. Activist and pioneer Harry Hay (one of the founders of the Mattachine Society and a longtime leader of left-wing gay liberation movements), for example, certainly wanted to be "tolerated" inasmuch as to be free from arrest and harassment, but he didn't particularly care about being "loved" by some putative "mainstream."[15] These concerns have been central to almost all major social movements of the 20th and early 21st century as minority populations (and majority ones, such as women) think through the complexity of demanding both rights and recognition with a majority culture that often wants them to have neither.

We are at a crossroads in the struggle for gay rights and, perhaps more importantly, for the ways in which sexual minorities are imagined in relationship to majority sexual identities. How is gay community or gay politics or even gay citizenship construed in this moment, a moment of such hope and possibility but also still chock full of such hatred and violence? What does it mean to emerge as gay—or queer—in an era when gayness is itself both a tool of marketing and an identity still in dispute? What is the path to full inclusion, and what would full inclusion look like?

What is even meant by "gay rights" is in question. The quest for equal treatment is often centered on a paradox. On the one hand, gays argue that gayness doesn't matter, that in making laws, taking a job, raising a family, it is irrelevant (as ethnic and racial minorities often similarly argue). It is, then, both singular and unimportant—a singular characteristic that has, or should have, little import in matters of law, employment, family formation, and so on. At the same time, these same minority groups have often embraced and articulated difference with a vengeance. The paradox is readily apparent in the history of ethnic and racial movements: the civil-rights-era "black is beautiful" symbolism, for example, is an immediate predecessor that defiantly signals an embrace of precisely that which has been deemed lesser by the majority culture.

Gay pride is part of that history, demanding rights *and* recognition, identity *and* inclusion. Are these two different goals—of both rights and recognition—reconcilable or intractably contradictory? Would "victory" be signaled by formal moves toward equality and equal access (e.g., marriage rights, equal-employment legislation), or is it a more abstract and elusive "liberation" that is being sought? Is "tolerance" and "acceptance" all that can be hoped for? Or is a vivid "rainbow" of civic inclusion the golden ring? What would it mean for America to embrace a "robust integration" that eschews simple assimilation and instead values the challenges and rewards offered by social and sexual difference? It is to these questions that *The Tolerance Trap* is addressed. They are hard questions, no doubt, and ones that may seem blind to the new, gay-friendly world being claimed by politicians and popular culture. Yet we must insist on wrestling with these deeper debates, because garnering basic civil rights is not the same as making the world a more amenable place for sexual difference. And tolerance is not the same as freedom.

# PART I

# *The End of Coming Out?*

If a bullet should enter my brain, let that bullet destroy every
closet door.                                    —Harvey Milk

The single most important thing you can do politically for gay
rights is to come out. Not to write a letter to your congressman
but to come out.                                —Barney Frank

Tom Cruise, this is Park County police! Please come out of
the closet. Everybody here just wants you to come out of the
closet, Tom. Nobody's gonna be mad, everything's gonna be all
right. Just come out of the closet.          —*South Park*

# I

# Once upon a Time

Back in the day, this was how it went. You sidled or ambled or strode into the gay bar. You were nervous but so very excited to be there. You found this bar maybe through the one gay bookstore in town. Leaflets pointed the way. Maybe you found it through those early cheesy guidebooks that you could buy at those precious bookstores or through the mail, wrapped ever so discreetly in generic brown paper. Maybe you just knew. And you'd go up to the bar and order a drink. If you were me, underage and clearly looking it, you ordered that beer nervously and probably a bit too loudly, never making eye contact with the bartender. You would sit and sip that beer and look around, trying not to seem too new, too obviously inept and green. And finally, after what seemed like a lifetime, she would come and sit next to you. If you were like me, young, she would probably be older by at least a dozen years. And she would bring you out.

Years later, or maybe years earlier, you would tell your parents. Or maybe not. And it would go surprisingly well, although everyone squirmed and looked at their feet. Or it didn't go well at all, and you were called names and told to leave. And there were tears and slaps. Or laughter. Or disgust or blame apportioned, probably to your mother. And you might tell friends, regale them with a story that you knew you were making up as you spoke it, a story that imposed a revelatory plotline even as you felt a bit uncomfortable with that linearity. You might, like me, speak it loudly and angrily (trying so hard not to look scared) to schoolmates in high school and watch those schoolmates shift uncomfortably in their seats and never really hang out with you anymore. You might fear reprisal or rejection, and you just might get it. But you also might feel that you just couldn't live if you didn't tell. Tell this story. Your story but not yours alone, which is what sometimes made it not only livable but thrilling. It was our pickup line, our bildungsroman, our coming of age, our grand narrative. Or so we thought. It was told in smoke-filled bars and in therapists' offices and in tears in the college dormitory. It was told to lovers old and new and to family biological and constructed. It was most easily told to strangers. It was our origins story but also our grand finale, and like all melodramas, it was as obfuscating and narrow and riddled with contradictions as such stories inevitably are. So here is my story.

———————

I was a snarly sixteen-year-old with a big secret before big secrets were TV worthy or at least fodder for drawn-out, media-friendly confessions. We were in London at the time while my mother—a family therapist—took a break from the rigors of working at a large urban clinic in Philadelphia to nip away at the recalcitrant hearts of the last true Freudians at the tony Tavistock Clinic for Psychotherapy. With my middle sister, we were living large in a very cramped basement apartment that had little to recommend it but for the gorgeous English garden that was ours to destroy. Our people had never been the gardening types, although I do remember my mother taking to the daffodils with gusto during her divorce. You could always tell when something personal was up with my mom: it was either vicious destruction of plant life or obsessive jigsaw-puzzle activity. There were more benign hobbies, like the endless stream of rainbow-colored ponchos that she knit for us, which would have been a big hit at gay pride festivals had I not developed a deep aversion to all things both poncho and rainbow.

Meanwhile, it was the height of punk and Rasta in London, and while I never indulged in either safety-pin piercings or dreadlocks (which I maintain no white person should do), I found myself flitting feverishly between those hardcore and hetero worlds and the vibrant feminist and nascent gay scenes, replete with disco clubbing and agitprop theater. I even became a doe-eyed helper with a women's theater troupe named Monstrous Regiment, and I think I may have directed some plays in that wonderfully open period of history when lack of knowledge or expertise posed no impediment to career choice.

Given that it was the mid-'70s, I looked terrible in my mannish and vaguely Virginia Woolfish (or perhaps newsboyish) tweed jacket and cap and artfully tied neck scarf, so I never managed to find the girlfriend I was sure would liberate me from the twin hells of teenage sexual confusion and '70s fashion nightmares. Directing righteous feminist plays or just drinking warm beer with the other vaguely newsboyish women was as good as it got.

How I had kept this one secret from my otherwise very tuned-in mother still mystifies me, although I do think the powers of parental denial kick into overdrive when the secrets being denied are sexual in nature. Come to think of it, though, for a very hands-on parent, my mother could morph into Nancy Botwin—TV's fave suburban mom-cum-drug-dealer on Showtime's *Weeds*—quicker than you can say "don't be home late." It's not that she herself was a drug dealer: she could barely finish the whisky sour I would helpfully mix for her when she walked through the front door as she came home from work. She wouldn't know a bud from a Bud Light. But it's just that—like Nancy—she was a curious mix of hyperprofessional competence and "hmm, where are my kids tonight?" maternal bemusement. Which is to say half the time she didn't know where we were or where we were headed, which was just as well because neither did we.

In my prepubescent tomboy days in Philadelphia, I frequently used to jump out of my second-story bedroom window and run away, with a Huck Finn–like stick and handkerchief of belongings perched jauntily on my shoulder. She rarely came after me, perhaps because she knew I was almost always in the nearby local park pretending hard to be (obviously gay) Harriet the Spy, writing furiously in my notebook and looking for clues among the tadpoles in the dirty stream that ran through Carpenter's Woods. Or maybe my mom just had other things on her mind. Is running away really running away if no one runs after you? Sometimes, however, she did notice, maybe because I made a racket banging my handkerchief pole on the window of my room as I delicately climbed out and made my grand escape. Then she would send Michael, my sister's six-foot-six black boyfriend, running after me to bring me home. It was always a test to see if he would get me before the police got him for chasing a little white girl while black.

"Can I see your driver's license and registration?" they would say when they would pull us over. Michael would dutifully provide these, and they would inevitably inquire, "Who is this child in the car with you?" Answering "My girlfriend's little sister," as he typically did, only led to more questions, usually focused on the handkerchief pole and long digressions on Harriet the Spy, which usually led to "Just get her home right away." A tall black man and a minuscule white girl sharing thoughts on Harriet the Spy with a burly South Philly Italian policeman produced not the expected arrest but enough confusion and disgust to allow us to slink home to my angry mother.

Even in London, when I was a more genuinely daring sixteen-year-old, she never did set chase on those nights I slipped out for activities a tad more nefarious than Harriet the Spy imitation, although truly some of the late-'70s gay bars did seem to contain an inordinate number of Harriet the Spy wannabes. Mom seemed to largely accept the lackluster excuses I offered even when they were patently silly. But at some point, all good secrets want to be told. And they don't usually get revealed out of stupidity or carelessness but rather the opposite, out of deliberate seeding of distrust and watering the delicate sprout of disbelief. I mean, I couldn't be a tragic gay teen without the audience. It was less important that she "know me" than that she be the one-woman Greek chorus to my epic tale of thwarted desire and flannel shirts. Without mutual hand-wringing and social disgust, this would devolve into a flaccid B movie. To be a full-fledged social-problem A-list extravaganza, one needed a torrid secret, a tortured secret keeper, and a revered receptacle for said secret.

I had dropped every hint I could muster, leaving books about "gay London" lying about the apartment, listening to Janis Ian records ("at seventeen I learned the truth . . .") on the stereo, and blaring the more-charming-than-it-sounds "Sing If You're Glad to Be Gay" anthem when Janis was off duty. I embodied as many stereotypes as I could gather into the body of one small sixteen-year-old. If hocking a loogie into a handy spittoon would have read "lesbian" to her, well I was up for that. But she just sang tunelessly along with "glad to be gay" and bought me another tweed jacket at the flea market. I was going to have to be more direct.

One night we were eating dinner in a fancy French restaurant with an American colleague of my mother's who was visiting London at the time. My mother barely knew this woman and I had only just met her, but that didn't stop us from airing our sexual linen in public. How apropos in a French restaurant! After civil introductions morphed into awkward pauses, my sullen silence prompted my mother to ask, "What's wrong?"

"Nothing," I said, the ever-ready adolescent response that can only inspire exasperation or maybe violence.

"Well, it can't be nothing," replied my mother. "You've been acting strange for weeks. Not to mention what you're dressed as." At this point, our poor dinner guest coughed nervously and said, "Oh, I do think those knotted scarves are quite fun." We didn't even look her way. This train was out of the station and on its way to gay town. And there was no conductor in sight.

"Really. This is enough. You need to cut this out and tell me what's wrong. I know there is something you want to say to me," said my mother as she struggled to wrest the garlicky snail from its dark shell. I bit into a frog's leg (it did taste like chicken!) and blurted out "OK. I'm gay." My mother, briefly looking up from her recalcitrant snail, met my anxious eyes with a neutral gaze and an imperious (not missing a beat) "No, you're not." A bit of a conversation stopper, it quickly sent our dinner guest off to the ladies' room, never to return or meet us again. Not a very good audience for this TV movie of the week.

I wonder if fundamentally new coming-out stories will be written in this changed era of gay visibility or if the power of shame and the status of the social outcast will continue to weigh so heavily on youth of the future. I'm no fan of shame and self-loathing, but it does make for a better life story than perky tolerance. I mean, if no one shoves your face into the school locker and instead competes with the other cool kids to have you as their gay best friend, a poignant melodrama is quickly turned into a saccharine chick flick and we're all bored.

But back in the pre-Ellen '70s, even my assiduously liberal mother greeted this announcement with disregard, if not contempt, and, upon our return to the US, hied me off to a child psychiatrist worthy of John Waters central casting. Much to my horror, he seemed transfixed by my breasts (and not in a nice, mildly pedophilic, admiring way) and kept asking me to identify my bra size in relation to that of my sisters. This was not a conversation I had with my sisters, so I was unable to answer, which must have meant I was in denial.

"How does it make you feel," he queried, "that your breasts are bigger than your elder sisters'?" I guess it made me feel like a raving homosexual. My mother had the good sense and professional expertise to snap me away from my mammary analyst (and do everything to malign his boob-based therapy practice) and finally begin to reckon with the love that may not often speak its name but had now taken up residence in her family tree.

While the good doctor didn't cure me of breast-based homosexuality, being an openly gay high school student in the 1970s did cure me of my need for high school. I rushed to complete it in three years, not from some burning sense of academic ambition (I was a theater buff at the time) or even from some anxious desire to leave home, but rather because high school for an openly gay teen in late-1970s Philadelphia offered little but scurried avoidance and furtive barhopping. Also there was the occasional snub and shove in the hallways of my liberal Quaker school.

I did, however, manage to turn the silent weekly "meeting for worship" required of all students and faculty into my own personal coming-out day. Usually we bad kids cut meeting (the Quaker version of a church service, although one without the preacher or the pulpit) for a toke and a hoagie, usually in that order. We might sidle in at the last minute, smelling suspiciously of sweet weed and oily onions. And, of course, the Quakers never punished us but patiently waited for the miscreants to find the light or finally graduate. So we would slouch in our seats during meeting, anticipating the heartfelt odes to community that usually came with regularity from one particularly devout teacher who seemed in a perpetual audition for *Little House on the Prairie.*

But one day I broke the slackers code and blurted out my secret to all attending. Maybe that is what the Friends meant by having God speak through you, or at least that was the interpretation of this Jewish kid in a deafeningly silent Quaker meetinghouse. I think I came out in the meeting as an act of social graciousness: *somebody* had to say *something* or the lull in conversation would be too deafening to bear. All that silence seemed to me a breach of etiquette rather than a sign of inner grace.

I never did understand the meeting protocols. I mean, you are supposed to sit together in silence in a state of "expectant waiting." But expecting what? Waiting for whom? Godot? Elijah? And then you are only meant to speak if the spirit moves you. You are not supposed to just chat away or offer random thoughts on current trends in fashion or the meaning of life but rather to give yourself over to having a message speak through you, from God presumably, or some other preferably nondemonic spirit that temporarily inhabits you, although hopefully not in a Carrie-like way. But one advantage of having the gay God speak through you in a Quaker meeting is that no one is allowed to beat you up or even whistle incredulously as you offer a homily on teen sexual identity. And if you change your mind later, and maybe become not so gay or perhaps even gayer, then you can always claim that shooting the messenger is never a wise choice when the messenger is the Messenger.

While quite alone in those pre-gay-support-group days, I was helped immensely by an openly gay, very tall and handsome, plain-clothes Quaker teacher. In this school, the students were instructed to call the male teachers "Master" and the female teachers "Teacher." So much for Quaker egalitarianism. I mean, it was easy to make "Master" funny (Master Bater being the best, but also "master" said like Marty Feldman from *Young Frankenstein*). "Teacher," on the other hand, was not only obviously lower on the totem pole of school hierarchy, but there was just no way to tweak that appellation into whimsy. Master Larry counseled me into "the life" as we lifted weights together in the basement of the school. Well, he lifted the weights and I watched him—alternately bored and confused by how cute he looked in his tight black shorts and clingy white muscleman T-shirt. He was at turns imposing and alluring, like the outcast progeny of the Village People if they had spent a dirty night in an Amish town. It's surprising, really, that I don't have a fetish for collarless shirts and suspenders.

Master Larry introduced me to my first girlfriend, although that might be a strong word for her, given that I can't recall her name. I do have memories of a skanky communal household where all the women seemed to drink cheap beer and wear kimonos but none of them were Japanese. These were not exactly pre-gay-pride days, but they sure were pre-gay/straight/bi/trans/queer/supportive/questioning high school support groups. So (Master) Larry found me some friends in a local university support group (itself pretty nascent), and the proverbial older woman welcomed me into the life, which seemed mostly to be about vague vegetarian casseroles served with the cheap beer while wearing inauthentic but fetching kimonos. It's gotten better.

I do remember that first moment, even if I can't remember her name. But let's call her Catherine in honor of Catherine Deneuve, who played a very sexy, Sapphicly inclined vampire in the '80s cult-classic vampire film *The Hunger*. So we're in her attic room in the communal household in West Philadelphia, and Catherine is wearing the confusing kimono and I'm feeling a little sick from the vegetarian food and cheap beer that, as a teenager, I'm still not that used to. We're sitting on the edge of her mattress on the floor, and she starts to take my clothes off. I can't really reciprocate because a kimono is supposed to just gracefully slip away, so I kind of just keep my hands to myself. That might have tipped her off. A more seasoned lover or the real Catherine Deneuve would, I guess, have taken the kimono in her bared teeth and gnawed it off her paramour's shoulders. So fake-kimono-wearing Catherine Deneuve stops and looks at me.

"Is this your first time?" she asks, with just a touch of nervousness in her voice. Just enough nervousness to make me really nervous that she will stop.

"Oh, nooo, of course not! I've even *made* barley bulgur kale casserole myself. All the time, really," I respond with more than a hint of false pride. When she looks at me less like *The Hunger* and more like *Halloween*, I realize—a little late—that she may have been referring to the bed/kimono activity we were about to initiate on the forlorn mattress and not the "meal" we had just consumed with the fellow kimono wearers in the fetid household. But, luckily for this initiate, food-based misunderstandings can never stop a kimono from getting what it wants. And so goes the story of one particular sixteen-year-old, coming of age and coming out in the late '70s in Philadelphia.

## I Want the World to Know

My coming out story is personal and idiosyncratic yet also so mundane. It is rooted in a particular time and place, vectored through intimate politics and family expectations, but nevertheless recognizable to strangers and friends alike. Silly, sad, and embarrassing but nevertheless a tale that marks me in ways both ineffable and predictably obvious. For me, and for others of my generation and those of earlier eras, this story figures mightily in our larger narratives of self and identity.

As Joan Didion famously wrote, "we tell ourselves stories in order to live."[1] A simple and uncontested truism is that all lives are narrated—by ourselves and by others eager to impose some coherence on the chaos of individual trajectory. For minority groups in particular, narratives are constructed as lifelines to each other and as insinuation into the larger stories of national identity and personal triumph. Often quite singular storylines are offered up as both the explanation and the antidote for marginalization and disenfranchisement. The larger social message now, however, is that coming out will promote tolerance. So the tolerance framework depends on coming out but insists that it be done quietly and correctly so as not to stir up or upset heterosexual equanimity. At the same time, and contradictorily, the fantasy of a newly tolerant world downplays the persistence of the closet and therefore conceals the continued strength of homophobia.

So one must be "known" to be tolerated. But not all ways of being out are equally validated, nor are all motivations for coming out similarly situated. In truth, we have different expectations of the people we come out to. Sometimes all we want is to be heard. Sometimes we want to be known. Sometimes we want affirmation of continued love. Sometimes we want to challenge what we understand to be the homophobia of the listener. Sometimes we want to cultivate a new ally. Coming out can be a confession or an assertion, a bold declaration of substantive difference or a quiet acknowledgment that nothing has changed. It can be a nod to the already known and a head-turning about-face. It can—especially in the media-saturated, nanosecond world of Twitter and Facebook and *TMZ*—be a way of heading off the inevitable outing by gossip columnists and bloggers. People can "receive" the coming out of a friend or family member as life altering, or they can hear it for a moment and then seemingly ignore its salience. Certainly, many gays report this response with their parents, when the utterance has only temporary meaning as it is actively disavowed in subsequent familial interactions or when admonitions not to come out to others (grandparents, relatives) are the immediate response.

While it is true that there are eight million (and counting) stories in the naked city, the coming-out story has long been offered as the master narrative of gay life. Indeed, the phrase "coming out" has so permeated cultural understanding that it has even moved from being a story gay people tell about themselves to others to a story multiplied through relationships (for example, when someone "comes out" as having a lesbian daughter or being the child of a gay man). This might be called the "six degrees of gay separation" game, much more fun—perhaps—than the "six degrees of Kevin Bacon" game.

Further, "coming out" has now become a generic phrase for any previously hidden self-revelation: coming out as HIV-positive, coming out as having cancer, or even the inevitable Oprah-ready coming out as bipolar. And it need not, these days, even imply a secret held with some degree of shame or discomfort: it can simply mean a benign disclosure, as in "last night I came out about my new shoes," although if they are Jimmy Choos, that might involve some small amount of shame at the exorbitant expense. This democratization or diffusion of coming out tells us a great deal about the declining—or at least changing—status of this particular theme of sexual emergence for gay people. Just as earrings on men or Doc Marten shoes on women were once irredeemably gay signs and are now fully banal parts of everyday straightness, the "de-gaying" of coming out speaks not only to transformations in gay life but to the ways in which gay signs have been both appropriated and accommodated by mainstream heterosexual populations.

Certainly, it was not always this way. The coming-out story—which now seems (at least in the West) almost synonymous with gayness itself—is actually of fairly recent vintage. Coming out as a representational form—as a genre and a tellable tale—really only emerges with the development of a movement for which coming out has salience. For example, the spate of coming-out films in the post-Stonewall period is predicated on that "post-"—on the assertion of a gay and lesbian identity as distinct, as narratively interesting, as a story to be told. In earlier eras, characters that were coded as gay might have been outed in the course of the film, but secrecy and misery were considered the fate of queer characters and most queer actors as well.

This is not to say that a hidden life was the only life available in pre-Stonewall America; people lived in all kinds of permutations of outness prior to the establishment of the coming-out story as the big gay saga of pop culture. History is littered with the marvelous few who insistently lived their lives openly, in the face of ridicule and censure, jail and death. But no one could really come out in films, for example, when *the closet* wasn't even an active metaphor. Certainly, internal struggles, self-revelation, and emergence to others existed in pre-gay-movement literature, film, and art. Iconic literary texts such as *The Well of Loneliness* from 1928 or the heartbreaking play and then film *The Children's Hour* or the '50s pathos-filled film *Tea and Sympathy* or the myriad pulp novels of the '50s and '60s spoke to such stories, even if elliptically. Of course, the pulp novels were unique in that they directly engaged proto-gay audiences with explicit tales of queer sex and romance, often centered around a coming-out theme.

But coming out as a singular process—and the closet as the paradigmatic metaphor for same-sex life itself—depended on the establishment of a gay identity and a gay movement to make it happen. In simple terms, one needed the very *category* of "the homosexual" to produce the story of coming out. As many historians and theorists have convincingly argued, the homosexual as a distinct category, a demarcated identity (rather than, say, a set of possible sexual acts or preferences) is a very modern invention, as is the heterosexual. Coming out may appear now as the transhistorical and transcultural story of gay life, but it actually was "invented" as recently as the early part of the last century. Like Google, it feels like it's always been with us because it has so permeated our understanding of gay identity.

## Society Girls and Rattling Bones

While it is not clear when, precisely, the term was first used, it certainly derives from referencing—by analogy—the coming out of a debutante into society. This analogy is interesting for many reasons, but what is most striking perhaps is that it prompts us to frame coming out in deeply social terms. This is somewhat at odds with more contemporary versions in which coming out is understood at least in part as an internal process of self-knowledge. Further, in contemporary (really post-Stonewall) parlance, coming out is linked to the idea of the closet, drawing now on a metaphor of "skeletons in the closet." So if the debutante analogy implied entrance into a specifically social world, with no necessary assumptions about what one was leaving (for the deb, she was making herself eligible for marriage and therefore, in that world, signaling her adulthood), the addition of "the closet" muddied the waters by imbuing this public display with a much more troubled and troubling assumption of shame.

The double analogy (coming out and the closet) marks a shift from a metaphor of social emergence to one of a deeply hidden personal trajectory at the same time that it reformulates the cost of social exclusion (homophobia) on the individual so hidden. Now forever associated, the closet frames coming out as a movement from a place of darkness, hiding, and duplicity. And the closet, now framed as something one comes out of, is understood as imposition and burden, as gay rights pioneer Donald Webster Cory (aka Edward Sagarin) poignantly noted when he wrote as early as the 1950s, "Society has handed me a mask to wear. . . . Everywhere I go, at all times and before all sections of society, I pretend."[2] So the closet, in this rendering, is a place one is forced into by the agents of what we now call homophobia. Leaving that place—coming out—must then imply an acknowledgment and rejection of that whole rubric of discrimination.

It is also vital to remember that the closet was not and is not the only way to describe historical forms of gay concealment. As historian George Chauncey and others have cautioned, we should be wary of understanding all forms of sexual disguise and subcultural life within the narrow terms of "the closet."[3] Other divisions (other than "in" or "out") can be more pertinent to an individual's self-definition and movement in the world. This has been particularly important in thinking cross-culturally but is also relevant to discussions of ethnic and racial differences here at home. In other words, the imperative to come out must be tempered by an understanding of other social factors that cross-cut our sexuality, especially ones such as race that may be impossible to "hide" in the first place. There are significant differences in how coming out resonates across racial, class, and ethnic lines. The discourse of the "down-low" (a term popularized in the late '90s to describe black men who have sex with men but do not identify as "gay"), for example, demonstrates that "coming out" as a framework for understanding gay identity is already infused with particular racial—if not racist—ways of thinking. So black men who don't declare a gay identity, who have sex with men but also with women, are given their own category (the down-low) that is then demonized as somehow worse, or somehow *more* duplicitous, than white men who do the same thing! And if coming out is also about coming into a gay community and if that gay community is configured as predominantly white, if not racist, well, coming out will then have different import across racial lines. Thus, many scholars have argued that coming out itself is a product not only of (racial, class) privilege (who, for example, can afford to lose jobs, family, support by the act of revelation?), but also of an outmoded notion of singular and unified identity (here is the "truth" of me). In other words, coming out was always a located and delimited phenomenon, reverberating differently across varying lines of identity, and not necessarily the sine qua non of gay personhood.

In addition, the very idea of the closet as simply and solely repressive has come under fire from any number of quarters, including scholars influenced by the work of the late French philosopher Michel Foucault and American feminist theorist Judith Butler. Acts of passing, hiding, duplicity, and the like are *productive* of identities and lifeways, not simply repressive of already existing (but denied/hidden) fully formed sexual identities. Sociologist Steven Seidman in *Beyond the Closet* argues that "practices of concealment not only protect the individual from the risks of exposure but create a 'protected' psychic space to imaginatively construct a gay self. . . . While some individuals conceal in order to avoid any public exposure, others pass as a strategy to make possible a public gay life."[4] Thus, the closet has had not only the "negative" function of repression and hiding but also the more positive one of creating alternative worlds and "safe spaces" for the management and construction of sexual identities. In addition, while passing is a relatively recent notion vis-à-vis sexual identity (because it depends on the modern idea of a true and singular sexual self that must do the passing), it has a long and complex racial history which intersects in some intriguing ways with sexual passing, ways that point to the centrality of "the visible" in our negotiations with social recognition.

For many gay scholars, then, "the closet" is a shifting and ambiguous phenomenon that is contingent on a multitude of complicating factors, including the importance of *other* aspects of one's identity in relation to the category and how centrally "gayness" figures in this self-definition. Judith Butler, for example, has wondered about the place of coming out in our own individual histories and in the pantheon of gay identity more broadly construed.[5] Further, some critics question the centrality of coming out because they believe that the social world has shifted so substantially that it renders "the closet" a minor note in gay identity and culture. Others argue that coming out inevitably mires one in producing the dualistic categories (in/out, gay/straight) that ensnare us to begin with. In addition, the act of coming out—and the attached identities it both assumes and creates—can serve as a sort of policing force, creating, as Seidman notes, "divisions between individuals who are 'in' and 'out' of the closet. The former are stigmatized as living false, unhappy lives and are pressured to be public without considering that the calculus of benefits and costs vary considerably depending on how individuals are socially positioned."[6]

While cultural theorists and historians ponder the fate of this persistent frame of reference, many psychologists have also been critical of the developmental models that undergird the coming-out story. The mainstream psychological frameworks often search for (and thus help to produce) a linear model of authenticity that presumes a simple trajectory toward "truth" and self-knowledge and singular sexual identity. Feminist psychologist Lisa Diamond, for example, has complained that many in her field too often seek to "uncover a true and generalizable trajectory of development," in which autobiographical consistency becomes the "marker of authenticity." These days, she claims, "researchers are increasingly challenging the notion that sexual identity development is an inherently linear and internally coherent process with an objectively discernible beginning, middle, and end, casting doubt on the notion that developmental psychologists should seek to discover or validate one or more discrete 'pathways' from heterosexuality to homosexuality in the first place."[7] So Diamond and other critics of mainstream psychology seriously undermine the assumptions embedded in the ways psychologists speak of and map out the process of coming out, taking issue with both the singularity (telling a story with one clear sexuality emerging in the end) and the linearity (telling a story that moves from falsehood and self-deception to truth and self-knowledge).

Both the cultural historians and the psychologists would also agree that the idea that "the closet" and "coming out" are one-off experiences is patently false. Not only is coming out an endless and recurrent process so that one is always having to reengage the questions one thought settled, but the closet is of course also a space of variability, inflected geographically and culturally. Someone's "life in the closet" may be another person's refusal to be pinned down. While you can't be a little bit pregnant, you certainly can be a little bit "out." What seems like a straightforward question ("Are you out?") will be answered by perhaps the majority of gays in long and meandering sentences rather than a single word. It might be answered emphatically ("Of course I am!") and then qualified in further conversation. Or it may be the proverbial open secret in which everyone seems to know but no one seems to be able to utter the words. While some are out to absolutely everyone in their lives, the majority of (nonexclusively heterosexual) Americans practice some sort of concealment of their sexual preference, and it is probably the case that all of us—gay, straight, bi, whatever—are even more withholding when it comes to revealing our sexual *practices*.

But, importantly, these partial or strategic forms of concealment or disavowal need not alter the sense of "outness." I have been out, for example, since I was sixteen years old but made a deliberate decision not to tell my elderly immigrant grandparents, not really for fear of their rejection but frankly because it seemed too much effort for little payoff. While this might have been a source of some internal conflict for me (and a source of repressed laughter between myself and my mother, when it became clear that my grandmother had constructed an alternative narrative of workaholic but heterosexual singledom for me), it did not alter my sense of being out, because for me that designation had everything to do with participation in a gay community and openness with people close to me. I saw my grandparents infrequently, so the management of that concealment hardly affected my everyday (and out) life. When they both died in their late nineties—without knowing I was gay—that omission seemed a negligible aspect of my overall sense of loss.

Or, alternately, there are situations when one's gayness is seemingly undermined by practices deemed irrevocably heterosexual. This has been the experience of so many gay parents whose parental role is perceived to be at odds with their sexuality. For example, years ago when I announced my pregnancy to the chair of my department, her response was both hilarious and horrifying: "But I thought you were a lesbian!" This reaction is diminishing of course and happens less often when two parents are present (I was a single mother), but gay parents remain "mistaken" for heterosexual all the time.

# 2

# Coming Out Is So Last Year

"Are you out?" is a question still asked by gays to other gays and to gays by straights, but it may not be the first question anymore or even the most important one. What seems like the timeless story of gay life has a fairly recent provenance and might even have a brief shelf life. There certainly is a sense that something has changed, that the stories we tell now are more varied, less full of pathos and internal self-doubt, less fearful of the response to revelation. That may be true—and more about that later—but I remain skeptical. Maybe it's just my generational sensibility, but I am suspicious of the claims that coming out and the closet have largely gone the way of the pet rock and the hula hoop. Or maybe it is like the hula hoop, whose original use (children's toy) has recently been reconfigured by adults eager to find yet another mode of weight loss and exercise.

While there is ample evidence[1] that the force of the closet is still an active part of American culture, it remains the case that all the vast changes of the past twenty or so years have chipped away at and altered the contours of the coming-out story. It should come as no surprise that new stories emerge out of changed circumstances, even as older stories still circulate. Undeniably, coming out retains a place in the lived experiences of many gay people, but there is no doubt that it has receded as "the story" in popular culture, even as it is clear it has not wholly disappeared. In this era of liberal gay visibility, contemporary culture has other motifs to choose from, and the coming-out story no longer represents both the beginning and the end of how gay identity is imagined in popular media.

Recent TV shows, certainly, have moved past the storyline of coming out as gayness becomes regularized as part of the everyday narrative. The shift from, let's say, *Ellen* to *Modern Family* was emblematic of that move. In the *Ellen* series, our heroine begins her sitcom life as ostensibly straight—although anyone with even a modicum of gaydar could read between those lines. Her transformation—from self-recognition to tortured closet case to revelation to close others to public coming out—mirrored exactly how we have come to understand the dual frames of the closet and the exit from it. By the time we meet the gays of the popular sitcom *Modern Family* (or *Glee* or *Happy Endings* or *True Blood* or . . .), they are introduced to the audience as "already gay." Their gayness is central to the series but not specifically in the melodramatic (or occasionally comic) form of coming out. *Modern Family* features a gay male couple who have just adopted a child; the least of their issues is coming out! Indeed, coming out is humorously situated in the past. Mitch and Cam might still have to deal with parental discomfort, but there is no hidden secret to be revealed or self-knowledge to be attained.

Similarly, the other major queer TV moments of the past decade—*Will & Grace*, *Queer as Folk*, *Queer Eye for the Straight Guy*, *L Word*—deal almost exclusively in the world of "already out" gayness. It is hard, in fact, to imagine another *Ellen* moment, in which the narrative revolves around the paradigms of closetedness and coming out. Even when we do get a signal coming-out moment (say, in the wonderful HBO series of the early 2000s *Six Feet Under*), we often see the conflict not simply as an internal one or one between a closeted person and his or her unknowing family but now between a closeted person and his or her out and proud lover. When out gay cop Keith of *Six Feet Under* is frustrated with closeted funeral director David, the struggle moves away from the narrowly familial and overly heterosexual to the larger canvas of gay activism and history. This shifts the terrain enormously and productively, I think, for coming out is thus rendered a profoundly social and political issue.

Other characters in hit shows such as *Grey's Anatomy* and *Desperate Housewives* are "already out" and fairly integrated into the main narratives. For example, when the overtly sexual and attractive surgeon Callie in *Grey's Anatomy* begins to feel an attraction for a woman—and then eventually gets involved with her—her response is both typically melodramatic (confusion, rejection, amazement) and surprisingly short-lived. There is little sturm und drang here, and most importantly, she does not then rewrite her entire sexual history to accord with this newfound desire. In a similar vein, when the gorgeous and ribald Dr. O'Hara in *Nurse Jackie* casually reveals her bisexuality, it causes a raised eyebrow or two but that's about it, particularly in a series that features a gay male nurse and a doctor inordinately proud of his lesbian moms.

There are already-out gay neighbors galore in TV land, and it seems almost every TV workplace has a token gay. *Brothers and Sisters*—a since canceled melodrama on ABC—featured a gay brother who has certainly evinced some discomfort with his "outness" but is now firmly in the out-and-proud category, along with his partner and, interestingly, his uncle, who only recently came out. In fact, that particular plot trajectory says a great deal about current frameworks. A much more traditional coming-out story (filled with self-doubt if not self-loathing), it perhaps could only ring true to contemporary audiences if it is located on the body and psyche of an elderly person. In fact, Uncle Saul consistently—and painfully—references the differences between this moment and his own past, when hiding and furtive encounters were all that were available to him. His diagnosis of HIV late in the series only further distances him from the dominant Hollywood rendering of contemporary gay life as free, easy, and largely unencumbered by either illness or discrimination. Even the campy, closeted, and largely miserable gay characters of AMC's critical hit *Mad Men* are framed as signs of a boozy but not so gay-friendly past when men who like men were pariahs or bore the brunt of office humor. Like the casual racism of the series, homophobia is assigned a place in the past.

In film, never as thoroughly "gayed" as popular television and always strangely a beat behind that more prosaic medium, the shift is evident as well. Most films that feature gay characters plop them down as "already gay" in a world in which everyone knows and nobody cares. In mainstream Hollywood—when gays are shown—they are largely depicted as already-out gay best friends. Tokens undoubtedly, but tokens largely open and easy with their sexuality. It is surely telling that it would be hard to imagine a major Hollywood film (like that 1982 taboo breaker *Making Love*) centering around a coming-out story. Even films set in the past—like *Brokeback Mountain*—might deal with the trauma of the closet and the price of repression but don't directly offer up the triumphant (or depressing) coming-out story as the narrative logic. And one of the few recent films to centrally depict gay characters—2010's *The Kids Are All Right*—features a pair of already-out lesbian moms who don't even reference a "non-out" past.

When a relatively "old-fashioned" coming out occurs, it is more of a send-up of uncomfortable homophobia than a heartfelt ode to the pain of the closet. In a hilarious scene from a 2008 episode of the satire *The Office,* manager Michael Scott outs employee Oscar Martinez to other co-workers when he loudly apologies for having called Oscar "faggy" earlier in the episode. This unleashes a bevy of homophobic and generally ignorant reactions from both Michael and other employees. In an attempt to deflate the situation, Michael calls a meeting where he outs Oscar to the rest of the staff and awkwardly tramples through an apology and a "tolerance training" that is as uncomfortable as it is insulting.

MICHAEL: The company has made it my responsibility today to put an end to one hundred thousand years of being weirded out by gays. All right, everybody in the conference room! I don't care if you are gay or straight or a lesbian or overweight! Just get in here, right now! Did you know that gay used to mean "happy"? When I was growing up, it meant "lame." And now, it means a man who makes love to other men. We're all homos! Homo sapiens. Gays aren't necessarily who you think they are, people. I mean anybody could be gay. Businessmen. Like antique dealers or hairdressers or . . . accountants. Oscar, why don't you take this opportunity to officially come out, to everybody here. However you want to do it. Go ahead. Stand up. I'm doing this for you.

OSCAR: Yes, I'm gay. And I didn't plan on sharing that part of my life with you today, so, whatever. Can I sit down now?

In the conclusion of the scene, Michael insists on kissing Oscar to show his acceptance of him, a gesture Oscar rejects, then begrudgingly complies with to appease Michael's hurt feelings.[2] Coming out is no longer treated with reverence and a kind of emotional saturation but instead has moved through our culture thoroughly enough to land on the barbed bed of satire and mockery. The gay character is no brave soul baring all for truth and self-knowledge, and coming out is sent up rather than cried over. And when *The Office* characters wonder where they can buy some "gaydar," we know we have entered a new realm of how coming out figures in American popular culture.

## Never In

Nowhere is this shift from coming out as the archetype of gay experience to coming out as one story among many more pronounced than in discussions about gay youth. In fact, the one TV venue where we still see coming out as a significant (and not merely ironic) storyline is, not surprisingly, in teen-centered shows. The coming-out story may have found new life in the hip narrative of the gay (or bi or questioning) teen, a staple of contemporary cultural fare. Showtime's quirky *The United States of Tara* has already-out gay neighbors but, more importantly, a teen gay son who tries valiantly to exercise a little heterosexual passion with an adoring girl but falls instead for the queeny, political, gay youth activist reviled at his high school. Hit series *Glee* (touted as the gayest show on TV) features the obligatory gay kid in the patchwork ensemble of difference, joined in later seasons by an already-out (and more macho) boyfriend, a pair of lesbian cheerleaders, and a cross-dressing diva. And almost to a one, these kids are greeted with positive embraces or a tepid "who cares?" For the boys of *Glee* and *The United States of Tara*, their gayness is an open secret: the audience knows full well that these adorable teens are a bit (well, a lot) sissified, and while the parents may be in some degree of denial, it is hard to imagine they are completely in the dark. When there is any struggle, it is quickly surmounted. In *Glee*, the coming out of the fashionable and effete Kurt is the inevitable waiting to happen. Even though he encounters some resistance from his manly single dad, a few episodes bring our boy thoroughly into the fold of both family and friends. Dad gets a serious life lesson in the process and becomes embarrassingly gay-positive to boot.

Gay teen Andrew is outed on campy *Desperate Housewives*, and his mother's initial homophobia is itself the source of humor, especially since his gayness is the least of her problems, given that he is a tad evil. In the series finale of *Ugly Betty* (already a gay-friendly show), young fashion maven Justin twirls around the dance floor with a classmate and finally reveals explicitly what was pretty obvious from day one of the series. The updated 90210 features a gaggle of gays, and *Gossip Girl* has a bisexual high school boy. The list goes on.

Indeed, the past several years have brought a deluge of articles and books heralding the coming of the "new gay teen." According to most of these popular accounts, "gay and lesbian teens are acknowledging same-sex attraction at ever-younger ages and questioning the concept of both 'coming out' and 'the closet.' "[3] Any parent who has traversed the school system can attest to this and to the numbers of youth who choose to dress in ways at odds with their assumed gender. While these issues are still highly fraught and debated in schools and households across the country, it was unimaginable only a few years ago that we'd witness the new sexual and gender freedom of youth to such an extent that girls take girls to the junior prom and boys wear dresses to second grade. I myself will never forget the time my then ten-year-old nephew looked across the Thanksgiving table and asked me, "Tante Suzie, are you gay?" When I replied in the affirmative, he easily continued, "I am too," and everyone went back to eating the dry turkey.

My sweet Lady Gaga/Marilyn Monroe–obsessed nephew is just one example, but it does seem to be the case that kids are coming out younger and younger—many in middle school—and coming into a very mixed situation in which tolerance is the mantra, but it is a mantra often at odds with the *experience* of queer youth. How we imagine the situation of queer youth reveals quite a bit about what gains we believe tolerance has won. For some commentators, the new sexual and gender fluidity of youth is a sure sign of the victory of a tolerant society. Writers like Ritch Savin-Williams—a longtime researcher on gay youth—seem to believe that fluidity and the refusal of singular definitions are more the rule than the exception and that this produces a world that is essentially "post-gay." As he states in the preface to his most recent book, "now at last I can hope that contemporary teenagers are bringing the sexual identity era to a close."[4] For Savin-Williams, "these kids are like straight kids. Straight kids don't define themselves by sexuality, even though sexuality is a huge part of who they are."[5] Replace sexuality with race in this equation, and you see what he's missing: of course straight kids don't need to declaim their sexuality—like whiteness, it's the default category. That's what we mean by "compulsory heterosexuality" or indeed any dominant and assumed phenomenon. That's what is indicated when every newspaper article refers to the "African American lawyer" or the "gay teen" or even, still, the "female candidate."

For many who study youth, this historical moment not only ushers in newly aware fluid queerness but in fact may push us beyond gay identity altogether. If gay youth encounter their "gayness" at the same time straight kids encounter their "straightness," then perhaps these developmental markers are beginning to merge. Some researchers state unequivocally that times have changed so dramatically that "teenagers are increasingly redefining, reinterpreting, and renegotiating their sexuality such that possessing a gay, lesbian, or bisexual identity is practically meaningless."[6] In other words, many critics, including literary theorist J. Jack Halberstam in her recent book *Gaga Feminism*, seem to believe we live in a "post-gay" world in which kids emerge into their "selves" without the strictures of singular identities.[7] Halberstam and others see "post-gay" in a positive sense, in which identity is proliferated and unmoored, expansive and fluid yet actively transgressive of heteronormativity. In this version, contemporary youth are actively countering the dominance of the hetero norm by a variety of gender-nonnormative behaviors and styles—that may or may not be tied to actual sexual practices or identities.

The problem with that story—one told by any number of researchers and popular journalists and one with some kernel of truth—is that it neglects the continued reality of homophobia and heterosexism. It may be the case that many kids are coming out younger and that the closet is no longer the place they emerge from. And it may also be the case that a kind of gender and sexual fluidity is seeping into the cultural waterways, albeit in ways that often appear glib. But it remains true that we still live in a world which radically prefers and values heterosexual "choices" over homosexual ones. Coming to a gay identity or same-sex attractions or even a gender-nonnormative style can never be a simple parallel to acquiring heterosexual identity or opposite-sex attractions. Even in this more open era, heterosexuality is the default, the assumed, the preferred, the promoted. It need not be explained, analyzed, or unpacked. No one looks for the straight gene or wonders if bad mothering turned a kid straight. No one talks about bravely tolerating the gender-normative, straight kids who brazenly flaunt their sexuality in class, on the playground, in the home. To argue, as many people seem to, that "life for the next wave of gay and lesbian students becomes more like that of their straight peers"[8] is to radically underestimate the centrality of heterosexual dominion. The post-gay story fits with the tolerance trap because neither one requires real examination of continuing and structural homophobia.

Savin-Williams and other commentators imagine they live in a brave new world where gayness is relegated to the proverbial dustbin of history and matters not at all in self-definition, or, as he says, "The notion of 'gay' as a noteworthy or identifying characteristic is being abandoned; it has lost definition,"[9] although he interestingly doesn't seem equally anxious to relegate heterosexuality to that same ash heap. So what, precisely, is the basis for the assertion of this new "revolutionary" nonidentity? In fact, much evidence exists to the contrary: both gayness as an identity category and homophobia as an active force on gay lives have not disappeared. While the research is limited on youth—and often quite contradictory—there does seem to be some solid work that challenges the idea that the "old" categories are wholly relics of the past for today's youth.[10] The persistence of, if not rise in, anti-gay bullying in schools and in the streets is surely at least some indication that old patterns of abuse and homophobia have not gone the way of the VHS, even as they are more challenged and publicized than in earlier periods. And it is true, isn't it, that the continued development of GSAs, gay-youth support groups, and the like speak to the persistent *need* for such resources? Just as you wouldn't need battered-women's shelters if women weren't abused, you wouldn't need a support group if you weren't still, in some profound sense, under attack. At the very least, those "support groups" would have different functions and meaning in a context of nondiscrimination.

In a *New York Times* piece about a longtime gay youth group in Long Island, all the contradictions of our current epoch are laid out, including the continued need for such groups given the persistent reality of discrimination after gay kids "go through a day of being called names or ignored or physically intimidated."[11] A young woman, who recently graduated from high school and now "runs peer education groups at Pride for Youth," recalls hearing homophobic remarks "every single day" when she was a student. "Walking through the halls, I constantly heard the word 'fag.' People would spit on me, throw pennies at me." She went on to found a GSA at her school and recalls that she was "terribly scared" and had to deal with "defaced or ripped down posters announcing meetings of the club." There is nothing new here, and this is not about a middle-aged woman but rather one just out of her teens. True, these GSAs are now "part of the school culture," but many of the kids attending a gay coffeehouse group in Long Island still do not tell their parents where they are going, and many live in group homes because they were kicked out of the house because they were gay—and I don't imagine this is a unique situation.[12] Some parents support their kid's participation in the group; others forbid it. Schools may be a more inviting place, but the closet may now operate much more selectively. While the *New York Times* and other national news sources might report on the newly warm embrace by gay-positive parents, many stories sound much more worrisome.

Certainly, things have changed since my own youthful coming out. GSAs (gay-straight alliances) now exist in schools across the country, although it is important to note that not even 5 percent of high schools have such groups.[13] Anti-gay epithets are often recognized—and supposedly prohibited—in most schools under the more general rubric of bullying and discrimination on the basis of sexual and gender identity. One cannot overestimate the effect these changes—and particularly the GSAs—have on both gay and straight kids, even those too closeted or too afraid or too unsure to join the club themselves. I think back to my own high school days, when the almost palpable feeling of singularity and isolation pushed me to join up with a local university's gay support group—and sped up my education to enter college a year early! I would have eagerly joined such a school-based support group, but I think even knowing it *existed*—and was legitimized by its institutional standing as a school club—would have taken at least some of the edge off my own loneliness.

So two things seem indisputably true. First, kids are no doubt coming out earlier. And, second, while violence and harassment and fear and shame are hardly phenomena of the past, the profound sense of isolation (what earlier generations may have understood as the "Am I the only one?") and lack of information have irrevocably changed. But disappeared? I think not.

## Only Boy Scouts Need Apply

While it might be the case that gay kids are less alone and isolated than previous generations (because of those GSAs, because of the new gay visibility), it is not necessarily the case that they are less vulnerable, more integrated, less taunted and harassed. Kids are still killed for being or appearing to be gay or being gender nonnormative in some way. Other kids just put up with everyday harassment, getting pushed into lockers, mocked and teased, called "fag" and "dyke," ostracized and left to sit alone at the lunch tables. It is not at all clear that schools and teachers are really tackling homophobia in the classroom, and "that's so gay" (as a stand-in for "that's so stupid," inevitably linking gayness with an intent to insult and demean) is still the schoolyard insult of choice. In the most recent (2011) report on the state of gay youth in our schools, the pioneering organization GLSEN (Gay, Lesbian, Straight Education Network) found distressing trends. Not only was generic "fag" name-calling an everyday occurrence for nearly all the kids surveyed, but "nearly nine-tenths of students (86.2%) reported being verbally harassed (e.g., called names or threatened) at school because of their sexual orientation. And two-thirds (66.5%) of students were verbally harassed because of their gender expression. Almost half (44.1%) of students had been physically harassed (e.g., pushed or shoved) at school in the past year because of their sexual orientation and three in ten students (30.4%) because of their gender expression." For some, victimization was even more severe—22.1 percent reported being physically assaulted (e.g., punched, kicked, injured with a weapon) because of their sexual orientation and 14.2 percent because of their gender expression. And all the expected repercussions of this continued taunting persist: absenteeism, poor school performance, lowered aspirations, even suicide.[14] However, it is encouraging that the presence of GSAs at a school does seem to lower the *rates* of harassment and, importantly, raise the rate of reporting of harassment to school authorities.

Given the persistence of anti-gay behavior in schools across the country, then, it is a bit jarring to read these accounts of happy-go-lucky gay youth, accounts that paint a picture of a wholly new era, when gay teens easily pass from "regular guy" to "bff" to prom king, a world of "the 'next wave' of gay and lesbian teenagers: adolescents who have grown up with openly gay teachers, television characters, neighbors, politicians, and even parents and who take for granted the acceptance that earlier generations struggled to achieve."[15] It must be true that all this gay visibility and gay activism has made it easier for today's youth, many of whom can't even imagine a time when fear ruled the day, but it may be too optimistic to claim that for these kids things are so copacetic that "gay marriage is more status quo than radical."[16]

In addition, some people have even blamed these young and out gay kids for their own victimization, pointing out once again how the framework of "tolerance" can easily morph into its opposite, especially if the person being tolerated is deemed, well, *too* gay. No case illustrated this so painfully as that of fifteen-year-old California youth Larry King. On February 12, 2008, Brandon McInerney, a fourteen-year-old classmate of Larry's, shot him twice in the back of the head in the school's computer lab, killing him. The killing became fodder for national news coverage, not only because of the youth of both the victim and the murderer but because the victim was a gender-nonnormative kid who came to school wearing women's clothes and makeup and was unabashedly flirtatious with other boys in the school, including perhaps the assailant. The trial ended in a plea deal for the young assailant, who is now spending twenty-one years behind bars. In a *Newsweek* piece, journalist Ramin Setoodah claims that "despite all the attention and outrage, the reason Larry died isn't as clear-cut as many people think." Gays, he argues, are everywhere—getting married, as characters on TV— "and no one seems to notice." For Setoodah, " 'the shrinking closet' is arguably a major factor in Larry's death," in that the earlier prohibitions that forced kids to closet themselves are giving way to a new openness around self-presentation. It is this new openness that journalists like Setoodah hold responsible for a display of gender and sexual difference that "invites" trouble. So, in this reading of the case, the closet and homophobia are no longer "the problem," but rather these kids themselves are in over their heads, "playing grown-up without fully knowing what that means." And schools (and the other kids who act violently against gay youth?) are simply "caught in between," particularly when it comes to a boy like

Larry, "who flaunted his sexuality and wielded it like a weapon [and] . . . push[ed] the boundaries so far that he put himself and others in danger." So Larry's death is not a horrifying tale of the effects of homophobic violence but rather reveals "the difficulty of defining the limits of tolerance."[17] Indeed. Because "tolerance" is so slippery and so much in the power of those who deem to do the tolerating, it can be posed—by journalists such as Setoodah— as something that is part of the problem itself: an overly tolerant society is here found culpable for the murder of a gay youth in that "our" supposed acceptance of his behavior ("pushing the boundaries") in a sense "provokes" the intolerant reaction. The framing of this as a tolerance question actively prohibits examining this as a homophobia question.

And many gay youth activists caution against reading liberal, northeastern urban experience into the rest of the country. As one social worker notes, "If you look at recent changes in our culture, one could presume that it is easier to come out. . . . But I am in New York. If I were in Oshkosh or someplace else where it is not so acceptable to be gay, it would be harder."[18] For all the stories of "easy out" gay kids, who blithely declaim their identity with barely a whisper of opprobrium, there are just as many (and of course many more untold) stories of kids afraid, harassed, alone. How do we square the new openness and outness of American youth with the continued reality not only of bullying and harassment but of teen suicide and suicide attempts, the rates of which are significantly higher in gay-identified youth: "gay and lesbian teenagers are two to three times more likely to attempt suicide than heterosexual teenagers, and homosexual teenagers account for 30 percent of all adolescent suicides"?[19] It may be the case that "gayness" has garnered a certain hip cachet in upper-class and urban settings, but out-of-the-ordinary sexual and gender configurations still bring on isolation and violence to most youth. I think again of my young nephew, whose penchant for "girls'" bathing suits and hair ribbons provoked concern on the part of his mother, not over his gender play itself but rather over his safety in the larger world of school and peers.

This much-publicized phenomenon of kids coming out ever younger prompts another, deeper, question: what does it mean to "come out" if one has never been in? Does an early recognition of "queerness" therefore undermine the "before and after" teleology of older out-of-the-closet narratives? And are contemporary youth both more open and nonchalant about sexual difference and reluctant to subscribe to the identity categories of earlier generations? Indeed, if coming out and coming of age (and into sexuality) are not sequential but synonymous, then the linear narrative that has so informed coming-out stories necessarily gets disrupted. This is enormously significant, although we won't know how far-reaching this is for years to come. If coming out has long been a "before and after" story, dependent on some period of "the closet" and hiding for its narrative logic, then these young kids—who simply can't have much of a "before"—may upend the very framework of coming out.

Tolerance has been undoubtedly tested by early-out youth and its limitations revealed. For our culture has no problem aggressively socializing even the youngest into heterosexuality (see baby stores and toddler pageants if you doubt this). Who hasn't heard a parent remark, of little Johnny's killer good looks, "he's going to break lots of girls' hearts one day" or watched two little toddlers on the playground and heard parents comment on their upcoming nuptials? Or heard a parent tease a little girl of six who is holding the hand of a little boy of seven, "Oh, Jane, is he your boyfriend?" We heterosexualize early and obsessively. But "accepting" queer youth or even youthful fluidity and experimentation evinces much more shock and awe, proving the limits of a tolerance that doesn't acknowledge its own (heterosexual) investments. And how, in this crazy new world of social media saturation, does the Internet figure into this equation, when kids can chat and interact with others without fear of identification and personal discovery?

## Virtually Out

A 2011 advice column in the gay weekly the *Advocate* reviews the protocol for online coming out. The young man seeking advice worries about the etiquette of declaring a sexual preference to all and sundry so impersonally, but the columnist assures him that his "one-click outing [is] as efficient as shopping on Amazon,"[20] even as he urges a more intimate approach to close family and friends. After the repeal of "Don't Ask, Don't Tell," twenty-one-year-old soldier Randy Phillips, stationed in Iraq, films himself coming out, tearfully, to his father. The video goes viral, and he gets his own Wikipedia page.[21] You can come out on Twitter in 140 characters, check out whenicameout. tumblr.com for niblets of advice and images, and view thousands of coming-out videos from around the world posted on YouTube and other social media sites. The end of "Don't Ask, Don't Tell," National Coming Out Day, and gay pride celebrations serve as hot points for revelations both mediated and more intimate. Basketball superstar Jason Collins makes headlines as the first major sports figure to come out while still in the game, and the tweets of support make their own headlines, even as negative tweets get dissed and recirculated.[22] Hunky newsman Anderson Cooper comes out in an email to journalist Andrew Sullivan, who posts it on his blog. It then gets reposted just about everywhere. Musician Frank Ocean comes out on Tumblr as having loved a man, and he prints some of his liner notes for an album on the site. After the Supreme Court decisions on same-sex marriage in June of 2013, teen star Raven-Symone tweets how happy she is that she can now get married, thus confirming long-circulating rumors about her sexual orientation.

Does anyone still sit mom and dad (or any combo of parental units) down with a stiff drink and tremulously stammer away, hemming and hawing, until some semblance of a story of sexual identity pushes through the excruciating metaphors and elliptical hints? My story and those of my peers sound so retro, like using a manual typewriter to convey your words instead of a keyboard or smartphone. Of course, lots of us noncelebrities do still come out the old-fashioned way since we don't have media platforms and, frankly, no one is interested but our family and friends. A coming-out Tweet makes no waves if the Tweeter has a following of five. But there is no doubt that the changing landscape of popular culture has itself shifted, with twenty-four-hour news cycles and the growing centrality of newer media forms such as the Internet and cellphone culture. These technological revolutions have profoundly altered the way in which we live our everyday lives and have dramatically changed both our official and unofficial culture. So what does "coming out" mean in an era of such new and expressive gay visibility? If once gayness was at least partially formed by its very absence in the public sphere, then how do we imagine people come to know themselves when they are visible in almost every venue of mainstream culture?

The most game-changing new venue is of course the Internet. The omnipresence of the Internet—with all that entails about communication, relationships, information, sexuality—must enter into our understandings of changing gay identity and community. How do we think about coming out in the age of Internet chat rooms and online avatars? If one is "out" online but "passes" as straight in the embodied social world, how are we to understand that person's relationship to any kind of gay identity? If one engages with other gays online but avoids physical and "offline" contacts, how might that form identity differently than for those gays whose sense of gayness is at least in part premised on that direct and public contact? And what about the potential, on the Internet, of simply "lurking" as a passive spectator?

First, of course, we need to acknowledge the obvious: on the Internet, coming out is (at least potentially) disembodied and removed from specific locales and even knowable identities. A process that was typically framed as a move from an internal understanding to an external declamation has become inevitably complicated by the mediating and often obfuscating space of chat rooms, message boards, and other virtual locales. Surely, whatever position we take on the Internet and its effects on identity and sexuality (and there are many arguments about this—running the gamut from utopian free space of blurred identities to recapitulation of old bigotries), there can be no doubt that it has supplied venues for recognition and revelation for people isolated either by geography or by familial or social location. Whether for rural youth in the US or urban adults in Iran, the Internet allows for casual contact, acknowledgment if not creation of identities, sexual assignations, and even political and social community when more embodied forms of communion are difficult or dangerous. These are not, of course, mutually exclusive. In other words, virtual coming out is not necessarily wholly distinct and separable from more embodied forms and is not solely the province of isolated youth or egregiously oppressed communities. The availability of virtual communication changes even those of us who entered our sexuality prior to its advent and serves individuals in ways both consequential and casual.

While all of us seem to use the Internet, its centrality for young people is incontestable. And for young people questioning their sexuality—where public spaces are simply forbidden or where fear and peer pressure reign—the Web can provide a unique space to "try on" identities and play out and perform them with a certain level of anonymity and freedom. Both youth themselves and Internet researchers see these gay-themed sites "as a practice arena for coming out, where the anonymity of the individual works to support the disclosure of traditionally anonymous sexual subjectivities."[23] There might not be a lot of agreement about the long-term *effects* of Internet use on youth, but it is surely the case that "the online world largely has been regarded as a site where queer young people are able to act in safety and privacy without the stigma associated with the experience of queerness."[24] The Internet provides—at the very least—access and information (and sexually explicit imagery and cybersex itself). In addition, given the context of continued prohibitions against even talking about gay sex (if you doubt this, see the initiatives in states like Arizona that would make it mandatory to "promote honor and respect for monogamous heterosexual marriage" when teaching sex ed and make it unlawful to "portray homosexuality as a positive alternative life-style"),[25] the Internet becomes a source of vital information, not just about safe sex practices but about the intricacies and variabilities of same-sex intimacy and identity. When schools still avoid the subject altogether or, worse, demonize gay sexuality as unnatural and dangerous, the Internet can provide vital and alarmingly basic information in the face of resolute indifference.

For those of us a bit older, part of the real pain of coming to terms with same-sex desire was the paucity of public information. That lack of easily accessible information was certainly a central component of the feelings of isolation and aloneness that so many of us experienced. I will never forget my own early attempts to access some kind of *detail* about the desires I was experiencing. It came in the form of paperback novels incongruously located on the shelves of the local drugstore and, later, in my terrified first steps into the local gay and lesbian bookstore—Giovanni's Room in my hometown of Philadelphia. Just being in the bookstore was both an act of information gathering and a tentative first step in coming out. Later, self-knowledge came in searching out that rare and coded film, covertly listening to that maudlin but gently empowering genre called "women's music," or walking into that bar or club. We were, to a certain extent, bounded by our own very real, very specific, and often very limited geography.

But the spaces of the Internet are seemingly endless, unlike "real" life, where if you don't like the one gay bar or the one gay community center, your social interactions may be limited. People jump from one Internet space to another, entering gay chat rooms and, when those turn out to be boring (or to not provide the certain something one is looking for), searching for others again and again. Surfing is the rule, not the exception. No longer bounded by the often depressing (and not very gay) realities of our towns and cities, where bars have often closed down as a result of both ever-higher rents and ill-conceived "public health" initiatives aimed at preventing HIV transmission, and bookstores, too, have largely disappeared due to mainstreaming and economic pressures (e.g., Amazon), the Internet offers a kind of mobility unimaginable in earlier eras.

And if kids are coming out ever younger, the need for information, community, and support in nonpublic places becomes even more pressing. As social media researcher Vikki Fraser notes, these online venues provide "young people with a space where they can experience a community in which they can test out and practice their sexualities." Further, these spaces are "highly necessary in contemporary society because people are exploring and identifying their sexuality at younger ages, thus rendering public spaces (e.g., pubs, bars, and clubs) traditionally used by queer people inaccessible for individuals at stages where they are most in need of support and community."[26] In this sense, coming-out stories have found a new life on the Internet, providing "a powerful source of group cohesion in the face of the continuing stigmatization of homosexuality,"[27] and kids are increasingly using the Internet both as a place to "try out" their coming out (before, perhaps, doing it "for real" with their parents) and to model coming out for others. One study even reports on a teen who developed a link on his homepage, where he had produced a kind of form letter for a coming-out missive to parents.[28] Of course, all of this does raise a bit of a chicken-and-egg question: Are kids actually "discovering" their sexual desires ever earlier? Or are kids coming out younger because there now exist relatively safe places and relatively easy access to information via the Internet? In other words, is the availability of new (and somewhat "safer") venues for coming out in a sense producing or inciting the phenomenon of earlier awareness and articulation?

In any case, it would be hard to overestimate the significance of the Internet and social media revolution, less for the actual formation of identities and communities than, more pragmatically, for the easy and simple accessing of information. Typing "gay" or "lesbian" or "queer" or "trans" into a Google search brings up thousands of possibilities. Certainly, the bar (or street or park) could and did serve as a singular space of coming out—or as an alternative space for being even as one traversed and lived in mainstream spaces by day. Yet surely it is true that coming out as both narrative and lived practice changes in a world in which one can Google "coming out" and find endless stories, resources, references, and chat rooms that provide a space not only to enact that ritual but also to locate it in a larger collective framework. There are archives and resources, stories old and new, tales from rural teens and urban elders, confessions from every possible region of the world in every conceivable language. These are, of course, of mixed provenance, and to get substantive and usable info takes some amount of work and familiarity with the Web. And it remains the case that not all kids—by any stretch of the imagination—have easy access to computers. But, in a keystroke, the possibilities to know, to hear from, to see, to talk, to touch "gayness" in some way becomes instantly possible.

Importantly, this kind of tentative searching can be done privately and anonymously, although surely kids worry that their parents will snoop on their computers and find links to gay sites, outing them in the process. What a different experience from my own, in which that paperback was—well—stolen to avoid the curious looks from the drugstore cashier (although I did fear my mother finding my stash of books, much as kids now fear that their parents will "stumble" on their Internet browsing history). And I remember gathering up my courage to walk into that bookstore and, later, that first bar. That profound sense of exposure shaped those early forays into gay spaces—exposure to others but also, through that simple act of walking into a bookstore, exposure to myself of myself. To search for gay life and information and stories on the Internet may entail some degree of trepidation, but it can't compare to that visceral sense of physical vulnerability felt by earlier generations whose own searches brought them not to the gay-friendly website but to the bar, the bookstore, the demonstration, the meeting. For before (and after) Stonewall, of course, those bars or meeting places were themselves dangerous places, subject to police raids, public exposure, and social vulnerability.

The Internet makes simple information gathering and access easier but also can alter the very process of coming out itself—for adults as well as for youth. If that linear story is already shaken up—by "already outness" or earlier sexual awareness—the Internet offers, as one researcher puts it, "a one-way window into a gay bar: the individual can observe but not be observed."[29] Caryn Brooks, writing in *Time* magazine, argues that forms of social media such as

Facebook shift coming out significantly, even though "the transparency that online social networking imposes is something that takes getting used to. For many people, exposing yourself to a potentially immense and judgmental community can be new and scary." Sites like Facebook can and do relieve the endless and reiterative burden of coming out. "Facebook," as Brooks writes, "is like drive-thru coming out: quick, cheap and open all night. Coming out used to be an exhausting process. You had to come out again and again and again to all your friends at different times. Nowadays, even with social networking, gays still have to come out, but one of the key differences between our pre-profile selves and our new online presentations is that now (finally!) the burden is also on our friends to discover and digest our identities. For the lesbian, gay, bisexual and transgender (LGBT) community, Facebook et al. have finally leveled the identity field, and it's kinda nice."[30]

Of course, in this era, not only do kids meet people and come out to others individually on the Internet, but the DIY YouTube phenomenon has spawned a home industry in coming-out videos, which in turn has spawned endless parodies and tangential renderings. Here, as in Facebook and other social media sites, we see an opportunity not only to come out en masse but to create forms of media that last beyond that fleeting moment of personal declaration. These direct camera addresses vie with made-for-YouTube "fictional" accounts of coming out to provide a new archive of coming-out documents available to anyone with a computer. Some, of course, become the stuff of celebrity, but others simply add to the ever-growing archive of first-person accounts.

The ready availability of information and the unavoidable presence of gay coming-out stories on the Internet can and does shift—for some kids—the sense of total isolation and aloneness that characterized earlier generations. In study after study, real kids say the same things: it was such a relief to know they weren't alone, to "meet" others like themselves, to talk with other kids about coming out, and so on. Kids also report a greater sense of freedom—particularly the freedom to make a fool of oneself—on the Internet. Not only is the experience of being mocked online perhaps less painful than in real-life situations but, unlike in their schools and with their families, kids alienated from a particular Web community can click quite easily to another.

Still, it is not at all clear that virtual communication makes disclosure *itself* easier or more available or less central to forming a gay identity. In one study of online use by lesbian youth, the author discusses how "the decision to disclose sexual identity is taken to indicate the successful completion of a stage of emotional maturity" and how kids clearly frame their own self-understanding in terms of where they are in the "coming-out hierarchy."[31] In other words, older paradigms and frameworks don't simply disappear when a new technology for expressing them insinuates itself into the everyday. I was struck by how familiar many of these coming-out stories on the Internet were to me. When you look at the endless compendiums of narratives now on the Internet—in gay chat rooms, generic Google searches, blogs—what is striking is how much they sound like the older stories. Of course, the sample is a skewed one, as we could surmise that many, if not most, of the kids who post their coming-out stories do so to relay a sense of struggle or difficulty. In other words, it would seem sort of beside the point, I guess, to write a coming-out story that basically said, "I thought I might be gay. Then I was sure. Then I told my parents, who told me they loved me and were happy. Then I told my classmates, who gave me a big group hug and marched with me in the next gay pride parade. The end." No doubt some of those stories exist, but those who come out with relative ease and assurance of continued support and love from friends and family don't often feel they even have a story to tell, although curiously that is the new story we are seeing portrayed in much of the mainstream media, even as these more heartrending self-authored tales populate the Web.

## My Avatar Has a Girlfriend

While not as transformative as we might imagine, these new stories on the Web are characterized by an openness produced at least in part by the newly available technology that allows people to be engaged yet anonymous. Many stories reference other stories set either in school, in families, at work, or now in the very virtual space in which they first utter the words "I am gay." Perhaps the profound sense of "I am the only one" is forever eradicated in a world of gay visibility. If that is the case, it is no small step toward an easier life for millions of gay youth. But the internal struggles, the sense of fear in telling parents, the harassment that shapes a life, the desire to be other than gay—these all crop up in first-person narratives today much as they did thirty years ago, when intrepid gay writers and editors started collecting such stories in volumes like *One Teenager in Ten*. Even the personal accounts told on *Coming Out Stories* of gay cable channel Logo don't seem light-years away from earlier tales. To a one, these young people share their deep fears of familial rejection. "I don't want to tell you," says one young woman; "you're going to hate me." Another admits she feels like she's "living a double life." The recent (attenuated and not to mention seriously odd) coming out of actor and director Jodie Foster at the Golden Globe Awards speaks to the persistent sense of loneliness and fear that marks even those we imagine "above it all." Her trepidation to utter the secret everyone already knew made the speech both bizarre and utterly poignant: "So while I'm here being all confessional, I guess I have a sudden urge to say something that I've never really been able to air in public. So a declaration that I'm a little nervous about but maybe not quite as nervous as my publicist right now . . . But I'm just going to put it out there, right? Loud and proud, right? So I'm going to need your support on this."[32] The kicker, of course, is that she then goes on to say "I'm single" instead of finally saying those much more troublesome words "I'm gay." I guess this was meant to be amusing, poking fun at those who have pressured her for years to speak about her sexuality. But her fear and anxiety seemed almost palpable. Why should she still, now, in 2013, in the era of gay marriage and rainbow love, need support and fear her publicist's anxiety? A woman of her accomplishments and stature and economic security? Even more worrisome is how these old/new coming-out stories merge with the "born that way" refrain of the medicalized moment and invoke a personal storyline that conflates "I've always known" with "it's not a choice."

Similarly, the early fantasies of the Internet as a site for the radical rejection of singular identities have been shown to be limited, as "fluid selves are no less subject to cultural hegemonies, rules of conduct and regulating cultural norms than are solid ones."[33] The "real world," with all its fears and bigotries and discomforts, doesn't disappear when we stare at the screen and disappear into the chaos of Web engagements. But it does—at least for those who use the Web on a regular basis and especially for youth—alter or expand the possibilities for "outness" and for identity formation. It has, "quite simply, revolutionized the experience of growing up gay. Isolation and shame persist among gay teenagers, of course, but now, along with the inhospitable families and towns in which many find themselves marooned, there exists a parallel online community—real people like them in cyberspace with whom they can chat, exchange messages and even engage in (online) sex."[34] In some ways, perhaps the bar and the website aren't so different after all, each in its own way a respite from social spaces that seem overwhelmingly heterosexual.

In an article on gay teens online, for example, the author connects with a young Christian boy, deeply afraid and pretty well isolated, for whom the Internet becomes refuge:

> He called a crisis line for gay teenagers, where a counselor suggested he attend a gay support group in a city an hour and a half away. But being 15, he was too young to drive and afraid to enlist his parents' help in what would surely seem a bizarre and suspicious errand. It was around this time that Jeffrey first typed the words "gay" and "teen" into a search engine on the computer he'd gotten several months before and was staggered to find himself aswirl in a teeming online gay world, replete with resource centers, articles, advice columns, personals, chat

rooms, message boards, porn sites and—most crucially—thousands of closeted and anxious kids like himself. That discovery changed his life.[35]

The boy goes on to tell the reporter, "The Internet is the thing that has kept me sane. I live constantly in fear. I can't be my true self. My mom complains: 'I can see you becoming more detached from us. You're always spending time on the computer.' But the Internet is my refuge."[36] Fear has, interestingly and sadly, not disappeared but can now be abated or managed somewhat by the "refuge" that is the Internet. For this kid, and for so many others, it is not only that the Internet provides information and resources to help him navigate his sexuality, but it allows him to connect with others in similar situations. This seems to me one of the most crucial transformations wrought by the Internet, and one that surely marks off the new era as so very altered from the info-starved days of yore. To know that there are others "like you" and that you can talk with them without leaving the safety of your home, well, changes the picture.

Along with that freedom and potential to simply watch comes a certain amount of safety; the Internet provides a "safe (from commitment, entanglement, abuse, embarrassment, stigma, exposure, and violence) environment to take the first steps toward becoming homosexual. . . . Anonymity and the ability to switch off the computer make for an environment where sexual issues can be explored with little fear."[37] This is particularly true for communities and individuals for whom the official mass media (TV, film, popular journalism) is both less accessible and less meaningful as a site for identity formation. As social media analyst Mary Gray convincingly argues in her recent book, *Out in the Country*, for many youth (rural and otherwise) the glam stories of gay life on mainstream TV just don't resonate. For one of her informants, it becomes clear that "the narratives of authenticity, of queer realness, that she found online reading coming-out stories from teens both in her state and living worlds away" mean more to her growing sense of identity than the mass-produced icons of mainstream popular culture.[38] For rural youth—and those in locales similarly isolated from visible gay politics and culture—the Internet becomes not only a site for becoming, for producing an identity, but also a crucial place of recognition and witnessing. Much as for earlier generations that first tentative step into the gay bar (or, sometimes, the gay bookstore) was an experience with multiple iterations (sexual, communal, social), so too the step into the Internet chat room alleviates the anxiety of aloneness that can still characterize gay coming of age, even in this era of new openness. It's not that other forms of media and other venues for identity formation aren't still relevant, but as Gray argues, the "realness found in online narratives as compared to fictional accounts in film and television indexes the limits of mass culture's ability to bring visibility to LGBT-identifying people in rural communities. They find comfort and familiarity in the narratives of realness circulating online because, more so than fictional characters situated in urban scenes where a critical mass of LGBT visibility is taken for granted, these stories resonate with the complex negotiation of visibility and maintaining family ties that consume rural young people's everyday lives."[39]

On the other hand, it is equally plausible that the practice of Internet coming out, for example, actively disables that same act in "real life." The earlier impetus to come out was premised on an alignment between aspects of self: bringing one's sense of "true" identity in line with the public presentation of that identity. What happens when a new platform emerges to present that "inner" identity but without any of the fears and challenges that typically accompany it (e.g., rejection, familial displacement, discrimination)? It is surely possible that finding a gay home on the Web could serve as a substitute for finding that gay home in the physical world; it could function as a sort of release valve, displacing the need to come out to embodied family and friends. If one has a vibrant and varied gay life in and on the Internet—without substantive risk or fear of rejection—then presumably that could provide all the (fun) gayness one needs, without any of the (unfun) discriminatory residue of the real. While some people might celebrate this (because it allows for an engagement with identity free of physical fear), I can only imagine this displacement or disconnect negatively in that it further strips us all of the need to develop vibrant *public* queer spaces.

Certainly, we do see all kinds of "Internet disconnects" where people engage in activities and assume identities (whether for online gaming or pornography or political blogging) that run counter to how they are perceived in the "real world." But it does appear that my fear—that queer youth may not just use the Internet as respite or "release valve" but may retreat from the social—is overblown and not supported by the evidence. On the contrary, many scholars have written about the relationship of the Internet or virtual world to the real or embodied world as a symbiotic one, so that actions and discourses in one arena impact and affect the other, or even construct, as Internet researcher danah boyd argues, new kinds of "networked public" spaces that need to be understood on their own complex terms, not just as stand-ins for "real life" off the disembodied net.[40] Youth researchers have also reported that gay kids online do use the Internet as a sort of intermediary step toward entering a series of gay communities in the "real world." In other words, the fear that Internet gay communities would undermine real-world gay communities may be unfounded, and coming out on the Net might very well support coming out in person.

# 3

# The Closet 2.0

I admit to some confusion. On the one hand, it does seem that "the closet" is neither as singular nor as significant as it once was. The combined forces of technological innovations and more expansive gay visibility have clearly undermined our reliance on this once-dominant storyline. On the other hand, as I think the preceding pages indicate, we've hardly entered into a brave new world of freely flung closet doors and easy-out everyday lives. Perhaps these singular stories have receded in the popular imagination, but I'm not sure that the lived experience of duplicity, of hiding, of demurral has really disappeared. We certainly have witnessed a waning of this theme in mainstream popular culture but not, perhaps, in the alternative worlds of gay films, festivals, and novels that are produced and consumed by a largely gay audience. So, curiously, many gay media audiences still find themselves watching these iconic tales while heterosexuals— when watching gay lives on TV or in film—are largely presented with a world of already-out gays whose coming out is either in the past or fairly inconsequential. It is likely, of course, that there are many things occurring simultaneously here and that we are living— no surprise!—in a deeply contradictory moment.

Thus, while the closet and coming out are and have been always narrower, more complicated, and less universal than typically construed, in the popular imagination they have often served as a sign of gayness itself. Part of what coming out does—either in its real-life forms or in its cultural representations—is to put a singular and intimate face on "gayness." Not only has this been the dominant theme in so many mainstream films, TV shows, after-school specials, novels, and magazine articles, but it has been a theme embraced and promoted by gay writers, filmmakers, journalists, and activists. Just a cursory glance at the gay section of any local megabookstore or at the gay genres on offer at Netflix or the websites of our major organizations shows that they feature coming out front and center. Even our T-shirts proclaim that we are "out and proud," although recent ones play on the closet paradigm by smirking, "Nobody knows I'm a lesbian." "Come out, come out wherever you are" has been the rallying cry of endless demonstrations and the goal of numerous political campaigns: gay pride inverts gay shame much as coming out undoes the closet. Almost every major gay organization includes guides to coming out as part of its basic arsenal of gay issues, and archives of coming-out stories flood the Internet. Every new celebrity or politician who comes out publicly is greeted by the gay equivalent of high fives (high snaps?), regardless of whether they take that opportunity to publicly embrace gay rights. National Coming Out Day is one of the signal events for gay and gay-supportive students around the country, and coming-out stories are featured in novels of gay youth and more generic teen fiction as well. Even one of the central political struggles of recent years—inclusion in the military—has centered around the framework of "in" or "out."

It actually took a bit of time for the coming-out story to become fodder for mainstream culture, even though it percolated through gay film festivals and gay novels earlier. It isn't really until the mid-'80s that it emerges as *the* way Hollywood can get its arms around gayness, partly because it jibes so well with the preexisting "social problem" genre found in both TV and film. So those very first films and TV specials with explicitly gay themes invariably centered on a coming-out story. These stories—in film, TV, literature—followed a typical trajectory, taking our incipient gay character on the well-worn path of confusion, internal torment, self-loathing, and resistance, followed by self-acceptance and emergence to oneself and others.

There might be variations on this theme—for example, maybe our nascent homo would assiduously and with disastrous effect attempt to straighten out—but master narratives do, well, tend to have fairly consistent trajectories.

I remember so well these emblematic stories. They were both exhilarating because they uttered our difference into existence and so filled with pathos and turmoil that they inevitably made entry into "the life" seem pretty damn scary. Sometimes they ended with real joy, as in the independent British film *My Beautiful Laundrette*, and sometimes they were revelatory and charming, as when Lianna's light bulbs go off in a lesbian bar in John Sayles's eponymous 1983 film or when the sad divorcée of 1985's *Desert Hearts* realizes she has a yen for tall country girls. But other times the coming out was itself wrapped in another layer of loss, such as when the poignant Philadelphia lawyer is forced out at the workplace as his AIDS becomes physically visible or when the lesbian mom faces a custody battle after coming out. On television, there were the maudlin dramas and after-school specials in which chagrined fathers, heads held down, revealed that daddy didn't love mommy anymore—he really loved Mr. Jones down the block. Often melodramatic and couched in a context of fear and furtiveness, they did nonetheless offer a full-on gay storyline, not just the ambiguous or stereotyped characters populating older films and TV shows.

So coming out as a personal process and as a political strategy has not been tossed out in this supposedly new era. Even as it has receded from public view, it has not been made redundant. If earlier dogma had it that coming out was the epitome of gay experience—both the social marker of political coming of age and the psychological imprimatur of mature identity formation—then the new queer dogmas perhaps invert that to champion not exactly coming out's opposite (the closet) but instead a more amorphous space of endless becoming or even a more banal fluidity. There is, however, an important distinction to be made between a decline of the coming-out plot as the master narrative of gay life and the broader thesis of the end of the closet per se. Steven Seidman clarifies that what he sees as the increasing normalization and "routinization" of homosexuality does not imply a new world wholly free of either self-doubt or discrimination. While he does believe that many gays do in fact live lives "beyond the closet," he seems to be implying not the disappearance of duplicity and self-management but the increasing specificity of it. His argument is that "identity management" still goes on, but the closet—as a broad and all-inclusive term that seems to define a life wholly lived in a place of doubleness and hiding—no longer rules the day. Gay identity, then, is understood as "more situation-specific than patterning of a whole way of life, as is suggested by the concept of the closet."[1]

While homophobia is obviously still alive and well—and many gay people still live in fear and trembling of it—an increasingly large number do not and live lives both mainstreamed and normalized. For many scholars, this has a paradoxical effect. On the one hand, gays no longer need to define themselves along that binary axis (gay versus straight) and therefore can avoid all the identity-politics detritus of ghettoization, separation, and the like. "Sexuality" as a primary definer of a social group thus has less play in these new supposedly uncloseted times. On the other hand, that normalization and identity dispersal can hinder social activism and community. If same-sex desire is reduced to any other minor aspect of personality— and therefore not the heart of a life project—then it matters not. For some people, we are in or rapidly approaching an era in which homosexuality simply won't matter.

But to what extent is this putative "beyond the closet" space dependent on a performance of homosexuality such that it doesn't look any different from heterosexuality? Post-gay, beyond-the-closet fantasies depend on sameness as one of the key underlying features of tolerance. Being seen as "normal" can only mean—in a world in which heterosexual identities are the norm—being relatively invisible as a gay person. In a study on workers in supposedly "gay-friendly" work environments, Christine Williams and her coauthors find just such a phenomenon: that the sense of "acceptance" and inclusion is dependent on being a particular kind of "gay," whereby "in addition to conservative politics, normal is equated with having a monoga-mous, long-term relationship."[2] One of the workers they interview, Max, says explicitly "that he wins over his straight coworkers because he is 'not the Queen of Sheba at work,' suggesting that he is not effeminate in his manner. In all of these ways, Max does not look or act gay, which he thinks makes him accepted as normal among his coworkers." Or, as another respondent claims, "I present a case of the things that the traditional, core group really like. I have a fam-ily. We have a house in the suburbs. We drive an SUV (laughs). So everyone can really relax. I go to church. It's just that my partner's a woman and that's about it. In all other respects, I'm just like them."[3] The framework of "tolerance" undoubtedly orients this discourse; this individual wouldn't want to "flaunt it" (whatever that means) because the limits of tolerance are almost always located at one of three places: gender nonnormativity, expressive sexuality, and politi-cal engagement.

Legal scholar Kenji Yoshino writes about this elegantly, recall-ing his early years as a law professor at Yale, where he was told to be "a homosexual professional" rather than a "professional homosexual." He immediately gets what is meant here, for "to be a 'homosexual professional' was to be a professor of constitutional law who 'hap-pened' to be gay. To be a 'professional homosexual' was to be a gay professor who made gay rights his work. Others echoed the senti-ment in less elegant formulations. Be gay, my world seemed to say. Be openly gay, if you want. But don't flaunt it."[4] For Yoshino, then, the closet doors had long been opened, but he found new impedi-ments to full expression.

While coming out may have changed in this new era of media visibility, Internet access, and tepid social embrace, it remains a pro-cess almost uniquely "gay" in its very essence. Because sexual differ-ence is not typically marked on the body (unlike racial and gender categorization), it must be uttered or performed or enacted to make it manifest to others (and sometimes to oneself). It must be made visible to be made legible. But also—and this is important to remember— because heterosexuality is so assumed, so much the default, so *not* in need of explanation, gayness is always placed not as the simple parallel to heterosexuality but as its hidden other. While both masculinity and whiteness are equally dominant in relation to femininity and "color," they are—by and large—visible. If you appear to be a woman, no one typically assumes you are a man unless you declare otherwise, and the same can be said for racial identifiers. Thus, the potential to pass is quite different along these axes. Interestingly, "coming out as disabled appears to have more in common with racial discourses of coming out or passing than with queer discourse, since the contingent (non)visibility of queer identity has produced a variety of nonverbal and/or spoken means to signal that identity, while the assumed visibility of race and disability has produced an absence of nonverbal signs and a distrust of spoken claims to those identities."[5]

This issue of visibility cannot be overstated here. Gays—unlike racial minorities but perhaps more like ethnic ones such as Jews—are assumed straight unless proven otherwise. This is simply to say that until "compulsory heterosexuality" and the assumption of heterosexuality are altered fundamentally, coming out or some version of a declamatory self-naming will always have to play a part in gay culture and politics.

Nevertheless, the decline of the coming-out story as *the* Hollywood story of gayness is of no small significance. Positively, the decline of these narratives signals queerness as less traumatic and less relational to heterosexuality. While coming-out stories are ostensibly about the gay person revealing "the truth" to him- or herself and then others, in practice (both in everyday life and in popular media) these accounts often focused exclusively on the horror of the parent/co-worker/husband/wife/friend who was told this "truth." In films and television and even popular literature, these earlier coming-out stories gave us glimpses into the internal struggles of gays but even more gave us endless depictions of heartbroken parents, bereft spouses, and confused co-workers. So, in this sense, the decline of coming-out stories may signal a move away from that focus on heterosexual reaction and—finally—allow us to imagine stories of gay life that aren't always seen through the lens of heartbroken and horrified heteros. Because "the focus on the closet, and the forms in which meanings are conveyed—as declarations/acts of identity/desire—has perhaps contributed to an under-appreciation of the importance of what comes after coming out,"[6] a shift away from this storyline might provide entrée into the richness of gay lives.

But I think we risk losing a vivid depiction of the reality of homophobia and heterosexism if we ditch this framework altogether. The coming-out narrative, in both a personal and a more social and cultural sense, forces an "audience" to witness rejection and discrimination and the effects of living a life not fully open. The new image of the fully formed fag may parry the slings and arrows of outrageous homophobia occasionally but is largely shown as accepted, loved, and embraced by both a benevolent family and a benign body politic. Alas, the body politic is not quite that benign. In presenting a world of already-out and always "accepted" gays, we might actually obscure or even cover up the persistence of both institutional and personal homophobia. For example, in an episode of the 2012 sitcom *The New Normal*, the two lead characters—a gay male couple starting a family with the help of a surrogate—find themselves the object of bigotry and derision as they embrace in a department store.[7] Kudos to the show for depicting the persistence of homophobia, but shame on it for not once mentioning the word. Since the animus is treated as a sort of *generic* bigotry, its specificity disappears. Of course, this cover-up is precisely what the framework of tolerance depends on, as heterosexuals can pat themselves on the back for their beneficent acceptance of their homosexual neighbors or as homophobia itself goes unmentioned.

As oppressive as "the closet" itself is and was, the *discourse* of "the closet" also allowed for an explicit engagement with self-hatred and shame, or what became called "internalized homophobia." Put differently, the story of coming out, in its more political versions, does reckon head-on with the costs of a life lived without recognition and with the everyday spectacle of misrecognition. It can connect us with shame—not of "being gay" but of being forced to not be gay. Or, again, with the shame of homophobia itself. In this genre's most moving forms, it depicts a coming *out* of something (denial, duplicity, the closet) but also a coming *into* something (gay community, self-identity, sexuality). This is part of the story that the groundbreaking play *Angels in America* detailed: the price of the closet (Roy Cohn) and the pleasures of leaving it ( Joe Pitt).[8] So the (modern) story of the closet and coming out typically does speak of a rubric of discrimination that enforces the closet and makes the emergence from it both difficult and necessary. Post-Stonewall, especially, coming out is celebrated not simply as a personal declaration of self-understanding but as a recognition of social solidarity in the face of both institutional and individual animus. Coming out was the antidote to self-hatred, the cure, the exit from the closet and the lie. It was what made Harvey Milk more than just a city supervisor and Stonewall not just an everyday riot.

There is also another quite interesting sense of coming out that may get lost in this new era, and that is the twinned trope of coming out into a community and being "brought out" sexually. When one spoke of who "brought you out," it was a particularly queer subcultural version of sexual initiation. Because it need not refer to one's first sexual experience (often, of course, with the opposite sex), the framework of being "brought out" has within it that dual sense of sexuality and community. One is "brought out" by another queer person and simultaneously brought into a queer community, or as historian George Chauncey notes, "Gay people in the pre-war years [pre–World War I] . . . did not speak of coming out of what we call the gay closet but rather of coming out into what they called homosexual society or the gay world, a world neither so small, nor so isolated, nor . . . so hidden as closet implies."[9] So coming out in these earlier and sometimes explicitly political iterations was understood as a process both personal and social, both confessional and performative, narrating a "shared fate" but also an "imagined community." As Seidman points out, "The narrative of coming out of the closet constructs gay individuals as suffering a common fate in a society organized around normative heterosexuality. Gay individuals are said to share an experience of secrecy and social isolation, the ordeal of refashioning a stigmatized identity, and negotiating social inclusion. This narrative shapes a common identity and politicizes it by making homosexuals into unjust social victims."[10]

## If Everyone's Out, Where Are All the Homosexuals?

Perhaps it is a fantasy of both privileged gay elites and paranoid anti-gay activists that the days of the closet are over or that coming out as a paradigm is mostly a remnant of the past. Or maybe a trickle seems like a flood when you're in a desert. Popular pundits and gossip columnists keep assuring us that "today's closet doors must be a bit easier to open. With the recent flood of stars coming out and embracing their true sexuality—Anna Paquin, Ricky Martin—Hollywood seems to be welcoming them."[11] A flood? A minor teen star and a washed-up pop star? Add to that tiny list the TV has-been Meredith Baxter, who revealed in *People* magazine that she, too, is a happy lesbian mom, and you have a veritable dribble of minor celebrities claiming queer credibility.[12] And, increasingly, these celebs are often outing themselves before the twenty-four-hour Twitter brigade does the job, attempting "to control their public personas by addressing personal issues directly with their fans."[13] Nevertheless, most celebrities still come out in the form of a magazine interview, often after being hounded for months or seeing the Internet gossip machine set in full motion. And, of course, after singer Martin revealed his sexuality on his own website (after, again, years of public speculation), *People* (and others) dutifully picked up the ball and ran with it. But that other message of caution shouldn't be lost. As *People* magazine notes, Martin was told that if he were to come out, "all the years you've worked and everything you've built will collapse."[14]

It's not to say that more stars (and politicians and business leaders and teachers and . . .) aren't coming out; all evidence seems to point to a growing number of out public figures and private individuals, even as the real numbers remain paltry. Yet to see this as the final triumph of a new openness and ease about gay life and sexuality would be naive. Again, I need to repeat a question that I can't help but chew over throughout this book: if that were the case—if coming out were so easy, so *not* a big deal—then wouldn't we simply see many, many more out-and-proud people at every level of public life? Why would people still kill themselves—like college freshman Tyler Clementi[15]—when their sexuality is made public? As critic Daniel Mendelsohn notes, "being gay is less controversial today than at any other time in American history, . . . and yet for many gay people, particularly gay youth, and especially gay youth of color, the acknowledgment that you're gay is still a process fraught with anxiety, if not terror and often violence."[16] It is just so hard to square these competing realities. Kids are coming out earlier and with more ease than in earlier generations, yet they still get kicked out of the home, bullied, even murdered. The larger social and cultural world "officially" greets coming out with a bored nod, yet still so few public figures do it. So, for example, in 2010, Republican hit man Ken Mehlman finally acknowledges what was a fairly open secret, and there is a flurry of activity and then it disappears. And yes, as one article states, that "new blink-and-you'll-miss-it style is an important hallmark of changing times."[17]

The coming out of TV anchor Anderson Cooper was no "news"—it had long been an open secret—but it illustrates well the curious and contradictory times we are in. It was on the front pages—admitted first in an interview with gay writer Andrew Sullivan—and then an active news story for several days post-admission. Cooper is hailed as brave and inspiring by gay and straight alike, and his admission becomes the opportunity to muse on the wonderfully positive changes in our social acceptance of homosexuality. So the *New York Times* writes that, until very recently, "to be identified as gay was . . . a potential career-killer."[18] But no more. For the *Times* and other venues, this moment indicated how far we have come; being openly gay, they now claim, is greeted with a "shrug" because it is so "unremarkable." Even further, a celebrity coming out is yet more evidence of our increasingly "tolerant" society, in which "most people didn't care" and "it just isn't a big deal anymore." But have we lost all sense of irony here, much less reality? Surely it is true that things have changed, but doesn't the fact that this is news fodder indicate that it remains some sort of a "deal" still, if no longer the biggest deal on the block? While praising Cooper for finally coming out, Mendelsohn, writing in the *New York Times,* indicts the "cozy omerta" that protects elite celebrities at the cost of countless others but also points out how even elites like Cooper "are still constrained by, and often internalize, the prejudices that oppress them"[19] either through nodding to privacy or scurrying away from political alliances. That Cooper declined to discuss this until his midforties, even though he claims that his gayness was nothing new to *him* and that he most assuredly was not ashamed of being gay, does seem curious if not disingenuous.

Indeed, *this* is becoming the new storyline: coming out is so yesterday. Of course, what I've been arguing here is that it is not in fact over, although it is changing. And, further, there are hidden costs to clanging the death knell of coming out. When Jim Parsons, actor in the TV comedy *The Big Bang Theory,* casually came out during an interview with a theater reporter for the *New York Times,* he claimed—and everyone seemed to buy it—that he was not coming out since he had never been "in." Instead, he argued, he was simply a private person. Of course, one might then ask why so many gay celebrities seem so much more private than heterosexual celebrities. And Parsons's insistence that he's "an actor, not a gay actor" is spun by the media as more dignified than those "gay celebrities [who] often use Twitter to champion same-sex marriage."[20] So this shrug of a coming out is better (and to be tolerated) because it doesn't "use" gayness as a platform to pronounce on either gay rights or anti-gay homophobia. Not only is this privacy argument contrasted with those "in your face" days of yore, but Parsons's ease is interpreted as one more sign of the "post-gay moment—meaning that public discussion about one's sexuality is so common now, so unexceptional in parts of America, that sexual orientation is akin to personal characteristics like race, ethnicity and religion. . . . Being known as gay seems like no big whoop."[21] These writers do often nod to ongoing closetedness, particularly among Hollywood film actors, but then sweep this under the rug with paeans to all the changes that are by now detailed by rote when claiming a new tolerant world. But rarely is the flip side mentioned: the persistence of discrimination, the inability to pass the Employment Non-Discrimination Act, the continued violence.

What seems unquestionably true is that coming out simply isn't as newsworthy as it once was or as inevitably destructive to one's career. While there are no doubt risks to coming out, many people have argued that in this more gay-friendly legal and political climate, what gets punished is not "outness" per se but rather those who "flaunt" their queerness or do not cover it under veils of privacy and discretion. And, truthfully, isn't it overstating the case to claim that "by daring anyone to overreact, the newest generation of gay public figures is making a clear statement that there is a 'new normal'—and it consists of being plainspoken, clear, and truthful about who you are."[22] But if no one cares, then why aren't more people out? Issues of duplicity, demurral, switched pronouns, and blurted revelations are not, alas, only modes of a closeted past. They remain with us today, even in our bright new rainbow world.

It is this doubleness, or rather continuation of older forms, that is so hard to get our heads around. For we must remember, even in this era of supposed visibility and openness, very few openly gay anythings (celebrities, politicians, etc.) circulate in our cultural imagination. Contrary to popular belief, the closet (or some semblance of it) is not a thing of the past in this country or around the world. For all the talk about the brave new world of open gayness, where we are supposedly everywhere, it remains the case that—at least in the space of the public square—surprisingly little has changed. The Gay and Lesbian Leadership Institute identifies roughly eight hundred openly gay public officials *worldwide*, with the vast majority being in the US.[23] While this is an increase from previous years, it still represents a drop in the bucket. There may be gay sheriffs and mayors here and there, but a quick glance at both local and national statistics reveals the paucity of openly gay political figures. Now, this begs any number of questions both about data gathering and about different cultural contexts in which "outness" is quite differently inflected. But in public life—celebrity culture, Hollywood, government, business—an assertion of an openly same-sex sensibility remains a minor note and one still marked by fear and trepidation. When country-music star Chely Wright came out in 2010, it might as well have been fifty years ago. As she told her story on the *Ellen* show, she described her fear of discovery and familial and fan rejection. It didn't sound so new. And neither did Ellen's designation of her coming out as a "brave" and risky thing to do, requiring determination and compelling need.[24] Growing up, this young woman desperately looked around for someone "like her" (which subsequently became the title of her book) and felt as alone and singular and isolated as earlier generations. While pop star Ricky Martin's coming out might have been greeted with a big yawn (Ricky Martin? Gay?? Impossible!), we do have to wonder what took him so long, and it turns out he was urged to be silent so as not to interfere with his growing career. Out gay actor Rupert Everett in fact declared unequivocally that "coming out as a gay actor ruined his career in Hollywood."[25]

So it presents something of a dilemma at this point: how to reckon with the reality of declining coming-out stories in popular culture (and the common belief among both gays and straights that coming out is no big deal anymore) and simultaneously with the continued reality of so few out gay politicians, celebrities, and just plain folks. The most recent (2013) Pew Research Center poll of LGBTQ adults showed, to the surprise of many observers, that large numbers report that they are not open about their sexuality; just over one-half report being out to their mothers, and the number is significantly lower when it comes to fathers. The closet has clearly not disappeared.

Many critics simply interpret this as a disconnect between personal life and structural and institutional life. Seidman, for example, has noted the dissonance between the changes at an interpersonal level and how (or how not) those changes have been institutionalized at the structural level. So in this sense, institutions and social structures simply need to catch up with the enormous changes being lived at the personal and individual level. This has some truth to it, and certainly some of what we're waiting for is perhaps really demographic: the growing up of this generation born into gay visibility and their assumption of leadership in corporations, legislatures, businesses, Hollywood.

But we need to further complicate this. It's not as if the closet no longer exists but structural homophobia does: both, alas, seem alive and well. For all the interviews that sociologists and ethnographers do with blasé queer teens and satisfied suburban gay couples, there are just as many stories of despair, of hiding, of aloneness, of violence. If, as our popular culture reports, everybody these days has a gay buddy/sister/ brother/co-worker, then why doesn't the world look different? And, more to the point here, why are there not more open gays at every level of public life?

Without a doubt, much political and social activism is still focused, albeit perhaps more obliquely, on the issue of coming out and the closet. The goal of dismantling "Don't Ask, Don't Tell" is precisely a critique of the cost of enforced closeting by the military. The policy itself was predicated on a recognition of the closet as a particularly gay reality—for no other group could we imagine such a strange mandate: you can be who you are as long as you hide it and do not "act" on it. Its admonition ("don't tell") is an explicit endorsement of passing. This is actually pretty astounding, since passing (especially racial and gender) is endorsed in no other way and has routinely been punished throughout American history.

Other social arenas assume the persistence of the closet and the need to remedy continued isolation. The growth of gay-straight alliances in schools and gay support groups in businesses and other social structures is in large part designed to create climates in which people can express their sexual sensibilities with some modicum of freedom. Indeed, even the old connection to the debutante "coming out" signifies this act or series of acts as very much about a public affirmation. Thus, there is simultaneously a personal and political aspect to coming out. The truth remains, doesn't it, that you can't have a mass movement without visibility, without some degree of "outness"? In addition, there must always be the recognition that this is never simply or easily a "personal decision." Gay activists have always stressed that coming out is vital not simply to live "true to oneself" but because coming out deeply affects others (to the extent that you are in the closet, you make me—my outness—more vulnerable and suspect). We often forget it now—in an age when workplaces often have LGBTQ support groups and openly gay people—but for many (both in the past and in the present) that experience of "being the only one" was/is truly awful. The pressure, the vulnerability, the spotlight, the expectations: tokenism has a profound effect.

So coming-out narratives have not wholly disappeared from mainstream popular culture, but they are often represented quite differently. In other words, that sense of "aha," of revelation and internal self-knowledge, seems almost gone. What does remain, however, in these newer coming-out stories is the struggle (albeit now somewhat briefer) with co-workers, friends, and family when presented with the new sexual identity. What has changed, then, is twofold. First, the transition into same-sex sexuality is depicted as more easygoing and less a radical break with the past than in previous eras. The sexuality of Sapphic surgeon Callie from *Grey's Anatomy*, for example, is depicted as "fluid, open-ended, and . . . determined by how she acts, rather than by what she professes herself to be."[26] For this character and many others, there is not a coming out *as such* but rather moments of engagement with astonished—or even blasé—heterosexuals and assorted strangers. And, second, the history of shame and self-loathing that has typified the coming-out narrative is reduced, if not wholly eliminated. This seems to me such an important and heartening trend, and one dependent on tentative steps by mainstream culture to show lesbians and gays as regular, integrated, unexceptional parts of the story. Thus, Callie and other fictional (and nonfictional) queers enter a world in which some versions of gayness have already been circulating—in other characters, in storylines, in the very ease of workplace life. Crucially, then, coming out is desensationalized in a cultural world in which gayness moves about not just as abjection or stereotype. This might just be the most potent argument against tokenism and for the end of coming out.

Coming out, then, has been understood as both the site of gay self-confidence and the sign of (heterosexual) cultural tolerance.

Coming out is always in a complicated tango with tolerance; how out we are allowed to be is often set up as the line in the sand. If earlier "tolerance" of gays depended on the force of the closet to exist (the secret that everyone knows but no one utters), then our current tolerance mode still holds the cards, insisting on outness but always in a form easily contained. Being "too out" (too noticeably, markedly queer) has long been the display of self that even liberal allies cannot tolerate. That's why the coming-out poster boys and girls are so relentlessly "normal": they are much easier for heterosexuals to tolerate if they are macho basketball players with impeccable masculinity credentials (Jason Collins) or willow-thin actresses with proven hetero allure (Cynthia Nixon). Perhaps tolerance traps gays in a different kind of closet after all.

# PART II

# *Do These Genes Make Me Look Gay?*

I'm beautiful in my way
'Cause God makes no mistakes
I'm on the right track, baby
I was born this way
                    —Lady Gaga

Let's be done with the biological and psychological nonsense that people are "born that way" and that there's nothing that can be done about it. Scripture and now research both say something quite different.
                    —Bryan Fischer, American Family Association

You were born this way. So just believe in yourself, and others will follow.                    —*Born This Way* blog contributor

The next time someone asks you, "Hey, how did you get to be a homosexual anyway?" tell them, "Homosexuals are chosen first on talent, then interview. The swimsuit and evening gown competition pretty much gets rid of the rest of them."
                    —Karen Williams, comedian

# 4

## The Medical Gayz

In a 2010 episode of the late, great medical drama series *House*, a young man faints, has a heart attack, and generally decomposes on his wedding day. His problem? He's gay and has gone through the full reparative-therapy regime. Blunt Dr. House assures him that "like so many other things, you were born that way," but the sick man insists, "we get to choose how we live our lives," and he has chosen hetero-sexuality and marriage. Of course, the dear doctor is dead on, and the dude gets dumped by his fiancée and embraces the queer inevitable, for the price of not acceding to that "truth" may just be his own death by dishonesty. This episode—unusually dramatic in its depiction of the perils of bucking biology—is by no means anomalous: it is rare indeed to find *any* contemporary depiction of gay identity that doesn't represent sexuality as predetermined in some fundamental way.

If marriage is conjured as the Oz of queer liberation, then biolog-ical and genetic arguments are the yellow brick road, often providing both the route and the rationale for civil rights. There does seem to be some evidence that increasing numbers of people are buying into the immutability arguments, although that may very well be more about the rapid popularization of genetic arguments for everything from happiness to shyness than it is about ideas of sexuality per se. But the polls are dramatic: in May 2013, Gallup reported that 47 percent of Americans believe that gays are "born that way," while 33 percent believe being gay is due to "factors such as upbringing or environment"—the largest gap ever seen since these polls have been conducted.[1]

Just as we have come to take it for granted that right-thinking people believe homosexuality is innate and hardwired (either through genetics or through some broader combination of genes and hormones), we have also come to believe that wrong-thinking people— either vicious homophobes or simply ill-informed onlookers—insist on gayness as choice and volitional "lifestyle." Or as sympathetic columnist Ellen Goodman reports, "Well, it turns out that the more you believe homosexuality is innate, the more accepting you are of gay rights. A full 79 percent of people who think human beings are born with a sexual orientation support gay rights, including civil unions or marriage equality. But only 22 percent of those who believe homosexuality is a choice agree."[2] It has become something of a truism in popular perception that a belief in immutability leads to more "accepting" (less homophobic) ideas. For example, a 2011 Gallup poll reported that Americans were evenly split on homosexuality's cause, but those who agreed that "people are born gay/lesbian" (a proxy for genetic or biological causation) were less anti-gay than those who agreed that "being gay/lesbian is due to environment." This same poll confirms that 87 percent of people who think homosexuality is inborn support civil unions or marriage equality, compared with 43 percent of those who believe it is caused by environment. For those who believe that sexuality is a choice, 65 percent stated they think lesbian and gay relations are morally wrong.[3]

Gays themselves are no strangers to the lure of the biological; many contemporary advocacy groups state quite explicitly that "born that way" is the way to go in arguing for gay rights. Truth Wins Out, an organization that focuses primarily on fighting the reparative-therapy movement (a constellation of activists and therapists committed to "turning" gays straight), argues that "at the core of these anti-gay efforts is a central truth: Polls show that people who believe homosexuality is a choice are significantly more likely to vote against gay rights. . . . The right wing has realized that the key to winning the culture war is convincing Americans that homosexuality is a frivolous and malleable lifestyle choice."[4] As sociomedical scientist Rebecca Jordan-Young point out, times have changed such that "the notion of innately different preferences in men and women was once politically suspect, [but] it is now often suggested that accepting these innate differences will encourage a more rational approach to equality."[5]

Indeed, the turn of the century seems to have provided a "perfect storm" moment in which the idea of immutability has taken hold of the public imagination. As Kate O'Riordan argues in an article detailing "the life of the gay gene," this idea, regardless of its scientific veracity or replicability, has taken on a life of its own, from newspaper articles and databases to T-shirts and song lyrics.[6] There is, inarguably, an overwhelming "born with it" ideology afoot that encompasses gay marriage, gay genes, and gayness as "trait" and that is—of course—used by both gay rights activists and anti-gay activists to make arguments for equality or against it.

At the heart of this debate are any number of erroneous assumptions, many of which I've discussed earlier. But underlying the "born this way" framework is a core commitment to an absolute "nature versus nurture" dichotomy. As Sarah Wilcox summarizes in her review of the media's contributions to the biological mantra,

> The dominant theme of biological discourse about sexuality was a dichotomy between being born gay and choosing to be gay. In this dichotomy, biology, genes, and being born gay are defined in opposition to choice and the possibility of change in sexual orientation. Key assumptions behind this dichotomy include: 1) biological determinism, or the idea that biology can only mean direct determination of a characteristic; 2) a conceptualization of homosexuality and heterosexuality as mutually exclusive and dichotomous categories; and 3) the idea that political and social change is dependent on proof that homosexuality is an innate and unchanging characteristic.[7]

So choice is configured as absolutely opposite to, or the inverse of, biological predestination, a framework which flies in the face of even the most conservative scientists, who generally believe in some level of "interplay" between social/cultural/historical factors and genetic and biological ones.

This is tricky, and I am well aware that I am heading into some rocky terrain here. A belief in biological immutability is now, much to my chagrin, the mother's milk of gay rights discourse. I have rarely been able to raise this issue—with gays or with allied straights—without causing an angry response and an insistence on both the truth of biological immutability and the necessity of framing it thus to access rights and social tolerance. If the public debate is set up so that "tolerance" is dependent on immutability and predetermination, it is hard to argue against both the larger frame of tolerance and the explanatory rubric of biological destiny. But argue we must. For while it is true that there appears to be a real correlation between believing in the born-gay thesis and supporting gay rights, that same thesis allows heterosexuals to, as historian John D'Emilio puts it, "quell their moral reservations about our lives and push aside their personal squeamishness about what we do"[8] because gayness is configured as something that just *is*, not something one actually *does*. The tolerance framework depends on these immutability arguments to embrace gays who just can't help themselves. Tolerance as a theme of contemporary gay rights is dependent on biological arguments much as plants need sunshine to flourish.

## Biology Is Destiny (Again)

Biological (and, more specifically, genetic and neurological and endocrinological) explanations for sexual orientation have a long history and have been thoroughly examined by any number of feminist and gay scholars, who have diligently detailed the rise and fall and rise again of these debates.[9] Surely, gays have been placed under the medical gaze since gayness itself was invented as a category not of behavior but rather of full-fledged and demarcated identity. The medicalization of sexual identity—and the search for a cause, if not a cure—has a long and infamous history, a history that includes well-meaning attempts by social activists to create a safe life for same-sex desire through the designation of inevitable and unstoppable difference but also, more ominously, includes the long and sordid history of incarceration, medication, electroshock "therapy," and numerous other attempts to rid the body (and mind) of its same-sex desires.

Notions of homosexuality as "inbred," innate, and immutable are therefore not new and were endorsed by a wide variety of thinkers and activists, including progressive reformers such as Havelock Ellis (who was also, of course, a devout eugenicist) and not so progressive doctors and scientists, eager to assert same-sex love as nature's mistake. Karl Ulrichs in the 1860s and '70s, Richard von Krafft-Ebing in the 1880s, and Magnus Hirschfeld in the 1910s and '20s—all pioneer sexologists and generally advocates of "toleration" or at least decriminalization—came to believe in some notion of innate homosexuality, whether through theories of a kind of brain inversion or through vague references to hormonal imbalances and other (unsubstantiated) anomalies. For Ulrichs, homosexuality was a congenital condition in which the gay or same-sex-desiring man (and most folks did completely ignore women in the search for causation; this lacuna continues today) is essentially psychically hermaphroditic: a female mind trapped in the wrong (male) body. Krafft-Ebing came to similar conclusions, seeing homosexuality as evidence of a sort of brain inversion. Ellis made a distinction between "true" inverts, who were characterized by some kind of biological immutability, and "homosexuals"—a rarer form of behavioral and situational identity. Even the designation of gays as a "third sex," a theory that held much appeal among a wide range of thinkers and activists, was premised on some reference to a biological substratum that produced such anomalous identities.[10]

The motto of Hirschfeld's Scientific Humanitarian Committee was actually "Per Scientiam ad Justitiam," or "through science to justice," an indication that for many of these early scholar-activists, science was understood to be the key not only to unlocking the "mystery" of sexuality but to opening the prison doors of criminalized "perverts" around the globe. And science itself was understood then—and even more so now—as the conduit to tolerance; if you are born that way, then you are worthy of freedom. In the early days of this nascent field of sexology, the supposed objectivity and "truth" of science provided a twofer: a justification of the inevitability of gayness for sex reformers and a justification for the field of sexology itself, now bolstered and propped up by the cultural authority of science. These ideas mostly had little traction—either within scientific communities or in the larger reform movements—and of course no reliable evidence whatsoever. And, needless to say, sexual science provided no immunity from persecution, particularly when the Nazis came calling.

These and other theories of the heritability or genetic or biological origins of gayness have ebbed and flowed during different historical and social moments, most obviously intersecting with the rise of eugenics and other determinist frameworks but also with reformist efforts both here and abroad. Arguments for immutability and biology are less popular, however, in historical periods that evince a broader skepticism toward scientific answers to social problems. For example, in an era that saw the emergence of gay liberation (and a challenge to older medicalized models of social identity more generally) like the 1960s and 1970s, heritability was not particularly on the radar screen for either gays or their opponents, and it was the *anti-gay* forces at the time that insisted on a sort of biological aberrance. As D'Emilio rightly points out, "In the literature produced by gay liberationists and lesbian feminists in the late 1960s and early 1970s, there is virtually a consensus that heterosexuality and homosexuality do not exist in nature, so to speak, but instead are products of culture . . . that emanate from an oppressive society."[11] Early gay rights groups such as the Mattachine Society didn't focus on issues of causation but rather on *rights*, explicitly defining gays as an oppressed minority group. Indeed, in the opening salvo of the 1971 manifesto "The Woman-Identified Woman," the authors declare that "a lesbian is the rage of all women condensed to the point of explosion."[12] Even further, they state that "lesbianism, like male homosexuality, is a category of behavior possible only in a sexist society characterized by rigid sex roles and dominated by male supremacy. . . . Homosexuality is a by-product of a particular way of setting up roles . . . on the basis of sex; as such it is an inauthentic . . . category."[13] So much for warped genes and predetermined desires. Thus, the early gay movement was committed to undermining the designation of homosexuality in pathological and medical terms, exemplified in the long battle to remove "homosexuality" as a disease category in the DSM (the *Diagnostic and Statistical Manual of Mental Disorders*, long the gold standard of classification for psychologists), finally achieved in 1974.[14] Implicit in that demedicalization—and *explicit* in much of the political organizing and thinking of the time—was an insistence that the question of "origins" (biological or otherwise) was the wrong question.

Not all post-Stonewall gay activists and thinkers were anti-essentialist or opposed to a biological perspective. Attenuated versions of essentialist[15] arguments have cropped up in the unlikeliest places. Even radicals such as lesbian-feminist poet and writer Adrienne Rich—through her concepts of the lesbian continuum and the woman-identified woman[16]—managed to make lesbian sexual desire less about desire for another woman per se and more about a kind of a political desire or even a biological drive. For Rich and some others of this period, lesbianism was less a "preference" than a force or, as queer theorist Jennifer Terry describes it, "somewhere between a natural drive and a moral imperative, while retaining elements of both."[17] Rich's position illustrates the many—often contradictory—sides of this equation. For, on the one hand, she offered up a naturalized version of lesbian desire that derived from a sort of primal mother-daughter bond or a continuum of woman identification and connection. On the other hand, she was one of the first to really articulate the idea of "compulsory heterosexuality" as essentially forcing women into traditional forms of intimacy premised on male domination. Her response to this compulsory heterosexuality, and the response of a vital branch of early radical feminism, was what became known as "political lesbianism," offering up same-sex desire as a positive and pro-woman *choice* that explicitly rejected both compulsory heterosexuality and medicalized models of homosexuality. For these activists, sexual and emotional *choice* was the radical mode that promised a freedom beyond mere tolerance. That there was really no gay male counterpart to this forceful notion of choosing lesbian sexuality speaks to the ways in which gender profoundly shapes the entire debate around gay etiology. This lack of symmetry between lesbians and gay men on the "choice" issue carries over into contemporary debates and even scientific research, as we will see later on. So a figure like Rich illustrates well this contradiction between ideas of choice and a belief in some determining "force," because she herself seems to have held both positions simultaneously.

There is no question, however, that the romance with biological causes for sexual "orientation" (really *same-sex* orientation, as the search for the hetero gene or the straight hypothalamus goes largely unexamined) has ratcheted up in recent years, due in no small part to the combined force of the gay-marriage debates and the increasing "medicalization" and "geneticization" of behavior and identity more generally. The public and scientific obsession with genetic origin stories, in particular, was spurred on by the initiation of the Human Genome Project in 1989, which furthered the already booming business—both popular and scientific—in genetic bases for behavior, personality, disease, and so on. The search for a gene for nearly everything (from shyness to sexiness) became a lucrative industry, and the early nineties produced a wave of studies that moved from the science journals quickly into the public eye.

Some of this impetus toward discovering "hard" scientific evidence of homosexuality has emerged as a reaction to social/psychological theories that predominated in the 20th century and that attributed homosexuality to some version of pathogenic family life: stunted development, bad mothering, absent fathers, or failed Oedipal resolutions. For many scientists—especially gay ones—this new science of sexual orientation was seen as a corrective to the glib psychology of the day, which tended not only to assume homosexuality as an emotional and sexual disorder of some kind but to place "blame" firmly on the already overburdened shoulders of mothers. In addition, this new moment has been marked by the (relatively unique) phenomenon of openly gay scientists conducting this research. Not only does this give added legitimacy to these studies, but many, if not all, of these researchers claim that they are doing this "for" gay people and in the service of furthering tolerance, if not gay rights. We will come back to this claim later.

## Girly Brains and Macho Digits

The two scientists most commonly cited in regard to the biological determinist theory of homosexuality are Simon LeVay and Dean Hamer, both of whom are openly gay and published their initial salvos in the "born gay" battle in the early 1990s. LeVay, a neuroscientist, and Hamer, a National Institutes of Health geneticist, have often explicitly presented their research as ammunition in the war for tolerance of gays and lesbians. In what independent scholar Nancy Ordover calls "The Great 1990s Medicalization of Queerness," both LeVay and Hamer published studies that ostensibly "proved" that homosexuality was biologically determined.[18] In 1991, LeVay published "A Difference in Hypothalamic Structure between Homosexual and Heterosexual Men" in the journal *Science*, announcing that a cell group in the interstitial nuclei of the anterior hypothalamus was twice as large in heterosexual men as in gay men, on the basis of an analysis of the brain tissue taken from the autopsies of forty-one subjects in New York and California. The subjects consisted of eighteen gay men with AIDS, one bisexual man with AIDS, sixteen "presumed heterosexual" men (six of whom died of AIDS-related deaths), and one woman with AIDS—a skewed sample whose problematic features did not go unnoticed. In 1993, Hamer and colleagues published their gay-gene manifesto, "A Linkage between DNA Markers on the X Chromosome and Male Sexual Orientation," which argued that a gene (which they suspected more than isolated) on the X chromosome influences male sexual orientation. Several other significant studies in the 1990s and early 2000s connected homosexuality and gender identity to biological origins, focusing on brain and finger size, various hormones and endocrine systems, maternal womb environment, and every permutation therein.[19]

Studies of twins have also played an important role in the medicalization of homosexuality and have become a highly debated area of experimentation. One of the most significant studies of this type was undertaken in 1991 by psychologist J. Michael Bailey and his collaborator, Richard Pillard, a psychiatrist. According to this initial study, "52% of identical (monozygotic) twins of homosexual men were likewise homosexual; 22% of fraternal (dizygotic) twins were likewise homosexual; 11% of adoptive brothers of homosexual men were likewise homosexual."[20] Bailey has since become one of the central, and most controversial,[21] players in the "born gay" debates and in sexuality studies more broadly construed, both for his methods—which have come under scrutiny from study subjects and researchers alike—and for his conclusions about gender, sexuality, desire, and identity. Bailey's research has been widely criticized for reinvigorating stereotypes of gay men as gender "inverts" and for claiming scientific definitions of sexual identity based solely on levels of penile arousal. And his work on transsexuals and bisexuals is equally reductive and controversial.

Another hypothesis that has garnered a great deal of popular press attention is the argument that men with older brothers are more likely to be gay. This is based (at least in part) on two studies by sexologist Ray Blanchard in 1997 and 2001 which found that "the more older biological brothers a man has, the more likely he will be gay because mothers become immunized against male-specific antigens by each male fetus so her anti-male antibodies interfere with the sexual differentiation of each successive male fetus's brain,"[22] suggesting that male homosexuality is "caused" by some event in the womb, perhaps the levels of circulating testosterone (although, of course, these can't be measured in the fetus, so this is just—in the end—guesswork). Other scientists have tried to link (male) homosexuality to female fecundity, as did Italian evolutionary psychologist Andrea Camperio-Ciana when he published studies suggesting that "homosexuality is a sex-linked trait" and that "female relatives of male homosexuals . . . produce more children."[23]

Without going into detail here, suffice it to say that these studies have presented any number of problems—from small sample size and constitution to embedded assumptions and unsubstantiated generalizations and the problem of replicability. Sexual desire and gender identity have often been conflated and confused and both have been understood as relatively clear and unambiguous categories. As Jordan-Young notes in her wide-ranging critique of the "science" of sex differences, the studies were deeply inconsistent and contradictory, particularly concerning the very unit of analysis (the "homosexual"), such that "one scientist's heterosexuals are another scientist's homosexuals."[24]

The past decade has seen the publication of similar studies linking homosexuality to genes or other biological factors, resulting in arguments concerning the effects of prenatal stress and the assertion that lesbians don't menstruate, have asymmetrical faces, and are good whistlers. It can get pretty silly: there have also been several studies linking sexuality to visible physical features such as the hands. One of these is called the 2D:4D effect, which claims that straight men and lesbians have shorter index fingers than ring fingers, but gay men and straight women have a smaller digit-ratio difference. [25] The trend is more pronounced in supposedly "effeminate" gay men and also apparently indicates whether he will be a "top" or a "bottom." And as if our deformed fingers and our whistling capacities weren't enough of a problem, in 2000, Martin LaLumiere and Kenneth Zucker published a study in the *Psychological Bulletin,* which concluded that homosexuals are more likely to be left-handed. While Zucker says the research provides empirical evidence that links homosexuality to left-handedness, he also adds, "we don't have a definitive answer as to why the relationship exists."[26] This caveat is repeated by many scientists linking homosexuality to genetics, including LeVay and Hamer. It seems that the difficulty lies in proving cause and effect: does homosexuality cause handedness, hypothalamus size, and strange little fingers? Or are left-handed people with varying finger length more likely to desire members of their own sex? And more to the point, do we want to limit the richness of our desires and identities to the discrete markers of the physical body?

## Bad Science, Bad Reporting, Bad News

There was a flurry of activity when these big studies of the 1990s came out, breathless reports in the weeklies and newspaper coverage extolling the "breakthrough" discovery of the "cause" of homosexuality. But at the same time, there was also a significant amount of critical and even skeptical attention, particularly from gay activists and scholars. In more recent years, however, the critical edge has worn down or moved solely into the academy, and the oft-repeated "most scientists believe" claim has become our collective common sense. Although many people have remained skeptical, the gay-gene story has come to have a "just so" quality, in which "references to the critique of the gay gene became diminished [and] the idea of the gay gene conversely became stronger."[27]

While scientists themselves are often culpable for overstating or misstating their findings, more often than not the problem lies in the reporting, which is quick to make (false) generalizations in the desire to promote a headline-grabbing "sea change" in research and findings. No scientists worth their salt claim a single determination (a gene, a hormone), yet this small cluster of studies has produced both a journalistic and a popular perception that gayness (specifically male homosexuality) is innate, immutable, predetermined in some finite and marked and knowable way. All nuance is thrown to the wind as evolutionary biologists such as David Barash declare that the "ship has sailed, and the consensus among scientists is that same-sex preference is rooted in our biology."[28] Note here the focus on *same-sex* preference as biological—no one seems to care much about *opposite-sex* origin.

The gap between a suggestion of possible biological *factors* and wholesale biological *determination* is narrowed to the point of invisibility. Stephen Jay Gould and other critics of deterministic and sociobiological frameworks have long insisted that we distinguish between *potentiality* and *determination.* This distinction, like that between heritability and immutability, is often lost in the public discussion of gay origins. Kate O'Riordan rightly points out that "the slippage between terms like *genetics, heritability, familial,* and *biological* is not only a feature of science news or popular science writings, but also of scientific databases, maps, and catalogues."[29]

Clearly, biological explanations have an enduring hold on our popular imagination, especially when it comes to sexuality and gender, and popular journalists have played a major role in this fascination, feeding "a popular appetite for deciphering human sexual relations by drawing parallels between animal mating patterns and human experiences of sexual attraction, dating, marriage, divorce, promiscuity, and homosexuality, often humorously simplifying or exaggerating the actual scientific findings."[30] Unfortunately, both the gay press and the mainstream media seem to take this stuff at face value. Given the motivation to promote tolerance, and the assumption that determinist ideas do this, it is unsurprising—albeit depressing—how few differences there are between the gay popular press and the mainstream popular press in this regard. But while some reporters attempt to modulate the "gay gene" mania—and do justice to the nuance and tentativeness with which many scientists make any assertions—most have jumped on the determinist bandwagon with fervor. This is due, in part, to the procedures of mainstream news reporting, in which bold headlines and controversial assertions are de rigueur and modulated ambivalence is a bad news day.

Even when reporters use numerous qualifiers (e.g., using words like "tend" and "appears"), the headlines—which almost always state categorically that gay brains or desires or preferences are ineluctably different from non-gay ones—mitigate against the more nuanced and tentative text of the article. One such piece in *Discover* magazine opens with a welcome willingness to assert that "the question remains unresolved."[31] Yet in the next sentence, this honest ambivalence is thrown to the wind because now we are told, "Whether or not a gay gene, or a set of gay genes, or some other biological mechanism is ever found, one thing is clear: The environment a child grows up in has nothing to do with what makes most gay men gay. Two of the most convincing studies have proved conclusively that sexual orientation in men has a genetic cause."[32] "Genetic" is thus set up in opposition to "environment" in a simple nature/nurture dichotomy in which behaviors are either singularly "caused" by genetic or other "predetermined" factors *or* behaviors are singularly "caused" by factors seen as social, cultural, or familial. Even more curious, this research apparently leaves open the possibility that *lesbians* may actually be "influenced" by environment and not, therefore, genetically programmed, a conclusion which seems rather incongruous, to say the least. Logically speaking, if sexual orientation is singularly produced through biogenetic factors, then women should not be left aside in the deterministic frameworks.

Not all studies, of course, have received the same attention. Indeed, one critic has argued that one study in particular has been sidelined because, "in contrast to LeVay's findings, which reiterated a traditional framework for equating homosexuality with femininity in men and with masculinity in women, [Dick F.] Swaab and [Michel A.] Hofman's research indicated that while the brains of homosexual men were different from those of heterosexual men, they did not resemble those of heterosexual women."[33] As Peter Conrad notes, "by trumpeting genetic discoveries on page one while relegating disconfirmations to back pages (if noting them at all), the media misrepresents the state of genetics. It amplifies the impression that genes for particular problems are being discovered, but is unlikely to correct that view when a disconfirmation occurs. This ultimately presents an overoptimistic view of the role of genetics in social problems and misinforms public knowledge."[34] Even here, though, gayness is easily situated as a "social problem" that merits attention as such, whether scientific or otherwise.

## A Homo Mystery Wrapped in a Gay Enigma

So many of these studies—and their reporting—begin with the designation of homosexuality as a "problem," a mystery to be solved.

The assumptions and perspectives of most popular representations and reporting on the "gay gene" are informed and framed by sociobiological and evolutionary psychological precepts and norms, such that, as anthropologist Roger Lancaster succinctly puts it, "sociobiology has become common sense."[35] It is surely the case that, as sociologist Martha McCaughy argues, "sociobiological explanations of human homosexuality wind up naturalizing heterosexuality by holding up homosexuality as a challenge for evolutionary theorists to explain—as if the legitimacy of evolutionary theory itself depends upon an evolved heterosexual human nature!"[36]

For those sociobiologists whose theories of evolution and zero-sum games often rule the day, the language can be even more stark. For psychobiologist Qazi Rahman of Queen Mary College in London, "Homosexuality is effectively like sterilization. . . . You'd think evolution would get rid of it."[37] In other words, since homosexuals don't reproduce (supposedly), then—evolutionarily speaking—they should have gone the way of the dinosaurs. Or maybe we'll just find out that all dinosaurs were a little light in their prehistoric loafers.

The immutability arguments not only set up a problem to be solved but rely on some sort of analogy to figure out this supposed problem: is gayness like handedness or hair color or height? Or is it more like intelligence or taste? Are gays like blacks or other minority groups? Or is it just set in stone? For some popular writers, homosexuality is not just a preference, but more like a compulsion, ineradicably written in our genetic codes and hormonal flows. *Washington Post* writer Marguerite Kelly claims that "most scientists think that a person's sexuality is the work of nature, not nurture; that it is as innate as the color of his eyes and just as immutable. A homosexual can no more be attracted to a member of the opposite sex than he can be attracted to a lamppost."[38] Tell that to all the attractive lampposts out there.

The arguments run in many directions; it is not as simple as social constructionists versus geneticists or biological determinists; social constructionists also find themselves at odds with the perspective of evolutionary psychologists who "hold that homosexuality is a

naturally selected adaptation, or at least a trade-off for such an adaptation."[39] Some have tried to find a "solution" to this debate by pro-
posing a sort of combined thesis, which often goes under the heading
of "evolutionary social constructivism," in which distinctions are
made between same-sex sexual behavior and sexual identity, and the
Darwinian hypothesis of "alliance formation" is utilized to "explain
how a socially constructed homosexuality is embedded in our evolved
nature."[40] The "alliance-formation" folks, say two academic critics of
the biological position, "argue that same-sex sexual behavior is an
adaptation that has been preserved in the gene pool because it promotes reciprocal altruism."[41] Others claim that it simply makes no
sense to be gay because it doesn't aid in the reproductive imperative
and would have, therefore, been weeded out over time. Some have
solved this dilemma by recourse to some variant of kin-selection
hypothesis, in which gay relatives are understood to aid in the reproductive success of their close kin, "thus enabl[ing] the gay gene to
proliferate through collateral lines of descent, even if its bearers did
not reproduce at all. In this model, homosexuals would be 'helpers at
the nest.'"[42] This handy-gay-uncle argument has very little evidence
to go for it and has the added problem of being wholly wedded to a
rather overly determinist reading of evolutionary theory, as well as a
particular view of family formation.

Both scientists and science reporters are often eager to prove both
the stability and always-thereness of gays at the same time that they
assert their minority status, their relative smallness in relation to the
general population. So gays are a stable but small population, always
there but always a minority. Timeless but bounded. Transcultural
but not transient. Of course, all of this work accepts the notion of
homosexuality as a mystery (or, in some cases, a Darwinian puzzle) to
be figured out. As one scientist opines, "If there is one thing that has
always seemed obvious about homosexuality, it's that it just doesn't
make sense. Evolution favors traits that aid reproduction, and being
gay clearly doesn't do that."[43]

# 5

# Dangerous Liaisons

Nowhere are the biases and limitations of the immutability argument more evident than when gender differences rear their tired heads. Repeatedly and consistently, theories of biological immutability rely on essentialist notions of gender difference and asymmetry and even sometimes outright sexist stereotypes. Or, as Simon LeVay crudely puts it, "most men can figure out their sexual orientation by consulting their genitals, but few women can do so . . . [because] sexual orientation is a 'higher-level' phenomenon in many women than it is in men, perhaps because it is embedded in relationship issues."[1] LeVay doesn't stop there. Like most scientists and science reporters deeply committed to the "born that way" mythology, he presents a veritable mother lode of gender stereotypes that hinge on the notion that gender differentiation produces sexual orientation. We "learn" from LeVay that boys engage in more rough-and-tumble play and have better spatial skills; that lesbians participate in more sports and gay men less; that gay men bond more with their mothers than do straight men; that gay men are more gender nonconformist as kids; and that, alas, lesbians have worse verbal skills than their straight sisters. All this and more is brought to you by early exposure to prenatal androgen![2]

The gay-gene story both begins and ends with deterministic ideas about gender. It is worth quoting *New York Times* reporter Nicholas Wade at length because he starts out by asserting ineluctable male/

female differences and then shifts easily to asserting the same for sexual desire:

> It is a misconception that the differences between men's and women's brains are small or erratic or found only in a few extreme cases, Dr. Larry Cahill of the University of California, Irvine, wrote last year in *Nature Reviews Neuroscience*. Widespread regions of the cortex, the brain's outer layer that performs much of its higher-level processing, are thicker in women. The hippocampus, where initial memories are formed, occupies a larger fraction of the female brain. Techniques for imaging the brain have begun to show that men and women use their brains in different ways even when doing the same thing. In the case of the amygdala, a pair of organs that helps prioritize memories according to their emotional strength, women use the left amygdala for this purpose but men tend to use the right. It is no surprise that the male and female versions of the human brain operate in distinct patterns, despite the heavy influence of culture. The male brain is sexually oriented toward women as an object of desire. The most direct evidence comes from a handful of cases, some of them circumcision accidents, in which boy babies have lost their penises and been reared as female. Despite every social inducement to the opposite, they grow up desiring women as partners, not men.[3]

The logic here is both tautological and dangerous: men and women are fundamentally different, and that difference is at least partly manifest in the "sexual brain," which means that the "male brain" desires women (naturally). Men who do not desire women therefore cannot be seen as having a "real" male brain, since they are then understood to be "like women" in their morphology. Or, alternately for some scientists, they are "like" women but still stereotypically male, as Dean Hamer repeatedly asserts when comparing male homosexual profligacy to male heterosexual profligacy. In other words, for Hamer and others, boys may be girls, but they still think with their dicks.[4]

## It's All About the Cheerleaders

To make the case for immutability, for example, as Hamer does when discussing the research on scent and arousal in gay men, inevitably relies on stereotypical assumptions about masculinity and femininity. In an interview concerning a new study of pheromones and sexual desire, Hamer argues that "gay men are a great control group for this kind of study . . . because they're pretty much the same as straight men except for that one factor."[5] The reporter "confirms" Hamer's assertion by claiming that "when the Swedish scientists ran the experiment this time, the results were striking: when gay men were exposed to male pheromones, their hypothalamuses lit up just like a woman's. Female hormones did nothing for them." Responding to the concern that this issue of smell and pheromones might not be so significant in humans, Hamer demurs, "They're certainly not as important as they are in the mouse, who can't rely on gawking at cheerleaders to get turned on."[6] So, for determinist advocates such as Hamer, "gawking at cheerleaders" is a universal sign of hetero male desire, not the socially constructed locus of gender norms. Gay men are "like women" in their brains (whatever that means) but just the same as straight men in their desire to objectify. And all these categories are themselves taken to be unproblematic.

And, again, choice is the enemy of neural truth because not only is our gender identity hardwired but so is our desire. Genes take on a life of their own—blindly following their evolutionarily determined course—and sexual desire (not to mention gender) is reduced to our organs. "If you can't make a male attracted to other males by cutting off his penis, how strong could any psychosocial effect be?" says Bailey, replicating here an age-old canard about men's brains being located, well, in their genitals.[7] Even further, science journalist Robert Kunzig concludes that, "by interfering with the masculinization of the brain, gay genes might promote feminine behavior traits, making men who carry them kinder, gentler, more nurturing. . . . Such men may be more likely to help raise children rather than kill them—or each other—and as a result, women may be more likely to choose them as mates."[8]

For many of these researchers, the assumptions of "feminization" (whatever that means) and "masculinization" (whatever that means) guide the framing of biological origins. As one critic notes, "Two background beliefs permeate the different fields contributing to the gay gene discourse. These beliefs are that (1) male homosexuality is a state of effeminacy and (2) male homosexuality is pathological."[9] Routinely—and circuitously—gay men and their (gay) brains are deemed gay precisely because they are not "real men," and real men are filled to the brim with testosterone (which is the marker of their real-manness). Gay men are gay precisely because they are feminized, and feminization means less testosterone. As one reporter asserts, "No one has yet identified a particular gay gene, but Brian Mustanski, a psychologist at the University of Illinois at Chicago, is examining a gene that helps time the release of testosterone from the testes of a male fetus. Testosterone masculinizes the fetal genitalia—and presumably also the brain. Without it, the fetus stays female. It may be that the brains of gay men don't feel the full effects of testosterone at the right time during fetal development, and so are insufficiently masculinized."[10] Pity the poor sissy brain, insufficient in its manliness. Or, as geneticist Eric Vilain wonders, "The big question has always been, if the brains of gay men are different, or feminized, as earlier research suggests, . . . then is it just limited to sexual preference or are there other regions that are gender atypical in gay males?"[11]

This gender essentialism seems to apply equally to genetic research and neuroendocrine research; the theorists who argue that homosexuality is "produced" in a male through some immune response in the mother's womb insist that this interferes "with the masculinization of his brain,"[12] turning a little would-be-macho fetus into a raving queen. Of course, no one bothers to interrogate what, precisely, they mean by "masculinization"; thus, the stereotypes themselves become actual *evidence* rather than something to be deeply examined.

Not only are the assumptions that go into gay-gene discourse jam-packed with sexist notions that assert gay men as feminized and gay women as masculinized (assumptions that go way back indeed), but other forms of gender binarism crop up as well. In this telling, men are hard and fast and singular in their sexual choices, while women are wishy-washy and "fluid." It appears, then, that "most of the scientists working on these questions are convinced that the antecedents of sexual orientation in males are happening early in life, probably before birth, . . . whereas for females, some are probably born to become gay, but clearly some get there quite late in life."[13] So straight or gay, a man's gotta be what a man's gotta be, but women just can't make up their minds! Or, as Marc Breedlove, a neuroscientist at Michigan State University, asserts, "Most males are quite stubborn in their ideas about which sex they want to pursue, while women seem more flexible."[14]

The link between this frenzied search for a "gay gene" and (equally frenzied) resurgent theories of biological/genetic differences between men and women is strong and sustained. Old beliefs about males as inherently more desirous of sex than females are is married to equally outdated and potent stereotypes about women's fluid sexuality or endless orgasms and about female vagueness (in life, in work, in bed). Thus, these stereotypes cohere in yet more rigidly defined sexual identities centered on gender oppositions.

The biological determinism of the gene mania rests therefore on a bedrock of gender essentialism, which obscures the fact that it is precisely our culture that gives meaning and content to gender, "that assigns nurturance, passivity, cooking, and clerical work to women; applauds independence, aggression, firefighting, and mechanical skills in men; and thus celebrates the tomboy and excoriates the sissy."[15] And just as a sexual orientation comes to be viewed as a core, an unchangeable and immutable part of self, so too does gender get depicted as stereotypically pink and blue, oppositional, dualistic. A whole series of equivalences are embedded in the mainstream biological narratives: natural = good = immutable = inevitable; male homosexuality = feminization; sexual acts = desire = identity.

I can't help wondering how this narrative structures social perception and the quest for equal rights. If tolerance rests on immutability and immutability rests on some black/white, gay/straight, male/female vision of clear-cut difference, then tolerance becomes the handmaiden to a *more* sexist society. Almost every single popular presentation of the gay-gene argument begins and ends with a narrative of "gender difference," thus effectively conflating sexual desire, sexual-object choice, gender identity, and gender performance into one neat and tidy package (and one wrapped with either a girly pink bow or a manly blue knot). As reporter Wade claims, "Desire between the sexes is not a matter of choice. Straight men, it seems, have neural circuits that prompt them to seek out women; gay men have those prompting them to seek other men. Women's brains may be organized to select men who seem likely to provide for them and their children. The deal is sealed with other neural programs that induce a burst of romantic love, followed by long-term attachment."[16] So straight men are hell-bent on cheerleaders, straight women are hardwired for sugar daddies, while lesbians (and bisexuals and . . .) sadly have no neural circuits whatsoever—and perhaps also no triumphant, romantic bursts either.

If men are from Mars and women are from Venus, then gay men are from Pluto and lesbians are from the land of hobbits and blue avatars. Or men will be men, gay men will be kinda like men but pinker, and lesbians will be an enigma wrapped in a mystery. What is completely absent here is any notion of the social. So there is "nature" (which is here configured as singular, determinative, genetic, immutable), and there is "nurture" (which is here configured as parental/maternal, psychological, didactic). Despite decades of feminist challenge, the assumptions of core binary gender continue to rule both scientific practice and commonsense ideologies.

## Toddlers in Tiaras

When not linking transcendent romance with neural bursts and macho brains, reporters regale us with stories of little boys who paint their nails, play dress-up with the girls, and choose pink over camouflage. Barbie inevitably provides the most damning evidence of little Junior's girlish proclivities. It is interesting to note that almost all these stories are of *boys'* gender nonnormativity. Tomboyishness is, I suppose, less indicative of sexual difference. Apparently a boy with Barbies is a big queen in training, but a girl with power tools might just be a handy housewife of the future.

The move from gender nonnormativity to specific sexual preferences and desires is not even a smooth segue; again and again the two are completely conflated. The story goes like this: from the earliest moments, Bobby always liked pink and frills. And dolls, not trucks like his big brother. While other boys his age played rough and ready, delighting in dirt and wartime make-believe, gentle Bobby preferred the company of girls and was squeamish about mess. His mother always knew he was "different," and so did he.

In a 20/20 segment ("Is My Baby Gay?") from April 2008,[17] the phrase "medical mystery" is repeated numerous times. The segment opens with a baby being swaddled, transitions to images of a toddler, and then on to a young boy. We hear a voice-over of a presumably adolescent boy: "I would say that I felt different as far back as kindergarten, first grade. I knew there was something about me that wasn't like the rest of the guys." The reporter then comes in with *her* strident voice-over: "Gay kids! How can they be so sure? It's a medical mystery. One of the biggest debates of our time. Is there a gene that determines whether you're gay or straight? Some scientists think it is mostly biological. Others say it's a learned behavior. Not that kids need science to confirm what they already know."[18] So here gay sexuality is framed as a "medical mystery." Further, this mystery pairs off "biology" (which is used as a stand-in for something we presumably are "forced" into) against "learned behavior" (which is a stand-in for choice). Nature versus nurture, immutability versus choice. And, even more problematically, that last line sets up the narrative arc: it *must* be nature because even the kids themselves (and their parents) "know" this to be true. Indeed, the next clip features what becomes the "argument" for a genetic immutability: the boy wanted a Barbie Dreamhouse! Even worse, this little gay boy had girls as friends, was (in the words of his mother) "prissy," "flamboyant," feminine, and—the sure sign of genetic gayness—he didn't like to get dirty. So presumably the evidence for genetics is simply the stuff of conventional femininity, and the parents reinforce this tautological conviction: "Zach's parents both believe that homosexuality was probably in their son's DNA. For them there is no medical mystery. But might a proven genetic link help other parents understand what they saw with their own eyes?"[19] Cut now to the lab coats and test tubes, reinforcing the scientific legitimacy of the storyline. This news report (and many others replicate this model) presents a medical mystery that we already know the answer to because the answer is in the behavior itself.

This "evidence" of ingrown girliness is held up as the "truth" of the medical mystery, as opposed to the "fiction" of choice, here configured as the misleading messages of the mass media: "Living in Greenville, South Carolina, a fundamentalist Christian community, Deborah was repeatedly taught that homosexuality was something little boys picked up from TV [cut here to *Will and Grace*] and movies [cut here to *Brokeback Mountain*], something they learned." But "real" gay boys "accept" this "medical mystery," or as interviewee David Hawkins says on this same program, "I think it will give gay children something to hold on to. Something to say 'I had no choice in this.'"[20]

It is clear that evidence is not only in our genes, but in our gendered behaviors. These kids were different precisely because they didn't look or act like little boys and little girls were supposed to act. The assumption, writes Lancaster, is that "if inappropriate acts, feelings, body types, or desires seem to throw us into the bodies or minds of other genders, it is because these acts, feelings, and so on are associated with gender by dint of the same all-enveloping cultural logic that gives us pink blankets (or caps, or crib cards, or I.D. bracelets) for girls and blue for boys in maternity ward cribs."[21] And of course this has shifted historically. Not too long ago, a (bourgeois, white) woman's desire to work outside the home was a sure sign of her masculinization, if not her outright queerness, and pink was most decidedly a manly tint.

## Pink Penguins and Lavender Lemurs

It's not just twee toddlers who evince ineluctable signs of innate queerness; so apparently do our furry friends. If one major problem with the gay-gene discourse is defining who, precisely, the scientists are talking about when they do their research, another major problem is the too-easy jump from the apparently very gay animal kingdom to human practices and identities. Along with the "discoveries" of gay genes and homo hypothalamuses, science reporting has fixated on the apparent perversity of the lesser beasts. These animal-based scientists probe not the apparently aberrant womb environment that produces sissified men who don't like dirt but the romantic entanglements of our hairy (or scaly) friends. This work—often by gay or gay-positive animal behaviorists whose studies of various animals (including our closer relatives, the primates, but also more distant creatures, such as worms, birds, fish, etc.)—leads them to believe not only that same-sex sexuality is common across numerous species but, importantly, that many animals can rightly be called "gay" in the sense of "choosing" life partners of the same sex. Coverage of the lavender animal kingdom brings out the anthropomorphs in even the most careful reporters. Some, of course, can't help but turn the animals into humans, claiming, for instance, that "Japanese macaques . . . are described as enthusiastic lesbians who mount each other frequently, although this behavior is somewhat ambiguous among primates for whom sexual mounting serves as a dominance submission display."[22] This same reporter later refers to "butch sheep" and the "orgies" of endless other animal species in a veritable frenzy of imputing human social and sexual categories onto every variety of fish, fowl, and livestock.

John Cloud, writing for *Time* magazine, sees nefarious (but cute) homo seduction, in which "straight" males get tricked by other wily straight males who dress in animal drag: male goodeid fish, for instance, sometimes have a black spot that resembles a spot that females get when pregnant. Dominant males then court them rather than fight with them. While the dominant guys are busy courting the subordinate, ladylike fish, the latter are able to "sneak copulations with females," prompting Cloud to claim this as his "Hugh Grant Theory: it's not always the most masculine guy who gets the most girls."[23] And almost all these journalistic accounts seamlessly merge gender stereotypes and sexual stereotypes to produce, for example, curious odes to "gay" and "straight" ferrets that act more or less "masculine." It does, of course, beg the question of what a manly ferret looks like: does it grab its crotch and swill beer and do manly (but not gay!) chest bumps with brethren weasels?

We are regaled with heartwarming tales of lesbian penguins or gay turtledoves and Valentine's Day encomiums to the love that dare not bark its name. That these scientists and their popularizers are often well intentioned does not lessen the problematic anthropomorphic tendencies of this line of argument or the slightly desperate edge it takes when translated into the language of human politics. One of the problems with the "animals do it" argument is that it is both scientifically and politically suspect to deduce from animal behavior to human behavior and social reasoning and choice. Surely, it is worthwhile to note that sexual variability exists in the animal kingdom just as it does among humans. And, certainly, many animal biologists seem more circumspect in their conclusions and are happy to document the expansive sexual variability among numerous species without necessarily using those examples to expound on human organization. In general, the animal researchers tend to be more careful in their claims than the geneticists, repeatedly resisting the immediate rush to deem their albatrosses or penguins as "gay" or "lesbian." Some, like biologist Marlene Zuk, actively resist the easy anthropomorphic tendencies of reporters and activists alike, arguing in her book *Sexual Selections* that "people need to be able to make decisions about their lives without worrying about keeping up with the bonobos."[24] Many argue, quite rightly, that the search for variation—either in the animal studies or in the work of Alfred Kinsey—is not the same as the search for causation or heritability and that knowledge of this variability is intrinsically interesting without necessarily linking it to vast claims about human sociability.

For many animal researchers, however, and even more so for the reporters who breathlessly cover them, the animal world not only gives us clues about how and why we are sexual beings, but provides a sort of translational reference point from the animal world to the human. It both proves and justifies. It shows not why we—humans—are gay but rather that since our brethren baboons and penguins seem to enjoy a bit of same-sex action, it must follow that it is "in nature" to exhibit same-sex desire. For those, on the other hand, who search not for the gay baboon but for the gay genotype, the goal is not one of homology or lineage but rather morphology and immutability.

There is no question that "this growing body of science has been increasingly drawn into charged debates about homosexuality in American society, on subjects from gay marriage to sodomy laws, despite reluctance from experts in the field to extrapolate from animals to humans."[25] And even the journalists acknowledge the political dilemmas of the homo-animals arguments. As one sharp writer notes,

> Gay groups argue that if homosexual behavior occurs in animals, it is natural, and therefore the rights of homosexuals should be protected. On the other hand, some conservative religious groups have condemned the same practices in the past, calling them "animalistic." But if homosexuality occurs among animals, does that necessarily mean that it is natural for humans, too? And that raises a familiar question: if homosexuality is not a choice, but a result of natural forces that cannot be controlled, can it be immoral?[26]

This jump from "gayness" as historically and cross-culturally eternal to gayness as present in the animal world to gayness as "natural" to gayness as "genetic" occurs in most of the popular reporting on the issue of possible determinants of (gay) sexual orientation. One

*Psychology Today* reporter makes just such a series of conflations when he writes,

> Others consider homosexuality to be unnatural, and they're simply wrong. Homosexual behavior has existed throughout human history; it exists throughout the animal kingdom; and it exists in every culture on earth—even in those that punish such behavior by death. The evidence is overwhelming that homosexual behavior is at least partially genetic in origin. More than 6 percent of male sheep, for example, are exclusively homosexual, and a 1996 study showed that homosexual behavior in fruit flies can be deliberately engineered by genetic manipulation. More to the point, concordance studies with humans suggest that male homosexuality is roughly 50 percent genetic in origin (compared with 5 percent for weight and 84 percent for height).[27]

But what does it mean to make claims for *human* gay rights on the basis of two female hens sitting on some eggs together or two male sheep snuggling and rutting away? It is one thing to say both the animal and human worlds evince an astonishing variability when it comes to matters sexual, although what is defined as "sexual" is itself part of the human lexicon. Kinsey said this, in so many words, and much of animal research reveals just such diversity. But that simple observation—for either humans or animals—gives us little help in 21st-century decisions about citizenship, civil rights, sexual freedoms. And easy extrapolations from animals are dangerous. As many critics have noted, many animals eat their young, toss aside their elderly and infirm, and follow only the strongest. Not to mention licking their genitals in public. Human social organization and values cannot be simply lifted from the animal world—nor should they be. In addition, lots of things are "natural" and have some bit of biological basis, including most disease and disability. This doesn't mean we don't attempt to alter or intervene in the "natural" course of disease growth and development.

These "in nature" arguments can, it is true, aid in "naturalizing" what religion and politics have combined to demonize as "unnatural," as one critic notes when he says that "regardless of the particular bio-logical mechanism through which homosexuality arises, it is a per-vasive phenomenon in the animal kingdom, a fact that discredits the common argument that it is 'unnatural.'"[28] But beyond that, animal analogies are dangerous, unless one intends to develop social policy and ethics directly from the antics and behaviors of our hairy (or scaled or feathery) friends, in which case we might begin by killing off the weaker among us and hibernating next winter.

## Immutability Amen!

If relying on randy rodents for social policy wasn't strange enough, imagine my surprise to uncover the curious courtship of biological immutability and religious revisionism. One of the more peculiar aspects of the born-gay discourse—a scientific discourse after all—is how it merges seamlessly with the religious argument that "God made me this way," marrying biological determinism with a kind of religious naturalism, all in the service of tolerance. From ardent gay activists to the (straight) man on the street to sympathetic theolo-gians, the "God made me this way" argument was bolstered by the new science of sexuality. Even uber-advice-columnist Ann Landers managed to merge religious benevolence with scientific immutabil-ity when she stated in a 1996 National Public Radio interview that "these people do not choose this 'lifestyle.' Homosexuals are born that way, and many of them are very content with their sexual ori-entation, and this is the way God made them."[29] It's as if sexuality were so essential that it is not even subject to evolution. The born-gay discourse is creationist!

If anti-gay activists rely on religion to demonize gays, then pro-gay activists have often relied on an unusual combination of religion and science to normalize gays. So you have, on the one hand, anti-gay activists claiming gayness as (unnatural) choice, as willful aber-ration that is explicitly condemned in the Bible, and pro-gay activists claiming immutability and God's love for all (his) children. A version of religious determinism has certainly existed prior to the rise of the

gay-gene discourse. However, in recent years, gay-embracing inter-
pretations of the Bible are bolstered with recourse to scientific "evidence" and personal testimony that attests to both the "naturalness"
and inevitability of homosexuality. Gay-positive religious figures
often rely on this "scientific" immutability argument to lay the justi-
fying groundwork for the theologically based argument that we are
all made "in God's image." There is almost a cottage industry in this
subject, which includes biblical reinterpretations, theological debates
about sexuality, and endless ruminations on Sodom, Gomorrah, and
associated biblical tropes of homo destructiveness.

One particularly revealing venue trumpets its position in its
very Web address: godmademegay.com. On this fascinating website, small-town pastor Bruce Lowe recalls a dinner in 1948 with a
parishioner, who became a lifelong friend. She eventually confided
to him that her "brother hates God because God made him gay, and
he knows he is going to hell, and I do, too, for that is what the Bible
says."[30] Motivated to examine the subject, Lowe comes to what we
can only call a "gay positive" perspective and writes the parishioner,
Louise, a letter, which is reprinted on the website. While moving and
powerful, the letter not only effortlessly merges the religious with the
scientific but foregrounds the scientific as its very first point in a list
of ten key conclusions the pastor has developed (after long study, of
course). For this pastor, as for so many people, "homosexuality is an
unchangeable nature; it is not a lifestyle choice." This is presented as
"an essential basis for understanding homosexuality" and for a tolerant attitude to those who are so imbued with this "nature."[31] As in
science journalism and television specials, the new science of homo
immutability is asserted as what tolerant and thoughtful religious
people agree on. While "there may still be a few knowledgeable people who do not believe this, . . . practically all behavioral scientists
now accept this statement as a fact," and therefore so should religious
leaders. "Advances in the sciences . . . in the last 100 years," claims the
same good pastor, "have shown that not all people are heterosexual;
some are homosexual, and their homosexuality is an unchangeable
nature, not a choice." So not only is it asserted unequivocally that the

whole civilized world of serious scholars believes in a "homosexual nature," but even the American Psychiatric Association's decision to remove homosexuality as a mental illness (referenced in the pastor's letter) is seen as a sign that *they* believe in immutability.[32]

Indeed, the pastor continues to marshal a dizzying array of "facts" to prove this idea of unchangeability, including

> (a) ten thousand suicides each year of young homosexuals unwilling to face life with that orientation; (b) the high percentage of homosexuals who go to psychotherapists desperately wanting to change their orientation, and then (c) the very small percentage of them reportedly being changed after hundreds of hours and thousands of dollars being spent in psychotherapy; (d) the millions of homosexuals who remain "in the closet," not acting like homosexuals and not wanting anyone to learn of their orientation; (e) the thousands who are reported as coming to pastors and counselors devastated to have to recognize their unchangeable orientation and wanting assistance in dealing with it.[33]

This is a fascinating list: suicides and the closet are here invoked as evidence of biological *determination*, not the terrible cost of *homophobia*. As the pastor notes, "scientists and sociologists do not know what causes homosexuality, just as they don't know what causes heterosexuality, but virtually all are convinced that whatever the cause, it is unchangeable. Homosexuals are homosexual by nature; it is never something they choose."[34] So "naturalness" is here applauded in ways that are seemingly contradictory and tautological: gays are natural because they exist everywhere and in multiple animal kingdoms, and gays are natural because they have no control over their desires in any case. This confusion of "natural" with "biological" with "immutable" with "determining" pervades both the religious versions of "born that way" and the scientific.

In some cases, religious determinism joined with biological determinism is used explicitly to counter the arguments of pious conservatives. In a typical piece, liberal columnist Nicholas Kristof challenges "religious conservatives" by arguing that "if homosexuality is utterly contrary to God's law, . . . why is it so embedded in human biology and in the rest of the animal kingdom?"[35] So here the evidence for the godliness of gayness rests on the shaky foundation of supposed immutability in both animals and humans, but of course the causal logic could just as easily flow the other way in terms of the incomplete, flawed, and inherently sinful essence of human (and animal?) being. In addition, the logic only plays out so far: would it be legitimate to say that God does *not* love homosexuals if it can be shown that sexual identity is a choice? Would that then provide ample counterevidence that it is "utterly contrary to God's law"? Would people then find justification *not* to tolerate if gays chose to love whom they love?

If progressive activists and gay-inclusive theologians embrace this combustible combo pack of religious and genetic determinism, religious conservatives seem to have little trouble either refuting the science or fitting the science into a consistent anti-gay theology. While some journalists seem to think that "science is stealing up on America's religious fundamentalists,"[36] making it more difficult for them to sustain anti-gay postures, many fundamentalists have no trouble reconciling the two. Mostly, they reject the contention of any biological basis. But the Reverend R. Albert Mohler Jr., president of the Southern Baptist Theological Seminary, drew a certain amount of ire from his fellow religious conservatives when he acknowledged the possibility that a "biological basis for sexual orientation exists."[37] For *Washington Post* writer Harold Myerson, discussing Mohler's argument, this presents a real problem, because "once you recognize homosexuality as a genetic reality, it does create a theological dilemma for the Mohlers among us, for it means that God is making people who, in the midst of what may otherwise be morally exemplary lives, have a special and inherent predisposition to sin. Mohler's response is that since Adam's fall, sin is the condition of all humankind. That sidesteps, however, the conundrum that a gay person may follow the same God-given instincts as a straight person—let's assume fidelity and the desire for church sanctification in both cases—and ends up damned while the straight person ends up saved. Indeed, it means that a gay person's duty is to suppress his God-given instincts while a straight person's duty is to fulfill his."[38] I applaud Myerson's attempt to tie the anti-gay Christians up in knots, but I'm not sure logical consistency is the mark of biblical literalists (e.g., a big thumbs-down to sodomy but seemingly no desire to stone adulterers or kill those who touch the skin of a dead pig). Surely, even if they accept the argument of immutability, they can argue—and do—that these desires (like others that may be "inborn") must be repressed and refocused in order to live a godly life.

Anti-gay Christians can often sound like the postmodernists in this debate. In contrast to the "God made me this way" religious progressives, who rely on a definition of sexuality that is both frustratingly gender dualistic and linear, religious conservatives often make the argument that attempting to construct personhood and identity on the basis of behaviors is akin to "building an identity on shifting sand."[39] In other words, they strangely invoke a sexuality that is less fixed and medicalized than the pro-gay Christians do. Of course, these anti-gay activists who adamantly contest the notion of "born that way" offer up a radically different version of social constructionism than that of secular progressives who embrace an expansive and multifaceted understanding of the vagaries of sexual identity and sexual desire.

For example, the Christian conservatives who champion reparative therapy as the "cure" for homosexuality frame choice through the twin constructs of family (largely maternal) dysfunction and sin. While conveniently and strangely ignoring lesbians, these conservatives largely dredge up tired old faux-psychoanalytic notions of overbearing mothers and distant fathers to explain the vexing pathology of male homosexuality. Curiously, like their biologically determinist opponents, right-wing reparative-therapy Christians rely heavily on stereotypical conceptions of gender, which just goes to show you that just about everyone thinks boys will be boys (and girls will be . . . mysterious). As Joseph Nicolosi, director of the National Association for Research and Therapy of Homosexuality and the author of the bible of this movement, *Reparative Therapy of Male Homosexuality*, argues, "Nature made man complementary to woman, and to cling to the sameness of one's own sex is to look at the world with one eye. . . . People are gendered. We are naturally gendered into male and female. So the male homosexual is trying to find his unfulfilled masculinity. . . . His homosexual attractions are a symptom of his desire to find his masculine identification and same-sex emotional needs."[40]

Of course, for most anti-gay activists, science is no impediment to bigotry. Evangelical leader Mohler, quoted in *Time* magazine, argues that "there has been among evangelicals a fear or a misunderstanding that if a scientific causation of homosexuality were discovered that that somehow removes the moral responsibility of the persons making these choices." But he has a nifty way out because "the Scripture doesn't say we are responsible only for the temptations we choose. The basic sinfulness of homosexuality, that wouldn't change."[41] Beyond such obvious dangers of adhering to biological determinist notions, we should be wary of the instrumental and selective yoking of religion to "science," a yoking that has a long and nefarious history in eugenics and other practices of racial annihilation and engineering.

# 6

# You Say Nature, I Say Nurture . . .
# Let's Call the Whole Thing Off

In our present political context, gay volition is like Voldemort—dangerous even to be uttered. Biological determinism is the new normal, yoked to tolerance claims much as magic hews to Harry Potter. As I have argued earlier, it was not always thus, but the determinist ethos began to insinuate itself into gay politics in the late 1980s or so. As sociologist Vera Whisman noted, as early as 1996, "the claim of 'no choice' is to a pro-gay stance as the claim of 'choice' is to an anti-gay one: a foundational argument. Anti-gay rhetoric uses the term 'sexual preference' to imply choice, while pro-gay rhetoric uses 'sexual orientation' to deny it."[1]

TV shows are full of characters invoking their biology when confronting their queerness, and Hollywood films depict immutability as unassailable truth in movies that present a "tolerance" thesis. No cultural moment, however, sums it up like the TV spectacle that took place in August 2007. Logo—the all-gay all the time cable network—joined with the Human Rights Campaign to host the first ever Democratic presidential primary debate centering on gay rights, with candidates Hillary Clinton, Barack Obama, and all the other major (and minor) Democratic contenders participating. At one point, the host, singer Melissa Etheridge (strangely representing "gay journalism"), asked the inevitable "born with it" question to New Mexico Governor Bill Richardson. Etheridge framed it in the now predictable way: "Do you think homosexuality is a choice? Or is it biological?" When Richardson responded in a way that was clearly "wrong" by saying "It's a choice," Etheridge was so shocked that she had to ask him if he actually understood the question. Richardson's attempt to follow up was one many of us would applaud ("I don't see this as an issue of science or definition") but one Etheridge was quick to correct, for how or why—she asked—would anyone *choose* to be gay? Obviously not satisfied with Richardson's clumsy attempts to follow her determinist lead, Etheridge managed to merge biological essentialism, religious fundamentalism, and the Constitution into one heady brew of homo immanence. "It's hard," she tells us, "when you are a citizen of a country that tells you that you are making a choice when you were born that way and your Creator made you that way and there's a document that was written two hundred years ago that says you are entitled to certain rights that you are not given." By the looks on the faces of Etheridge and the other hosts, Richardson had patently erred and, sure enough, follow-up questions attempted to get him to rectify the situation.[2] Coincidentally, three years earlier, John Kerry had made the same essentialist case in speaking of Vice President Dick Cheney's lesbian daughter, Mary Cheney. "We're all God's children," said Kerry when asked a question by the moderator. Referring to Mary Cheney, Kerry said, "She would tell you that she's being . . . who she was born as. I think if you talk to anybody, it's not choice." Strangely enough, it was his opponent—George W. Bush— who said of the choice question, "I just don't know," once again demarcating the nonessentialist position as the conservative one![3]

Or, more recently, poor Cynthia Nixon—*Sex and the City* alum and newly minted lesbian activist about town—discussed her sexuality in a way that threw the biological determinists into a tizzy. In the context of an interview with the *New York Times*, Nixon made the seemingly innocuous (and personal) statement that, for her, being gay was a choice and actually pushed the point to make a more radical argument against ceding choice to, as she said, "the bigots who are demanding it" because "it doesn't matter if we flew here or we swam here, it matters that we are here and we are one group and let us stop trying to make a litmus test for who is considered gay and who is not."[4] Well, you would think she had declared that baby pandas were ugly and the moon was made of green cheese: she was attacked from all quarters, most vociferously by gay leaders and the gay press. While she didn't back down entirely, she did "clarify" her remarks in an interview with the *Advocate* to the effect that since she was *bisexual*, it was a choice to be with a woman, but nonetheless, she said, "most members of our community—as well as the majority of heterosexuals—cannot and do not choose the gender of the persons with whom they seek to have intimate relationships."[5] This episode illustrates vividly the complexity of the relationship between these "by nature" arguments and tolerance (and, of course, intolerance as well) and how easily these biological arguments can be yoked to either side in these debates, depending on the political context.

## What's the Matter with Choice?

"Choice" has gained such negative valence that even a serious opponent of biological reductionism such as pioneering feminist biologist Anne Fausto-Sterling balks at the term, seeing it not only as dangerously open to political misuse but erroneous in its presumption of a fungibility of sexual desire. She states that "even those who argue that being gay is a choice would vehemently deny that they could make such a choice."[6] In truth, she is here echoing the very common anecdotal reports from gays themselves. In conversations with friends and family, we certainly hear a lot of "but I always knew something was different" or "I always felt gay" or something to that effect. These are, unquestionably, very real feelings for many (although assuredly not all) gay people, and I don't want to deny the experience of that "inevitability." But given the way in which genetic and biological determinisms frame everyday discourse, it is just too easy to jump from this inchoate "feeling" to assertions of immutability and biological imprinting. Perhaps, as cultural critics Janet Jakobsen and Ann Pellegrini argue, the born-gay sentiment "is a way of describing this feeling of unchosenness, this sense that the 'I' could not be any other way."[7] Believing that one is born gay can also become a handy weapon against the harsh treatment by family and society and an explanatory tool to combat internal self-loathing and doubt. There is clearly some real comfort for gays—particularly those who have navigated the waters of hatred—to come to land on the supposedly solid shores of biology. As the homo puppets of the hit Broadway musical *Avenue Q* chime in,

> *Nicky*
> *You can count on me*
> *To always be*
> *Beside you every day,*
> *To tell you it's okay,*
> *You were just born*
> *That way,*
> *And, as they say,*
> *It's in your DNA,*
> *You're gay!*[8]

It is certainly true that very few gays would claim that they chose to be gay (or heterosexuals that they chose to be straight, for that matter—not that anyone is interested), in the way we imagine choice as a deliberate and straightforward act, like choosing to eat lobster or buy a pair of Nikes. No gays would argue that they simply woke up one day and made a conscious decision to sexually desire members of their own sex. So part of the problem in this whole gay-gene discussion is that "choice" is referenced in a narrow way, and most of us do not think of our sexual desires or identities as akin to that almost consumerist notion of choice. But it is a big leap from thinking that homosexuality is a deep part of one's sense of self to asserting that particular sexual formations and desires are biologically *predetermined*. This is a leap made regularly by science writers, journalists, pundits, and the rest of us, including Truth Wins Out founder Wayne Besen, who asserts unequivocally that "biology, psychology and empirical wisdom strongly suggest that sexual orientation is an intrinsic part of one's nature."[9]

Yet even constructionist and radical gay activists find themselves forced to rely on "nature" when facing off against those who deem gays both unnatural and immoral. Particularly in the sound-bite world of public discourse, it is almost impossible to articulate a notion of queer choice or even just queer "being," because it is certainly the case that "the long-standing demand, made by religious conservatives, distraught parents, and liberal helping professions alike, is but this: *change your unnatural desires.* Time and again, the response is given: *I can't change them—They're part of my nature.*"[10] But for most of the scientists and, more to the point, science writers and popularizers eager to sell the born-gay thesis, innate gayness is offered as the antidote to help "dispel the idea that gay behavior is a matter of fickle choice subject to 'correction.'"[11] The language here is revealing. Choice is considered to be fickle (and obviously "lower" somehow than its opposite—the inevitability of biological determination), and the assumption is that if in fact it is a choice, then it can be "corrected."

Would it be as convincing to own one's sexuality in a voluntary fashion or, as Roger Lancaster sardonically notes, "to take to the airwaves to argue the legitimacy of one's feelings without recourse to the depths of an inner nature?"[12] For anyone who has had to be on the public stage as a "professional homosexual"—as a speaker at a conference, a panelist on a talk show, an interviewee on the radio—the question "Is it a choice?" almost invariably pops up, no matter what subject you are addressing. And all too often this is the question addressed to you by sympathetic friends, eager to "understand" your life (of course, gays rarely ask those probing questions of heterosexuals). The gay author Eric Marcus had just this combination of personal and professional experience, prompting him to write a witty and breezy book answering "the most frequently asked questions about gays and lesbians."[13] Not surprisingly, topping the list: "Is it a choice?" to which, again unsurprisingly, he answers with a definitive no.

Even more damning evidence of immutability is offered up by those words quoted earlier from Melissa Etheridge and echoed by so many gays themselves and their allies as well: why would anyone "choose" to be in a socially vilified position? For Marcus, Etheridge, and countless others, *homophobia* is the evidence of the immutability of gayness. Gay inevitability is therefore posited as the narrative of our lives; one does not "become" gay but rather either simply represses or alternatively accepts what is always already there.

In this way, as in so many others, determinist ideas rest under layers of other determinist ideas. The behavior/identity distinction is thus particularly relevant when it comes to issues of heritability or determination. Can anyone make a claim that *genes* (or the endocrine system) produces an *identity* (e.g., a queer identity)? The most anyone can do is indicate possible behaviors or predictions of desires, and even categorizing those behaviors as part of an identity schema is problematic. Even serious scientists, such as National Institutes of Health neurobiologist Vittorio Gallo, admit that "the definitions of heterosexuality and homosexuality are ambiguous; therefore, a scientific sample population is nearly impossible to create."[14]

Simon LeVay's study, in particular, has come in for criticism on precisely these issues, because

> the medical records of post-mortem individuals contain insufficient data to reliably allocate those individuals to different categories of sexual identity, . . . LeVay's use of the categories "heterosexual" and "homosexual" is modeled on outdated notions of sexual identity, . . . the post-mortem brains of many of the subjects may have been modified by complications from AIDS, . . . LeVay conflates male homosexuality with femininity, . . . the sample size is too small for reliable comparisons between groups to be made, . . . LeVay's hypothesis can only be supported when data from the brains of homosexual women are included in the comparative schema, and . . . LeVay's assertion that studies of rodent and primate sexuality offer useful behavioral and neurological homologies for humans is not valid.[15]

Critics of the gay-gene dogma have detailed just how fraught this problem of definition is. For example, legal studies scholar Ed Stein conducted a revealing interview with psychiatrist Richard Pillard, coauthor with Michael Bailey of one of the most celebrated—and debated—studies of so-called gay twins. In response to a question concerning his sample, Pillard responds,

> What we did was to put out advertisements for gay men who had a twin brother—either gay or straight—or an adopted brother, adopted into the family at an age less than three. Then we interviewed the men who volunteered to be sure what their sexual orientations were. They volunteered as gay people—and that's generally what they were—but we tried to quantify this in a rough way by asking, "Are you bisexual? That is, are you attracted to women too or just to men?"[16]

So Pillard assumes that if they say they are gay, then they are and again assumes that a singular definition of "gayness" is shared by all concerned. But, perhaps more importantly, how differently that definition ("gay") and identity circulates (between different ethnic and racial groups, generationally, etc.) seems unaddressed. In other words, we have a tautology here, a sort of circular argument that "proves" an identity through its utterance and then uses that new "truth" to make analyses about that identity. In addition, "bisexuality" is assumed to be a simple doubling process of "attraction" and thus rules out being "gay."

But can't we imagine and don't we know loads of people who identify as gay (and who would therefore answer Pillard's question in the affirmative) but, at the same time and often unproblematically, find members of the opposite sex attractive, even sexually alluring? Are they then not gay? Are they less gay and their genes therefore less interesting? These are just a few of the many, many problems—problems that are mostly not addressed and often actively ignored—in simply assuming that "gay" is a self-evident category.

Laypeople and scientists alike do fervently believe that "scientific research can help dispel some of the myths about homosexuality that in the past have clouded the image of lesbians and gay men,"[17] thus perhaps opening the door to more "tolerant" attitudes. But I do wonder what myths they think immutability arguments dispel. Certainly, one myth they may dispel is the simplistic mother-blaming of

psychology or the equally simplistic conservative fantasies of a deca-
dent culture that "produces" gayness, along with associated evils such
as feminism, rap music, and thongs. Logically, the only other myth
that could be dispelled in this scenario is the "myth" of choice, as
immutability is configured as its opposite. As critical biologist Garland Allen remarks sarcastically, "'It's not my fault,' is supposed to be
a liberating conception."[18]

## The Cure around the Corner

A quick examination of the progressive response to the so-called
reparative-therapy movement to "cure" gays by turning them straight
reveals the limitations of the gay-gene mania. Since the reparative-
therapy dogma relies on a notion of choice and therefore changeabil-
ity, the progressive response has been to insist that, no indeedy, we
cannot change. In other words, reparative therapy is wrong not simply or only because we are happy to be gay (and therefore there is
nothing to cure) but because it will inevitably fail: a leopard can't
change its spots. Pillard, author of the twins study discussed above,
argues that genetic discourses will "get psychiatrists away from trying to convert sexual orientation":

> That's an undertaking that should be given up; it didn't ever work,
> but it did lead to conflicts and people feeing bad about themselves.
> Also, I think parents will realize that their children aren't gay because
> of something wrong that they did. I have had opportunities to talk to
> parents who have more than one gay person in their families, and they
> are relieved by this realization. They wondered if they were poisoning
> their children in some awful way. The answer is no. So in those ways I
> think studies like mine can be useful.[19]

But for all Pillard's beneficent intentions, how chilling it is to see the
set of assumptions wrapped into this simple statement. Conversion
therapy is bad because it doesn't work, and parents are now liberated
because they realize they didn't poison their kids. So being gay is

equated with having a poisoned interior, and how much poison can the body politic tolerate? When Alan Chambers, of the conversion group Exodus International (the standard-bearer for the "ex-gay" movement), changes his tune, it is not to embrace a "gay is good" ethos but rather to embrace a model of unchanging "urges" that are "inborn." And our friend Wayne Besen of Truth Wins Out responds to the news that Exodus is disbanding by saying, "it really highlights the futility of trying to change your sexuality,"[20] rather than rejecting the very desire to be "ex-"gay. Besen wages his war on reparative therapy through another war on the "notion that one can change,"[21] essentially ignoring the real culprit of anti-gay animus itself.

The disease model permeates this framing with an underlying definition of gayness as "something wrong," an aberration that no one, no parent, would ever desire or choose for his or her child. So these scientists not only see themselves as providing vital ammunition for the larger culture wars but assert that their work can relieve grieving parents of their inevitable guilt over having somehow "caused" this horrific thing called a gay child. But as Timothy Murphy argues in his book on the ethics of sexual-orientation research, "what has really killed most interest in sexual science therapy is not proof of the genetic origins of homosexuality, but the rejection of the notion that homosexuality is a condition that needs to be 'cured.' "[22] Tolerance as a goal leaves the door open for the curative "solution" (and therefore "born that way" ideas) because that "thing" that is generously tolerated would not have to be tolerated at all if it was done away with.

Pro-gay celebrities and pundits are the most insistent that choice is the enemy of freedom and civil rights, a strange argument to make for those who are also, well, *pro*-choice when it comes to reproductive rights. "Born that way" is the preferred theme for most celebs when they recount their coming out or when they support gay causes. When design superstar Nate Berkus had a heart-to-heart with Oprah in 2013, he recounted the moment his father began to "understand" his gayness. As recounted to Oprah, he reportedly told his dad, "Why would I choose to make my life more difficult—why would anyone choose to make their life more difficult? Do you think I would choose to have this hair? Do you think that I would choose to be five-foot-nine? I would have been six-foot-one. It's the exact same thing. The truth of the matter is being gay is the way I was born. I believe this to the core of my being.'" His dad, supplied now with this glowing endorsement of same-sex love, replied, "If you say you are born this way, and you didn't have a choice, then we are good." For Berkus, "that was really the moment": "Then, I knew if I had this base level of respect that I could move forward."²³ So pops can respect him if he can't help himself, and he compares his sexual identity to his hair.

In a June 1, 2009, episode of the popular morning chat show *The View*, liberal host Joy Behar claims of gays, "The main thing about it, I think, with people who don't want them to come out and who don't want them to have their rights is that they believe that it is a choice. As soon as people get over the fact that it is a choice, it will be a nonissue. It is not a choice. It is what people are. . . . No one is choosing to be vilified by people." Well, what a confusion here! Not only is it simply asserted (by a heterosexual woman, moreover) that gays don't choose to be gay, but homo*phobia* and homo*sexuality* are confused. Of course, no one would choose to be vilified, although bigots do clearly choose to be bigoted. But the presence of hatred says nothing about the desires and practices and identities one might choose to engage in. Using the pain of homophobia as evidence that gayness is not chosen is as spurious as arguing that no one would ever choose to be black or to be a woman or a Jew since all of these carry with them onerous histories of discrimination. It's insulting and patronizing. Yet because tolerance governs our thinking about gay rights, such phrases trip off the tongue with nary a whisper of concern. Can we imagine the issue of choice and immutability being central to the discussions concerning other civil rights?

## Will the Real Homosexual Please Stand Up!

Of course, making the determination of the "cause" of homosexuality begs the question of how to determine if one is a homosexual.

This gets to the heart of a real problem: in searching for a biological basis for homosexuality, most scientists cannot help but reinscribe the most constrained definitions of sexual identity, definitions that have been vigorously challenged by theorists and historians for decades. LGBTQ theorists have long disputed the easy assumptions that link behaviors with identities. The assumption of "gay" as a category clearly delineated and easily knowable is challenged theoretically, historically, and cross-culturally. It is by now axiomatic in gay studies—and generally accepted—that while all kinds of sexual practices have existed throughout history, "homosexuality" and "heterosexuality" as distinct identity categories (e.g., "I am a homosexual" rather than "I sometimes engage in sex acts with someone of the same gender") are products of the modern era. We learn this from the groundbreaking work of the late French philosopher Michel Foucault but also from the diligent, detailed work of a wide array of historians, including Jonathan Ned Katz, George Chauncey, and others.

The most telling examples come from ancient history, when male-male sexual behavior was common and accepted (at least in normative forms, with an elder citizen acquiring a youthful male lover) and when that behavior neither established a particular identity (gay) nor contradicted other practices of opposite-sex love and marriage. Still other cross-cultural examples indicate much more elaborate systems of classification than "gay" or "straight" seem to encompass. In many Latin and Central American contexts, for example, more emphasis is placed on an individual's relationship to particular sexual acts than to some totalizing identity, so who penetrates and who gets penetrated may—in some contexts—be more determinative of identity than "sodomy" itself. Or in many South Asian cultures, such as Thailand, sexual identities are formed much more around specific kinds of *gender* comportment, which does not translate easily into the simple moniker "gay." And US Native American concepts of "two-spirit" or "berdache" don't fit easily with the normative concept of homosexuality as a unique minority identity either, as it indicates an understanding of gender identity quite at odds with the mainstream American model of mapping gender onto sexed bodies.

So when this nuanced and complicated historical and cross-cultural work confronts the recent obsession with immutability and biological origins, we have a serious set of problems, if not real contradictions. For this historical and scholarly work details the very contextual, historically specific, and complicated reality of what we now call "sexual identity": it proves that the very notion of "sexual identity" as singular, transhistorical, and transcultural is simply not supported by the anthropological and historical evidence. Homosexuality did not simply "evolve" from preference to identity in some singular linear way; contemporary "homosexuals" vary widely in terms of how their desires do or do not construct/produce/define identity.

How we experience our sexual identity is produced in and through a multitude of factors, including our political commitments, our geographical locations, and our racial/ethnic identifications. And, to add to the complexity, desire itself shifts and changes over the course of a lifetime. We might have a bit more in common with the Greeks than we imagine, in the sense that seemingly contradictory sexual practices coexist, even as we insist on their absolute separability. Even further, classifications actually produce and create identities; they don't merely reflect already given reality. So the invention of a gay identity does help funnel desires into those categories: one is no longer someone who likes a little this or a little that, but one *is* a gay person, part of a "class" or even species of person. And this is even more the case for heterosexuality as an identity, as the groundbreaking work of Jonathan Ned Katz has amply demonstrated.[24]

Given that indisputable truth (that "gayness" is hardly a self-evident and internally coherent category of behavior *or* identity), the scientific search for causality becomes even more fraught. This question of naming, identifying, and classifying is vexing to say the least, and scholars have insisted that we be much more circumspect in our systems of sexual classification. Furthermore, this work is made more challenging by the insistence that we cannot—tautologically—claim that which we intend to prove. If scientists working on the "gay gene" presume this identity they call "gay" as if it is a self-evident, easily definable, and uniform fact of social existence, it is in direct contradiction to the work of most gay scholars, who have insisted we historicize social and sexual identities and not assume that the presence of certain acts were always a sure sign of an entire personal (or social) identity.

Most scientists have "resolved" this very serious definitional problem with a combination of subjects' self-reporting, declared homosexual experiences, and measured physiological reaction to visual stimuli. For many researchers, responses to stimuli are the real test—but this begs any number of questions: Does attraction connote identity? Always? Does it imply action? "By what criterion," asks Rebecca Jordan-Young, "is blood flow to the penis a better indicator of desire than someone's subjective state of arousal?"[25] Our responses to sexual images, for example, are cross-cut with any number of complicating factors: our relation to visual (and sexual) imagery, the dominance and pervasiveness of heterosexuality, how racial/ethnic and gender differences play out in watching sexual imagery, and so on. Finding something pleasurable to watch—and even getting aroused by it—does not automatically indicate action, much less identity. I can't tell you how many lesbians (longtime, unambiguously defined lesbians) love gay male porn.[26] It doesn't mean they're secretly straight. A woman who defines herself as exclusively heterosexual might get seriously turned on by a gorgeous gay man (or woman), but this says little about her own self-identification or her own actual sexual behaviors and practices (which, in turn, may say little about her identity). So if one reports that one is gay (let's say, for a scientific study) but in fact has never had same-sex sexual behavior, then how is that measured? Is that person "gay" for the sake of the study? How gay? Or if one has same-sex desire but never acts on it? Or engages in same-sex acts but never defines oneself as gay? Or engages in acts that scientists define as gay but that they themselves do not? Or sometimes has same-sex sex but also has (pleasurable, active) opposite-sex sex? What is the cutoff point?

And what of changes over the life course? Not only does our sexuality change as we age, but our perceptions of it alter and shift. How we tell the story of our sexual identities and lives is affected by any number of factors, including of course the larger social world in which we live. So, for example, even to name oneself as "gay" is dependent on a social movement, a language, a set of identity politics in which "gayness" has some meaning (as opposed to, say, certain tastes or preferences or practices). And it is also the case that these studies presume—and therefore reinforce and produce—the assumption that what matters is sexual-object choice. But, says sociologist Martha McCaughy,

> What of variations in sexual preference other than object-choice—such as scripted vs. non-scripted sex, sex in public vs. sex in private, orgasmic vs. non-orgasmic sex, sex with one person vs. more than one? These variations seem not to concern evolutionary theorists precisely because such preferences are assumed to be less intrinsic or fundamental to our being than the gender of object-choice. That variations in sexual preference that do not revolve around sex categories are ignored suggests that evolutionary theorists presume and perpetuate a sex binarism that queer theorists and "postmodern" feminists have analyzed as central to a disciplinary regime of heterosexuality.[27]

Two other points must be stressed here. First, there are much more complicated and contradictory stories of sexual identity out there that are just not captured by the choice/determined dichotomy, as any conversation with a random group of gays will tell you. And, second, we cannot even begin to imagine how we come into sexual identities outside of the overwhelming force of heterosexual dominance. In other words, how can we think of "choice" (or coercion) in the context of what many people have called compulsory heterosexuality? How does one factor in the reality that we live in a world that privileges heterosexuality, that relentlessly advertises it, that naturalizes it yet provides endless benefits (both ephemeral and manifest) for participation? In other words, how do we know what range of bodies and practices we may desire in a world in which one way of desiring is seen as, well, so desirable and in which others are demonized, criminalized, mocked, ghettoized, or simply invisible? In a culture so thoroughly heterosexualized (from day one, from the way we think of our fetuses and infants to the supposed fruition of hetero marriage to the way we imagine loss, grief, and death), it is hard to think that our "preferences" aren't at least in part framed by this overweening reality.

In truth, very few articles even delve into these definitional problems that—to many of us—invalidate these studies from the get-go. "Brain organization research on sexual orientation," argues Jordan-Young, "is fraught with internal contradictions. In particular, scientists' extremely different ways of measuring 'homosexuality' have contributed to a network of studies that look convincing and mutually supportive on the surface, but in fact are fundamentally at odds with one another."[28] Gallo's earlier point, that a serious scientific sample population is almost impossible to imagine when dealing with the complexities of sexual desire, practices, preferences, and identities, goes almost unexamined in the rush to determine etiology. No wonder, since admitting the fluid and complex "nature" of sexuality would undermine the very terms of the scientific discourse and simultaneously trouble tolerance, itself dependent on a gay/straight clarity. A binary opposition between clearly demarcated "homo" and "hetero" does the double trick of maintaining the "purity" of the majority and containing fears of contagion while, at the same time, further cordoning off complicating social factors. These are just a few of the many, many problems—problems that are mostly not addressed and often actively ignored—in simply assuming that "gay" is a self-evident category.

## Playing with Fire

Leave it to the humor magazine the *Onion* to reveal the darkness at the heart of the gay-gene obsession. With a headline screaming "Gay Gene Isolated, Ostracized," it reveals,

> Scientists at Johns Hopkins University isolated the gene which causes homosexuality in human males, promptly segregating it from normal,

heterosexual genes. "I had suspected that gene was queer for a long time now. There was just something not quite right about it," said team leader Dr. Norbert Reynolds. "It's a good thing we isolated it; I wouldn't want that faggot-ass gene messing with the straight ones." Among the factors Reynolds cited as evidence of the gene's gayness: its pinkish hue; meticulously frilly perimeter; and faint but distinct, perfume-like odor.[29]

Similarly, a satiric news website states that "gay scientists claim to have isolated the Christian gene" and goes on to replicate—in exact form—every trope of the gay-gene discourse, including the relieved parents who say, "Well, we'd always worried that if we'd done something different, our child wouldn't have ended up a Christian but now we know we didn't have any choice."[30] Not to be outdone, in an episode of the animated series *Family Guy*, Peter is injected with the "gay gene" and comes home swishing uncontrollably and wearing a jaunty scarf, one of the few mainstream pop-culture examples that parodies rather than promotes biological essentialism.[31]

These are humorous examples—an outsized take on the gay-science mania. But there are real dangers inherent in the biological explanations of homosexuality, many of which I've discussed in the previous pages. Indeed, if homosexuality is some kind of genetic or brain aberration, then there must be interventions to make homos "normal." As Jennifer Terry says, most, if not all, of the scientific commentary is and has been interventionist, "linked to larger agendas concerned with what ought to be done not just about homosexuality but about the sexual and social phenomena to which it has been attributed."[32] A quick romp through recent history reveals the results of biological determinism, particularly when meshed with religious ideologies. As Stacy Chinn argues, "Hereditarian arguments about nonnormative sexuality, which were immensely popular in the first decades of the twentieth century, encouraged thirty states to enact sterilization statutes that in some way aimed at limiting the transmission of sexual excesses. Countless queers were subjected to any number of different 'treatments,' ranging from genital surgery and sterilization to electro-shock and lobotomy."[33] It is hard not to see the ugly specter of eugenics once again raising its head.

We would be foolish to believe the fantasy that somehow "proving" immutability would easily and automatically nullify anti-gay animus and homophobia and lead to tolerance. On the contrary, biological arguments about immutable differences and inherent otherness have long been used to demonize, discriminate, and otherwise victimize those who are deemed inferior by "nature" of their birth (Jews), skin color (African Americans), and sex (women). Not surprisingly, women in general and lesbians and feminists in particular have approached the biological arguments much more cautiously than men have. As neurobiologist Neena Schwartz argues,

> It is instructive to contrast the stance of feminists and gays with respect to theories of biological etiology. For members of both groups, the overt biological phenotypes are "normal," and both groups have supported changes in the laws, urging equal treatment. But feminists have argued that women's biology, acknowledged to be hormonally and genetically different from men's, at least with respect to sexual phenotype, is *not* definitive and that the differences do not impact one's ability to do certain types of work (like math!) or to run for political office. In contrast, many gays have argued that our biology *is* different and determinative, that gayness is no more a "choice" than is gender or eye color. Clearly, this might make a difference to some non-homosexuals.[34]

The idea that discovering biological causation leads simply and automatically to an erosion of discrimination is patently false and has been challenged repeatedly and insistently by any number of critics. As noted earlier, this born-gay doctrine was certainly not the mantra of '60s gay radicals and liberationists, and scholars continue to take issue with the determinist argument from any number of angles. But I'm always rather surprised at the persistent and naive commitment to this fantasy, a commitment that seems to fly in the face of most of our history, in which biological theories of difference have been marshaled not in the service of liberation but rather in the service of categorization, medical experimentation, and even annihilation.

And the biological model can always be turned—easily—on its head. One of the most perturbing aspects of the biological argument is that it can't be controlled. "We" may want to use it to promote civil rights, but it can just as easily be used to further medicalize and promote eugenic policies and may therefore have serious unintended consequences. For some people, the prospect of a "gay gene" provokes a nightmare scenario, in which tests are performed in utero to detect said genes and abortion and gene "therapy" initiated to rid the world of the plague of gay infants. Just such a scenario has been imagined in a 1993 Broadway play and film, *The Twilight of the Golds*, in which genetic testing reveals to a pregnant woman that she is carrying a gay fetus.[35] This fear of the eugenicist uses of scientific knowledge has prompted some (gay) researchers such as Dean Hamer to patent their research in the perhaps futile attempt to mitigate against its use by those who would "cure" or "eliminate" homosexuality. As Robert Brookey points out, in a wonderful book detailing the rise of the gay-gene framework, "the greatest danger that the biological research on homosexuality presents is the ability of politicians to interpret the research as proof of pathology."[36]

Gay as biologically predetermined and therefore benign can easily morph into gay as biologically aberrant and therefore diseased. Maggie Gallagher, a dedicated foe of same-sex marriage, asserts that "there is rather powerful evidence that human beings are a two-sex species, designed for sexual rather than asexual reproduction. If this is true, then the absence of desire for the opposite sex represents, at a minimum, a sexual dysfunction much as impotence or infertility."[37] Even more worrisome, of course, is that biologically determinist arguments *for* gay rights can always be turned on their head to argue *against* gay rights. Anti-gay-marriage groups, for example, invoke not only "choice" to invalidate gay claims but also, simultaneously, a kind of strange Darwinist perspective in which gay marriage is illegitimate because it is counter to the "natural" reproduction of the species. In other words, the notion of gays as a "biological error" is a close cousin to the more supposedly benign notion of biological immutability.

A statement by the Ramsey Colloquium—a religious think-tank of sorts organized by the Institute for Religion and Public Life—illustrates vividly how the "revelation " of immutability can easily be sidestepped or integrated into a broader anti-gay perspective. The authors of the piece claim,

> We cannot settle the dispute about the roots—genetic or environmental—of homosexual orientation. When some scientific evidence suggests a genetic predisposition for homosexual orientation, the case is not significantly different from evidence of predispositions toward other traits—for example, alcoholism or violence. In each instance we must still ask whether such a predisposition should be acted upon or whether it should be resisted. Whether or not a homosexual orientation can be changed—and it is important to recognize that there are responsible authorities on both sides of this question—we affirm the obligation of pastors and therapists to assist those who recognize the value of chaste living to resist the impulse to act on their desire for homogenital gratification.[38]

And, of course, when Christian conservatives get ahold of the "science," there is no telling what pretzels they will turn themselves into. When Rev. Mohler began raising the "What if your baby is gay?" question on his blog, he did so both to acknowledge the sway of genetic arguments on the general public and to find a way to continue to navigate the ship of homophobia through those new waters, "to draw attention to a very real threat to human dignity that lurks as a possibility on our horizon, . . . that, if a biological marker (real or not) is ever claimed to mark homosexuality in prenatal testing, widespread abortion of such babies might well follow."[39] So abortion is still bad, but a little hormonal tinkering not so much; Mohler believes "that Christian couples 'should be open' to the prospect of changing the course of nature—if a biological marker for homosexuality were to be found. He would not support gene therapy but might back other treatments, such as a hormonal patch."[40] And DNA discoverer James Watson was quoted—early on in the gay-gene mania—as saying, "If you could find a gene which determines sexuality and a woman decided that she doesn't want a homosexual child, well, let her."[41] Of course, it seems to go without saying that it would be the homosexual child she would abort! Dishearteningly, even some openly gay science writers such as Chandler Burr look on the possibility of a "gay gene" as providing the silver bullet to end the homosexual desire that—apparently—they despise. Burr has directly reached out to conservatives in advancing the immutability argument by saying that he himself would seek a "cure" if one could be found.[42] The assumption here, of course, is that the silver bullet has "straight" written on it; as an ABC news story of December 2007 frames it, "switching" can only be that of a gay person potentially switching to straight.[43]

In addition, almost wholly absent from so-called scientific work on sexual preferences is any attention to issues of power and inequality. More specifically, the willful refusal to examine how normative and compulsory heterosexuality organizes, impacts, and structures the possibilities of deviations from that norm is itself enough to throw serious doubt as to the validity of such studies. Or, as Roger Lancaster says, "the search for gay identity gradually finds its closure in the normalcy of the norm as natural law."[44] The biological approach therefore "leaves in place, and even cements, the status of heterosexuality as natural and normative and, further, the status of scientific stories as value-neutral accounts of human nature."[45] Of course, it is also obvious—but important to note—that when scientists talk about the "search for the origins or causes of sexual orientation," they are, almost to a one, looking for the causes of one particular sexual orientation (and even that is usually male). So we begin the whole gene saga from a starting place of normalizing heterosexuality and assuming homosexuality as a problem to be figured out, a medical (if not evolutionary) mystery, in which male sexuality is the norm from which female sexuality diverts.

Despite the dangers of biological essentialism, one can imagine some compelling strategic merit in attempting to prove immutability, and many gay activists have taken this route, even when they feel a deep discomfort with hinging their arguments on biological predetermination. For many of the more virulent Christian conservative groups, such as Focus on the Family, gayness is both choice and contagion, each dependent on the other for reciprocal validity. So for these groups to posit contagion—to construct gays as able to seduce/contaminate people they come in contact with—they must also posit sexual desire and identity as choice, for one couldn't be deviled into the lifestyle by the sinister homo teacher (it is usually the teachers in this scenario) if sexuality were already predetermined. An immutability argument might undermine the contagion premise, robbing one of the great marketing tactics of anti-gay activists ("they're out to get your children") of its potency. Undeniably, the geneticist arguments address one of the greatest fears propagated by anti-gay activists: that gayness is/can be "promoted" (e.g., the so-called gay agenda), that it is "catching" in too sexually open environments, and that gays "recruit" the young into the "gay lifestyle." Armed with "born this way" ideas and a goal of mere tolerance, gays can argue back at these folks, saying instead that if it is genetic/predetermined, then no social and cultural factors can influence a person's sexual choices. In other words, your (presumptively straight) children are safe with us! Understandably perhaps, gay activists fear that in eschewing immutability, they open up the Pandora's box of contagion and a kind of viral understanding of gayness. So they maintain instead a self-limiting version of benign homosexuality, in which gayness cannot (and the implicit assumption here is that it should not) "spread" because the gene itself limits its propagation.

As with so many other political struggles, gay rights strategies are often adopted in reaction to attacks. In the early 1990s, when the Christian anti-gay movement began sharpening an approach that painted gays as willfully choosing a sinful/evil/aberrant life *and* able to change through reparative therapy, the gay response—that we're born this way—was in some sense preordained. It's inevitable that these debates have both political origins and political repercussions.

As noted earlier, 19th- and early 20th-century sex reformers attempted to use notions of biology and immutability to coax both their fellow scientists and social leaders toward more "tolerant" views of homosexuality. This strategy met with little success but, clearly, continues in new forms to this day. Contemporary gay legal activists have also made arguments that ideas of immutability can be harnessed to the equal protection clause of the Constitution to help make the case for suspect-class status and thus higher degrees of legal protection. On the television program *Nightline*, lawyer and psychiatrist Richard Green—author of the irritating book *The Sissy Boy Syndrome*—could not have been more explicit in his conviction that immutability leads to liberation:

> Well, legally, I think, [the LeVay study] could make a very big difference. In American constitutional law, groups that are prejudiced against or stigmatized are given special protection by the courts if the feature for which they are discriminated is what's called immutable or innate or essentially unchangeable. . . . So if we can find—the scientists can find that a specific part of the brain is primarily responsible for sexual orientation, then the stigma and the legal discrimination against gays and lesbians in this country should fall.[46]

LeVay and Hamer were immediately recruited (and offered themselves up) in testimonials in gay rights litigation. As early as 1992, Hamer testified in the challenge to Colorado's Amendment 2, arguing that homosexuality was not a choice (like polygamy) but rather an immutable trait. As this case continued in the courts, Hamer was not the only biology guru summoned to the stand. Psychiatrist Green and notorious homophobe Judd Marmor also testified to the stressed-out fetuses, large clitorises, and temporal-lobe pathology of homosexuals. Interestingly, when this Colorado case reached the US Supreme Court (in 1996), it saw fit to overturn the amendment on grounds that did not rely on these immutability arguments.[47] And similar arguments have been used in later cases, including the gay-marriage case in California. For these activists and scholars, the "discovery" of immutability provides both the essential ingredients for gay rights and the scientific justification for self-understandings of sexual identity as predetermined, always there, singular, embedded.

Part of this legal strategy hinges on the fantasy of immutability as the tie-in to including gays in Fourteenth Amendment protection. One problem is that other supposedly immutable characteristics are not protected (eye color, hair color, etc.), so the assumption that simply proving (if one even could) immutability would lead automatically to designation as a "protected class" and that designation to full civil rights is weak, to say the least. The other criterion is that you have to show bias and discrimination, which doesn't happen with eye color, making that particular analogy (used surprisingly often by gay rights advocates) not a very helpful one. In addition, as the anti-gay forces are quick to point out, having a biological "fact" does not justify behavior: we can and do discriminate on the basis of behavior that may have "natural" causes but that has been socially determined to be dangerous or unhealthy. Also, immutability is by no means the only route to civil rights; other identities (religion, most notably) are protected but not immutable. The continued reality of persecution and discrimination (around race, around gender) in spite of immutability claims should serve as a cautionary tale. Of course we need to pursue legal protections even if those legal protections fall short, which they often do. My point is that legal protections based on immutability not only fall short, but are also dangerous.

A narrowly determinist position can be challenged on many grounds: the veracity of the studies themselves (small sample sizes, not replicated, definitional issues from the start, etc.); the gendered assumptions that are built into the very studies and the idea of causality; the inability to account for competing narratives such as bisexuality, changes over life course, gender differences, and so on; the fact that most of these studies, in searching for "gay" causality, leave heterosexuality and its compulsory nature unexamined. Addressing these complex challenges is more important in the fight for real inclusion than the short-term tactic of exploiting essentialist arguments for political gain. But if the public debate (and much of the legal argumentation) is set up so that "tolerance" is dependent on immutability, it is hard to challenge either, because they become wedded to each other in a relation of means (immutability) to end (tolerance).

My intention here is not simply to reject the biological or to play off social constructionism against biological determinism. That is a stale debate, one that has been replayed over the years. Reformulating this as a "nature versus nurture" debate similarly gets us nowhere, for the typical "nurture" arguments are no less deterministic and limited and usually end up in a "blame the mother" scenario. Progressive scientists and committed social constructivists have a shared dilemma: how to recognize and account for the truism that homosexuality as an identity is a social construction—a creation—at the same time that they acknowledge the "truth" that same-sex sexual behavior not only has existed historically and cross-culturally for quite some time but finds expression in a variety of animal species as well. Perhaps it is the case, as many people have argued, that the study of same-sex sexual *behavior* (in humans and in animals) is wholly separate from the study of same-sex sexual *identity* and, even more, community.

In any case, I am more concerned here with a rather different issue: why we—as scientists, as scholars, as a nation—ask certain questions and not others. Or, more to the point, why is it that certain "issues" get framed a particular way, and how does that shift over time? What is most troubling to me is not that determinist and biological ideas are offered up as an "answer" to the supposed conundrum of homosexuality, for we have seen this impetus rear its (mostly ugly) head throughout history—through slavery, through the Holocaust, through the seemingly endless years of male dominion. What is most troubling now is, first, that this framework has so captured both the academy and the everyday, both the intimate and the social worlds, that other frames get pushed to the side or marginalized. And, second, it is worrisome to say the least when a sort of perfect storm develops that marries biological determinism with a religious explanatory framework. What gets lost when "Is it a choice?" become *the* question we ask of homosexuality? Whither fluidity? What about bisexuality? What about transformations over time? What about our own complicated volition? Is "Is it a choice?" the most important question we should be asking? Isn't the most important question one of how we achieve real integration and secure rights for a minority population? And to the extent that so much gets hinged on this choice debate, do we subsume or even banish other questions or concerns?

And what kinds of assumptions—about gender, about family, about sexuality, and, most importantly, about civil rights—are embedded in that seemingly innocuous formation? The genetic frames undermine both Kinsey's continuous model of sexuality and gay radicals' models of fluidity. They rely on binary and bimodal models of both sexuality and gender, at least when it comes to men. As Ed Stein notes,

> Linking human rights to some scientific theory as yet completely un-proven is risky. All that you'll get with the gene theory is the right with things you don't choose, but homosexuals want things they do choose: to be openly gay and hold a job and have same-sex marriages. . . . My concern is that as soon as we start to encourage and embrace as part of a political agenda scientific research in this area, we lead to remedicalization of sexual orientation. . . . Jumping on the genetic bandwagon is hurting our cause. The point is, nothing's wrong with homosexuality, so why try to take it on with science?[48]

Indeed, what for gays may be simply a case of benign biological imperative may take a more dangerous turn, says Brookey, for "the greatest danger that the biological research on homosexuality presents is the ability of politicians to interpret the research as proof of pathology."[49] Science (or some version of it) and politics have always been strange bedfellows. As Valerie Rohy points out in a fascinating article on "homosexual reproduction," anti-gay-marriage groups not only invoke choice when making their arguments but also wrap themselves in a strange Darwinian flag, claiming that same-sex marriage is illegitimate because it is counter to the "natural" reproduction of the species,[50] proving once again that theories of biological immutability are close cousins to theories of biological error. It is no accident that in the face of these neo-Darwinian arguments, gays proclaim both immutability and the family unit as a productive (and reproductive) counterpart to heterosexual futurity.

The political uses of the born-gay thesis have ratcheted up in recent years, in part as a response to the increasing number of legal cases, from the historic 2003 *Lawrence v. Texas* case that overturned anti-sodomy laws to the numerous marriage-related cases circulating around the country. One of the most closely watched cases, the California Supreme Court trial of Proposition 8 (the 2008 anti-gay-marriage proposition that the California electorate voted in after a brief moment of marriage rights in the state) engages with the argument for immutability. As Dean Hamer and Michael Rosbash explicitly argue, "One key issue should influence every aspect of the . . . proceedings: What makes people gay? Is it a choice or is it innate?"[51] So granting gays equal civil rights comes down to this? Not justice? Not inclusion? Not equality? And, again, the framing is a simple— too simple—binary: choice or innate.

And, of course, the "from nature" argument could go both ways. If gayness is found to be "not natural," then being gay is going "against nature" (which is wrong). As John D'Emilio puts it, "What will happen when the shallowness of the scientific evidence is exposed? How will allies react when our messy complicated life histories get a fuller airing?"[52] Or, as critic Mark Simpson puts it in a blog post wittily titled "Bored This Way," "It's as if someone decided to remake the *Rocky Horror Picture Show* as a GLAAD public service announcement."[53]

The naturalistic fallacy is at play here, with the assumption that what is "natural" is somehow simply good. As Jon Mooallem argues in the *New York Times Magazine*, "Those wanting to discriminate against gays and lesbians may have roped the rest of us into an argument about what's 'natural' just by asserting for so long that homosexuality is not. But affixing any importance to the question of whether something is natural or unnatural is a red herring: it's impossible to pin down what those words mean even in a purely scientific context."[54] Even PFLAG, a fairly mainstream gay rights support group, refuses the easy "biology is destiny" argument, instead noting,

> No one knows exactly how sexual orientation and gender identity are determined. However, experts agree that it is a complicated matter of genetics, biology, psychological and social factors. For most people, sexual orientation and gender identity are shaped at an early age. While research has not determined a cause, homosexuality and gender variance are not the result of any one factor like parenting or past experiences. It is never anyone's "fault" if they or their loved one grows up to be LGBT.
>
> If you are asking yourself why you or your loved one is LGBT, consider asking yourself another question: Why ask why? Does your response to a LGBT person depend on knowing why they are LGBT? Regardless of cause, LGBT people deserve equal rights and to be treated fairly.[55]

Would that this were the reigning discourse!

If we do believe that sexual desires and choices are fluid and complicated, then surely we must assume that a world in which heterosexuality is not the default norm—not promoted—would perhaps open up the door to a wider variety of sexual expressions and choices. And isn't it the case that difference does, in point of fact, matter? In other words, wouldn't it be logical to claim that more openly gay people would provide positive role models for those who are still ambivalent about their own sexuality? For example, if little girls never saw other girls and women in positions of authority and expertise, they would find it much more difficult to aspire to do those things. In other words, it should and does make a difference if real diversity is what our children see everyday in the classroom. That's one of the reasons we believe in racially integrated environments. While gay teachers may not "turn" kids gay (just as my hetero parents failed to turn me hetero), can't we also offer up the possibility that openly gay teachers (or neighbors or mothers or firefighters or whatever) may create environments that encourage expansive thinking about sexuality and gender? I think many heterosexuals fear a kind of homosexual replication, an insinuation into all areas of life, a reproduction, a contagion. "Born this way" counters these fears by making of gayness a stable (and thus containable) minority. As Rohy notes, "faced with antigay paranoia, gay and lesbian activists have labored to disprove the idea of contagious or communicated homosexuality" and have taken a rhetorical strategy ("born that way") and turned it into a truth claim to argue that "homosexuality . . . is not acquired, but innate and immutable, fixed at birth, and impervious to influence."[56]

Challenging both the fear of homosexuality and the ideology of immutability that attempts to refute that fear depends on a very different set of assumptions: that being gay is just fine, thank you very much; that gayness is not a problem to be understood or solved or even tolerated; and, more to the point, that there is a positive benefit to an expansive and open approach to human sexuality and gender. In other words, the framing of "gayness" as an issue of nature versus nurture or destiny versus choice misses the point about sexuality and about civil rights. It's not our genes that matter here but rather our ethics.

# PART III

# *Citizen Gay*

I have no doubt we shall win, but the road is long, and red with monstrous martyrdoms. —Oscar Wilde

The world spins only forward. . . . We will be citizens. The time has come. —Tony Kushner's *Angels in America*

Is it worth being boring for a blender? Gay marriage: you might as well be straight. —Dyke Action Machine poster

Marriage is the most important relation in life. . . . It is the foundation of society. It is essential to the orderly pursuit of happiness. —lawyer Ted Olsen

Gay adopted parents with minority babies, you can get into any school you want. You're diverse times three. —*Modern Family*

# 7

# Homeland Insecurities

What does it mean to be a citizen? At first glance, this seems an obvious question with an equally obvious answer. Citizenship is, we are told, both a right and a responsibility. One can be born into it effortlessly, thinking very little of its meaning, or struggle for it relentlessly, risking life and limb to access that imprimatur of belonging. One can marry for it, cross dangerous borders for it, treat it casually, or cling to it fiercely like a lifeline or like an embracing mother. One can cynically dismiss it as meaningless or idealistically invest it with futuristic fantasies. It can be symbolized by the gun, the flag, the ballot box. It is wrapped up in something called "nation" or, variously, "state," but its meanings are often vague and ill defined or, alternately, fought over by those who want it and those who want to keep it from them. It can be dangerously perceived as the sole purview of inhabitants of the righteous mother/fatherland or more generously conceptualized as the province of borderless cosmopolitans.

In a general sense, though, the quest for citizenship includes an insistence on equal treatment in employment, housing, education, and law and the right to participate fully in the political process. But of course, feeling fully included in the society in which you live entails more than the formal acquisition of legal equality. For so many minority groups, legal or formal equality is but the starting point of a more thoroughgoing struggle for substantive inclusion. A truly vital citizenship does not merely encompass this combination of shared responsibilities and shared rights but rather signals a deeper sense of belonging. Throughout US history, minority groups have struggled to acquire both that formal equality and the often more intangible substantive equality offered through full citizenship and inclusion. This process has been both explosively violent and, at times, imperceptible and under the surface of public life. Museums are founded to remember its history, or, alternately, that history is neglected or pushed aside.

Citizenship is therefore wrapped up with memory, particularly that larger sense of citizenship that I like to refer to as a sense of belonging, or social membership. To become a citizen in a new land, for example, often has meant actively and expressly repudiating other histories, other stories, other national attachments. It can take the form of language (the insistence on speaking English, for example, not simply to get by but to lose the past in asserting one's place in the present). Or it can take the form of pledged allegiance (to *this* country, to *this* flag), manifest in military service and, sometimes, death. Political rights always invoke complicated reckonings with history, with personal and institutional memory, with stories of trauma and the fear of forgetting that trauma. Who has not heard—by an elderly black activist, by a seasoned '70s feminist, by a veteran of early gay rights struggles—the slightly put-off, kind of irritated admonition to the younger generation? "You take it all for granted," we (yes, I admit to this myself) say to those youth who seem to wear their freedom so easily and loosely. "Do you know what we did to make that available to you?" These mutterings are often cranky and annoying (to the young particularly), but they do serve as reality check (you think *this* is bad?) and warning to those who think the present always triumphs over the past.

Because questions of citizenship are often so tied up with concerns about immigration and legal inclusion, the issue of civil rights for those who are already deemed citizens is typically understood outside of these now classic histories of border crossings. In other words, the citizenship status of gay and lesbian Americans appears to be a nonissue. At the very least, it seems significantly less pressing than the current dilemmas of, say, undocumented Central American workers or even earlier claims by the waves of immigrants who found their way to these shores. I daresay my Russian-immigrant grandparents would have looked at me quizzically if I started in on *gay rights* as a question of *citizenship*. It thus might seem incongruous at first to discuss gays and lesbians in the context of debates around national identity. Nevertheless, the gay movement has much in common with earlier social movements in a shared focus on the simple but frustratingly elusive goal of equal membership in the legal sense. Full citizenship was on the radar even in those pre-Stonewall days of yore. In 1951, the Mattachine Society—one of the earliest gay rights (or "homophile") groups—framed its goals around this concept, claiming that its desire was "the heroic objective of liberating one of our largest minorities and guaranteeing them self-respecting citizenship."[1] Or, as founder Harry Hay explained in one of his last interviews, the group organized out of a desire to "be respected for our differences not for our samenesses to heterosexuals."[2]

## Threat Level Lavender

But aren't gays—as gays—still citizens, unlike those who breach borders in more tangible ways? True, the gay person next door is no less a formal citizen than is her heterosexual neighbor. She does not have to petition for entry or prove herself to vote, although until recently she did have to lie about herself in order to serve her country in the military. But nations—and here the United States is no exception—often reckon with what we might call "internal aliens," or "strangers," as the great sociologist Georg Simmel deemed such groups and individuals who were both a part of a nation-state but also somehow deemed illegitimate members of that community. Strangers—or the others within—are in a different structural and psychic relation to the more obvious and discrete category of "outsider" or "immigrant."[3] For Simmel and many other social theorists, Jews (particularly those of the diaspora) were the ultimate strangers—a part of the everyday life of a nation yet also excluded from its privileges. African Americans—originally brought here against their will and kept in slavery and then in Jim Crow servitude—provide yet another example of strangers within. The recent discourse surrounding the "origins" of President Barack Obama is a troubling indication of the continued salience of internal otherness to American politics. Even those who "defend" him as a "real American" couch their discourse in a language of presumed citizenship, berating the "birthers" for insinuating that "President Obama is not one of us" (as liberal MSNBC host Chris Matthews repeatedly phrased it), with the implicit assumption being that we know who "us" is. Matthews and others may not say it explicitly, but the inference is clear: "us" is presumptively white.

Women, for whom basic citizenship rights (e.g., voting) were a fairly recent acquisition, can also be understood as strangers in their own country, having been denied many of the outward signs of citizenship (voting, property ownership, ownership over one's own labor and body, etc.) but also treated in more general ways as "second-class" citizens, which is really not being a citizen at all. This is truly how the tolerance trap works—by framing social justice and equal rights as a kind of "gift" bestowed on an assumed "us" to a minority "them."

In addition, we must remember that these categories are never discrete and isolated from each other: gays are black and white, male and female, Latina and Asian. And the same holds true for other strangers: they may experience their claims to citizenship quite differently according to how these cross-cutting identities play out. So, for example, the Russian Jewish woman of the mid 19th century may have felt even more "other" in her actual homeland, because she was not only excluded from meaningful citizenship by the Russian anti-Semites but demeaned by the patriarchal practices of traditional Judaism which prevented her from engaging with the collective study of religious texts because of her gender. Or the white, educated, professional gay man might feel a surety in his citizenship status because his class and racial (and gender) status "trumps" his experience of beleaguered gayness.

It gets more complicated. Citizenship rights can be variously understood as freedom *via* the state (freedom to develop one's life fully, to participate in every aspect of social and political life, to take advantage of all rights and opportunities) or—to the contrary—freedom *from* the state (from state intrusion into one's private life, into one's sexual life, from state differential treatment, from punitive state action). Gay activists and theorists fall on both sides of this equation and everywhere in between. Many, particularly around issues such as marriage equality or hate crimes legislation, demand that the state actively intervene to redress structural inequity or bigoted violence. Others are in fact are working with the latter notion of rights (freedom *from* the state) and actually reject moves such as employment-discrimination legislation because they believe that "private morality" (e.g., the right to hate gays) should somehow be allowed to coexist with state freedoms.

Even gaining legal rights is sometimes a mixed blessing, as it carries with it the weight of normative ideologies of family and relationship that seep into even the most "gay-positive" rulings. The justly famous *Lawrence v. Texas* decision of 2003, which overturned all statewide anti-sodomy laws and unequivocally chastised the earlier decision in the 1986 case of *Bowers v. Hardwick*, didn't so much legalize "sodomy" or any act per se but rather couched its ruling in terms of the right to engage in long-term intimate relationships. Ironically, of course, the case in question was no such thing but rather a casual encounter. The *Lawrence* case, involving two Texas men (John Lawrence and Tyron Garner) who were arrested in the home of one of them and charged under the "homosexual conduct" provision of the anti-sodomy laws of the state, was undoubtedly a watershed moment in the history of gay rights litigation and civil rights more broadly construed. The *Lawrence* ruling can be interpreted in many ways, but surely at its core was the strong and new assertion that gays have a right to sexual expression free from overreaching state intrusion, even as it couched this sexual expression in the language of "commitment" and "love." It will be interesting to see if *Lawrence* holds for casual encounters that refuse to be "misread" as long-term attachments.

So *Lawrence* rejected the flawed ruling of *Bowers v. Hardwick* and recognized directly the anti-gay animus motivating anti-sodomy laws. This can and must be applauded. But the ruling makes this recognition by turning a casual sexual encounter into a matter of (straight-like) intimacy, privacy, and "long-term relationships" and thereby paradoxically granting gay rights through a discourse that renders the historical differences of (particularly male) gay sexuality even *more* invisible. In other words, the deliberate interest in sexual freedom unmoored from the dictates of family and the private sphere are erased in granting gay rights through the tolerant "acknowledgment" of a queer sexuality that resembles—at least in the legal telling—that of its straight brethren. Interestingly, the earlier gay rights decision in Colorado (*Romer v. Evans*, 1996) was more helpful in countering anti-gay discrimination in that it clearly understood that the only rationale for the statute was "the desire to harm a politically unpopular group" and that this desire "cannot constitute a legitimate government interest."[4]

Undoubtedly, legal progress has been made, and that progress—however attenuated—does of course contribute to increased social inclusion and justice. But legal redress is so often a double-edged sword, and remains a highly debated strategy for minority groups attempting to find both citizenship in the broader sense and simple equality and redress in narrower terms. There is a longstanding dispute both in academic (especially political science) literature and within various social movements themselves about the efficacy of pursuing legal strategies for obtaining substantive social transformation and about whether the courts lead or follow public opinion. Further, it is not at all clear that we can easily measure progress by the striking down of punitive laws or the establishment of reparative ones. For example, sociologist Mary Bernstein argues that we can't judge the success of social movements by simple reference to specific changes in laws and notes, counterintuitively, that "between 1961 and 1977 eighteen states enacted legislation overturning sodomy laws; in contrast, despite increased activism regarding decriminalization, no states overturned their sodomy laws between 1986 and

1991."⁵ There is often only an attenuated or tangential relationship between the dismantling of formal or legal impediments to equality and the active production of a more inclusive and egalitarian culture, although clearly failures to pass anti-discriminatory measures are some evidence that gays have not achieved full citizenship. Legal victories don't easily translate into substantive social change, but, conversely, social change does not always manifest itself in legal cases. Some scholars have even argued that pushing for identity-based rights through the courts inevitably invites a backlash that is more trouble than it is worth. And the framework of tolerance, I contend, only further muddies the waters, for it explicitly argues that you can still disapprove of or even hate "gayness" while simultaneously tolerating it.

Still others are working both within law and outside it to develop broader and more radical notions of "sexual citizenship," arguing that if citizenship has historically been yoked to heterosexuality (and, in particular, the heterosexual nuclear family idealized but rarely actualized in contemporary culture), then gays and lesbians challenge the core of what we mean by "citizen" by demanding full access to it. For these theorists, freedom *from* state repression is certainly important but hardly guarantees freedom *for* sexual and gender nonconformity. Just as "tolerance" rests on a weak version of acceptance instead of a full-bodied quest for integration, the "live and let live" version of liberal citizenship hides or mystifies the presumptions of heterosexuality at the core of state formation itself. So while keeping the state out of all our bedrooms is an important corrective to the differential ways in which anti-sodomy laws were applied (and does give the imprimatur of legitimacy to some kinds of gay sexual life), it doesn't address those deeper questions about the relationship between sexuality and family, kinship and the state, bodies and power.

Recourse to the courts thus puts minority groups in a curious position: arguing for "rights" typically requires the construction of a class of citizen (in this case, an "ideal gay" who is all too often imagined as white, male, middle class, partnered) that belies and in fact can undermine the lived complexity of human lives, particularly sexual ones. So, for example, many of the cases concerning gay rights (whether marriage rights or employment or equal protection) rely on amicus briefs that paint a singular picture of a gay identity predetermined, immutable, unchanging. Some of this has to do with the way the law works (by precedent, by analogy to other groups deemed worthy of strict or even heightened scrutiny), but it also reflects a powerful belief that rights depend on tolerance and that tolerance depends on seeing sexual minorities as equivalent to heterosexuals and, at the same time, biologically different.

While these debates about gays and citizenship circulate, we increasingly—particularly in the West—equate citizenship with consumerism. Many of us are urged to identify more, alas, with what brands we buy than with our abiding political beliefs or orientation to a nation-state. Over half a century ago, the famous Nixon-Khrushchev "kitchen debates" of 1959 played out the Cold War through a game of consumer one-upmanship; the "freer" and happier citizen was the one who could access the snazzier kitchen appliances. The consumer-as-citizen ethos has only gotten worse since that iconic moment, and gays and lesbians are no strangers to this corporate sponsorship ("Celebrate Pride with a Bud Light!") that promotes faux citizenship in an era when who you are is increasingly what you wear or drink or drive.[6]

These different theories of citizenship matter greatly both in a symbolic sense and in a deeply practical sense; how we imagine "citizenship" will frame the kinds of legal and political strategies we employ to get it. If citizenship is measured by corporate sponsorship or being courted by employers, then (some) gays are doing pretty well. If citizenship is measured by an increasing insistence on equal treatment under the law, then the tide is turning, although unequal treatment is still widespread in large areas of life and law. If citizenship is measured by a modicum of public tolerance of a group formerly wholly excluded, then, well, we've made some sure strides. But if citizenship is measured by that admittedly slipperier and murkier sense of social belonging and inclusion, then we are still a far way off.

Significantly, when you Google "gay citizenship" these days, 90 percent of what you come up with is marriage. While this is just a rough generalization, it remains true that marriage and immigration are the only topics covered in the first twenty-five links when I "do the Google" on gay citizenship, although of course Google caters search results to the individual surfer, so there will be some amount of variation. Gay marriage as political goal, legal strategy, and ideological front line has so captivated the public and political imagination that most of us turn solely to that issue when we ponder the question of gay rights. Particularly since *Lawrence v. Texas*, and even more so since the 2013 Supreme Court rulings on DOMA, same-sex marriage rights appear to be the cornerstone of gay inclusion. In a deeper and more pernicious sense, gay and lesbian political rights are rarely brought into public debate in anything other than a discrete debate over marriage equality or, alternately, a broad discourse on normalcy and morality. In other words, like abortion rights and women's rights more generally, lesbian and gay rights are whittled down to single issues and dismissed by both Left and Right as "special interest issues," "wedge issues," or remnants of "the culture wars."

## Visibly Different

So citizenship is itself a shifting terrain: how to access it, what its icons are, and what it signifies in a larger social sense are all points of contestation and debate and shift as the tides of politics and history themselves ebb and flow. This is all to say that citizenship is no simple matter, and neither is "otherness"; there are many different ways in which a social group can be made to be "strange" and outside of the possibility of full inclusion. Sometimes exclusion can be as ugly and explicit as literally calling people "aliens" (or perverts) and marking them off as threats to the nation-state. Other times, of course, we are "made strange" in convoluted and elliptical ways, in ways that are not immediately apparent or obvious. Part of the reason citizenship claims or feelings of real belonging are often so opaque is because not only is citizenship wrapped up with rights and responsibilities, but it is something we "do" all the time. We "perform" citizenship constantly, much in the way we perform or enact or display our gender. To be a citizen, then, is to follow the rules but, moreover, to internalize the rules so that "self-policing" and self-control become the markers of good citizenship.

We see how this issue of self-policing can play out with gays—those who discipline themselves in ways that resemble the heterosexual norm are granted more meaningful belonging than those who refuse that self-policing. We self-police by trying to act "less gay": for men, less "effeminate," less swishy, less flamboyant; for women, less "butch," less confident, less athletic and strong. Self-policing is almost always about refuting stereotypes and making oneself over in the image of the norm. In that sense, gay access to deep citizenship depends at least in part on what the current contours of acceptability are at any given historical moment. So if marriage, for example, has historically been (in the US but not necessarily elsewhere) a sign of citizenship (indeed, it remains the easiest way for an immigrant to become a citizen), then gay access to that institution signals to the world that *these* gays (the ones who want to marry) are at least recognizable as potential citizens.

Gays and lesbians have of course been a particular *kind* of stranger to heterosexual society and have been denied specific kinds of citizenship rights. For most minority groups, citizenship claims are wrapped up in the politics of representation, if only to counter the most obvious stereotypes and absences that are inevitably produced by the dominant culture. Being seen in popular culture is often mistaken as the sure sign of social inclusion, and while this is an overstatement, it is undeniable that complete cultural invisibility or stereotypical denigration makes it difficult to advance claims for political inclusion. Gays are no different from other minority groups in this regard.

But gay "strangeness" vis-à-vis the popular imagination is a bit distinctive. Because we can more easily hide—be unseen and mistaken—the very act of "being visible" becomes heavy with meaning, heavier perhaps than for groups whose "difference" is marked on their bodies in explicit ways. While the gay-black comparison is the one most often trotted out (by supporters and anti-gay activists alike), I've always found the gay-Jewish analogy to be particularly revealing and especially helpful in uncovering the mechanisms of anti-gay sentiment. Like Jews, gays are pilloried as cosmopolitan dandies and intellectuals, mocked as rootless wanderers drawn to urban centers, and feared as signs of social demise and contagion. And like Jews, but importantly *not* like many other groups (e.g., African Americans, women), gays can hide, can shield their identity, and can easily pass as that which they are not. And like Jewish identity (and particularly American Jewish identity), gay identity is slippery and contested. It is at once a definable singularity ("I sexually desire members of my own gender"; "My mother was Jewish and thus by some quirky matrilineal law am I") and yet always exceeds that narrowness, or at least that "overflow" is up for debate and discussion. So being a gay person can mean simply this "thing," this singular sexual desire, and feel irrelevant to one's larger sense of purpose and identity. And being a Jew can, for many, be an equally random and innocuous marker of birthright and vague religious affiliation. But for many— Jews and gays alike—these terms connote much more, even as that "much more" is as confusing and contested as the singularity. So being Jewish, then, can speak deeply to a person's sense of self, of history, of place in the world, of ethnic identity and sensibility. It can be palpable and ineffable simultaneously. And being gay can similarly tell a story of the furious mix of identity and desire, a tale of subculture and history and community. It can resonate. It can mean. It can matter. That's one reason why the phrase "the gay lifestyle" is so demeaning. Not only does it seem to assert that there is a singular way of "being gay," but it demotes the richness and range of gay culture and identity to what sounds like an ad for a retirement village. Certainly, few would speak of a "Jewish lifestyle," although other stereotypes, alas, abound.

There's a reason, in other words, that gays have focused so thoroughly on attaining visibility in popular culture and in everyday life via coming out. Our national organizations and strategies are inordinately engaged with garnering a visible public presence. Even Vice

President Joe Biden got in on the act when he declared, on national television, that *"Will and Grace* did more to educate the American public than almost anything anybody has ever done."[7] We might ask, educate them about what? That sassy, straight, urban women can have enduring friendships with equally sassy but surely desexualized gay men? Joking aside, Biden's point is not insignificant; cultural visibility matters to queers in profound and far-reaching ways. And, as Biden's words make clear, it matters to straights, many of whom get their dose of tolerance through the silver or the flat screen.

In addition, gays are "internal others" in another unique way—through the complexities of family and kinship. Because gays are both in and radically out of normative familial structures, the politics of kinship looms large. Gays are largely raised by people who are sexually different from them, and the families they construct implicitly undermine the models of male-female nuclear structures. And if the nuclear family and the reproductive imperative are central to dominant conceptions of citizenship and the nation, then gays are immediately construed as radically other. Our citizenship rights are tied in with an insistence that heterosexuals imagine queer love and, even more challenging, queer sex. In speaking of the difference between gay rights and black civil rights, one critic notes that "the gay civil rights struggle is about preventing discrimination based on our proclivity to love, as distinct from the messier foundation of racial discrimination, which primarily has to do with protecting white privilege and wealth. . . . Love and sex were not, as is the case with gay civil rights, unambiguously the heart of the matter."[8]

The very moniker of a radical activist group, Queer Nation, implied that we were seeking and demanding something that we didn't already have, some sense of belonging that was kept from us. Simultaneously, it suggested that queerness might need its own "nation" of sexual difference to flourish, implying therefore a sense of citizenship both inside and outside the normative nation-state. It is interesting, too, to remember that immigration itself has long been tied to heterosexuality. The infamous 1952 Immigration and Nationality Act (often referred to as the McCarran-Walter Act) explicitly speaks of homosexuality by excluding "persons afflicted with psycho-pathic personality," a designation generally read as including homo-sexuals and other so-called sex perverts. A 1965 amendment to that law added "sexual deviation" to ensure that there would be no doubt as to its intent to solidify gay exclusion from legal immigration. This exclusion was not formally removed until 1990. Even today, sex-ual preference marks immigration in complex ways—from cases in which gays attempt to claim political asylum due to discriminatory and violent realities in their nations of origin to those of gays who are married abroad and seeking legitimation in this country, for whom a federal law until recently prohibited such recognition.

## Work It

The right to work as a marker of citizenship has always been a more complicated issue than simply crossing a border, as the US (and other countries) has often welcomed in cheap temporary labor while simultaneously denying these workers full national status. Work-place equal access is a battleground for our internal others—see the women's movement and the civil rights movement, if you doubt this. Now, while it is true that it is technically legal in most venues to fire someone on the basis of his or her sexual identity (since the Employ-ment Non-Discrimination Act—ENDA—is still not passed), formal workplace discrimination is not primarily the source of gay discon-tent, although it certainly exists and is not to be minimized. Indeed, while employment discrimination has never been seen to be at the core of gay grievances, it is by no means incidental. Currently it is legal to fire or refuse to hire workers on the basis of sexual orientation in twenty-nine states and gender identity in thirty-four states,[9] and a recent study by the Department of Housing and Urban Development discovered persistent discrimination against lesbians and gays in the housing market, particularly the rental market.[10] This discrimina-tion is—unsurprisingly—more marked in states and cities where there are no legal protections for gay workers. The number of pri-vate corporations that include nondiscrimination policies has risen in recent years—at last count, 1,411 with sexual orientation protections and 727 with language on gender identity[11]—yet there remains a broad swath of the labor force that is not covered. Broken down to the individual level, three out of every five citizens currently live in areas *without* employment protection on the basis of sexual orientation.[12] Additionally, queer people of color are disproportionately impacted by employment policies that don't protect against discrimination on the basis of sexual orientation. For example, black and Latino cohabiting same-sex couples are more likely to hold public-sector jobs and therefore do not benefit from the growing number of policies offered by private companies.[13]

There is also a considerable level of income disparity between heterosexuals and sexual minorities. The National Center for Lesbian Rights reports that lesbians typically earn 14 percent less than heterosexual women do, even when controlling for occupation and training. According to Eden King and Jose Cortina, in 2007 gay men earned up to 23 percent less than their heterosexual counterparts of the same occupation and rank. Others studies have suggested the number is somewhere between 10 percent and 32 percent.[14]

Many LGBTQ people will assure you that they have in fact experienced discrimination in the workplace; a 2003 poll from Harris International Witeck-Combs Communications showed that 41 percent of gay respondents said they were discriminated against at work.[15] Until recently, discrimination was in fact openly deployed in jobs considered "sensitive" (e.g., that required a security clearance). A more recent large-scale overview of scholarly research on LGBTQ workplace life found that "between 25% and 66% of LGBT employees reported that they had experienced discrimination, with higher rates being reported by individuals who had disclosed their orientation."[16] This indicates, I think, that workplace integration and equity can be a potent site of push-back against the limitations of tolerance because it demands something more of straight co-workers than begrudging acceptance or assimilated sameness. Like struggles for gender equity in the workplace, queer inclusion in this venue (as opposed to, say, access to marriage rights) forces heterosexuals to directly and proactively reckon with sexual difference and with the results of institutionalized exclusion and homophobia.

As evidence of just that, the enforcement of the closet in many cases makes overt discrimination a moot point. To be out at work almost always has meant to be vulnerable. Polls consistently show that while more and more people are out at work, it is often selectively done so that supervisors and bosses are kept in the dark, because of workers' desire to immunize themselves from punitive action or covert discrimination. Even those explicit forms of discrimination (say, anti-sodomy laws) were more powerful for the fear they inspired and the message they sent than for the actual instances of enforcement.

The persistent fact of gay invisibility, then, alters how these citizenship claims play out. For example, regarding job discrimination, one must first be seen and identified (even falsely, even against one's will, even through rumor) to be discriminated against. Thus, for gays, employment discrimination begins *before* employment, in the displacement of (sexual) identity in order to be admitted to civil society, the public sphere, and workplace culture. There are very few gay people who haven't practiced the art of passing or "covering" when at work—through a casually changed pronoun, the omission of a partner's picture on a desk, the avoidance of the company picnic, the gender-appropriate attire so as to avoid suspicion. Unlike women and people of color (and Jews), for whom job discrimination was deep, structural, and socially legitimated, the possibility of gay passing renders issues of outright exclusion more problematic.

## Pink Camouflage

Nowhere has employment discrimination been so explicit and legitimated than in the US military. Indeed, "Don't Ask, Don't Tell" (the policy that formally excluded gays and lesbians from a central expression of national citizenship) is a *particularly* anti-gay form of discrimination and pretty much unimaginable as a strategy of exclusion for other minority groups. You can only "not ask" if there is something that is not immediately evident; military exclusion depends on the closet and on the possibility of a life lived in it, hidden from view.

The attempted repeal of the odious policy of military exclusion emerges in this context of increased gay visibility, new "normalization," and a more generalized integration of lesbians and gays into American culture.[17] How significant have changes in the larger cultural milieu been to the decision to—finally—get rid of "Don't Ask, Don't Tell" (DADT)? While surely the relationship between current ideologies concerning "gayness" and military policy is not a singular and linear one, changing ideologies of immutability, identity, citizenship, and public perception have played a part in the push to integrate. While polls have just recently tipped over to a slight majority in favor of equal marriage rights, they have for some time shown much stronger majorities (between 65 and 75 percent) favoring open military service, although these polls—like many others—show deep divides by gender and age in particular. Apparently, the general public is more "tolerant" of gays dying than of gays loving.

Many allies of the US have had an open policy for years, with no "dire consequences" for morale or military effectiveness. And, surely, the more general cultural shift—reflected in polls but also of course in the by-now-banal visibility of LGBTQ folks in everyday life— makes it more tenable to repeal DADT ("the American people want this") and pushes the military to match more closely the tenor of the times. Recent court rulings—easier in the wake of *Lawrence v. Texas*—have also prompted the president to move on this, lest he seem both behind the times and out of sync with current legal reasoning. And, if the polls are to be believed, it was easily the most unpopular of discriminatory policies, with consistent majorities supporting open gay service and even international pressure coming to bear from nations whose example gave further evidence to the weakness of the US exclusionary policy.

Unquestionably, this policy began to have the look of an albatross around the neck of any administration committed to it. Our humorists couldn't resist poking fun. In 2007 and 2010, the satirical news site the *Onion* put out two pieces "responding" to President Obama's goal of repealing "Don't Ask, Don't Tell." In the first, a video, a faux general gets on the faux news channel to argue against open service, saying "gays [are] too precious to risk in combat." "Gays of America," gravely intones the general, "are the only group left untouched by war. They're special, pure, and rare, like a gleaming diamond or a snow-white colt. We must protect them. . . . We love them too much."[18] The headline of the second piece warns, "Repeal of 'Don't Ask, Don't Tell' Paves Way for Gay Sex Right on Battlefield, Opponents Fantasize." The article goes on to quote a "soldier," who argues, "The last thing I need after a 12-hour reconnaissance patrol is to know I'm hitting the showers with some guy who might be checking me out and who might, after seeing what I have to work with, find himself wondering if I too long for the firm yet tender embrace of another man."[19]

Jon Stewart also skewered the anti-repeal diehards like Senator John McCain in segments portending the "Gaypocalypse." When Stewart objected to the treatment of ejected service member (and now activist) Dan Choi and wondered how this could possibly be legitimate, his *Daily Show* comrade John Oliver countered Stewart's confusion by repeatedly insisting (with handy signs), "He is gay, Jon!" as if the simple reality of his gayness was, at heart, what McCain objected to in Choi's presence.[20]

And, of course, our own national history of racial segregation in the armed forces added to the ease with which comparisons could be trotted out for ethical argumentation. Arguments for gay rights have—unsurprisingly—long been couched in analogical terms. With both the military and marriage debates, analogies have been hard to avoid, particularly given the history of both institutions in this country as rife with segregationist ideologies and mandates, and the trope of tolerance is most often tethered to historical comparisons and analogies. No public or legislative discussion around either can avoid analogies and historical comparisons, most potently—and perhaps most problematically—around race. Analogies, and even comparisons, are complicated rhetorical moves and even more fraught when used explicitly in legal and political contexts. I do not want to go into a long discussion on the merit of such analogies, but I am interested in how pliable and fluid they seem to be in the case of discussions around DADT. The analogical move itself becomes the playing field—with some commentators, like revered military icon Colin Powell, decrying the analogy in order to displace the gay claim on historical struggle and others arguing that, to the contrary, the lessons of the past are key to overturning the ban.[21] Much ink has been spilled on debating the merits of analogies and comparisons between blacks (and other racial and ethnic minorities) and gays, particularly around the marriage and military debates in which both anti- and pro-gay advocates weighed in on the salience of the analogy. It was, no doubt, the first time many white conservatives found themselves focusing on the "uniqueness" of the civil rights movement and black history, an irony that should not be lost on anyone.

When making comparisons and analogies, we typically focus on the difference of visibility that marks out the gay experience as dissonant from that of its most frequently analyzed counterparts—women and blacks. There is good reason to do so, for having difference marked on your body matters a great deal. You don't always have to be seen to be targeted for victimization, but it sure makes it easier for those who want to do you harm! Therefore, the place of visibility and recognition figures mightily here. Entry into the public eye becomes itself the sign of gay inclusion precisely because gays can assimilate so well and can hide with such ease.

Gay exclusion, then (at least in the military), depended on passing and indeed required it. Further, passing was situated as legitimate and mundane; it was not seen as a form of discrimination. This is radically at odds with how passing and other ways of "being what you are not" have historically been used to punish those who cross, for example, the color line. Or, even further back, the forced conversion of Spanish Jews to Catholicism (the *conversos*) is now conceptualized by historians as having been a result of anti-Semitic institutions and policies. Gay passing during DADT, on the other hand, is seen not only as a requirement for legitimacy and inclusion but as not itself a mode of discrimination. In other words, gay passing for straight was the very terms of tolerance within the military.

These analogies have undoubtedly been useful and hold some merit. They have been embraced by many, African Americans included, who see the "basic equality" questions that open service raises as similar to those faced by other oppressed minorities and women.[22] For gay rights activists eager to locate military inclusion in the long trajectory of civil rights struggles now canonized as shining moments of American tolerance, reference to the history of racial and gender integration of the military is necessary. It justifies gay inclusion and makes the contiguous argument that open service will—like the integration of blacks and (partial) integration of women—have generally positive effects on military readiness.[23] While segregation and exclusion are not exactly the same as closeted presence and formal rejection, they are close cousins, both in their structural motivations (to instantiate second-class status, to legally discriminate) and their experiential effects (resentment, fear, isolation, loss of employment). The arguments used in both instances retain striking similarities, with opponents invoking stereotypes of gays in a manner similar to stereotypes of blacks and women used in earlier eras. Similar antagonistic sentiments were expressed around racially desegregating the army, including arguments about isolation, unit cohesion, morale, and so on. Surely, part of the resistance to the integration of blacks into the armed services derived from a prejudicial insistence by (some) whites that they not associate in such "close quarters" with blacks. Similar objections to openly gay service members invoke this "close quarters" argument as well, creating a heady mix of contagion fears, infiltration anxiety, and the sullying of the purity of (male, heterosexual, white) military culture. Of course, in the sexual-orientation case, the fear of sexual desires (yours, mine, and ours) is added into the mix.

What is striking, however, is how the military—now faced with a president who has insisted on the full inclusion of openly gay service members—manages to create a *hierarchy* of analogy in order to maintain the legitimacy of anti-gay animus, while at the same time acknowledging the need for "tolerance." In the Department of Defense (DoD) report that emerged from the most recent congressional hearings, the military brings up the analogy of homosexual and racial integration only to make sure to differentiate the two:

> In drawing parallels to racial integration in the 1940s and 1950s, there are similarities and differences between that experience and repeal of Don't Ask, Don't Tell today that we must acknowledge. First, skin color and sexual orientation are fundamentally different. That said, the concerns expressed in the 1940s about the effects of integration on unit cohesion and effectiveness sound much the same as those voiced in this debate.
>
> Second, there is a religious component to the issue of homosexuality that generally does not exist on matters of race. Many hold a sincere religious and moral belief that homosexuality is a sin. Many military chaplains today express opposition in religious terms to allowing gay men and lesbians to serve openly in the military. By contrast, there was no significant opposition to racial integration among military chaplains. In fact, the historical record of the period indicates that the military chaplain community, for the most part, encouraged followers along the path of racial integration.[24]

According to the DoD, then, the analogy has weight yet also does not hold water. The fundamental flaw that these military analysts—as well as many conservative and mainstream writers on gay rights—find in the analogy is that, at bottom, the analogy doesn't logically "work." The animus against blacks, and the stereotypes underlying the animus, were proven to be simply and undeniably false and based on prejudice, whereas the animus against gays apparently has merit. Moreover, visibility enters directly into the debate because "race is an obvious identifier; sexual orientation is not. Even if the law is repealed, it is likely that gay men and lesbians will continue to be discreet and private about their sexual orientation, as in civilian society."[25]

So the official line from the military was that, while it is true that older arguments against blacks serving alongside whites in the military sound curiously like those used today against gays, one should not forget the absolute difference between sexual and racial integration into the military. The absolute difference is based on two linked arguments. First, that sexual "orientation" and race are radically different forms of identity. As Colin Powell argued in an earlier iteration of the debate, "Skin color is a benign, non-behavioral characteristic. Sexual orientation is perhaps the most profound of human behavioral characteristics. Comparison of the two is a convenient but invalid argument."[26] For Powell, race is different because it is meaningless, the emptiest of signifiers, while sexuality is seen as core, as deep, as the essence of self. Yet, for others, including the DoD, race is different because it is much *more* meaningful. It is the ultimate signifier of *illegitimate* social exclusion, historical victimization, and discrimination.[27]

Second, more elliptically and perhaps more dangerously, the race-sexuality analogy is challenged because the moral and religious justifications for anti-gay animus apparently have merit and need to be respected.[28] The DoD report repeatedly assures readers, soldiers, and the public that moral and religious objections to homosexuality deserve respect.[29] The difference now (with the end of official discrimination) is that those who have objections (objections seen in this context as legitimate) must nonetheless treat "them" fairly. In other words, if you are morally and religiously opposed to homosexuality, the military will not "turn its back on you," and your legitimate animus toward gays will not be a problem at all, although you will now be required to treat "them" equitably. In fact, in May 2012, Rep. Todd Akin (more recently infamous for his strange musings on female anatomy) sponsored a bill to "protect the conscience of all armed services personnel who disagree with homosexuality" and to ban the use of military facilities for same-sex weddings. The bill was tacked on to the 2013 National Defense Authorization Act and passed the House Armed Services Committee 56–5. As Akin stated in his defense of this bill, it is vital to "allow people to have those kinds of beliefs without being worried that they're going to get demoted or run over because they believe in something. . . . Chaplains and service members should not face recrimination or persecution in the military for standing strong on their religious beliefs in opposition to homosexuality."[30]

Now again we see how the assumptions underlying the analogical moves are different. It is hard to imagine a military report assuring soldiers that it is really okay if they think blacks are inferiors who are immoral and simply wrong. Here is where the hierarchy of analogies becomes even more head-turning; the same report seems to indicate that resistance to women in the military had/has some legitimacy as well—and, in fact, women's historical exclusion from combat roles is yet one more indicator of the acceptance of this ideology. Thus, anti-black animus is deemed a full-scale relic of the past and motivated wholly by prejudice and irrationality.[31] Conversely, anti-woman animus is deemed old-fashioned but legitimately motivated by "traditional"—and therefore sanctified—understandings of the different "roles" of men and women in the world and the supposedly different physical capacities for warfare.[32] Righteous anti-gay animus, however, is justified by reference to unchallengeable religious and moral objections that tautologically are backed up with the simple phrase from Jon Oliver of *The Daily Show*: "But he's gay!" Therefore, heterosexual military men's enforced "tolerance" of gays in "their" army coexists with official military tolerance of homophobia and anti-gay animus. In the DoD report, anti-gay animus is explicitly addressed as legitimate, and its legitimacy is framed largely through reference to morality, religion, and traditional values. Of course, racism and slavery were long legitimized through religious arguments; the DoD is wrong about this history as well.

We might do better to make nuanced, historically specific comparisons rather than overarching analogies. Queer studies scholar Siobhan Somerville, for example, argues that instead of analogizing between race and sexual orientation (which inevitably occludes the ways in which these phenomena are interrelated and often inseparable), we would do better to "look sideways" to consider how these categories were produced simultaneously.[33] In making the analogical case, it is hard to avoid the argument that gays are "like" blacks because, like skin color, gayness is something one does not choose;

it is something one is born with through "no fault of one's own." Of course, the easy analogy conveniently obscures race itself as a social construction, a fiction, even as it has material consequences.

In addition, the analogy can't help but reassert the troubling assumption of gayness as whiteness and blackness as heterosexual. This shores up the old opposition (all the women are white, all the blacks are men, as feminist women of color Gloria Hull, Patricia Scott, and Barbara Smith put it years ago) that refuses to see not only the constructedness of these categories but also their overlapping or intersecting nature (e.g., some of those gay soldiers are black, Latino, etc.).[34] Here, I fear an analogical move that effectively causes black lesbian and gay service members to disappear. The easy and glib use of analogy can make racial and gender discrimination appear a thing of the past—a triumph of brave integrationism and tolerance over (now formally delegitimized) old-school prejudice.

## To Do or Not to Be

If the debate over the validity of analogies is slippery, it surely hinges on a strange bifurcation largely invisible in the earlier moment of racial integration: the status/conduct distinction. Unlike other "suspect class" categories, the question of causation (i.e., "What causes homosexuality?") almost always enters into discussions of gay rights, whereas for women and blacks, the discussion centers more on the *meanings* of race and gender in terms of access, identity, behaviors, and the like. Gays are inevitably caught up in a public discourse that engages both cause and effect and inevitably links the two—particularly in a moment of biological obsession. As one analyst succinctly put it, "Prior to the 1940s, dismissal was based on conduct, that is, the commission of an act of sodomy; in the postwar era, the attention shifted to status or identity, that is, to sexual orientation."[35]

Many writers have thoroughly critiqued DADT about the dubiousness of the status/conduct distinction,[36] but it seems that the various versions of that faux "tolerance" (for example, "love the sinner, hate the sin," which is itself a variation of the status/conduct distinction) have been largely supplanted by another—perhaps uniquely American—normative theme. This theme—the "born with it" idea discussed earlier—has transformed into a kind of everyday truth, with enormous consequences both legal and political.

It is intriguing, however, that immutability arguments—so generally pervasive and utilized so deliberately in many legal and social battles, including the marriage battle and earlier arguments to overturn the anti-sodomy laws—seem oddly absent when it comes to the discussions around DADT and open military service. In the entire DoD report, there is not a single reference to issues of etiology, whereas, in the legal proceedings of gay-marriage statutes or sodomy laws, immutability arguments stand front and center. For a complicated set of historical reasons, the question of etiology was more salient in earlier iterations of the debate over gay military service. In the 1993 hearings around the beginning of the policy of DADT, key witness and longtime sexuality scholar Gregory Herek addressed the "born with it" question rather carefully but nonetheless endorsed it:

> Regardless of whether they are homosexual, heterosexual, or bisexual, people generally experience their sexual orientation as an essential part of their core identity, their sense of who they are sexually. Scientific research has not established why anyone develops a particular sexual orientation, but we do know that whether they are heterosexual, homosexual, or bisexual, people generally do not choose their sexual orientation. Rather they discover it and come to understand it through a long developmental process.[37]

The question of what a gay "is" (i.e., the question of "identity") marks this debate in ways that are contiguous with the immutability debates but not reducible to it. So while the military largely avoided weighing in on the quagmire that is the "born with it" discourse, it certainly couldn't avoid questions of identity itself. Defining "gayness" becomes, then, part and parcel of tolerating gayness. And these definitions—while not always tied irrevocably to biological origin stories—cannot help but corral "gayness" into a knowable entity that can then (if we are obeying orders!) be tolerated.

Largely cohering around the status/conduct distinction—which is the cornerstone of DADT—and challenges to it, the identity question also crops up in the issue of "unit cohesion."[38] The current arguments against inclusion (excluding for the moment ones that express a simple and unadorned hatred of homosexuals) focus on this red herring as well.[39] This is where the analogies of race and gender do make some sense, to a point. The argument is that many service members do in fact feel uncomfortable with, if not antagonistic toward, gays and therefore will not be able to function to the best of their ability if openly gay people serve beside them. This has prompted at least one judge, in ruling against DADT, to note that "the known presence of homosexuals may disrupt the unit because heterosexual members may morally disapprove of homosexuals. This is an outright confession that 'unit cohesion' is a euphemism for catering to the prejudices of heterosexuals."[40] Sometimes, the (fake) unit-cohesion argument gives way to an alarming honesty, as in 2007 when General Peter Pace, then chairman of the Joint Chiefs of Staff, offered a different rationale, when he stated that he believed "homosexual acts between two individuals are immoral and that we should not condone immoral acts."[41]

Of course, acts—specifically sexual acts—have always figured prominently in both gay rights acquisitions and discrimination itself. Identities (such as they are) have been brought into being, policed, punished, and legitimated through reference to specific acts. DADT hinges precisely on this status/conduct distinction: that one can "be" gay without "acting" (performing) gayness. But what is often ignored in this discussion is that acting "not gay" (but being gay) requires a performance of another kind, and not simply the performance of the closet or of dissimulation. If gayness is conduct unbecoming an officer, then straightness is conduct becoming an officer, and straightness is not just marked through sexual acts but through the displacements of those acts into soldiering, into killing, into male bonding, and into brotherhood.

The unit-cohesion argument is the military parallel to the marriage-disintegration argument: let gays in the military and all hell will break loose, and brave (hetero) soldiers will no longer be brave. Let gays get married and all hell will break loose, and hetero couples will find their own relationships—and clearly, the institution itself—wrecked on the shoals of homo love and lust. Ah, would that it were so! But of course, gay activists on both issues respond almost identically: gays in the military will only enhance unit cohesion and military readiness by allowing for openness and—importantly— utilizing every willing soldier in the worldwide battle to make the world safe for "normal" heterosexuality and unfettered military might. The argument that ultimately carried the day was that the military—and the nation—were suffering as a result of gay exclusion, as evidenced by the selective "stop loss" actions, when gays were deemed too essential to discharge over a stupid policy, and by the loss of so many Arab translators.[42] In other words, discrimination against gays is not just bad in a moral sense; it is actually bad for national security and the economy. As we will see in the next chapter, a similar argument emerged around marriage: same-sex marriage will not alter hetero marriage one bit but will rather enhance the cachet of this rather tattered institution by pledging more bodies and lives to the altar of normal family life.

The arguments against gays in the military not only claim that gays will disrupt unit morale and effectiveness (by their very difference, their free-floating and unmoored desires, their effeminate or—alternately—their overly manly nature) but also claim that they are not "fit for service."[43] Underlying both these objections is an argument about performance: gays cannot perform soldiering because they are not heterosexual, because they are aberrant, because they are unmanly, because they are too manly, or because they are morally corrupt.[44]

And the "pro" arguments generally respond in kind: gays are absolutely fit for service. They may not be heterosexual, but they also can be fighting machines—ready to die for God and country like any other normal, red-blooded American who signs up to serve.

"Pro" arguments are filled with tales of hetero service members supporting their brave gay brethren because they have seen firsthand how very soldierly they actually are. Because the military is seen as a "special" institution—not one open to all on a democratic basis but rather the few, the chosen, the Marines—the basic equality claims are invoked less frequently than, say, around marriage or employment rights. So gay soldiers have to be hypersoldiers—exemplars of military rectitude—to merit recognition from their straight comrades. And gays who want to marry need just be seen as "humans" worthy of equal rights, albeit humans whose lives look as similar to their straight counterparts' as possible.

Even though anti-military activists have questioned gay activist organizations' focus on repealing DADT, it is the marriage movement that has elicited much more lively internal gay debate.[45] There are many reasons for this discrepancy, but surely one is the simple fact that repealing DADT has direct consequences for those who are already serving in the military, and doing so in conditions that place them in positions of great vulnerability (as employees whose income is dependent on hiding their identity).[46] In other words, the military is an *employer* and, moreover, an employer of largely working-class and minority youth.[47] While the economic benefits of married life have been well documented, entrance into it has largely been argued on intimate and symbolic grounds.[48]

While marriage and the military differ along these and other axes, they both retain enormous symbolic importance, particularly as icons of citizenship and the belief that victory in these venues would signal a new era of tolerance and acceptance.[49] Like so many of the arguments for ending the ban on same-sex marriage, proponents of ending the ban on gays in the military advance a sameness argument (i.e., we just want to serve our country or we just want to raise a family *like everyone else*). Colonel Margarethe Cammermeyer, a retired lesbian army officer who successfully challenged the military's ban on homosexuals, stated this sentiment clearly years ago when she argued, "What I hope to represent is a part of the normality of being homosexual, of not being in leather or shaving my hair, but rather

showing how much we are all alike. . . . If people can see the sameness of me to you, then perhaps they won't have the walls that makes
it so they have to hate us without a cause."[50]

It is also the case that the movement for open military service is
predicated on an understanding of "gayness" as a discrete, knowable,
legible, and utterable identity.[51] To oppose DADT means you assume
there is something clear to be asked and to be told. This is, undeniably, one of the persistent dilemmas of civil rights legislation and litigation around stigmatized minorities: how to gain rights, access, and
freedoms while at the same time not enshrining (and creating) the
very categories of identity that many people believe to be partially
responsible for the very abridgement of those freedoms. What happens, in other words, when Foucault goes to court? Or, to paraphrase
another gay icon, poet Walt Whitman, it just might be that an army
of lovers can only make war, not the queer new world that our elec-
tric bodies demand.

# 8

# Better Put a Ring on It

Should I or shouldn't I? Will they or won't they? It's hard to bring up this subject without getting personal. Even if marriage is a profoundly social (and legal and economic) institution, it is also one that carries more than its share of emotional weight. I remember when I was pregnant with my (now grown) daughter, and my mother threw me a lavish baby shower. It wasn't really her style, but she claimed it was justified since I would never be getting married. It wasn't only my gayness that seemed a deal breaker on the marital front, but my earnest feminism rendered me unfit for that particular form of bliss called matrimonial. At the time—1994—I didn't think twice about her assumptions, for they were my own. I didn't want marriage for myself personally (too normative, too hetero, too state and church sanctioned, too white-wedding consumerist, too mired in a nasty history of ownership and property, too many tacky dresses and even tackier music) and couldn't imagine it as a central demand for the gay rights movement. It wasn't on my personal radar and didn't seem much on the national one either.

My, how times have changed. As I sit down to finish this book, the Supreme Court has weighed in on two of the signal cases concerning same-sex marriage: *United States v. Windsor* (the case relating to the constitutionality of the Defense of Marriage Act, or DOMA) and *Hollingsworth v. Perry* (the case concerning the standing of California's Proposition 8). In the first, the Court found for the plaintiff (the eighty-three-year-old widow who was hit by a huge inheritance tax because of the lack of legal recognition of her partnership with another woman) and essentially called out DOMA for the crass bigotry it was. In the second, the Court ruled that the petitioners did not have "standing," which basically upheld the lower court's ruling on the unconstitutionality of Prop 8, returning same-sex marriage to the state of California. Both decisions were momentous and historic, and it is hard to imagine that they won't realize Justice Scalia's worst nightmares and pave the way for full legal married status for gays in every state in the union.

Wherever you stand on this issue (and, as I will elaborate, it's not the simple pro/con that is mostly presented in the mainstream media), it has utterly changed the political landscape since those baby-shower days of yore. What was once unthinkable (by both gay activists and anti-gay conservatives) is irrevocably part of the political discourse. And many of us who found it unimaginable for other reasons have either changed our tune (that's what makes an ideology dominant: it's pretty damn hard to just say no) or are a cranky minority vigorously waving the flag of feminism and sexual freedom as the bridal bouquet gets tossed and the honeymoons taken.

In case I seem too antagonistic to marriage, let me be as clear as I can: as a civil rights issue, same-sex marriage is a no-brainer. To deny individuals access to any social and legal institution simply by virtue of their "gayness" is patently discriminatory. There is, it can safely be assumed, no debate about that within the gay community. That said, we need to reckon with why gay marriage has become the sign of all things gay—for advocates and opponents alike. Why did a walk down the aisle replace a walk on the wild side, and why does marriage and family rhetoric hold such powerful sway?

Even for a card-carrying feminist like myself, I have to admit it has crossed my mind, albeit with a fair amount of chagrin. When milestones are reached (say, the legalization of same-sex marriage in New York), it is hard not to feel something, even if the thrill of a civil rights victory is cross-cut with much more ambivalent frustration over how this issue has edged so many others out of the spotlight. And I'm embarrassed to say it, but I diligently read the *New York Times* wedding announcements, turning to those pages even before I indulge in the fantasies of the Travel section. I read them for a confused and multiple set of reasons; because I want to see how many matchy-matchy, same-haircut, same-name, richy-rich gays are getting married ("John and Jon met at a timeshare on Fire Island!"), because I am jarred to see an old girlfriend (or two) show up in wedded bliss, because I want to see how many met at a bar or at a gay pride parade, because I am fascinated by the cultural marker this is. But mostly, I think, I read them because I can. Because it does remain astonishing that this has happened. And then I (figuratively, of course) slap myself upside the head and berate myself for thinking marriage is any sign of real social inclusion. And I smack myself again for being "grateful" to have gained (in a few states, in such an attenuated way) the most basic of civil rights. Something we really, really shouldn't have to be fighting for. And then, of course, when I come to after all the slapping, I think of my partner and my love for her and how meaningful it might be—especially at the ripe old age of fifty-one—to publicly announce it. To name her as something different than "girlfriend." To provide for each other financially and to protect each other's children. To be the one—without question— making decisions at the hospital if that becomes necessary. And, most importantly, to get the presents and honeymoon. But then I hear her voice (and my own voice, and the voice of many, many critics, and the voice of my own snarky feminist daughter) reminding me that love is not more legitimate or good or valuable if the state makes it official. I hear the voices of my friends who have pledged that they will not take part in this rush to the altar. I hear the voices of the poor, the disenfranchised, the gays of color for whom marriage is hardly the golden egg or prized victory. I am sickened— again and again—by the wedding industry that bilks billions out of those who need those resources for health care and housing and everyday life. I shudder at the resources (both of the movement and of individuals getting married) that go to this industry while HIV/ AIDS remains a national crisis. I am reminded, again, of the vexed history of this institution and its stubbornly gendered and racial-ized parameters.

And as I watch the commentary on the nightly news, my eighteen-year-old daughter on the couch next to me, I am appalled that the plaintiffs, attorneys, and pundits alike intone joyously that *now* children of gay parents will feel that they are *legitimate*, will feel that they are in *real* families, *just as good* as those of their friends. My straight, gay-positive, feminist daughter shakes her head in wonder and no small amount of disgust: "Huh," she says. "I feel pretty legitimate without you being married."

I laugh at myself too, knowing that I have always felt no one should have a wife; I can't imagine being called that or calling anyone else that. To paraphrase Gloria Steinem, a lesbian needs a wife like a fish needs a bicycle. On the other hand, we all need wives (if not fish or bicycles) if being a wife means taking care of someone else, putting that person's needs before your own. And that's precisely why "wife" is so bankrupt a term. Sigh. What is a besotted feminist to do? Because, like so many marriage-wary gays, I am lost in the romance and the longing for that which has been denied us, but I also know that something being locked away may make it more tantalizing but does not make it a worthy or good thing. And it certainly does not make it the pinnacle of gay liberation.

Do I sound confused? Are you thinking, dear reader, this feminist doth protest too much? Am I secretly yearning for a white wedding, even as I publicly denounce our current obsession with all things nuptial? I admit to some more sappiness than originally intended. Or, rather, I find myself less able to easily dismiss the marriage desires of others. I want to boycott the festivities, but my heart isn't in it. I see how others' hearts are so tied to this iconic event that raining on their parade seems downright churlish.

Yes, I too cry at weddings. And cry in amazement at the gay ones for sure. Marriage takes what might be an invisible identity and makes it visible, at least visible to many heterosexuals who live lives willfully isolated from gay cultures. In fact, for many same-sex couples, that is the emotional virtue of marriage: not to increase already established commitments but to announce their love *in public*. I see the genuine love at work in many gay couples who desire marriage and, even more, respect their need for the financial and legal security that is (wrongly but still) tied to this particular configuration of care. Love is no less genuine for being wrapped up in all the messiness of shallow notions of social legitimacy. As we sociologists are wont to repeat (endlessly and pedantically), a phenomenon is no less experienced or lived or felt if it is socially constructed. The heart wants what it wants, even as we recognize that wanting marriage per se is less a product of the heart than of a culture that has consistently sold and marketed it as sign of maturity, a marker of commitment, a testament to the values of family, faith, and country.

Still and all, people—gay, straight, whatever—do want to get married. But that doesn't mean that this single-minded focus is good for creating a future for full-bodied gay liberation and gender equity. What follows will hopefully open up a little chink in the armor of marital certitude and engage a wide range of critiques of marriage itself and the focus on marriage strategically. And it will become clear that gay marriage is the perfect Trojan horse for the tolerance trap, sneaking in retrograde ideas in the guise of simple civil rights advances.

## Marriage Mania

As contemporary social issues go, you can't get much more zeitgeist than gay marriage. Its resonance goes high and low, wide and deep. It graces the cover of the elite *New Yorker* (a rainbow White House, two brides in wedding white, Bert and Ernie snuggling before a TV lit up with the Supreme Court after DOMA was overturned) and shows up in lowbrow reality TV (*Four Weddings, Say Yes to the Dress*) and *People* magazine (Ellen and Portia). The April 8, 2013, issue of *Time* magazine featured two alternative covers—each with a same-sex couple leaning in for a close-up kiss and with the emphatic words, "Gay Marriage Already Won . . . The Supreme Court Hasn't Made Up It's Mind—But America Has." *Jersey Shore* phenoms Snooki and JWoww give the president "props" for his stance on gay marriage, and literary lions and soigné celebs (George Clooney, for one) host parties celebrating pro-marriage victories. Viral videos attack gay marriage, and spoofs on those attacks become even more popular on the Internet. A star-studded cast puts on East and West Coast performances of 8, a play about anti-gay-marriage Proposition 8 in California; a movie is in the works. The cute gay brother in the long-running nighttime soap *Brothers & Sisters* has an uber-supportive wedding to his even cuter boyfriend, and *Sex and the City* alum Cynthia Nixon marries her sweetheart in New York and our (well, my) fave (and gorgeous) lesbian doctors on *Grey's Anatomy* are joined in wedded bliss, baby to follow. Celebrities rush to champion marriage equality, more and more national political organizations and corporations voice their support (including most of the major labor unions, the NAACP, the National Council of La Raza, Starbucks, Amazon, Apple—the list goes on), and a sizeable number of national politicians step into the fray to declare their support for those who want to tie the pink knot. As one blogger puts it, "supporting gay marriage is fashionable."[1]

The literati, intellectual gatekeepers, and even the celebrity lightweights of low-rent pop culture may deem gay marriage fashionable and the sexy new civil right, but it remains an issue still ferociously debated. The list of those who inveigh against same-sex marriage may seem like the cast of a Fox News playlist or a passion play of the medieval era, but one would be hard-pressed to say they have no support whatsoever. However you cut it and whatever direction one imagines the wind is blowing, the vast majority of states have "mini DOMAs" that prohibit same-sex marriage, even as thirteen states and the District of Columbia have legalized it (and more have passed bills that have yet to go into effect). True, DOMA is pretty much dead, but we are facing years of litigation ahead when this new federal freedom comes in conflict with state-enshrined discrimination. What will happen, for example, when a couple married in a state that recognizes same-sex marriage (say, Massachusetts) moves to a state that doesn't (say, South Carolina)? While the Department of the Treasury and the IRS, with the explicit support of the Obama administration, has assured gays that all legal same-sex marriages will be federally recognized for tax purposes regardless of where the couple currently lives, it remains unclear how much of this will play out when state laws come in conflict with federal rulings.

Legal or not, religious leaders—from popes to local pastors and clergy—assure us that Adam and Steve tuxed out on top of a wedding cake is the sign of the Apocalypse. Reputable politicians on the local and national scene assure their constituents that gay marriage will ruin all marriages and take us on a slippery slope whereby folks will be serving up their perky fox terrier as their life mate of choice at the local city hall.

In other words, same-sex marriage may be au courant and validated in some venues of contemporary culture, but vast swaths of the nation (and millions of individuals) remain deeply appalled at the prospect of Janet and Sally united in holy matrimony. Some preachers predict fire and brimstone, Republican leaders largely march in lockstep with the party line against it, and "family" organizations split their hatred now between pro-choice feminists and marrying gays, both of whom seem to be responsible for natural disasters such as Hurricane Sandy. We're noticeably behind a number of other countries on this issue; at last count, fifteen countries (including France, South Africa, the Netherlands, Belgium, Spain, and Canada) recognize same-sex marriage as a point of national law, and many others come pretty close to it. And the National Organization for Marriage (the main group fighting same-sex marriage)—with its indefatigable leader, Maggie Gallagher (who famously intoned, "It is not discrimination to treat different things differently")[2]—doesn't seem starved for resources or volunteers.

Nevertheless, after the debacle of the 2004 elections, in which, arguably, anti-gay-marriage amendments helped ignite the Republican Right to defeat Democrats along with the wedding plans of millions of taffeta-loving homosexuals, it appears the tide is turning or at least creeping up a bit. Gay bashing has lost none of its allure, but it has less legislative sway in the context of never-ending war, lobbying scandals and corporate chicanery, and an economy that continues to widen the gap between rich and poor. The polls have shifted, particularly among the young, and many observers simply believe that once these young people become the majority voting bloc, gay marriage will be a done deal. As Margaret Talbot puts it in the *New Yorker*, "Same-sex marriage is a historical inevitability," and "if you are under thirty-five, you are more likely to have come of age knowing people who were openly gay—or at least to have seen then on TV—and less likely to get the arguments against gay marriage."[3]

It would be a mistake, however, to see the shift in support for same-sex marriage as reflecting only a generational divide; in a Pew Research poll of Americans in October 2012, every age group showed marked increases. For those under forty-seven, the shift in favor was to a slight majority or even a strong majority for the youngest of those, the so-called millennials. But even for the baby boomers and seniors, support has grown. Growing support for gay marriage is therefore not just the result of an aging out of a recalcitrant older population but rather reflects broader social change. As legal scholar Michael Klarman notes, "the percentage of senior citizens supporting gay marriage has increased by 15 percentage points over the last five years,"[4] a remarkable achievement to be sure. Most reporters attribute these shifts largely to the growing reality of knowing someone who is gay. One CBS/*New York Times* poll (of May 2012) shows 69 percent of adults reporting a gay relative, friend, or colleague, while that number was only 44 percent in 2003.[5] The percentages get even higher for younger respondents.

What is crystal clear, however, is that this issue dominates our current historical moment, crowding out any other battles in gay rights. It is curious to note that same-sex marriage emerges as a hot issue right at the historical moment in which marriage as an institution is in decline. While it remains the case that the vast majority of Americans will get married at some point over their lifetime, statistics reveal that marriage rates are at an all-time low (51 percent in the 2011 US Census report; it was 72 percent in 1960), and these rates vary dramatically by race and ethnicity. While the Right claims that same-sex marriage will hasten this decline and kill off an increasingly fragile institution, marriage equality advocates say, conversely, that opening it up will rescue it.

It is in this climate that gay marriage pops on the national stage and has come to represent gay rights writ large. Every major gay organization features this issue front and center, and many others have sprouted up in recent years that focus solely on marriage equality. And you can bet that any casual conversation with gay *or* straight friends will come around to "the marriage debate" when gay issues are broached at all. Gay pride parades still have their fair share of scantily clad dancing boys and righteous drag queens and tough and topless lesbian activists. But marriage-equality posters and banners far outweigh the others and have pride of place in the parade route, right behind the gay cops and the gay soldiers. Rarely have we seen social movements so identified with one single issue and that issue then become so all encompassing that it becomes synonymous with the struggle itself. Surely, abortion rights have been central to feminist demands, but they've never wholly crowded out other important concerns such as violence against women, pay equity, family-friendly workplaces, and so on. Voting rights were a centerpiece of the civil rights movement, but the moral gravitas of the struggle was never reduced to simple access to the ballot box but to a whole range of rights both practical and ineffable that came under the rubric of racial equality.

But for the vast majority of Americans, two things seem indisputably true; first, most gays want to be married, and second, most gays believe marriage equality to be the single most important issue facing gay activists today. While there is little hard data on this, the few polls we do have that ask people (gay and straight) to list the most pressing issue facing the LGBTQ community consistently have marriage equality at the top of the list by a strong margin.[6] I remember being congratulated by straight friends when New York legalized same-sex marriage and noting their discomfort at my own ambivalent reactions. Not a semester goes by without a student being either perplexed or downright angry when I voice some criticisms of the marriage-equality movement. "But aren't you *gay*, Professor

Walters?" they say in amazement. It seems not getting on the marriage bandwagon might result in the revocation of one's gay card. The upshot of such a singular focus and singular association are troublesome, to say the least. Rendering gay rights synonymous with gay marriage reduces the complicated range of legal and social and sexual demands to a single institutional right and, in so doing, makes those complicated demands disappear right out of view.

## Get Your Marriage On

So what's going on here? Some of the singular focus on marriage is the product of how mass-media outlets eschew complicated analysis in favor of the simple sound bite. For the mainstream media, "gay marriage" can be easily framed within a pro/con, two-sides opposition that is most favored by media organizations and the punditocracy. As a topic for mass popular consumption, same-sex marriage couldn't be sexier and safer at the same time; it mixes up religion, the state, kids, and romance in a way that links love and legitimacy. And, more to the point, same-sex marriage is very easy for liberal straight allies (who yearn to be "accepting") to glom on to; supporting gay marriage proves how uber-tolerant one is but cannily avoids getting caught up in the messiness of gay difference, gay sex, gay liberation. The gauzily iconic image of the wedding can replace the debased image of the (take your pick) gay bar / drag ball / dykes on bikes and is a win-win: gays get their marriage, and straights get their feel-good pat on the back. Same-sex marriage can be easily analogized to the repeal of miscegenation laws and can be framed in the language of love. It is a media-friendly issue tailor-made for straight support. Let's face it: liberals love them some gay marriage. Nothing warms hearts looking for an easy cause to tout their tolerance like a video of a strapping young Boy Scout extolling the virtues of his two moms, who want nothing more than to marry and be left alone.

Like a *Daily Show* episode gone awry, we have, in one corner, the brave warriors of the Christian Right (especially certain closeted and self-loathing leaders of evangelical megachurches), defending marriage against those devious gays whose hitching instincts are sure to bring down Western civilization as we know it and will inevitably take us down the slippery slope of polygamous, animal-loving anarchy. In the other corner is our newly minted hero of civil rights—I picture him tanned and about 165 pounds—joined at the would-be altar by his life partner of many years. Their lovely child only wants to see them decently wed in front of God and family.

For most gay leaders, straight allies, and anti-gay activists alike, marriage is the last frontier in the fight for gay inclusion. It is often framed, erroneously, as the next step in a simple historical progression, ignoring that same-sex marriage only really became a concern for the gay rights movement in the 1990s and that, furthermore, the sexual revolutionary origins of the gay rights movement explicitly argued against investment in such normative practices and institutions. But this historical reality doesn't stop pundits such as Paul Waldman, writing for the *American Prospect*, from arguing,

> Though the larger culture war continues, one by one these controversies can get settled, and we reach a consensus on which side was wrong and which side was right. Today, the hottest culture war issue is gay rights, specifically marriage equality. Although most conservatives will be loath to admit it, this battle is over, and they have lost. Not that there won't be plenty more arguing, and fights in courts and legislatures and at the ballot box—there will be, and it will take years before there are no more skirmishes. But the outcome is no longer in doubt.[7]

Other pundits echo the centrality of marriage rights, if not the surety of achieving it.

Nowhere has this liberal mantra of marriage as the temple of all that is good and moral been more front and center than on the West Coast. It seems somehow fitting that the most controversial gay-marriage case would take place in California, home of celebrity five-minute marriages and TV reality programming that depict marriage as Coney Island freak show. The rollercoaster ride that has been gay marriage in California really began in 2004 when then-mayor of San Francisco Gavin Newsome—in a move that has made him a hero in gay rights circles—issued some four thousand marriage licenses to same-sex couples in just over the period of a month. Lawsuits against the state predictably followed, eventually finding their way to the state supreme court, which in May (effective in June) 2008 began formally issuing same-sex marriage licenses based on an equal protection argument from the plaintiffs.

And then the anti-gay-marriage forces began work in earnest and successfully passed Proposition 8—a ballot proposition and constitutional amendment that stated, "only marriage between a man and a woman is valid or recognized in California"—after a bitter battle that was largely funded by out-of-state "family values" activists. But the tussle over marriage in California didn't stop there. In August 2010, District Court Judge Vaughn Walker ruled that Prop 8 was unconstitutional, and higher courts upheld Walker's ruling. As we now know, in June 2013 the US Supreme Court, claiming that the supporters of Prop 8 had no legal standing, made same-sex marriage once again legal in California.

The California case brought together any number of hot-button issues for the gay community. With gay marriage thought to be an easy win in liberal California, many people were surprised at the passage of Proposition 8, and accusations flew between local and national activists and, most perniciously, at African American and Latino communities that were somehow blamed for the passage of the homophobic amendment. And, being California, the issue elicited more than its fair share of celebrity buy-in, with prominent actors, producers, and directors filming supportive ads and very funny online videos mocking the fearmongering of the pro–Prop 8 crowd. The plaintiff's lawyers (the "dream team" of Ted Olson and David Boies, previously on opposing sides in the Bush-Gore recount and later representing the plaintiffs before the US Supreme Court) and amicus briefs hammered home the themes of tolerance, diversity, economic benefit, and sameness to heterosexuals that are the hallmarks of the marriage mantra. As Margaret Talbot presciently reported in a *New Yorker* piece written before the trial,

The case has involved some unexpected staking out of positions—as though both sides had been reading up on the work of postmodern academics and come to opposite conclusions. Olson's team will argue that marriage is a malleable institution, shaped by shifting notions of gender, race, and property, while sexual orientation is innate. And the defendants will likely argue that marriage is immutable, and sexual orientation is a performative act, a chosen identity.[8]

How accurate this turned out to be, as gay marriage advocates embraced all manner of biological determinism in the rush to use immutability as the legal and morally persuasive tool to gain civil rights.

Add odes to commitment and picket-fence uniformity into the immutability stew and you get a discourse that effectively takes the gay out of gay marriage. Even one feminist economist begins her book on gay marriage by declaring that "the summer of 2008 was the summer of love and commitment for same-sex couples in the United States."[9] So are we to understand that, prior to the summer of 2008, gays had little love and no commitment? I don't mean to be facetious here, but declarations such as these are legion in the gay-marriage literature and help to frame the story as one of rootless and commitment-phobic gays finally being able to join their hetero brethren on the path of monogamy and family (and let's forget for a moment the obvious irony here when one glances at hetero divorce rates). The move to "normalize" and sell same-sex marriage as suburban humdrum comes through at every level of this campaign—both national and local. As Marc Solomon, who directed the marriage campaign for Equality California, argued, "We're not necessarily the gays in West Hollywood or the Castro but the gays around the corner in Bakersfield or Fresno—maybe the couple you've seen walking their dog or watering their lawn."[10]

On the other hand, it is hard not to be moved by the statements of the couples represented in the lawsuit and by the teary-eyed and jubilant courthouse weddings in that heady moment between mayoral action and voter reaction. Racially and ethnically diverse, diverse in age and longevity of relationship, these couples represent needs both prosaic and sacred. Some just want health care, the right to make decisions, legal responsibilities. Others want the more ephemeral but no less powerful (perhaps even more powerful) imprimatur of legitimacy. And when New York legalized same-sex marriage in the summer of 2011, that imprimatur was even more dramatic. Championed by both the governor and the mayor of New York City, it was enabled at least in part by key Republican support and canny political organizing, pointing to potential bipartisan "consensus" on this issue. The celebrations in New York were tremendous indeed.

## (Not) Everyone Loves a Wedding

Not all are so sanguine or celebratory. The *public* stance of gay rights is now firmly on top of a wedding cake, but there has been a healthy debate *within* the gay movement over both strategy and the value of marriage as an institution. Gay opinion about marriage runs the gamut from "can't wait to buy the dress" to "wouldn't mind the benefits" to "not for me" to "over my dead body." It may seem to the general population that marriage rights are all gays want and all they think about, but, in truth, gays have taken a wide variety of opinions on this topic,[11] not that you'd gather that from the mainstream media coverage. This has been framed so thoroughly as a tolerance issue and in such simplistic terms that there has been little room for more complicated analyses, particularly outside the hallowed halls of academe. My own daughter, raised to be a feminist critic of marriage while of course supporting it as a basic civil right, has often found herself being accused of homophobia when she voices any criticism of the marriage mania. She can—and does—pull out the "Hello? Do you know who my mother is?" card to quell those charges, but it is sadly true that to be gay or gay positive and simultaneously be critical of the ethos of gay marriage is to be rather freakish, if not oxymoronic.

Those who see homosexuality itself as dangerous and aberrant may see this newly configured marital dyad as a threat to national unity and "family values." But many *gays* perceive a different sort of threat, as the marrying couple pushes aside other gay and queer folk who seek not marriage but perhaps something else, what we might call (for old times' sake) sexual and gender liberation. There are serious and sustained voices of opposition, some in the name of gay liberation of the old-school variety, some in the spirit of feminist critiques of the nuclear family; still others are more pragmatic in bent, fearing that the focus on marriage will derail other struggles and issues. That discussion is largely lost in recent books and the general media maelstrom.

Feminist and gay radical writers of all stripes have long been dubious of the centrality of marriage in national gay rights struggles. Some of the most critical are older activists and theorists, such as Australian scholar Dennis Altman, who grumpily acknowledges, "We used to worry about being beaten up in the street. . . . Young queers now worry about the cost of wedding receptions."[12] While criticism of gay marriage (from gays) does not follow a strict generational divide, it is the case that many veterans of the hand-to-hand combat of early gay rights battles find little appeal in joining hands at the altar. Most recently, beyondmarriage.org (a website and position paper) engaged a wide group of activists and intellectuals in broadening the national dialogue. Op-eds by scholars such as Stephanie Coontz (writing in the *New York Times*) urge us to reach out to larger communities of intimacy and care rather than invest wholly in marriage as the place of all sustenance.[13] The historian John D'Emilio, in *The Gay & Lesbian Review*, argues that the marriage movement has been a dismal failure on any number of counts and that we should push to "further de-center and de-institutionalize marriage" rather than lining up at the chapel door.[14] Even those who have been called to testify in court cases surrounding same-sex marriage, such as sociologist Judith Stacey, have "had to squelch . . . serious qualms about some of the arguments that same-sex marriage advocates make and, more importantly, about the limited visions of family diversity that the campaign fosters."[15]

And legal theorists such as Nancy Polikoff have passionately argued that we move beyond both gay *and* straight marriage in delinking a particular form of relationship (marriage) from the whole panoply of rights and benefits associated with it (health care, inheritance law, Social Security benefits, etc.). For Polikoff and many others, one shouldn't have to marry (gay *or* straight) to have one's family supported legally and respected socially.[16] As the statement from beyondmarriage.org argues, "Marriage is not the only worthy form of family and relationship, and it should not be legally and economically privileged above all others."[17] Amen to that. Or, as feminist journalist Katha Pollitt notes, "For outmoded historical reasons, our society makes marriage the key to a host of social goods, from health insurance and death benefits to the right to make medical decisions for a loved one. . . . That system was always inadequate and today makes no sense at all."[18]

Even more radical groups have emerged to challenge the focus on marriage. Against Equality—an online archive and blog that recently published a collection of articles—explicitly and aggressively takes on the gay-marriage movement from the left, claiming that it is deeply destructive to gay freedom and particularly burdensome for gays already marginalized by class and racial strictures.[19] In this reading, the marriage mania is not just a distraction or an overly assimilationist strategy but actually *hurts* gays as real funding and resources are diverted from, say, local youth groups to statewide referenda battles and national initiatives. Over $44 million was spent in 2008 attempting to defeat Proposition 8 in California, and from 2004 through to 2012, other battleground states spent roughly the same amount in their combined efforts for gay-marriage rights.[20] You don't need to be an economist to realize that the pie can only be cut so many ways and that the funding of gay-marriage initiatives has effectively taken money away from a whole host of other gay rights causes.

## Strange Bedfellows

The focus on marriage has also had the unsalutary effect of creating a new group of donors and supporters who wholeheartedly champion same-sex-marriage rights (often because they have a gay relative) but have little to say about gay rights and freedoms more generally or, for that matter, related civil rights concerns. Here again is the tolerance trap at work: because "tolerance" allows broader anti-gay animus to go unaddressed, single issues can emerge that straight allies can be "tolerant" about without altering their more general beliefs about sex and gender. Case in point is billionaire hedge-fund dude and stalwart Republican Paul Singer, who helped underwrite the successful push for marriage equality in New York and has now joined with other Republicans to form a PAC focused solely on gay marriage. Singer has funded some of the most heinous causes in recent years, from the kind of campaigns that "swift-boated" presidential candidate John Kerry to reapportionment initiatives for the presidential campaigns of George W. Bush and Mitt Romney.[21]

Incongruous support for gay marriage is not limited to conservative Republicans but has trickled into the business community, which has determined that "diversity" and the appearance of tolerance is good for profit margins: more than two hundred megacorporations (including Apple, Citigroup, Alcoa, Disney, Microsoft, Amazon, AIG, Starbucks, and Pfizer) signed on to an amicus brief for the Supreme Court regarding DOMA and argued "that the federal Defense of Marriage Act imposes serious administrative and financial costs on their operations."[22]

Most dramatically perhaps, David Blankenhorn, anti-gay-marriage activist and founder of the Institute for American Values, recanted in a *New York Times* op-ed and now says he *supports* same-sex marriage, largely because he'd "like to help build new coalitions bringing together gays who want to strengthen marriage with straight people who want to do the same." He goes on to join with supposedly more liberal gay advocates of marriage in making the conservative family-values case, hitching marriage to a particular vision of family life. "Might we also agree," he opines, "that marrying before having children is a vital cultural value that all of us should do more to embrace? Can we agree that, for all lovers who want their love to last, marriage is preferable to cohabitation? Can we discuss whether both gays and straight people should think twice before denying children born through artificial reproductive technology the right to know and be known by their biological parents?"²³ He follows up with "a call for a new conversation on marriage" that enlists a wider array of signatories to support new dialogues to strengthen marriage because, as the "call" claims, "families are the seedbeds of civil society, and marriage is the basis of the family," thus now including those "good" gays who see the superior virtues of marriage over all other forms of human communion. One conservative signatory—Jonathan Rauch—hopes that this new initiative will provide "the family values agenda for the postgay world."²⁴ Even notorious right-wing moneybags David Koch told a *Politico* reporter that he supports gay marriage. Worse, this is reported by gay journalists as a good thing!

This isn't just a case of political pragmatism but rather the kind of (very) strange bedfellows that should make the hardiest of gay-marriage advocates scream in terror, because it argues for a single civil right while embracing a politics that would deny many other rights to a whole range of disenfranchised groups. Of course, most supporters of gay marriage do in fact locate it within a context of gay rights more broadly conceived and, unfortunately less often, a broader agenda of civil rights. But marriage equality is uniquely ripe for cherry picking, as when *New York Times* columnist Frank Bruni writes, alas without irony, that "marriage equality, which in fact gets government *out* of the business of controlling and casting judgment on people's private lives, is consistent with conservative principles."²⁵ Or, as Paul Singer himself says, supporting gay marriage "fit within my framework of freedom. . . . [It promotes] family stability."²⁶ Of course, that won't stop him from supporting Republican causes or casting his lot with anti-gay-marriage presidential candidates such as Mitt Romney. As gay Republican Robert Stevens said, when queried at the 2012 Republican National Convention about his support for an anti-gay ticket, "I understand I'm going to be subject to certain limitations. . . . I understand I won't have equal rights. But I also want to be filthy rich, and I think the Republican ticket can get me there."²⁷ Perhaps the Brits are a bit more straightforward that marriage equality is a conservative issue: David Cameron, the Conservative prime minister, recently said, "I don't support gay marriage despite being a Conservative. . . . I support gay marriage because I am a Conservative."[28] Even many Americans—and gay rights activists themselves—frame this issue as a fundamentally conservative one. Frank Bruni, writing in the *New York Times*, argues that we are successful in this battle because

> the wish and push to be married cast gay men and lesbians in the most benign, conservative light imaginable, not as enemies of tradition but as aspirants to it. In the quest for integration and validation, saying "I do" to "I do" is much more effective—not to mention more reflective of the way most gay people live—than strutting in leather on a parade float. We're not trying to undermine the institution of marriage, a task ably handled by the likes of Tiger Woods, Arnold Schwarzenegger, John Edwards and too many other onetime role models to mention. We're paying it an enormous compliment.[29]

Indeed.

Many marriage-equality strategists have embraced—often quite successfully—an approach that aims for "tolerance" and an appeal to a supposedly generic family ethos instead of a more full-throated call for civil rights. One can certainly look at the turnaround in Maine as an example of just that shift. In 2009, Maine voters rejected a same-sex-marriage bill, but in 2012 they reversed that vote almost to the percentage point, in large part due to an effort that, as one journalist notes, deliberately "moved beyond abstract appeals about civil rights," focusing instead on airing "television commercials [that] presented loving, committed gay and lesbian couples or endorsements from straight, respected people from unexpected corners of the community, like a firefighter."[30] And a 2013 "technical report" from the American Academy of Pediatrics, used to great effect in the Supreme Court cases testing gay marriage, couched its support of marriage *equality* in a language of marriage *promotion* ("marriage supports permanence and security, . . . the basic ingredients for the healthy development of children") and the perils of single parenthood—a move that would please "family values" conservatives the world over![31]

For conservative writers like Jonathan Rauch, in *Gay Marriage*, and Andrew Sullivan, in *Same-Sex Marriage*, the good of marriage is self-evident, the magic elixir that will cure society of its feckless amorality (Rauch), the taming influence on innate gay (male—these lads have little to say about lesbians) promiscuity (Sullivan), or the glue that holds together the social fabric (both). Rauch begins his book by asking us to "imagine life without marriage," which is not only like a day without sunshine but is a post-apocalyptic hell filled with unfeeling and loveless zombies only out for a good time because, as he asserts without even a twinkle of irony, "true love means, first and foremost, a love which ends in lasting marriage." Pity the poor homosexual, adrift in a world "less healthy, less happy, . . . a world of fragile families . . . in some respects not civilized, because marriage is the foundation of civilization."[32] Rauch wants to enlist rascally and pathetic gays in the grand effort to shore up the declining fortunes of marriage—a plague on alternatives, a plague on single parents, a plague on singles everywhere pretending to be whole. For "if marriage is to work, it cannot be merely a 'lifestyle option.' It must be privileged. That is, it must be understood to be better than other ways of living."[33] This explicit paean to marital bliss (Kardashians take heed!) hints at some difficult contradictions and absences in the arguments put forth by gay-marriage advocates.

Well-intentioned and nuanced historians such as George Chauncey, in *Why Marriage?*, and Stephanie Coontz, in *Marriage, a History*, challenge the right-wing canard that marriage is an unchanging force, a singular certitude through the vagaries of time. Instead, they argue that it has been a markedly changing and adaptable institution. But I suspect the pro-gay historians overstate the case for progressive potential. While surely these eminent scholars have now corrected the historical record, it is also true that the record is largely one of state control, gender-based divisions, ownership, slavery, and so on. Coverture (the common law understanding of a wife as the merged property of her husband) and marriage may no longer be indistinguishable, but they did unfortunately have a long courtship that bears inevitable scars. While Coontz is certainly correct that "companionate" or love marriage is a modern invention (as are the very concepts of "homo" and "hetero" as singular identities), that does not mean that this changing institution has no baggage or that the "equality revolution within heterosexual marriage," as she calls it, has created a radically new kind of marriage—free of gender roles and discriminatory divisions of labor.[34] Neither is it endlessly elastic. Certainly, we might question whether it is elastic enough to incorporate the claims of minority populations.

Gay-marriage advocates believe that in order to make their case, they need to challenge the "misconception" that marriage is in crisis, torn from its traditional moorings by rising divorce rates, secular feminists, birth control and abortion, and—most threatening of all—gays. Instead, these commentators see no crisis but rather an institution in flux. For Coontz and others, what is radically new is not gay inclusion per se, or even changing gender roles, but the idea that marriage is based on love and individual choice. Marriage, no longer fundamentally an economic necessity, becomes from the late 18th century on more defined by ideals of mutual affection, love, and choice. These historians aptly chart the decline of marriage as the central economic unit, but that does not mean that the *ideology* of marriage—or more broadly a kind of hetero-centered and gender-normative version of family—has lost its social and cultural *authority*. While the liberal cultural analysts are careful to illustrate the ways in which marriage has disempowered and isolated women, they also are anxious to treat the institution of marriage as sort of empty of meaning, or at least enormously shifty. It may be true, as Coontz asserts, that marriage wasn't "created" to oppress women in the way that slavery was created to oppress Africans, but it sure has done one hell of a job of contributing to that oppression. The prevalence of battering in heterosexual marriage doesn't mean all men are batterers or all heterosexual marriages potential battlefields, but it should push us to question just how equitable, peaceful, and gender-neutral such institutions can potentially be in a world marked and defined by gendered violence and inequity. The fact that the World Health Organization estimates that at least 30 percent of all women experience intimate-partner violence should give us pause, at the very least.[35]

*Conservative* marriage advocates, on the other hand, see an institution only superficially changing but essentially timeless in its social and cultural utility. Gay access to marriage is therefore akin to access to civilization or even to essential humanity itself. So which is it? Pliable, modernizing set of practices with an unfortunate history, as the pro-marriage liberals would have it, or transhistorical uber-institution of eternal value, as the pro-marriage conservatives contend? Further contradictions accompany such argumentation: in responding to the fear that gay marriage will shift the terms of marriage itself and somehow harm heterosexual marriage, most advocates insist that gay entry to marriage will not alter the institution a whit. Economist Lee Badgett, in a book that covers gay-marriage issues cross-culturally, claims that the evidence thus far is that "gay people will not change marriage in any significant way."[36] For Badgett and others, "same-sex marriage is more of a cosmetic makeover of the old institution of marriage than structural reconstruction," and this is to be applauded as "ideological opposition to marriage is likely to fade in importance as new couples form."[37]

Still others want to have it both ways and argue that gay entry into marriage will make it more equitable and less rigidly gendered. Conservative or centrist gay writers such as Rauch, Sullivan, and Yale law professor Bill Eskridge excluded, most of our pro-gay-marriage pundits would readily concede that point. But here's the rub: you can't have it both ways. Marriage can't be the sign of true inclusion, maturity, and citizenship and simultaneously be just one item in a vast menu of sexual and relational configurations. And, yes, it is galling to have these (mostly male) writers wax poetic on the virtues of wedded bliss and neglect wholly the contemporaneous attack on reproductive rights, not making the connections between control of one's own body and control of one's own relationship status.

## Don't Change a Thing

But shouldn't we make a much more provocative claim: that gay marriage will and should alter heterosexual marriages? As Liza Mundy says in a piece for the *Atlantic*, most gay-marriage advocates argue "that married gays and lesbian will blend seamlessly with the millions of straight Americans," but she wonders if that isn't short-changing both sides of the equation. She asks, correctly I believe, if same-sex marriage might in fact change marriage per se, although in a *positive* way not imagined by its critics. Mundy echoes many feminists in wondering if "by providing a new model of how two people can live together equitably, same-sex marriage could help haul matrimony more fully into the 21st century, . . . providing an example that can be enlightening to all couples."[38] Even National Cathedral dean and Episcopal priest Gary Hale argues strongly that gay marriages can and do affect straight ones. "When [conservatives] say that gay marriage threatens my marriage, I used to say, 'that's ridiculous,'" says Hale. Honing right in on the gender dimension, Hale now says, "Yeah, it does. It's asking you a crucial question about your marriage that you may not want to answer: If I'm a man, am I actually sharing the duties and responsibilities of married life equally with my wife? Same-sex marriage gives us another image of what marriage can be."[39]

This gets to the heart of the problem for gay-marriage advocates. How can both these things be simultaneously true? Can gays reasonably argue that gay entry will not alter the social fabric but just gently expand it, while at the same time claiming gay marriage as a fundamental civil rights issue? If it is basically a civil rights issue, then shouldn't we take the *strong* position: that integration of an institution (a school, a neighborhood, a workplace, a relationship) radically changes that space, alters both its interior and exterior geographies?

At its simplest, legalizing interracial marriage (here we think of the problematic analogizing to the central case of *Loving v. Virginia*, the 1967 Supreme Court decision invalidating state laws against interracial marriage) legitimated existing and future couples and protected them from state-sponsored harm. But *Loving* (and the "issue" of interracial marriage) was part of a larger project of integration, which is all about deeper change and challenging automatic privilege. The fact that we now live in a nation filled with multiracial children (themselves the subject of policy and census debates) points to the flaw in the "it won't change anything" argument. It also shows how analogies with interracial marriage are somewhat off the mark. For interracial marriage *did* augur the potential and possibilities of integration in the very intimacy of everyday married life. The fear of "race mixing" by those earlier activists opposed to "miscegenation" was precisely a fear of integration, of the blurring of distinct racial lines, lines that were crucial to maintaining structures of dominance. Gay marriage, on the other hand, is surely a civil right that must be won, but what it offers toward the project of integration is more tenuous and more complicated.

Is it inevitable that, in demanding marriage rights as fundamental civil rights, marriage advocates will invoke sameness, traditional family values, and the sanctity of the couple? If marriage is raised to the level of core right—indicative of full citizenship—then doesn't that elevate one particular form of intimacy to a level that should rightly be reserved for claims such as health, liberty, free speech, freedom from hunger, and so on? For Sullivan and others, what flows from the marriage-as-citizenship assertion is that marriage (and the military) is theorized as the last vestige of legal discrimination and social abjection.

But what are we to make of the sad fact that the Employment Non-Discrimination Act that would protect lesbians and gays from workplace abuses has been in limbo for eons? That gays and lesbians and transgendered people are still beaten up with impunity and still legitimate fodder for election mockery? That self-hatred is still rampant (see Mark Foley and Ted Haggard for that sad story) and that "gay sex scandal" is still enough to get you on page one and in rehab? Should I even mention here that we are still unable to pass the Equal Rights Amendment? So we are to have gay marriage but no gender equality? This chillingly reprises the 19th-century battle for women's enfranchisement, seen as separate from and exclusive of black male enfranchisement. Only a very few radicals held out for both.

More troubling still, in arguing for marriage as the brass ring of civic inclusion, we risk consigning a utopian vision of sexual and gender freedom to the dustbin of history. We may, I fear, pave the way for a new gay class system, in which wealthy gay insiders can play ball with the hetero big boys, the gay couple becomes the sign of gay legitimacy, and other gays become further marginalized by a gay movement eager to squelch its swishes and dim its dykes in order to get just a smidgen of tolerance and acceptance. While progressives Chauncey, Coontz, and Freedom to Marry leader and lawyer Evan Wolfson would certainly not be pleased to be put in the same camp as neocons such as Rauch and Sullivan, the truth is that it is hard to champion marriage (by depicting it as an endlessly pliable and flexible institution) without at the same time, well, championing marriage. Otherwise we really wouldn't need all these books. We'd just say the obvious: civil rights for all. Not a very long book. Thus, progressive advocates of gay marriage can't just leave it at the civil rights point or push it to the critically feminist and queer point of questioning gender stereotypes and the primacy of coupledom. They're perched uncomfortably betwixt and between. The progressives might not be as explicit as Rauch and Sullivan in trumpeting the inherent benefits of marriage to children, world health, and civilization, but they can't help being benign cheerleaders for an institution that may not be responsible for international terrorism but that surely is troubling to people committed to gender equity, social justice, the flourishing of children, relational diversity, and sexual freedom.

It's hard too for these progressives not to join in the chorus of cultural conservatives bemoaning the high rate of divorce, single motherhood, and nonmarital cohabitation. To say, for example, that divorce is not inherently a negative social phenomenon, that single-parent households are potentially more constructive of egalitarian family life, that serial relationships are not necessarily a sign of emotional pathology—well, that would put *all* pundits far outside the acceptable range of cultural discourses. When Wolfson, for example, pitches marriage as "in the best interests of the children," he, unwittingly perhaps, assumes a heterosexual model of two parents.[40] Eskridge more deliberately inveighs against single mothers in his argument, but almost all the "gay marriage is good for the kids" pleas (and legal arguments) explicitly assume two parents and implicitly push aside, if not demonize, other forms of family construction. To speak of "families of choice," envisioning a world of various and diverse intimacies and ways of living in which marriage doesn't loom as the mack daddy of institutional legitimacy, is simply beyond the pale of contemporary political discourse. That explains a bit why queer and feminist analyses are so notably absent from the treatises of the major gay proponents of gay marriage, even when they know better. Marriage advocates wax eloquent (and problematically) on the black civil rights movement, analogizing and comparing, invoking Martin Luther King and company to their hearts' content. Fair enough. But those same advocates are deafeningly silent about gender and feminism.

## You Can Have Your Gay Marriage . . . but Not Your Feminism Too

Have no doubts about it, gender is at the very heart of the matter. Rulings and arguments against same-sex marriage (and adoption and foster-care rulings as well) invoke the absolute necessity of opposite-gender parents in the raising of healthy children, building off the ready-made diatribes against single mothers permeating our culture. In the Supreme Court arguments around Proposition 8, Charles Cooper—the lawyer defending Prop 8—asserted that "redefining marriage as a genderless institution could well lead over time to harms to that institution,"[41] thus explicitly stating the gender norms at the heart of the whole discussion.

Arguments *for* same-sex marriage either skirt the gender issues at the center of the debate or, more problematically, assure anxious Americans that lesbian moms do indeed provide their progeny with hearty masculine models in the form of manly uncles, ball-tossing buddies, and virile grandpas. With the exception of (feminist) historians such as Coontz, most seem to blithely disregard that the very reason for the exclusion rests on *gender*: gay marriage is only gay because both members of the couple are of the same gender. It seems patently illogical to debate gay marriage without engaging theories of gender and power when its very difference is predicated on gender. Maybe feminism is the (pink) elephant in the wedding chapel of gay marriage: the obvious challenge to the fantasy of the equitable marital institution but one that many people willfully ignore.

That might be the very reason why gay marriage gets everyone's knickers in a twist. Not one of these gay-marriage books speaks at length on questions of gender equity, much less reproductive rights or workplace issues. Some of this is due to the rabbit hole of single-issue politics (mustn't mix 'em up!), but I think it bespeaks a stronger resistance to placing the issue in the broader context of the politics of gender, sexuality, and family. For example, *Gay Marriage* by Eskridge and corporate attorney Darren R. Spedale challenges "defense of marriage" arguments using same-sex-marriage data from Scandinavia. The authors note the radical critique of gay marriage only to subsume alternative families into an emerging "menu of relationship options." The authors' prototypical couple (Jack Baker, the "dashing engineer-turned-lawyer," and Mike McConnell, the "dimpled librarian") are compared favorably to (viciously anti-gay and anti-feminist) Sen. Rick Santorum and his wife, Karen, who, the authors claim, share the same values of idealized and romantic marriage as do our gay couple.[42] Yikes! It's hard for these marriage advocates—even the smart, historically minded ones—not to narrate a story that starts with marriage as an unequal and even sexist contractual obligation and ends with its transformation into a fluid, open, egalitarian exchange of love and commitment, even when all our national data still show the unequal division of labor in the home.

In fact, one sign of the pernicious pull of marriage as a meta-institution is the almost complete absence (Brangelina aside—and even they seem to have given in to marriage) of any large-scale heterosexual boycott of marriage in the name of equality. There's a de facto boycott in many of the European and Scandinavian social democracies, where social benefits accrue to everyone regardless of relational status and there are millions of straight couples raising kids without ever marrying. Yet we have little evidence that this is being done in *concerted* response to marriage's gender exclusions, especially here in the US. It is interesting—and telling—that the only major response to the exclusionary nature of marriage has been to open its borders. Very few gay-marriage advocates (gay or straight) have strongly insisted on a boycott of the institution until it is integrated, even though there are some heterosexuals who refuse to marry on precisely those grounds.

But, of course, many people did organize substantial and structural boycotts in other similar cases of social exclusion. At the height of the civil rights movement, many (not enough but some) whites refused to eat in segregated luncheonettes or join whites-only clubs or live in neighborhoods with "covenants" keeping blacks out. True, those who are fighting to be included have always been the ones forced to put themselves on the line for social change; it is unusual for the people in power to forgo it in the name of equality. Sure, some couples—gay and straight alike—are forgoing marriage because they oppose it for all or some of the reasons I've elucidated. But even broaching something like a boycott—around this particular issue— seems ludicrous to people. I can't tell you how many times I have said to my straight students (who are all on board with same-sex marriage) that I assumed they wouldn't get married until all people could get married, and they shift uncomfortably in their seats and look away. Or look at me like I am crazy and raining on their parade. The reaction isn't much different with my straight *adult* friends, who may festoon their marriage services with rainbow flags but rarely forgo the thing itself. This is not unlike the experience many of us have when we query women about taking their husband's name upon marrying: the vast majority still do, and my experience is that they just won't reckon with the blatant sexism of it, even when questioned. To add insult to injury, many gay couples are following suit and taking up a single name when they wed. True, that decision (to have one shared name) is at least unmoored here from the masculinist assumption that the woman will take the man's name. But I am always surprised when I raise this to same-sex couples who are pondering a name change, and the origins of that tradition—and all it symbolizes about loss of self and individual identity in the concept of a merged couple—go unexamined. Bringing it up, as I am wont to do, is the surest way to get uninvited to the wedding festivities.

## Altared Expectations

What I hope I've done here is to reframe and recast the marriage debates, first, by bringing to light internal voices of dissent that challenge the focus on this issue and, second, by dethroning gay marriage as *the* civil rights achievement that will signal the death knell of homophobia and discrimination. It is crucial to shake up the reigning assumption that equates gay rights with marriage rights. For no other minority group do we imagine this: do we think misogyny has been vanquished now that legal gender discrimination is a thing of the past? Do we think anti-Semitism is gone because Jews no longer must wear the yellow star? Has the integration of women into the labor force eradicated sexism? Has the election of a black president and the end of legal segregation slain the scourge of racism?

Marriage rights may be at the heart of the tolerance trap; legalizing same-sex marriage has now been constructed as the test of heterosexual goodwill and alliance. When the equation becomes gay rights = marriage, the tolerant society allows its others access to its institutions in exchange for a quiescence on more troublesome exclusions. It is at the top of the list of all the gay rights groups and is the cause that unites celebrities and (some) politicians in a warm haze of beneficent tolerance. And tying gay rights and gay citizenship to a specific social institution undermines the likelihood of detaching those rights and treating them as, well, inalienable and not yoked to membership in the marital club.

We are in a bit of a bind. As sociologist Joe Rollins remarks, "Proponents minimize the imagined differences between gay and straight couples, opponents are striving to render an image of same-sex marriage as a cultural and political monstrosity, and the critically inclined worry that we are making a Faustian bargain."[43] Almost all gay rights activists, in making the case for same-sex marriage, insist that marriage is a "fundamental right" and even one central to both the nation in a more ephemeral sense and the Constitution more specifically. Even the Universal Declaration of Human Rights declares marriage thus, and in more recent years it has been interpreted to include freedom to marry regardless of sexual orientation. On the face of it, this seems straightforward enough—who shouldn't be able to marry the person of his or her choosing? But poke a bit more and it begins to unravel. Isn't it curious that we may have come to a social place, in the US at least, where marriage is considered a fundamental right (akin to life, liberty, and the pursuit of happiness) but health care is not? A place to rest one's head is not? Enough food in one's belly is not? I respect the idea of same-sex marriage as a basic civil right, but one more fundamental than these others? Of course, supporting gay marriage doesn't necessarily lead to setting this priority, but it has in practice often done so, because of a confluence of legal, political, and ideological factors. And, worse, gay-marriage advocates can't seem to avoid the language of "just like you." Time and time again, our leaders claim that we are just as capable of making committed relationships as "you" are and that our marriages are no different.

So is it possible to be pro-gay and pro-civil-rights and still be anti-gay-*marriage*? I don't mean anti-marriage in the "I hate gays and this is an institution only for one man and one woman" kind of way. I mean, can one support the civil right as obvious and necessary while simultaneously decrying both the undue emphasis this has in the gay movement *and* being critical of the institution of marriage itself? Certainly many people do just that, as I have elaborated in this chapter. Few gay activists would begrudge another's marriage, although surely there are some whose critique takes that form. But a small and unfortunately largely unheard minority not only would question our priorities in championing this above all other issues but would go deeper to challenge the linking of a particular kind of relationship with both legal rights and social legitimacy. When gay rights become synonymous with marriage rights, these nuances and internal criticisms become confined to the background, as tolerance of (marrying) gays becomes the top priority for an enlightened public.

One of the central arguments of straight supporters of gay marriage reveals this tolerance motif at work. "How," they ask with righteous moral authority, "does Jim marrying Bob in any way challenge or undermine my wedded bliss with my wife?" And here's the conundrum: if it doesn't challenge your life, it's not very radical, and if it does challenge your life, we won't get it. It is inevitable that the hysterical response to same-sex marriage will be couched in both political and personal terms. Politically, gay rights advocates argue that this is a cut-and-dried (albeit difficult to achieve) civil rights issue, analogous to ending miscegenation laws years earlier. Personally, they argue that gay marriage won't hurt or change or alter "your" marriage a bit. The upshot? We ask nothing of you. There's the rub and there's the trap. Marriage as a right is a trap, at the heart of the tolerance project. The overweening emphasis on this—not just as an obvious civil right but as *the* sign of gay inclusion—is a contraction of the expansive potential of sexual freedom imagined by earlier activists.

For many gay critics, the response to the rise of the good, married, respectable gay couple is to trumpet the opposite (promiscuous, nonmonogamous, sexually and socially marginalized) in the name of resisting assimilation. For them, gay marriage is the nail in the coffin, firmly snuffing out sexual liberation and social freedoms. Other critics focus more on questions of political priorities (How about national health care based on individuals, not marital status? Peace? An end to gender discrimination in the workplace?). One of the reasons that the US state is so resistant to gay marriage is not only the strength of Christian conservatism in this country but the linkage of marriage to social-welfare provisions, health care, and other state and federal rights and privileges. No wonder European social democracies have been quicker to move on gay marriage.

Still others resist marriage in the name of feminist or even anarchist commitments to alternative forms of intimacy and kinship not bound by the state or by a narrow understanding of "family." The radical argument that progressive gays and their allies should be focusing on more important matters is correct but doesn't in fact go far enough into unpacking the tolerance trap that undergirds the marriage focus. Instead, we need to reckon with why marriage has such enormous meaning for people and then perhaps attempt to undo or challenge or redirect some of that meaning. If we can all agree that people are not born with some inherent drive to marry (or even, perhaps, to partner exclusively), then we would do well to think about how to unlink desires for connection and support and intimacy (which all of us do seem to have) from a particular and singular social institution.

The gay Left is certainly on the mark in its (our) critique of the marriage mania, but it may be missing another point—the robust integration point. I'm no fan of either the military or marriage—two institutions yoked historically to violence and xenophobia, ownership and gender roles. But maybe we don't know what can happen to these institutions with new players, players who have been not only excluded from but defined against those very structures. If marriage is, well, married to gender opposition and gender role, then what does marriage become when that binary framework and all that comes with it is undone? I'll date myself here, but I remember a much-argued-over 1981 book, Zillah R. Eisenstein's *The Radical Future of Liberal Feminism*, which posited the transgressive (unintended) potential of seemingly simple liberal demands for equity and inclusion. There could of course be a sort of "trickle down" cultural effect of legalizing same-sex marriage. To see gays as *marriageable*, as "worthy" of this institution that has such symbolic resonance, can have the effect of chipping away at the "otherness" of gay people.

While surely the focus on gay marriage caused backlash (e.g., the Defense of Marriage Act, statewide marriage initiatives) and diverted resources from a host of other issues, it also, as Michael Klarman argues, "forced Americans to discuss and form opinions about a social reform that previously would have struck most of them as incomprehensible."[44] And it was not just the conservatives such as

Paul Singer who climbed on board the marriage train; the public airing of such a contentious social issue has certainly pushed liberals to get off the fence and gays themselves to become more engaged in the political process more broadly conceived. Still, for many radicals, gay marriage seems the nadir of queer liberation.[45] But maybe it is the Trojan horse in the war against gender inequity and sexual subordination. Or maybe that is wishful thinking in a cultural context in which "liberation" is a term more associated with "hands-free device" than political futures. Coontz, Chauncey, and even Wolfson go a long way toward debunking the myths of marriage and pulling the rug out from under the right-wing arguments. But few of our marriage mavens are willing to embrace the "radical future of liberal gay marriage," to claim that gays may actually alter an institution that—for all its variability—has historically been defined by sexual inequality, gender rigidity, and sometimes outright violence.

But here's my caveat, and it's a big one: as long as marriage rights are framed as the pinnacle of gay liberation and, simultaneously, no challenge to hetero business as usual, then the jaws of the tolerance trap will have snapped shut, keeping out the more transformative possibilities. The very shift to a language of "marriage equality," rather than "same-sex" or "gay" marriage, indicates a desire to take the messiness of sex out of the picture, to remove the specter of homosex from the hominess of marriage. Just as the main pro-gay-marriage organization has the bland name "Human Rights Campaign," effectively nullifying the specificity of queerness in the very title, so too does "marriage equality" implicitly de-gay our inclusion in that institution, making heterosexual unions the default point of comparison.

The real lavender threat is not most (gay) marriages. Some gays may or may not alter the institution by gaining access to it. The real lavender threat, perhaps symbolized by marriage but certainly not subsumed by it, is that gay kinship, gay sexual frontiers, gay intimacies will disrupt the norms of heterosexual family life. Now that would be a revolution worth all the tulle in Massachusetts and all the confetti in Hollywood.

# 9

# In the Family Way

In the early summer of 2012, right on the heels of President Obama's announcement that he supported gay marriage, deep in the midst of an ugly election season that saw no shortage of anti-gay animus, a new study emerged. In this one, purportedly scientific and vetted by scholarly peers, sociologist Mark Regnerus claimed he had definitive proof that kids raised by gay parents are worse off than kids raised by straight parents.[1] It ignited a firestorm of controversy. Critics claimed it was bad science and worse sentiment, fanning the flames of homophobia in the guise of "research." Supporters hailed Regnerus as a brave new hero in the continuing culture wars, a scholar who has offered up the evidence they so desperately want to "justify" discriminatory practices.[2]

Shift now to a few months later, to the glitzy Emmy awards. *Modern Family*—the breakout ABC hit comedy that features a gay male couple with an adopted daughter—sweeps the awards, as it has done since it debuted in 2009. Universally lauded as both well written and socially progressive, *Modern Family* situates its token homosexuals firmly—even stereotypically—in suburban family land. Mitchell, finicky lawyer son of macho family patriarch Jay, and Cam, campy show-tune-singing farm boy, are icons of marital normalcy and anxious 21st-century parenting. Or glance over to Fox and see *Glee*, where the heartwarming relationship between gay teen Kurt and his (macho) father provides some of the more moving moments in the series. In 2012, not to be outdone by strangely gay-positive Fox, NBC launched *The New Normal*, a sitcom (now canceled) about two ridiculously wealthy, white, and handsome gay men whose biological clocks kick into high gear, prompting them to acquire a gorgeous blond surrogate, replete with wise-beyond-her-years, sitcom-ready preteen and cantankerous, homophobic, racist grandma. Conspicuous consumption, Archie Bunkerish bigotry, and laughs ensue. An interracial lesbian couple are raising a truckload of kids over at ABC Family in *The Fosters*, and hit thriller *Scandal* features an ethically challenged (but out) gay father. And as of this writing, actor Sean Hayes of *Will and Grace* fame is set to play a gay dad raising a teenage daughter in a new NBC sitcom.

Inevitably linked to the media-friendly story of same-sex marriage, Hollywood gay parenting has also emerged as the feel-good sign of all things tolerant. The adorable progeny of Ricky Martin, Cynthia Nixon, Jane Lynch, and other gay luminaries are featured in *People* magazine cover stories, and news of gay couples having kids becomes integrated into the everyday life of celebrity gossip. Or look at the heartwarmingly banal pictures of gay parents and their children rolling Easter eggs on the White House lawn, greeted with a yawn by the press, or get teary-eyed as Boy Scout Zach Walls, the son of two lesbian moms, testifies in the Iowa anti-marriage debate of 2011, insisting, "the sexual orientation of my parents has had zero effect on the content of my character."[3] Both gays with kids and parents of gays get wild applause at pride parades, and the stroller brigades compete with the "I love my gay son" T-shirt-wearing mamas for accolades and a warm embrace. Indeed, new genres seem to have popped up in a market ever ready to commercialize sentiment: sperm-donor stories, odes to alternative parenting, memoirs of growing up gay (or trans or bi or queer or . . . ). There are endless blogs and magazines devoted to gay parenting, and even a glance at the Internet reveals a treasure trove of resources, providing advice on coming out to the principal at little Charlie's preschool and curricular aides for an inclusive kindergarten.

Move away from celebrities and photo ops and back to reality and the picture is not quite so pretty: while courts have been uneven in recent custody cases and restrictive laws regarding adoption and fostering have mostly retreated, at least seven states actually prohibit second-parent adoption, and a few still won't allow gays and lesbians to foster or adopt or make it very difficult to do so.[4] It's heartening to see polls that report more Americans in favor of allowing gays and lesbians to adopt children, with 54 percent stating they are in favor or strongly in favor versus 40 percent who say they oppose or strongly oppose gay adoption.[5] But that 40 percent opposed should still be terrifying information to all prospective parents. The beliefs that undergird that opposition are outdated but persistent: that gays and lesbians are predatory and perverse, unfit for family life. A poll a few years earlier from the Pew Research Center found that 43 percent of respondents felt that more gay and lesbian couples raising children was bad for US society.[6] And as Bryan Fischer, prominent evangelical preacher and host of the daily *Focal Point* radio talk program on AFR Talk, a division of the American Family Association, claims, "Children growing up in homosexual households have been shown to be more likely to experiment sexually, and as same-sex unions (as well as cohabitation) become the norm, this will only become more pronounced, producing more heartache, more children born out of wedlock, and more sexually transmitted diseases."[7] Or as Catholic League president Bill Donohue puts it by way of praise for the tainted Regnerus study, "If we know that there is a gold standard—is the father and mother—why would we want to treat it as a relativized? You know, pick from one, pick from two, then you get to the point where we're at today. . . . Marriage is about children. Nature has ordained, and nature's God, that only a man and woman can have a family. Gay people have been disqualified from nature."[8] These are common, if wildly unsubstantiated, beliefs. And we can't forget that even the "right" to second-parent adoption is a burden and financially troublesome. I'll never forget when a dear friend of mine had to hire a lawyer and endure a home visit by a social worker in order to "adopt" her own child. When they went to city hall to finalize it and the judge offered them congratulations, she remarked, "Congratulations?

For having to expend thousands of dollars to legally tie myself to my own child? No thanks."

Like the debates about marriage, this one gets personal pretty quickly. I'm a lesbian mother and a single parent at that—both coming in for derision and debate in the ever-more-annoying "family values" tedium. While I am pretty ambivalent and maybe even a little depressed about the rush to the altar and the inordinate focus on marriage rights, I am unabashedly a partisan for the rights of gay parents. My family doesn't look at all like *Modern Family* (more Showtime than ABC, I think), but I take a certain pleasure in seeing those boys parent and a certain pain in attacks on parents who look more like them than like their hetero counterparts. Since this is personal, here is my story, the story of how I became a "modern family."

———————

Cliché though it is, I had always wanted children. And when I was ready to embark on parenting and started considering it seriously, I was adamant about wanting to do it as a single parent. For most people, that's like saying they always knew they wanted to undergo abdominal surgery without anesthesia, but there you have it. I loved being in relationships but saw the "relationship story" as separate and distinct from the "parenting story." I mean, the great mama movies like *Stella Dallas* and *Mildred Pierce* and *Mommy Dearest* and *Aliens* are all about the mother-daughter bond and put aside the secondary boyfriend storyline, unless you count Ripley's relationship with the extraterrestrial host. I wanted to build a family, therefore, like Ripley's, and while not as buff as Sigourney Weaver, I did feel competent to take on alien intruders both inside and outside my womb. Child and I would be the Martha Stewarts of queer family life, assuring anxious gals and some guys that with a little pluck, a lotta friends, a decent income, and the right kind of adhesive, we could remake the world.

So nineteen-plus years ago, with the help of a friendly sperm bank, I became a lesbian single mother. Well, I was already a lesbian, but the single-mother part required the child. So in order to make myself even more of a pariah, I gathered my hopefully ripe eggs about me and headed on down to the Watergate Sperm Bank. Yes, the Watergate Sperm Bank. When the director didn't laugh at my "anyone but G. Gordon Liddy!" joke, I knew that the barrel of giggles I anticipated as motherhood might be more difficult to attain than originally thought. And to make matters worse, the doctor who performed the insemination was similarly unimpressed with my request for a peck on the cheek as my derriere was propped up ignominiously post-insemination. "What, no kiss?" I queried. She glared and grunted, "Can I get you a magazine or something?" "I think we're a little late for the magazines," I replied, trying for a little donating-sperm wit. "*Time* or *Newsweek*?" she insisted, willfully ignoring my attempts to lighten up what was really already a pretty light moment. I gave in and resentfully accepted the stack of outdated newsmagazines.

Timing is everything. Since I was in the midst of a difficult tenure battle as an openly gay person at a Catholic university, I thought it only appropriate to throw caution to the wind and add pregnancy to my other obvious advantages. I was clearly the Antichrist in their eyes (Jewish, without an obvious male master, filled with suspicious joie de vivre), so why not fashion myself a Madonna-Satan hybrid? Justify my love. Surely they could get behind this, family values and all that. This was the closest thing these priests would see to an immaculate conception.

Today, artificial insemination is an exercise in Internet access, with banks posting detailed descriptions of donors in a *Dating Game* meets Human Genome Project sort of way ("Hi, I'm Brian! I love music, long walks in the park, and pleasuring myself for financial remuneration. All this and my ebullient personality are genetically transferable!"). Friends in the process of inseminating regale me with sperm-bank stories as they surf the Net for good swimmers with nifty hobbies and high SATs. Donor catalogues now go way past listing height and weight and banal hobbies and give excruciating details about the dreams, study habits, and visions for world peace of a young man who has just expelled his effluvia for a few bucks and a free magazine. You can even hear tape-recordings of Joe Six-Vial earnestly evaluating the meaning of life and detailing his favorite movies, mostly predictable noir classics or World War II paeans to staunch masculinity.

But back in the old days, this whole artificial insemination thing was a fairly routine endeavor. Now they call it *"alternative"* insemination." While I know the new designation is much more politically right-on, I do prefer the odes to artificiality. Like "artificial sweeteners" and "artificial limbs," they are great additions to modern life. "Alternative" makes me think of vegetarian restaurants and shaggy-haired boys earnestly playing discordant music. I prefer the clean and utterly made-up image of artificial Splenda to grungy alternative indie-rock when I order up my family jewels. But artificiality aside, the whole process was pretty low-tech and essentially consisted of a few visits to a sperm bank (or "fertility center") where one flipped through faintly musty and not very detailed catalogues of potential donors that revealed basic medical information but little else. It didn't take me long to peruse the dusty folder that contained only a few entries and was as easy to navigate as an old Sears catalogue. Come to think of it, implementing a stamp-book system into sperm-bank management might be a great way to increase business and reward frequent users. Something like the old S&H Green Stamps that we had as kids, where we got the stamps at the supermarket checkout, eagerly pasted them into the stamp book, and then redeemed them for necessary prizes such as tent poles. Or we could even have a whole TV episode centered on them, like *The Brady Bunch* did, although I'm not sure what special redeemable gifts one should get with a sperm-bank green-stamp system.

Why I chose the Watergate Sperm Bank remains a mystery. No one else I know has used this facility. I've never heard the phrase "Watergate Sperm Bank" uttered in a sentence. I'm not even sure it really exists—perhaps my daughter, Emma, truly was an immaculate conception. I'm starting to believe that maybe I broke in, stole some hot sperm, and repressed the whole experience to save my country. But if my memory is correct, I did in fact make a few visits to this den of burgled sperm and quickly picked out donor-boy with the help of the bank director, an extremely diminutive Greek man who laughed heartily at my request for a tall Jewish guy. I don't usually speak in that teenage-girl questioning voice, but here I was stumped.

"Uh, hi? I'm looking for some, uh, sperm?" I said to the diminutive Greek man.

"Of course you are," he said forcefully, gripping my hand in a firm and manly shake. "Is your husband joining us today to help make the choice?"

I always get strangely flummoxed at such conversations, because it was true enough to just say, as I did this day, "No?"

"Fine, fine, no problem," he said and winked at me as we sat down. "Here is the catalogue." And he placed the dusty folder in my hands. "Any special preferences?" Another hard question that left me a little confused for a bit until I realized that he was referring to the sperm biography.

"Oh, well, Jewish actually," I finally spluttered. "Kinda eastern European but in a 1940s resistance fighter way, not a Gorbachev sort of way. Although I loved Gorby. Not the map on his bald head. Sad, really. And that would look strange on my child, especially if it was a girl." Now the director began to stare at me, all hint of a wink gone from his worried eyes. But I continued, "And tall? because, like, ha ha, obviously . . . I'm not?"

The diminutive Greek director hesitated a moment, took the folder he had given me and replaced it with a much thinner one and said, "Here we go. Shouldn't take you too long to make a choice," and left me in the office to pick out my resistance fighter on my own. Jewish men are squeamish enough about their bodies, so the Chosen Donors are few and far between. But tall *and* Jewish? It seemed an impossible request. We are generally a short people, albeit with tall aspirations. So I settled for a five-foot-eleven-inch hunk of Hebrew manhood. The choice was a tough one: a five-foot-four stamp collector or a five-foot-eleven swimmer. Of course, given my conviction that stamp collecting and swimming (and all hobbies) are handed down generation to generation, I thought I'd take my chance with the Mark Spitz wannabe. After five home tests proved it, I called my mother. "Ma, I think I may actually be pregnant."

"Oh please, that's not how it happens," she replied.

"We've already been through this. A husband is not an option," I said, eager to insist on my fertility.

"That's not what I'm talking about, you idiot," she interjected. I don't think you should call the mother of a resistance fighter an idiot, but she went on anyway. "It just doesn't happen that quickly. There'll be many tries and lots of disappointment. Trust me. I tried for—"

I cut her off. I knew this story. "Ma," I said forcefully into the phone, "it is not written in the Bible that thou shalt inherit thy mother's uterus. I know we're a lot alike, but I have a feeling here."

I could hear her sucking her teeth and snorting and sighing on the other end. "Well, we'll talk about your feelings after you've seen the doctor."

"Midwife," I corrected.

"I'll take you to the doctor tomorrow," she said as she hung up.

When she finally admitted she was wrong and we did not in fact share the same uterine fate, my ever-gracious mother pointed out how lucky I was to be gay as otherwise we would have a family large enough to populate a small Aleutian island by now. I was one of those jolly pregnant women, rarely sick, pinky, and very healthy. However, the one downside of being pregnant was being endlessly mistaken for heterosexual. I wanted to wear a big pink triangle, preferably etched in my maternity clothes so it would grow to enormous proportions with my ever-expanding girth. When I finally decided to alert my sure-to-be-disapproving Catholic colleagues, I made an appointment with the chair of the department, a stout and stern woman who had, years ago, taken me out to the woodshed (faculty club) for a "talk" in which she asked me if I could "tone it down." I was confused, as I didn't really look like Liberace or Rosie O'Donnell. So I'm not sure what the appropriate bar of gay flauntiness was for her. We were not on very good terms, but I thought I should tell her anyway.

"Well," I started in, "I just thought I should let you all know that I am pregnant." And I smiled, in what I assumed was a "we're all women here" beatific way.

She looked at me quizzically, leaned forward in her seat, coughed a bit, and then said, "Suzanna! I'm so surprised. I just, umm, you know . . ." I just stared at her, unclear where she was going with this. "What I mean to say is, did you *intend* to get pregnant?" I stared even harder until it dawned on me: this was confirmation for her that I was not, in fact, a lesbian but rather a more recognizable fallen woman.

"Oh, you know how it is," I murmured. She nodded back in sisterly sympathy now. "I lost my head, had a bit too much to drink, had my way with a bunch of sailors and forgot, you know, to use . . . 'protection.'" A sharp intake of breath from her and a tight headshake. What Catholic girl couldn't understand that old story? Oh, those wacky lesbians! So unable was she to reckon with my lesbianism and my pregnancy simultaneously that one had to disappear, and since my belly wasn't going anywhere . . . I simply didn't fit into her mainstream narrative of parenting. After years of being on the outside, I was now being pulled into a sisterhood I wasn't sure I wanted to join. It's like protesting to gain entrance into the restrictive country club and realizing that you don't play golf.

If I was mistaken for hetero by confused liberals, my dear friend Deborah got a chance to take a walk on the abject side when she agreed to be my birthing coach and accompanied me to the Lamaze classes. At first I didn't notice what was going on, because I was hugely pregnant and only concerned that Debby show up, infamous as she was in her uncompromising lateness. Debby was a sixties refugee with a heart of gold and a head a bit hazy with too much Dylan and drugs. I trusted her totally and breathed a sigh of relief when she miraculously wandered into the Lamaze class on time. Debby is one of those gorgeous and graceful blondes whose bemused affect keeps everyone slightly off guard and allows her exceedingly sharp mind to do its work without showiness. Looking like Goldie Hawn without the plastic surgery and insipid smile. Spacey, but the kind of woman you'd trust with your life or your firstborn or your first bail bond. We eagerly joined the earnest couples at prenatal class. Debby—a mother of two—consistently challenged the nurse's dire predictions of the hell of childbearing. Perhaps you really do forget the pain if you are stoned.

"Now, Joan," she would say, the only one who addressed the Birkenstocked nurse by her name, "Let's be real here." She would take a long breath and stare—in an Earth Mother sort of way—at the anxious and very pregnant women sitting uncomfortably on the floor. "Of *course* there is some . . . *discomfort*. But," and here she took another long pause and tossed her beautiful blond head side to side, "it really is quite . . . *miraculous*." Every woman in the room wanted her to deliver their babies.

Not only did Debby displace the nurse as resident birth expert, but she understood what it was like—for a few weeks at least—to be a lesbian. Of course, everyone assumed we were a couple. We didn't help matters by camping it up a bit, and her tongue in my ear might have indicated something to our fellow travelers, although really it just made my ear wet. While the other presumably hetero couples bonded in anticipatory natalism, no one chatted us up. At first Debby—so used to an easy kind of mother bonding assumed by most straight women—didn't understand why no one put their birthing pillows next to us as we gathered uncomfortably in a circle on the floor. Perhaps they were afraid that if they got too near, they would catch the lesbian mother disease. This alienation was a shocker for my well-meaning companion. So I kept urging Debby to slap one of the fathers-to-be on the back and give him a leering wink ("Hey, bud—these women are *bigggg*!"), but her giggly blond girliness prevented such a display of stereotypical manly pride. She was, though, inordinately interested in the vending machines in the hospital, and we often could be found sneaking out between "possible birth defects" and "how to clean a bellybutton" to ponder the classic and always unresolved question of ice cream sandwich versus Fritos. Just like a straight woman, I eventually gave birth.

## Love the Child, Hate the Movement

It worked out pretty well for me, but family remains a vexed or contradictory site, at once the place of continued stigma and rejection and the expansive location for creative new configurations of kinship.

Just like ideologies of marriage, ideologies of family are heavily freighted and carry with them loads of historical and emotional baggage. We typically have a higher bar for our family connections then we do for our social ones. Generally, we don't ask for "tolerance" from siblings or parents but rather yearn for a deeper acceptance and sometimes even a real love. Some of us older homos even remember when asking if someone was "family" was a coded—and particularly poignant—way of ascertaining the person's sexuality. One of the reasons we referred to each other that way was not just to encode our sexuality, but to claim a term, or a structure of feeling, that was so often kept from us. Our grand narrative ("coming out") is itself situated so deeply in the familial; we come out to friends and co-workers, but the source of so much strife and stress (and joy and relief too) has been in the revelation to family members.

As feminist sociologist Judith Stacey notes in *Unhitched*—her wonderful history of marriage, love, and family life—even though the *Leave It to Beaver* family is no longer (if it ever was) the reality for most Americans, "the word *family* continues to conjure an image of a married, monogamous, heterosexual pair and their progeny."[9] Just as Alfred Kinsey showed us that *sexual* diversity is perfectly normal, so too are contemporary family researchers proving without a shadow of a doubt that *family* diversity is normal as well, even if our ideologies insist otherwise.

But embracing family "diversity" as a benign nod to a newly tolerant society is easier said then done. Further, tolerating different sorts of families is assuredly not the same as embracing them. Even further, tolerance comes at a cost, as I will elaborate throughout this chapter. For unlike other minorities (Jews or blacks, for example) whose encounter with bigotry typically takes place outside the family home, queers often experience their first taste of fear and loathing at the family hearth. A 2006 study by the National Center for Lesbian Rights found that over 30 percent of LGBTQ youth reported physical violence by family members after they came out, and 26 percent were forced to leave their families because of conflicts over sexual or gender identity.[10] The statistics on gay kids in foster care are even starker. One study shows that 78 percent of LGBTQ youth in foster care were either removed from the home or ran away due to hostility concerning their sexual or gender identity, and similar studies document the continued rejection and violence against LGBTQ youth in their families of origin or foster families, violence that prompts a disproportionate number of queer kids to end up on the streets.[11]

For all the new family formations and work of groups like PFLAG, it remains the case that these other stories still persist: stories of familial rejection and even violence or more benign but still hurtful marginalization of gay parents at the local PTA or neighborhood picnic. One could even argue that rejection by one's family is a sad, perhaps even unique, hallmark of the gay experience.[12] A popular bumper sticker proclaims that "hate is not a family value" in an attempt to "reclaim" the family-values terrain for a tolerant (nonhateful) attitude toward gay families. But that sticker has it all wrong: not only is hate central to the family-values discourse (for what do these organizations promulgate but deep animosity toward every type of family structure that doesn't look like Ozzie and Harriet?), but families themselves have been the source of so much pain for gays and other sexual minorities, as writer Sarah Schulman so aptly describes in her 2011 book *Ties That Bind: Familial Homophobia and Its Consequences.* In the rush to claim victory over homophobia, the (older) stories of familial (and institutional) discrimination have faded in the face of overly optimistic prognostications and fantasies of a benign new embrace.

It is undeniable that our culture is filled with stories of changed hearts and minds following a family revelation. It has become something of a truism that having a gay son or daughter—or having a gay parent or sibling—is the basic stuff of transformation. It is surely no accident that one of the most enduring and active gay rights groups consists of parents (and friends) of lesbians and gays: PFLAG. Examples are legion here, from the politician whose push for gay marriage seems motivated by his love for his lesbian sister to the PFLAG parents who champion their progeny to the mom of a murdered gay youth who dedicates her life to gay causes. Certainly, these family-inspired shifts seem most pointed when it comes to previously anti-gay Republican stalwarts like Ohio Senator Rob Portman, whose change of tune regarding marriage equality was laid firmly at the feet of his gay son. These moments are significant and give truth to the continued necessity of coming out, being visible, being known.

Sometimes, for sure, family love can morph into substantive and thoughtful advocacy. My own mother, a strong feminist and progressive but one who had never really thought much about gay rights, became a fierce advocate after I came out at sixteen. Not immediately—in that, she was like so many others (shocked, upset, confused)—but over time the politics of gay rights and inclusion became for her the mark of a true radical. And my daughter, raised not only by a lesbian mother but in a broader community of mixed provenance, has emerged, inarguably, more committed to equal rights than she might have been had she been raised in another kind of family. This is always interesting to note when defenders of gay families plead for "tolerance" by pointing out that kids of gay parents are not "harmed" by them; the point seems quite different to me: kids of gay parents have unique opportunities to be more thoughtful and curious about difference and, yes, about sexual choice than others.

Most of us believe—and the mainstream gay movement certainly makes the argument—that the simple reality of actually knowing gays as family members will chip away at bigotry. The story so often told is this evolutionary one: a child comes out to her parents, the parents experience fear and dismay but come to love their gay child. They declare, "We love you no matter who you are." They say, "It doesn't matter if you are gay. You're still our daughter." Or, in another scenario, little Aidan plays with his schoolmate Tom. When Tom's heterosexual parents encounter Aidan's two daddies, they realize (cue warm fuzzies) that they're all "just parents" after all and that Aidan's daddies are just the same as they are. We trot out our lesbian moms to display our tolerance even as we insist that they are no different from those "normal" moms down the street.

This is the tolerance trap hard at work, measuring gay kids and gay parents by their similarity to their heterosexual counterparts.

This is the *fallacy of familiarity*,[13] which imagines a "natural" relationship between knowing a gay person (through family ties, for example) and a real critique of anti-gay sentiment. Familiarity can undoubtedly breed empathy, even in the most recalcitrant individuals. There is no doubt that the polls are conclusive on this: knowing someone who is gay is a powerful predictor of social shifts. In 1985, only 25 percent of people said they knew someone who was gay, and more than 50 percent claimed they never met anyone gay. By 2010, 77 percent said they knew someone gay, and the numbers are even larger the younger the sample group.[14] I applaud the change of heart of folks like Senator Portman, but the ethical imperative only became apparent when it became personal. One has to wonder how deep that commitment to gay rights will be if it is rooted only in the (tolerant) love of a family member.

But familiarity can also breed contempt or, more to the point, can produce a sentiment of individual love—"I love my gay son" or "I love my two moms"[15]—that may or may not translate into a changed social consciousness. Indeed, what is meant by that T-shirt or the similar one "I'm proud of my gay son"? Is the pride in the gayness itself? Could we imagine such a T-shirt for another minority identity? ("I love my Jewish daughter"?) Don't get me wrong—I'm all for the love! Much better than the alternative—an alternative that way too many gay kids have experienced when they come out and get viciously rejected by their families of origin. But it does hint at the limitations of a change of heart that is motivated by individual familiarity rather than social solidarity.

## (Not) All in the Family

At the same time—and this is what we are beginning now to see really percolate through popular culture—gays themselves are more and more constructing their own families, whether through donor insemination, surrogacy, or earlier heterosexual marriages and relationships. There is little accidental and much creative in these new kinship structures, although you'd hardly know that if your knowledge about queer families was brought to you through popular culture.

If the *Will and Grace* / *Ellen* / *Queer as Folk* zeitgeist of the years running from roughly 1994 to 2005 brought queerness into the family home largely through the familiar tropes of friendship, coming out, and—to a lesser extent—the politics of community, then this new wave of gay visibility moves in some decidedly different directions, largely eschewing the "gay pals" motif in favor of the gay family story. These new family images are wrapped up in—and compromised by—the current tolerance framework in which gay rights is signified almost completely through the political acquisition of same-sex marriage and the theoretical buy-in of biological immutability.

Gay family images, moreover, are emerging as the sanitizing counterpart to gay sexual liberationist images. By and large these images are of churchgoing, nuptial-desiring, station-wagon-driving, pet-loving, PTA-attending, suburban-dwelling, two-parent-and-child households. In the current mainstream "pro-gay" zeitgeist, gay marriage plus gay parents plus gay genes plus gay soldiers equals victory. This media-friendly version of sexual-minority inclusion is predicated on an erasure of feminist and queer critiques of gender normativity and the nuclear family.[16] The mainstream visibility of the unthinkable possibility (gay marriage) hinges on mainstream invisibility of a more unthinkable and more threatening possibility (feminist, queer families) and helps to bolster the liberal, assimilationist models of "acceptance" and "tolerance" of queers. There is in fact a troubling erasure of queer difference (and particularly feminist and lesbian difference) in the seemingly benign and inclusive depiction of gay parents and gay kids. This erasure—or cleaning up—is precisely what tolerance enables in lieu of a deeper embrace of gay family difference.

Gay family images may be au courant in our current media culture, but they all too often follow a depressingly simplistic storyline. There are essentially three themes playing out in contemporary family images (and here I am talking about images of gay *parents* as well as ones of straight parents and gay *kids*), most of which depend on the framework of tolerance and acceptance to provide both the motivation for action and the happy ending. First, there is the *universalist* theme that depicts gay families as not really so different after all. Second, we have the *still abject adolescent* theme (e.g., the TV series *Glee*, which features an array of sexual- and gender-variant youth; news stories on teen suicides; the "It Gets Better" project) that does at least speak of continued homophobia even as it assures us that progress is most assuredly being made. Lastly, and perhaps most promisingly, is the charmingly innovative *hey kids, let's make an alternative family!* theme, best illustrated in TV shows like *Modern Family* and *Brothers and Sisters* and mainstream magazine stories on the everyday wonders of brave new families.

While an improvement on invisibility for sure, these media images often produce a series of *displacements*, much as tolerance displaces the challenge that gay inclusion offers up to us all. First, *homophobia* is displaced or ignored. This is most vividly illustrated when our dominant cultural message, embraced and promoted by straight allies and gays alike, is that the battle for gay rights is largely over and all that remains is to tidy up the marriage laws and tone down school bullying. In so many contemporary TV programs and popular movies that feature gay families, homophobia appears as a relic of the past. And, interestingly, homophobia is now wholly located in adolescence: it is youth who experience it and youth who perpetrate it. Families of origin and society at large (much less the state) are let off the hook. Second, gay difference is displaced through a strategy of benign inclusion and tolerance married with universalism. And third, thoughtful *feminist* reimaginings of kinship and intimacy are decidedly disappeared in the rush to normalize gay families through recognizable gender binaries. And no recent representation is more guilty on this last count than the critically acclaimed film of 2010 *The Kids Are All Right*.

## California Dreamin'

*The Kids Are All Right* comes with all the appropriate indie credentials as well as the commercial Hollywood bona fides. Directed and co-written by Lisa Cholodenko—known for the lesbian-themed indie film *High Art* and herself a lesbian mom—and starring Julianne Moore, Annette Bening, and Mark Ruffalo (all A-list Hollywood celebrities with more than a touch of indie hipster cred), it was poised (like *Brokeback Mountain* before it) to be *the* zeitgeist movie on gay families. It was inevitably overburdened as the first mainstream Hollywood film about lesbian moms and their kids. The fact that it featured major stars and garnered critical and popular attention as well as accolades and awards situates it as one of those "symptomatic" texts that exceed their particular moment in history.

*The Kids Are All Right* tells the tale of a long-term lesbian couple, Jules and Nic, with two kids, Laser and Joni. The couple's already frayed relationship is put to the test by the entry into their world of Paul, their sperm donor, who proceeds to bond with the kids and have an affair with Jules, the stay-at-home "wife" of masculinized workaholic/alcoholic Nic.[17] While acclaimed high and low by the mainstream media and the more-Hollywood-friendly gay media (e.g., the *Advocate*),[18] the film did come in for its share of criticism from the more skeptical blogosphere and academically based writers. The recurring theme in this more disapproving discourse centered on the affair between Jules and Paul and what it intimated about lesbian life and sexuality. Feminist and queer academic J. Jack Halberstam, writing in the blog *Bullybloggers*, summarized many of the critiques when she claimed that the "film loads sexual inertia, domestic dowdiness and bourgeois complacency onto the lesbian couple and leaves the sperm donor dad in the enviable position of being free, cool and casually sexual."[19] The irony of glam gals Bening and Moore as sexless and dowdy either points to our cultural inability to imagine lesbian passion (that isn't porn) or our cultural inability to sacrifice hetero star cred at the altar of that passion. In either case, it should go without saying—but I will say it anyway—that as much as I am not the marrying kind, I would of course willingly settle down in miserable (but California sunny) domestic not-bliss with either Annette Bening or Julianne Moore (or, for that matter, the dashing Mark Ruffalo). They are rich, famous, beautiful, and straight: just the way we like our lesbians.

But, to be serious, there is much to concern us here. While the couple's use of gay male porn for Sapphic sex play or the launch of a hetero affair by a putative same-sexer are fairly humdrum and not at all bothersome in some global sense (at least to those of us fairly catholic in our sexual tastes), in the context of the narrative arc of the film, they are troublesome to say the least. For example, had the couple been able to actually use that porn to good effect, it might have been an interesting moment in opening up our imaginations about the diversity of sexual iconography. But like every potential sexual moment between the two women, this one too is short-circuited. They start . . . and can't seem to finish. Every attempt (and there aren't many) of sexual play between the women fails. Now, true enough, one could see this as a commentary on the perils of long-term coupling: the long term derails the coupling, or so we are told. But this is not the desultory disinterest of disaffected dykes but rather the slapstick inability to maintain even a modicum of romantic gravitas. First—contrary to popular opinion—middle-aged lesbians do in fact have sex, and often with each other. Even middle-aged lesbians with children have sex. Really. Alas, not in Hollywood, even when the lesbians are hetero-pretty Moore and Bening. Paired, of course, with the antidote to this lesbian desert of no-desire (hot, penis-happy, passionate hetero romps, replete with lush Garden of Eden fertility imagery), our lesbians suffer not so much from the proverbial bed death but rather its more gruesome second cousin: bed rigor mortis.

Critically, though, this tired phallic narrative (revealed most laughingly when Jules genuflects before Paul's penis) is framed by an even more retro one that situates the film as old-fashioned and horribly sexist in its understanding of gender. In other words, the couple becomes recognizable, if not sympathetic, by trading on one of the most reliably anti-feminist shibboleths of all time: the cold, controlling, and hard-drinking working mom from hell. *The Kids Are All Right* regenders (normatively) what could by all accounts be a queerer (and more feminist) family form. Two women become, in this film, mom and dad, worker and lover, fire and ice, recuperating normative gender roles in a veritable bonanza of binary oppositions.

Further, the abhorrent gender politics of this film provide the vehicle for the equally abhorrent universalizing politics.

One critic inadvertently reveals the gender politics of the film when he writes, "As Nic, the more patriarchal half of a same-sex married couple in Lisa Cholodenko's high-strung comedy *The Kids Are All Right*, she [Bening] wears a short, blunt haircut; drops her voice (she purges the tinkle); and presents to her teenage children, a boy and a girl, a façade of stability, of someone who values structure above all. Nic's political agenda is unspoken but implicit: that two mothers (the other is Jules, played by Julianne Moore) can create a home that's every bit as traditional as one with a mother and father."[20]

One particular three-part scene is emblematic of this overweening (and curiously unnecessary) linkage between lesbian sexual failure, assertive masculinity, and maternal comeuppance. This scene of sexual failure is bookended by two others that reveal the ideological intent. Here, then, in the middle scene, Nic is attempting to romance Jules with a candlelit bath and the hint of more to follow. She is solicitous but controlling and slightly hysterical, a mode carried throughout the film. But amour is not to be, as Nic responds to a phone call from a patient and leaves Jules alone in the tub, frustrated and angry. When Jules finally stalks downstairs, she finds Nic pouring herself a glass of wine and conferring with a patient, having seemingly forgotten the romantic interlude she herself initiated. This moment of clichéd romance derailed by "workaholic" (and possibly alcoholic) behavior is preceded by what can only be understood as the "ball transfer" scene. Here, gently macho Paul has bonded with the teenage son Laser and, in the course of but a few hours, has managed to both diagnose and address Laser's acquiescence to his obviously brutish best buddy, whose rough-and-tumble relationship with his own father sparks poor Laser's desire for daddy action. The mothers— true to form—have been ineffectual in getting Laser to reevaluate his relationship with the clearly unstable young man, but, you know, they don't have balls, so they can't transfer that power to the son. The ball-transfer scene precedes the failed-lesbian-romance scene, which is then followed up by the heterosexual-revelation scene. Here, we witness the first kiss between Jules and sperm man Paul, when they find themselves in a sweaty embrace after working together in the garden—signifying her "natural/real woman" status and sensual fertility in contradistinction to the unnatural, mannish, sterile Nic. So lesbians fail once again at even the most tired clichés of romance. And they fail because mannish working gal Nic can't tear herself away from her work (or her wine). This also, of course, sets up the narrative justification of Jules's betrayal: if Nic had just paid more attention to her (like a real man), she wouldn't have strayed.

## Not-So-Modern Families

So a gender normativity and retro anti-feminism haunt the seemingly delightful *Kids Are All Right*. But equally worrisome is the reliance—both in the film itself and in the reviews—on a universalist framework that effectively "de-gays" this supposedly gayest of films. Like its (non-family-centered) predecessor *Brokeback Mountain*, this universalizing move can be seen most explicitly in both the advertising and the reviews. That "cowboy love story" won over hearts and perhaps even some minds with precisely this strategy of titillating with the new while simultaneously reassuring with the assertion of a universalism of a generic love story. Of course, generic and universal in this sort of a context always really means that heterosexuality is secured as the default point of comparison. *Brokeback Mountain*, then, was sold and marketed and reviewed as the film about gay cowboys that wasn't really about gay cowboys because it was about "love," which is, inevitably if implicitly, heterosexual. In much the same way, *The Kids Are All Right* circulates as both a radically "new" representation of "gay families" while embedding this newness in an overarching universalist discourse of "family." Audiences can tolerate both—the queer cowboys and the lesbian moms—because they are reassured that these stories are not *really* queer stories after all but straight tales in gay drag.

Here, Hollywood wants to have its homosexual difference and contain it too: these movies are marketed as a "new" twist on a universal (read: straight) story of a family trying to make it work and a couple trying to rekindle the flame. So much of the PR (including interviews with the stars, critical reviews, and blogosphere pontificating) went down the well-worn universalist track. Almost every review follows a similar template. So, for example, film critic Roger Ebert tells us that " 'The Kids Are All Right' centers on a lesbian marriage, but is not about one. It's a film about marriage itself, an institution with challenges that are universal." He opines, "I refuse to call it a 'gay film.' I toyed with the idea of not even using the word 'lesbian' and leaving it to you to figure out that the couple was female. This is a romantic triangle happening to involve these three people."[21] A. O Scott, in the *New York Times*, captures perfectly this frisson of difference that titillates even as it reassures us in its normalcy: "But its originality—the thrilling, vertiginous sense of never having seen anything quite like it before—also arises from the particular circumstances of the family at its heart. There is undeniable novelty to a movie about a lesbian couple whose two teenage children were conceived with the help of an anonymous sperm donor. Nic and Jules, a couple with two children, a Volvo and a tidy, spacious house in a pleasant suburban stretch of Southern California, are a picture of normalcy."[22] So what we see here is novelty in the service of normalcy, or as another critic notes, "Genders aside, you know this couple; one of the more satisfying jokes in 'The Kids Are All Right' is that good intentions and parental cluelessness are beyond sexual orientation."[23] Another article, titled "Same Sex—with the Same Family Issues," assures us that " 'The Kids Are All Right' isn't about a gay family; it's about all families."[24] For another critic, "The guiding joke in *The Kids Are All Right* is not that Nic and Jules are a same-sex couple, but that they're so utterly conventional—the kind of healthy-eating, meticulously recycling, solid citizens you might find in any affluent metropolitan enclave."[25] Yes, exactly, and the joke is on us. Or, as the director herself says, "Our intention wasn't overtly political. The subversion, as we saw it, was to be nonpolitical, and just to make this human story that was about a family that people could relate to, no matter what your identity or your sexual preferences were."[26]

Other critics can be even more directly universalizing: "Let's start by getting past any hesitations or reservations about the lesbian household premise on which 'The Kids Are All Right' is based. The issue of gay marriage is not what's on the table here. At its heart, this is a movie about how families, whatever their composition, stay together, love each other through difficult times, and weather the particularly storm-tossed seas that come when the kids hit their teen-age years."[27] Of course, universal means normal means hetero means universal. It's hard to imagine anyone saying, "This is not a film about heterosexual marriage. It's a film about marriage." Not-gay must mean heterosexual, because of the binary we are locked into. So if this is *not* about same-sex marriage, it must be about heterosexual marriage. In this logic, as one reviewer says, all marriages are really heterosexual after all: "More than anything, *The Kids Are All Right* is a film about marriage. Not about gay marriage in particular, though the portrait of this couple's decades-long bond underscores the absur-dity of the debate about what to call same-sex unions. Cholodenko, who has a donor child with her partner, isn't making a rah-rah com-mercial for alternative families—in fact, some gay viewers may bris-tle at the movie's less-than-orthodox take on lesbian sexuality and the complications of donor parenthood. What Cholodenko has aimed for, and achieved, is something bigger: a serious and funny film about the simple yet incomprehensibly fraught act of moving through time with the person you love."[28]

So "something bigger" is of course not something gay or, god forbid, lesbian—that would be a special instance (a special right?). Lesbian relationships are therefore the particular; they point to something else more generic and more important (such as "love" or "marriage," which is universalized as heterosexual). Or, as Howard Bragman, a Hollywood publicist known as the "coming-out guru" for helping gay celebs go public, says, "It's the perfect post-gay film. . . . Gays are just part of the landscape, which is where we want to be."[29]

Even gay pundits were largely celebratory, arguing, as nation-ally syndicated gay columnist Dan Savage did, that the director was brave for engaging in some hard "truth-telling" about the lesbian community. As he says, "Ms. Cholodenko dramatizes some truths about lesbian sexuality and identity that many lesbians are uncomfortable discussing among themselves much less seeing portrayed in a film intended for a general—mostly straight—audience. (A lot of lesbians watch gay male porn; some lesbian-identified women are also attracted to men and sometimes sleep with men. Discuss.) Ms. Cholodenko also portrays a boy raised by a lesbian couple as hungry for male attention. Considering the right-wing attacks on same-sex parents, that's also a brave bit of truth-telling."[30] Hmm. Since when is understanding masculinity as a necessary patrilineage a bit of truth-telling? Seems to me "father knows best" has a quite sturdy hold on American social consciousness and has actually been presented as such a truth that it needs no telling at all.

My issue with *Kids* therefore is not the hetero romp Jules has with Paul (although had it been paired with a lusty lesbian life, it would have been far more interesting) or the use of gay male porn to attempt to spice up the women's sex life or even the depiction of a long-term relationship as sexually and emotionally . . . dry. Really—the affair with the donor is both ludicrous and sad. It is ludicrous because her adoration of his penis is so over the top as to render their first encounter slapstick and cartoonish. But it is also sad because it thoroughly diminishes her as a parent. Truly, the affair itself is not of concern to me, nor is the fact that she has one with a man. But it does defy both logic and some basic tenets of parental decency to embark on an affair with the previously anonymous sperm donor, given that there is a world of men/women out there more than willing to have affairs with gorgeous but neglected lesbian housewives. So our paradigmatic queer moms are crappy parents, crappy lesbians, crappy lovers, crappy everything. To top it all off, these women are not even self-conscious about their "casual" racism, which is most painfully exemplified by using Jules's firing of the hardworking and blameless Mexican gardener to cover up her indiscretion with Paul as the premise for a throw-away joke. While a minor note, it is a telling one in which the single character of color is used as minstrel-show fodder for high hilarity and narrative emptiness.

No, my problem is much more with the reliance on universality, which entails—almost always—a de-gaying of gayness, which gets to the heart of the tolerance trap. This tolerant de-gaying relies on stereotyped gender paradigms so that the women are depicted as—really—just like our neighbors down the street, where daddy goes out to work and mommy stays at home. Lesbian culture and lesbian friends are invisible, and the film erases the extended queer kinship networks that most of us do construct out of both need and desire.[31] This last issue remains—for me at least—the most persistently troubling. If invisibility and sad stereotypes were the problems of the past, then a new glib tokenism and erasure of community seem to be the signs of the difficult present. Gayness is the motivation for these plots but is emptied of any specific (gay) meaning. Instead, these stories offer up a liberal universalism that acts as a cultural pat on the back for tolerant heterosexuals and an accepting hug for assimilated gays.

## Homo Is Where the Heart Is

There is, of course, some value in the normalizing and universalizing move, in demystifying and even accepting that which has been hidden and rejected. In other words, normal and tolerated looks pretty good compared to weird and excluded! But the sociopolitical costs are many and variegated. In the case of this film, the cost is feminism certainly but also any sense of queer parents emerging out of and living within queer communities and culture. The cost of de-gaying gayness—of making it tolerable—is the flattening out or even eviscerating of the deep and abiding intersection of gay social critique with feminist ones. What is also lost is a *critique* of the limitation of heterosexual family forms as well as a *validation* of how queer and feminist families can model challenging alternatives for all of us.

Couldn't we—for a moment—imagine that children of gay parents might indeed walk in a world of more gender play and fluidity, more gender sophistication, and (dare we say it) more righteous political anger? Might we imagine that they not only encounter homophobia along the way but also perhaps a different kind of kinship?

Couldn't we imagine, then, that the kids are not all right but actually better off?[32] Sociologists Judith Stacey and Tim Biblarz have, for example, found just that; in summarizing the research to date, these scholars learned that "more women than men desired egalitarian parenting and work responsibilities," but more relevant to us here, "lesbian coparents seemed to come closer than heterosexual coparents to achieving this."[33] Moreover, gay men didn't just double down on traditional masculinity; rather, the few studies available show "gay men less inclined than heterosexual couples to promote gender conformity in children."[34] Even earlier work by pioneer family sociologists illustrates that gay couples practice more egalitarian relationships.[35]

All this reality is for naught in this particular film, of course. While the queer family *is* reconciled at the end—it takes a male figure (and his overweening phallic presence) to bring them together: he is the catalyst that both disrupts this homo home and gets it back on some semblance of an even keel. He is also the catalyst that prompts the son, Laser, to reject his bullying best friend and the daughter, Joni, to stand on her own two feet: it takes a man, therefore, to set a lesbian family straight.

So these are our lesbians of the moment, mired in anti-feminist tropes of old, rendered sexless and significant only by their reference to universal and normative heterosexuality. But at least, I guess, we are finally seeing some *lesbians* as parents; it remains the case that most gay families represented in popular media consist of male parents who are—by and large—in a lot better shape and are of course most definitely *not* looking for love in all the wrong genitals. Given that lesbian moms remain a far larger segment of the population than gay male parents, this is a curious phenomenon and may have much to do with the potentially more challenging configuration of a home without male presence and dominance. I should also add that the lesbians of contemporary media (including of course our penis-happy Jules) are oddly depicted as endlessly sexually fluid and polymorphous in their desires. Almost all the lesbians are kinda bisexual—you know, that fluid wishy-washy girlie sexuality that just can't make up its mind—while the men, not so much. So our current pop moment connects messy lesbian sexuality with ineffectual parenting and sets this up against sexually stable gay male identity and competent parenting.

If the California mothers are hapless and harried and stereotyped (and living in a world devoid of other queers), then the gay dads of the hit TV sitcom *Modern Family* at least seem to have an occasional homo friend or two and share a giggling awareness of their own embodied stereotypes. The big queen is of course the stay-at-home dad but also the sports-watching handyman. Their mutual embrace of gay effete sensibilities at least pokes fun at the artifice of all sexual identities, even while the show dare not depict even a modicum of physical affection, let alone full-on sexual passion. *Modern Family* too traffics in the universalist tropes in which the gay dads are the tokens that add to the quirky, multiculti stew of "contemporary family life," albeit a very monied one. But while *The Kids Are All Right* hyper-heteros the lesbians (even their tepid butch/femme performance is more reminiscent of '50s housewife/husband relationships than anything found in actual queer intimacies), Cameron and Mitchell are devoutly queer, have at least some modicum of a queer-centered social life, and infuse their parenting with a skittish gay sensibility and (over)awareness of themselves as the stereotypical white gay dads with the adopted Asian baby. Several episodes play this up, most hysterically when they attempt to play "the gay card" in the kindergarten admissions battle and are bested by the interracial lesbian couple with a handicapped child.

The gay marrieds of the nighttime soap *Brothers and Sisters*, on the other hand, are refreshingly physical and surprisingly complex. In the 2010–11 season, they first attempted surrogacy, then adopted an older child, and even expanded their family when the supposedly failed surrogate turned up with a baby in tow. More importantly, the show resists the tokenism that troubles contemporary culture by revealing that the beloved uncle—everyone's surrogate father and go-to guy—is himself gay. Here, as in *Modern Family* but not in our Hollywood indie hit *The Kids Are All Right*, gayness is more richly integrated into the ongoing narrative. The gay dads of *Brothers and*

*Sisters* are not desexualized hetero parental clones but amorous lovers, engaged sons, devoted siblings. They seem to live and love in a world not wholly circumscribed by heterosexuality, and their parenting practices seem at least somewhat informed by alternative sensibilities. These TV fathers fare much better (as parents, as lovers) than the lesbian moms of the big screen. But in all of these, gay parenting is itself rendered both unproblematic to the public at large and not structurally or socially different from heterosexual parenting. Yet scholars have persuasively argued something quite different: that the cumulative research proves unequivocally, first, that gay and lesbian parents "favor comparatively egalitarian and flexible approaches to sharing childcare and breadwinning" and, second, that the belief in inevitable and inherent gender differences is simply unsupported by the evidence.[36]

It is only when we get to gay teens that we are allowed entrée into the persistence of homophobia and the difference sexual difference makes—even as that is eventually and quickly swallowed up in the warm love of family acceptance. Emily of *Pretty Little Liars* and Teddy of *90210* have a moment of closeted turmoil but push open the closet door pretty quickly. Even in *Glee*—where we actually do see homophobia and its effects on the young Kurt—his coming out to his father provides only a simple moment of challenge.[37] Dad's initial difficulty is overcome in one single episode (a queer-positive reeducation faster than a Lindsay Lohan relapse), and he becomes not only open and "accepting" but a brave warrior dad defending his gay son. Indeed, Kurt's gayness is in many ways signified as analogically identical to any of the outsider statuses that the *Glee* kids inhabit—from fat girls to wheelchair-bound boys to teen moms. But at least here, queer kids are not nullified by normalcy: Kurt is the over-the-top, sensitive, show-tune-singing fashionista we all remember fondly from high school drama club. And his encounters with hetero family life don't sacrifice his queerness at the altar of acceptance. His queerness changes others—most dramatically his father—whereas the queerness of the lesbian moms is either an empty sign or a drag on both kids and sexual pleasure. And, later in the series, when sharp-tongued Santana avows her love for the hysterically deadpan cheerleader Brittany, she struggles mightily both with that old interior desire to hide and with the vicious rejection from her beloved *abuela*. We know (this is a sitcom after all) that all will be wrapped up with a song and a dance (in this case, "I Kissed a Girl and I Liked It"), but at least we see queerness *mattering*—to the kids who come out, to the family members who may or may not respond well, to the culture of a school in which anti-gay taunts are still as common as scribbled love notes on a bathroom stall.

Whether in *Ugly Betty* or *Glee* or *Brothers and Sisters* or *The Good Wife* or *Desperate Housewives* or any number of films with the obligatory gay character, hip acceptance and blasé embrace are the rule, not the exception. In most of these worlds, the parents and other family members are benignly embracing of the production of queer families. Now this presents something of a dilemma, for on the one hand only depicting horrified sisters or grandparents refusing to acknowledge their grandchildren would do a disservice to the very real changes in social consciousness that have had very palpable effects on everyday life, including family life. But the rosy picture is not only disingenuous; it can help to present a false sense (which, by the way, many progressive pundits—gay and straight—contribute to) that the battle for gay rights and deep sexual freedom is somehow won or at least largely over. In other words, these family images largely present a world beyond both the closet and serious homophobia. In addition, these images of all-embracing kin help to remythologize family (even after all these years of feminist critique of family life and structure) as the haven in a homo's world. Homophobia is narratively externalized and displaced *outside* the family unit and put on the doorsteps of the Internet (cyberbullying), the judiciary and other institutional locales, and individual "bad" people. Paradoxically, as queer families become more visible, queerness becomes a way to reassert a homogeneous vision of family life.

We need, instead, images of gay kinship that push at the boundaries of "traditional" family values instead of just painting the picket fence in rainbow hues. Why are we seemingly so stuck on imagining queer families as benignly "alternative" and "diverse" instead of force-fully different? Why can't gay parents ever get laid (by the same sex they supposedly desire)? Most illogically perhaps, why are most of the parents we see in popular representations male even when the statistics tell us otherwise? Why are all (televisual, cinematic) parents so wonderfully "accepting" of their queer progeny even as we know queer kids are still getting kicked out of their homes in the "real world" of not-so-hip family life? Perhaps we would do well to queer Tolstoy for a moment: all happy gay families sing show tunes together; every unhappy gay family is unhappy in its own straight way.

Of course, some independent films can and do show queer families in a different register—I think particularly of that wonderful early indie *The Incredibly True Adventures of Two Girls in Love* from 1995, in which you actually were able to lay eyes on the unthinkable: lesbian kids and lesbian parents represented as *different* from their hetero counterparts. But there are glimpses even in mainstream media and mostly in television and not film of a more complicated and interesting take on queer families. I want to mention just two examples. The first is from the brilliant Showtime series *Nurse Jackie*, which features a rich panoply of sexual reprobates. What is important here is that the whole narrative world has already been queered: heterosexual family life is shown as riven with duplicity, there is a strangely macho but also queeny gay male nurse, and the upper-crust British doctor is bisexual (or just promiscuous) and shown with both male and female lovers. Family queerness enters into the workplace when it is revealed that odd duck Dr. Coop has two moms,[38] who then later surprise him with a devastating divorce. Queer family life, then, is woven into a richer tapestry of sexual difference.

Interesting representations of truly queer kinship crops up in unusual places. Probably the most unlikely source is the long-running nighttime soap *Grey's Anatomy*. There have been a number of gay and lesbian characters in this series, but its queer quotient has been ratcheted up in recent years as two of the main female characters navigate a fairly complex relationship, made all the more difficult by differing desires when it comes to reproduction and family life. In a bizarre sequence of events, the lesbian couple (both doctors) end up in their own ER—having spectacularly crashed their car right at the moment of a marriage proposal. To make matters more televisual, lesbian orthopedic surgeon Callie is both gravely injured and blissfully pregnant by her male best friend, the ne'er-do-well with a heart of gold Mark (aka Dr. McSteamy). During the course of numerous episodes, the three of them try to figure out a way to imagine a kind of kinship that includes them all. In one critical scene, Arizona—the girlfriend of injured Callie—and baby daddy Mark (a plastic surgeon, of course) are arguing over Callie's medical care. In true melodramatic style, the car crash has created a medical crisis that may turn on a "save the mother" or "save the baby" decision. Mark, in arguing his point, declares that he is the father, that he is the only one that matters, and that she (Arizona) is "nothing." Now, what is intriguing here is that the series refuses to present the crisis as revolving around a (hetero) couple united by their unborn child. In addition, *homophobia* is made visible, and made visible in a character that is central and that viewers are encouraged to admire and like. Mark does come around and recant (and he realizes that his fatherhood does not trump their shared motherhood), but we can applaud the naming of a persistent homophobia even as we are pained by its explicitness.

These exceptions aside, what remains depressingly the same is the rarity with which queer lives are shown as their own stories, not as signs of hetero hipness or the decline of Western civilization. Those stories still exist but have now largely been ghettoized either to all-gay-all-the-time cable programming or gay film festivals or the rare series such as *Brothers and Sisters*, *L Word*, *Orange Is the New Black*, and the like. The question is, can we have it both ways? Can gay families—particularly feminist, lesbian ones—be radically challenging, deeply different, unmooring our certitudes of kinship and care while at the same time being wholly normalized and unthreatening to hetero family business as usual?

It is no accident that so many of the debates around "gay rights" have been understood as concerns about family and kinship. There are several reasons for this. First, especially in relation to marriage and raising kids, gays counter stereotypes by locating themselves firmly in known family structures. Second, the tragedy of AIDS not only raised the profile of gays more generally but also brought home the life-altering issues of legal rights and access. For those who were turned away at the hospital door after years of caring for a sick partner or who didn't receive survivor benefits or who found themselves cut off from funeral proceedings, the stark reality of legal second-class status hit home. In addition, AIDS of course brought many gay people—many unwillingly—out of the closet to their parents, many of whom then cared for them and watched them die.

Gay families therefore exist in a complicated *context*, and we need representations of these multilayered communities: we need images that depict the work that goes into making communities happen. Still and all, what we largely see is the lone queer (or now queer family) navigating her way through the thickets of hetero life and missing out on that broader social and political community. In other words, these gay families might be shown to refuse to reduce queer struggles to "gay rights" or—god forbid—"gay marriage" or "gays in the military." A more prosaic and multilayered queer politics should be part of the context of these familial images instead of the sterile world of deracinated lesbian suburbanites we see in *The Kids Are All Right*.

We need to imagine, perhaps, a different relationship between being seen and being known. As queer theorist David Halperin archly complains, "Is the whole purpose of gay politics, or gay culture, to return gay people to the fold of middle-class heterosexual family life, with all its obligatory rites and rituals—to enable us to reproduce the worst social features, the most ghastly clichés of heterosexuality?"[39] We need, instead, to insist that our families might just be radically different (not just modern or California hip) in ways that upend heterosexist business as usual and provide a template for imagining kinship in the future tense.

# PART IV

# *Escape from the Tolerance Trap*

Heterosexuality is not normal, it's just common.
—Dorothy Parker

What do you mean, you "don't believe in homosexuality"? It's not like the Easter Bunny, your belief isn't necessary.
—Lea DeLaria

And now I will tell you what we want, we radical homosexuals: not for you to tolerate us, but to understand us. And this you can only do by becoming one with us.        —Martha Shelley

A minority is only thought of as a minority when it constitutes some kind of threat to the majority, real or imaginary. And no threat is ever quite imaginary.        — Christopher Isherwood

# IO

# Is That All There Is?

In 2013, the Organization for Economic Cooperation and Development released a report that concluded that equal rights generally make for happier citizens. No surprise really, but perhaps a bit more interesting is the finding that "all of the highest ranking countries are accepting of homosexuality, support equal rights and have laws protecting gay people. All of the top 10 countries have legislation in place to protect citizens against discrimination based on sexual orientation."[1]

I can imagine a future—perhaps one I will live in—that looks something like those countries, where all the major structural impediments are gone. Where all those official markers of civic inclusion are, finally, shared by gays and lesbians. I look forward to that day. But I don't for a moment think that day will, in and of itself, herald that deeper citizenship we all yearn for. That citizenship is not measured merely by the removal of official condemnation and official door opening. That citizenship is not (only) a vote, a job, a march to war, a marriage. Belonging is not measured thus. We all experience the difference between formal inclusion and deep belonging every day. At the best of times, we feel that belonging in our families—those of choice or of origin—where we feel we are known, are even adored sometimes. We can feel it with a lover; indeed, the language of official romance is riddled with that undoubtedly mythical but always iconic sense of affiliation to and for another. We can feel it in the workplace, sometimes, when we experience a meaningful and productive connection with our co-workers, an abiding sense of mutual appreciation. We often experience it in political movements, when our hearts and souls are joined in shared struggle. Tolerance doesn't come into the equation. What we might call "substantive citizenship" is not captured by the weak language of acceptance or the tepid embrace of tolerance but rather by the richness of real inclusion and robust integration and investment.

So what constitutes full citizenship for lesbians and gays? Repeal of anti-sodomy laws? Hate crimes legislation? Gay marriage? Formal nondiscrimination policies in employment? And what of global gays and the relationship between local battles for civil rights and assumptions of human dignity on a transnational scale? What of immigration and political asylum? Debates over citizenship in fact provoke further debate around the political goals and strategies of the LGBTQ movement. That in turn raises the issue of what is the cause or motivating factor for the subordination of LGBTQ people. Is it some aversion to same-sex desire and sex? Is it the challenge to gender norms that inevitably arises when relationships move outside the "different but complementary" ideology of heterosexual attraction? Is it because the nonprocreative potential of gay life renders gays supposedly unfit for marital/family life? Is it—at core—religious in origin? What fantasies of the "nation" are being "protected" against the incursion of these Others? What relationships are imagined as being threatened by legalizing other types of intimacy? What kind of sex is understood as "good" when some forms are subject to the penalties of the law?

In other words, digging through the explicit issue of citizenship rights forces us to go both beneath and above—to think through what underlying animus motivates discrimination and what overarching principles structure possibilities for inclusion. This is not to say that animus is necessarily rational; it is often predicated on myths and perpetuated by unfounded stereotypes and outright falsehoods. Even deeper, it can tap into terrors of sex, of the dirty or wretched, of the very stuff of the body. But it is to say that thinking through how humans turn other humans into outsiders who must be pushed out, limited, denied, vilified requires attention to both the intimate and structural levels.

## A Glass Half Full

So have the battles largely been won in America? Are gays full citizens? Surely, they vote, they hold passports, they move freely, they live in the suburbs and the cities, the country and the rural enclave. They can run for office and hold most jobs. Other signs are even more promising: looked at from a purely quantitative level, there has been a steady shift in public attitudes toward lesbians and gays. As political scientist Paul Brewer notes,

> One point is already clear: public attitudes about homosexuality changed dramatically over the course of the 1990's. . . . The percentage of General Social Survey respondents stating that "sexual relations between two adults of the same sex" is "always wrong" was fairly stable from 1973 to 1988; if anything, there was a small increase in hostility toward homosexuality during this period. From 1992 onward, however, such hostility decreased rapidly. In 1992, 71% of the GSS respondents chose the "always wrong" option; in 1994, 63% did; by 1998, only 54% did.[2]

The same shifts—by and large—hold true about specific issues, such as service in the military and employment rights.

The most recent polls on public attitudes toward lesbians and gays show even more encouraging change, particularly among young people. These changes are linked to any number of factors, including the increasing visibility of gays in the public sphere and, most dramatically, the concurrence between personally knowing someone who is gay and having more "accepting" views of gays in general. Signal events like the murder of Matthew Shepard or the suicide of a gay teen or—less dramatically—the Supreme Court decision of *Lawrence*—all shape as well as reflect public opinion. Some people

attribute the growing "tolerance" of straight men for gay men as produced in part because straight men don't want to be associated with
anti-gay attitudes, since there is certainly a prevalent "notion that
homophobia in some men could be a reaction to their own homosexual impulses."[3] So, in that sense, if homophobia equals homosexual
tendencies, then it is most decidedly uncool to be anti-gay!

As discussed earlier, the shift around marriage rights has been
especially dramatic. A May 8, 2012, Gallup poll showed that 50 percent of Americans support legalizing same-sex marriage, down a bit
from a 2011 poll which showed a majority for the first time. The
most recent polls pull it into "strong majority" category, ranging
anywhere from 52 percent to as high as 58 percent. This majority
becomes significantly larger when we look at younger respondents,
who are noticeably more "accepting" of lesbians and gays around a
variety of questions from marriage to, as the polls put it, "moral legitimacy" (whatever that is!). Indeed, even this notoriously immovable
question (of the "legitimacy" of homosexuality) has shifted in most
polls, so a slim majority no longer deems gays and lesbians morally
reprehensible. Another strong sign of the shift on marriage is the fact
that of the thirteen states (plus DC) that now allow same-sex marriage, three—Maine, New Hampshire, and Vermont—legalized the
practice through a vote by the state legislature, without prodding by
a court.[4]

There are more gays and lesbians serving openly in public office
—from the city councils to the statehouse to the Congress and federal government. The Victory Fund, an organization which works
to get openly gay candidates elected at all levels of government,
documented the dramatic shift from 257 openly gay and lesbian
elected officials in 2001 to over 500 in 2012. Of the 180 candidates
the organization endorsed in the 2012 elections, 123 were victorious—a strong showing by any measure. Many of these officials are
in unlikely places—as sheriffs in Texas, mayors in towns small and
large, southern and eastern—and the Fund now claims that there
is an elected openly LGBTQ official in all fifty states, including of
course the first open lesbian elected to the Senate, Tammy Baldwin of

Wisconsin. In schools throughout the country, gay-straight alliances have blossomed, and anti-bullying mandates that include gender expression and sexual orientation have become part of the everyday practice of much of the country. Many state governments and the federal government prohibit employment discrimination against gays and lesbians; at last count, twenty-one states and the District of Columbia had such laws, and over 140 cities and counties have enacted such bans. The shifts on the state level seem to be some of the most profound and fast moving, with one researcher arguing that "issues of gay rights are mainly state issues, so the focus for activism is going to be on the local level."[5] Gay voters are courted as a significant political bloc in both national and local elections, and politicians regularly solicit gay donors and gay votes at fundraisers and political events. Gay Pride Month is celebrated from the streets of San Francisco to the grandeur of the White House.

The world of business, once a redoubt of the closet, now is just as likely to include a gay and lesbian staff association as a bowling league. The Fortune 500 compete for "most diverse" workplace and proudly wave the rainbow flag as a sign to both potential consumers of their products ("Buy from us! We're hip and gay friendly!") and potential workers ("Work for us! You can bring your domestic partner to the corporate picnic and no one will care!"). And if being commodified is one, sad perhaps, sign of citizenship, then things are moving along at a rapid clip. From gay-wedding planners (or, should I say, planners of gay weddings, who may or may not be gay, . . . although my money is on gay all the way) to corporate sponsorship of gay pride marches and gay film festivals, "gay" money is courted, solicited, sought after, particularly in political campaigns. And this is to say nothing of the continued presence of gay and lesbian and, to a lesser extent, transgendered characters in prime-time and cable TV and indie and Hollywood films. Though these characters are still an afterthought to the main drama of heterosexual lives and too often tokenized as the happy-go-lucky homo friend every hip (hetero) girl or guy should have, it is nevertheless a long way from the days of backhanded stereotypes and predictable invisibility.

## Or Mostly Empty?

But just as surely as times have changed, gays continue to be excluded from a number of central social institutions in which citizenship has often adhered. While it may not happen often, gays can be fired from jobs and have little recourse legally, unlike other minority groups. In some states, gays cannot adopt children. In others, they cannot foster them. Until recently, we still had the discriminatory military policy known as "Don't Ask, Don't Tell" and the obnoxious Defense of Marriage Act (and even that has not been fully repealed), and there are local DOMAs in place in states around the nation. The Employment Non-Discrimination Act has not yet passed. Gay kids are still disproportionately likely to commit suicide and to be homeless, and hate crimes stubbornly persist.

And our political culture continues to operate either in typically homophobic ways or, alternately, through a self-congratulatory tolerance of a minimum of gay rights. Truly, blatant forms of mainstream anti-gay activism have not disappeared from the political scene. The Republican governor of Virginia, Bob McDonnell, began his tenure in 2010 by removing sexual orientation from state anti-discrimination protections, and a few news organizations covered it; but, you know, he did it and did not get drummed out of office for such an aggressive act of discrimination. His attorney general (now gubernatorial candidate), Ken Cuccinelli, has gone even further, "urging" the state's public colleges and universities to rescind policies that ban discrimination on the basis of sexual orientation. A mayor of a small town in California is deposed by the city council when she moved to sign a proclamation declaring June a month of gay pride. A few years ago, Scott Brown—the Massachusetts miracle boy adored by mainstream America—attacked fellow state senator Cheryl Jacques for her decision to have a baby with her female partner, saying the situation was "unusual for two women . . . in terms of what's normal in today's society."[6] If that's not open homophobia, I don't know what is—and yet it has hardly held him back in his move through political life.

Michele Bachmann, a *Daily Show* joke but a member of Congress and, for a bit, a viable presidential candidate, said, "If you're involved in the gay and lesbian lifestyle, it's *bondage*. It is personal bondage, personal despair and personal enslavement."[7] And her fellow Republican primary candidate (and senator) Rick Santorum offers an endless supply of anti-gay epithets, including a remark he made on the stump about the nonexistent rights of lesbian mothers: "A lesbian woman came up to me and said, 'Why are you denying me my right?' I said, 'Well, because it's not a right. It's a privilege that society recognizes because society sees intrinsic value to that relationship over any other relationship.'"[8] The remarks—both casual and deliberate—from politicians, elected officials, TV anchors, sports figures, Hollywood celebrities, and religious leaders would fill up this entire book—and several more.

Indeed, outright opposition to gay equality—whether in the form of marriage equality, workplace equality, or service equality—seems not to be a barrier to political legitimacy at all: quite the contrary. Just look at the president on marriage equality (he was against it before he "evolved" and became for it) or on the ease of inviting anti-gay leaders into the fold of official legitimacy. One way in which gays have been no different from any other minority group clamoring for their rights is in their deep disappointment with political leaders who—only recently to be sure—have promised much and delivered little. From Bill Clinton caving in on gays in the military to Barack Obama's drawn-out dismantling of it, gays have often found themselves taken for granted in (Democratic) party politics, prompting longtime activist Richard Socarides (ironically, the son of the late Charles Socarides, a psychiatrist and founder of the National Association for Research & Therapy of Homosexuality, who spent his entire career arguing that homosexuality could be changed) to ask of the Obama administration, "Where is our New Deal?"[9] For many, Obama's indecisiveness and reluctance to act aggressively on any number of gay rights issues (from ENDA to DADT to gay marriage to the insult of inviting anti-gay pastor Rick Warren to give an invocation at his first inaugural) is particularly galling, not only because he promised so much but because—in the estimation of many—the time is particularly ripe for substantive movement on these issues. Socarides and many others felt early disappointment with Obama and urged him to "champion comprehensive, omnibus federal gay civil rights legislation, similar to the Civil Rights Act of 1964, outlawing discrimination based on sexual orientation and granting a basic umbrella of protections in employment, education, housing and the like (rather than the existing piecemeal approach to legislation). Such a bill should also provide for federal recognition of both civil unions and marriages as they are authorized by specific states."[10] Like other minorities who have pinned their hopes for redress on a Democratic Party that at least claimed some degree of sympathy, gays found themselves profoundly disappointed.

The historic election of Obama was itself a site of much bitter irony. Here was the first African American elected to president in this country—supported overwhelmingly by LGBTQ voters who celebrated wildly on election night and, later, at the inauguration. I was among those celebrants. That same election night victory coincided with a stunning defeat, as California approved Prop 8, overturning the state's previous decision legislating gay-marriage rights; Arkansas passed a ban on same-sex adoption, and Arizona and Florida easily passed bans on same-sex marriage.

Or let's consider the 2012 brouhaha over the anti-gay-marriage comments by Chik-fil-A president and longtime anti-gay donor Dan Cathy. The comments themselves were of the run-of-the-mill kind, invoking God's wrath on heathen homos everywhere (and the straight heathens that love them too). Activists and political figures condemned Cathy's remarks and tried to find ways to distance themselves from the chain and its products, yet more than six hundred thousand RSVPed on Facebook for a "Chik-fil-A Appreciation Day" initiated by former Arkansas governor and candidate for president Mike Huckabee. The chain reported record sales (even though "kiss-ins" by gay rights groups tried to undercut the Appreciation Day efforts), and many of the Facebook posts echoed those of one commentator who stated, "It's a shame that the gay community that asks for tolerance is so intolerant of other opinions." Tolerance trap indeed!

Another stunning example of the tolerance trap at work is the recent decision to allow gay youth to serve as Boy Scouts. This vote was a long time coming. And there was some real dedicated activism on this issue, particularly from Scouts who had been booted out in the past, and online petitions to change the discriminatory policy garnered over two million signatories. In addition, many of the corporations and organizations that had historically supported the Boy Scouts had already pulled funding in response to earlier Boy Scouts reiterations of anti-gay policy. In particular, big guns Merck and Intel had ended their financing because the Boy Scouts' policies violated their own nondiscrimination policies. More corporations and more localities have anti-discrimination policies or anti-discrimination legislation on their books, so it became more difficult for them to do business with an organization that explicitly discriminated.

On the one hand, this is a victory; a discriminatory organization has stopped discriminating. But, of course, it's only partial. The Boy Scouts wouldn't even bring up the question of gay Scout *leaders*, for fear of a mass exodus from the organization. This message implies that gay *kids* can be Boy Scouts because they're "just kids," but grown-up homosexuals remain a threat, remain a danger. All the animus against gay *adults* is allowed to fester and stay strong and is thus displaced rather than eliminated in the move to allow gay youth in but continue to exclude adults.

But the words of Wayne Brock, the Boy Scouts of America's chief executive, illustrate the tolerance frame of mind. He reportedly said, when asked about the change of position, that "this is not about what's legal but what's compassionate, caring and kind."[11] What a paternalistic sentiment. Actually, *it is* about doing the legal, right, ethical thing, and kindness and compassion have nothing to do with it. It's about following a basic ethic of citizenship. We're all created equal. We pay our taxes, we are citizens. We should have the right to marry, the ability to serve in jobs without fear of discrimination, the same legal rights as anyone. Civil rights are about equality and ethical inclusion. But so much of our contemporary discourse about gay and lesbian lives is couched in this language of tolerance, acceptance, compassion, and caring. And who doesn't like those things? Yet that is not what a meaningful civil rights movement is based on. It is based on deep integration, inclusion, the rule of law, the celebration of difference, and substantive equality.

## Post-Gay or Just Tepid Tolerance

The preceding section provides just a few examples of continuing discrimination, but they are important ones to indicate that real structural impediments keep gays from achieving entry into these iconic institutions, an inclusion which is not in itself the sign of full citizenship in any case, as I've been arguing throughout this book. We can and must applaud all the amazing movement forward. But look a bit deeper, and the picture—even at the polling level—becomes much more troubling. Let me start with the headline of one Gallup poll. If you came across this in your email inbox, it would be hard not to mistake it for a caption from the satirical magazine the *Onion*: "For third year, majority says gay/lesbian relations are morally acceptable."[12] I don't know whether to laugh or cry at such a declaration. Have no doubt, this is being reported as a good and tolerant trend, or as the bigger Gallup byline says, "U.S. Acceptance of Gay/Lesbian Relations Is the New Normal." So someone—not gays presumably—is adjudicating the moral acceptability and normality of gayness.

And here is the tolerance trap at work; as gays are "accepted," they are reminded that their very *legitimacy* (their acceptability) is contingent on someone else deeming it so, someone else who needs no accepting, whose moral certitude needs no certification, someone whose citizenship (US) precedes and excludes gayness because gayness is something that they can decide whether or not to accept, whether or not to tolerate.

How strange that the very question of gay rights still hinges on whether or not heterosexuals deem gays morally acceptable. And how far this is from earlier challenges to anti-gay discrimination such as that of gay rights pioneer Frank Kameny, whose petition to the Supreme Court in 1961, protesting his 1957 dismissal from the

US Map Service of the US Army, "asserts, flatly, unequivocally, and absolutely uncompromisingly, that homosexuality, whether by mere inclination or by overt act, is not only not immoral, but that for those choosing voluntarily to engage in homosexual acts, such acts are moral in a real and positive sense, and are good, right, and desirable, socially and personally."[13] Here, way back in 1961, his strong words express not only the *absence* of a quest for tolerance or acceptance but the *presence* of a "gay is good" positivity.

The confusion between laws, public policy, court rulings, and public opinion is profound. The majority of Americans now support same-sex marriage, the Supreme Court gives it a tentative green light, and yet state laws continue to oppose it. For years, polls have shown strong opposition to discrimination against gays in employment, yet we still are unable to pass ENDA. All right-thinking people of course believe in equal rights and love their gay neighbors, but even the most optimistic polls reveal that almost half still don't think gays should marry or adopt, although they are certainly happier to see gays carry a gun into battle! And, importantly, when asked more general questions about the "morality" or general "goodness" of homosexuality, an even stronger minority firmly comes down on the "gays are immoral deviants" side of the equation.

So it is hard to get excited by finally crossing the 50 percent mark of folks who find "gay and lesbian relations" morally acceptable. That means half don't or, if we're being more generous, half are less apt to fully assume gay equality. And what is even meant by "gay and lesbian relations" (and what is meant by "morally acceptable")? The very fact that these questions are framed thus undermines the salience of the result. But for the general public, these polls—along with the happy-go-lucky gay characters on TV and same-sex wedding announcements in your hometown paper—serve as collective signs of victory over anti-gay bigotry. The prevalent cultural narrative—among both the Left and the Right—is that the battle for gay rights has largely been won, that this particular battlefront in the culture war is no longer a viable one. Not surprisingly, it is conservative and lukewarm liberal pundits who tend to see the glass as much more than half full, particularly when comparing the 2004 election cycle (in which gay rights played a significant part) to the 2008 or 2012 cycles, in which gay rights issues seemed less significant. For these writers, "the cultural backlash against gay equality is far from over, and the marriage fight, in particular, has years to go. But the core message of legal equality has gotten through."[14] For conservative gay writers such as Jonathan Rauch, gays themselves need to imagine a shift because "the civil rights mind-set, with its focus on antidiscrimination laws and court-ordered remedies, has outlived its usefulness."[15] In this view, gays are no longer an oppressed minority and therefore need to focus less on classic civil rights agendas (e.g., ENDA) and more on what Rauch—and many others—see as the pièce de résistance of gay integration: "the culturally transformative family agenda."[16]

Liberal allies couldn't help joining in on the chorus that declared gay rights a done deal. *New York Times* columnist Frank Rich argued that "there is now little political advantage to spewing homophobia. Indeed, anti-gay animus is far more likely to repel voters than attract them. Now that explicit anti-gay animus is an albatross, those who oppose gay civil rights are driven to invent ever loopier rationales for denying those rights, whether in the military or in marriage.[17] And Leslie Savan, reliable progressive writing for the *Nation*, similarly claims that "the Republican Party that won the White House in 2004 by vowing to protect us from homosexual terrorists has simply lost on the entire issue."[18]

Some critics want to have their post-gay and deny it too. Rich, who seems to personify this ambivalence, at times argues that we are in the death throes of anti-gay bigotry. But when an explicitly anti-gay event pops up—such as the removal of *A Fire in My Belly* (a film by the late gay artist David Wojnarowicz)—from a 2010 National Portrait Gallery exhibit, he claims that "the incident is chilling because it suggests that even in a time of huge progress in gay civil rights, homophobia remains among the last permissible bigotries in America."[19] In the same article, he claims that this is a "throwback to the culture wars we thought we were getting past now" but then later tacks again, arguing that we have "an unwritten rule in estab-lishment Washington that homophobia is at most a misdemeanor."[20] So anti-gay animus is now, in Rich's words, an "albatross," but it is nevertheless "among the last permissible bigotries in America." I don't mean to pick on devoted ally Frank Rich here but rather to suggest that his ambivalence about the state of gay rights is framed in by the goal of tolerance; tolerance traps us in a false storyline in which the end is always in sight and "setbacks" are merely bumps in the inevitable road forward.

If reputable journalists like Rich are quaffing the post-gay punch, then Linda Hirshman—author of *Victory: The Triumphant Gay Revolution*—has added some vodka and a twist. While a wonder-ful compendium documenting the trials and triumphs of the move-ment from the early pre-Stonewall days, through AIDS and to the present, *Victory* paints a portrait too rosy by half. By relegating dis-crimination and violence to the sideline, continued anti-gay animus becomes merely a footnote in the quest to tell a simple story of prog-ress and redemption. She tellingly ends the book with iconic images of marriage and the military, followed by a tepid epilogue in which she gives the briefest of afterthoughts to continued homophobia.

For many popular writers, politics has simply not caught up with the changes on the cultural level. Adam Nagourney, writing in the *New York Times*, claims our current moment is paradoxical: "Even as cultural acceptance of homosexuality increases across the country, the politics of gay rights remains full of crosscurrents. . . . Yet if the culture is moving on, national politics is not, or at least not as rapidly."[21] Rich agrees that "we've come a long way in a short time, but . . . glee for gay people in America still does not match 'Glee' on Fox. Until the law catches up with the culture, the collec-tive American soul should find even June's wedding Champagne a bit flat."[22] For these pundits, the political lag is mostly just strategic realpolitik and at odds with a fundamentally changed social reality. Many politicians and political consultants, such as Virginia Demo-cratic adviser Dave Saunders, agree with the pundits that, while big-otry still abides, there "are signs that the issue is not as pressing or toxic as it once was." Saunders echoes a dominant political sentiment when he claims that being gay or being strongly for gay rights is not "the political deal-breaker it once was" because "most people out here really don't care because everybody has gay friends."[23] Gay leaders such as former Massachusetts congressman Barney Frank seem to echo this optimism by claiming, "the diminution of the homophobia has been as important a phenomena as anything we've seen in the last 15 years."[24] And many claim politics will eventually, automatically, inevitably "catch up"—not only because "everyone knows someone who is gay" but also because they see a huge generational divide on this issue, with younger voters less and less prejudicial against gays.

Many analysts, therefore, want to have it both ways: to argue that—as a nation—we are ripe and ready for full gay rights, that the change is there for the taking, and, simultaneously, that we are still second-class citizens. All these arguments, however, depend on a shared assumption: the vast majority of Americans are more "tolerant" toward gays and lesbians than ever before, our cultural world is more open and visible, and it is just legislation and craven political posturing that keeps us from achieving full citizenship for lesbians and gays. Rich argues that politicians need not be so timid, as "the cultural climate is far different today. . . . Gay civil rights history is moving faster in the country, including on the once-theoretical front of same-sex marriage, than it is in Washington."[25]

Alongside this "politics will catch up" idea is the underlying thesis that even recalcitrant politicians will eventually see the light as they get to know gays personally. As Rich again assures us, "As more gay people have come out—a process that accelerated once the modern gay rights movement emerged from the Stonewall riots of 1969—so more heterosexuals have learned that they have gay relatives, friends, neighbors, teachers and co-workers. It is hard to deny our own fundamental rights to those we know, admire and love."[26] Polls have in fact shown a steep rise in the numbers of people who say they have a family member or close friend who is gay or lesbian.[27] While this certainly has some truth to it, there are a number of problems in this formulation—many of which I discussed earlier around the "familiarity" arguments. Mass coming out—and the intimate sites where this takes place—can and does change attitudes and might even challenge more deep-seated homophobia. It is a necessary, but not sufficient, condition for social change. One can break bread with a gay neighbor, love a gay sister, share confidences with a gay co-worker but still frame that embrace in a benign tolerance that lets the structural dominance of heterosexuality go unexamined.

Surely, as has been well documented in this book and others, there have been enormous changes in civil rights for gays and lesbians, hard-won over decades of activism. But it is equally true that we must challenge this too-easy triumphant story that posits a "post-gay" world of almost-achieved acceptance or that sees "setbacks" as evidence of a few recalcitrant retrogrades. The evidence is simply much more tenuous and fractured and the depth and range of anti-gay animus too potent and wily a force. The reality, therefore, is that the face of emergent gay citizenship is deeply contradictory.

The bottom line remains this: wouldn't the world look different (like, perhaps, more openly gay politicians, teachers, CEOs, even actors!) if real citizenship had been achieved? In truth, the closet (or some more modern and comfy version of it) remains the place many, many—if not most—gays remain. If we were truly living in a brave new gay-friendly world, wouldn't it be, well, more gay? Wouldn't there be more than one Ellen out there? More than one Barney Frank? Wouldn't pollsters stop asking about "our" tolerance of "them"?

## Does It Get Better?

In 2008, a fifteen-year-old gender nonnormative gay boy was shot to death in his junior high school by a classmate. In 2010, a college student jumped off a bridge to his death after he was surreptitiously videotaped having sex with another man. In 2010, again, two gay teenage boys in the Midwest killed themselves. In 2011, a twenty-one-year-old Portland, Oregon, lesbian youth activist was brutally beaten while witnesses neglected to come to her aid. In January 2012, eighteen-year-old Jeffrey Fehr of California hanged himself outside his parents home. Though he had been out for several years, his parents said the harassment he had faced wore him down.[28] In June of that same year, sixteen-year-old Brandon Elizares from El Paso, Texas, committed suicide the day after getting threatening texts from a classmate. His mother said he had been harassed at school and by his family since coming out two years earlier.[29] In May 2013, a thirteen-year-old openly gay boy from California was beaten by a group of four boys while he was walking home from school. He said he didn't recognize any of them, but they knew his name and hurled anti-gay epithets at him while they beat him.[30] The list doesn't begin there and surely doesn't end there either. And the lines of simple causality are always murkier than immediately apparent, rendering the line from teasing to bullying to abuse to death often circuitous and hard to pin down. But there were and are many more incidents, most of them ignored by the media. Some make headlines, some go to trial, and others are just footnotes in the story of everyday violence. This is at least some part of the story of gay life today.

In response to these and other cases of suicide, bullying, and murder, gay columnist Dan Savage and his partner, Terry Miller, uploaded a video on YouTube designed to impart a message of hope and possibility to gay youth. The message was quite simple: acknowledging the extra hardness accompanying the lives of queer kids but at the same time assuring them "it gets better," that adult gay life carries with it less sadness and brutality and is, well, easier and even happier. The rest, as they say, is viral. The "It Gets Better" project was born, rebirthed countless times, debated, lampooned, laughed over, cried about. Politicians and celebrities—including the president and Lady Gaga—recorded their own "It Gets Better" spots, and a social media moment entered into the record books. For some people, it was a crucial opportunity to bring straight "allies" into the fold, to enlist people of goodwill (and good celebrity cred!) into the battle for the souls of queer youth.

Others were more critical. For many gay activists and academics, "It Gets Better" was a campaign both phony and potentially dangerous. On the one hand, it posited gay youth as inherently in crisis, always on the brink of abuse or self-annihilation. So, in that sense, it painted an overly *gloomy* picture of what it is like to live as gay (or trans or bi) in the world as we know it. And on the other hand, it painted an overly *rosy* picture of adult queerness, fully embraced, successful, freed of the ugliness of anti-gay animosity. A new picture curiously like the poster-boy images of white, male, urban, successful entrepreneur Dan Savage himself. So maybe the (unintended) message was really that it gets better if you are white, male, normatively gendered, and middle class. Moreover, the "It Gets Better" campaign, however it began, was quickly rolled into a slick media trajectory that itself became the story, so that the nitty-gritty and complicated situation of life for so many gay teens got lost in celebrities' rush to associate themselves with a trendy new "message."

Nevertheless, one of the benefits of an Internet campaign like this is that it is uncontrollable—the critique itself becomes part of the discourse, and new campaigns emerge to address the absences in the original, campaigns such as "Make It Better" and "We Got Your Back Project," which are both more action oriented in their approach to gay youth and more cognizant of how racial, class, and gender difference plays out in the context of bullying and anti-gay violence. My take on it all is that "It Gets Better" was mercifully more expansive and complicated than its originator, Dan Savage, whose hubris comes through when he claims that the project "brought the old order crashing down."[31]

It is curious that in the age of the suicidal (or harassed or bullied or murdered) gay teen as public figure of pathos and presidential concern, we are also in thrall to Kurt, the kinda tortured but mostly show-tune-happy dandy of *Glee*, the teen TV phenomenon. Perhaps Kurt himself embodies the glib "it gets better" ethos, turning ostracized anguish into empowered identity politics in the move from sophomore to junior. So is the gay citizen boy or man, girl or woman? Is our reference point the bullied and wounded child, for surely the child is the citizen-to-be? Or is it the integrated and happy adult, stronger for having weathered the slings and arrows of outrageous homophobia?

# 11

# When the Rainbow Isn't Enough

In the great—and pretty gay—musical *Rent*, a rousing and poignant song marks the death of a character from AIDS, asking us, "How do you measure a life?" Of course, since it is a Broadway musical, the answer is "love." But how do you measure the success of a social movement? The gay rights saga is, like so many other stories of integration and inclusion, complicated and filled with contradictions. Truth be told, I can't make up my mind about it half the time! I am torn, like many people, I think, between a celebration of the real changes and despair over the persistence of anti-gay animus. I may be ambivalent about breaking out the champagne just yet, but I am absolutely *unambivalent* that tolerance and acceptance forestall any real victory; they will never really reckon with that animus or open the door to a new world of free gender and sexual expression. As I've detailed throughout this book, the triumphant story of a fully tolerant and inclusive society is just plain wrong on so many counts. Tolerance is the wrong goal, and inclusion is only an attenuated reality.

Nevertheless, I do know this world is assuredly better than those fashion-challenged and isolated late '70s when I came out. I was particularly struck by this when I took a look at the Democratic Party platform and convention of 2012—in which marriage equality, passage of ENDA, and the end to anti-gay discrimination were central and unequivocal. When speaker after speaker proclaimed the right to marry whom you love as a core value of being American (and gay speakers were themselves part of the lineup), you did have to shake your head in wonderment. As gay historian Eric Marcus noted, the convention participants were "actually wearing their pro-gay agenda as a badge of honor. What a transformed world from my youth."[1] Headshaking for me, too. And the second inaugural speech of President Obama brought tears to the eyes of many when, for the first time in the history of inaugural addresses, he eloquently invoked Stonewall in the litany of historic civil rights watersheds and further staked his claim by declaring, "Our journey is not complete until our gay brothers and sisters are treated like anyone else under the law— for if we are truly created equal, then surely the love we commit to one another must be equal as well."[2]

Let's stay with these political watersheds for a moment, for although they are bits of highly choreographed theater and at times seem more infomercial than democracy in action, they are also spaces for the public display of national belief, at least national belief as embodied in the major political parties. Of course, I cannot help but throw a bit of cold water on these happy occasions. For it is worrisome that, in the inaugural address, Obama's rhetorical move is from Stonewall to a generic call for equal treatment and then to the manifestation of that equality in marital love. Once again, even in this historic moment of presidential recognition, the vast panoply of sexual and civil rights is reduced to access to one institution: marriage.

But back to those convention speeches. At the Democratic one, gay rights were embraced in the form of marriage equality and military service. Freedom to marry and freedom to serve are the watchwords of the these movements; both rely on classic liberal egalitarian and civil rights arguments to make the case for gaining access to these two social institutions. Both discourses depend (variously) on notions of immutability, discretion, and blending in to argue that gays in the military, or gays in marriages, will not "damage" the institutions themselves or even fundamentally alter them. For these convention speakers—and for many activists, writers, and politicians—given the centrality of military service and marriage to national status and citizenship, these two represent the nail in the coffin of institutionalized homophobia and the sign of full inclusion.[3] Now, this is wholly understandable given how marriage in particular has become the litmus test for all things gay. The symbolic and iconic value of victories such as the two *m*'s of the military and marriage are heady indeed but, I would argue, not singularly or unambiguously positive.

There are two stories to be told here. The one that is most obvious is that while the Democrats pulled gays and lesbians into a warm election-year embrace, Republicans doubled down on a long history of enshrined discrimination. The two platforms couldn't have been more different when it comes to gay rights or, for that matter, minority rights of any stripe. And given that our country is about evenly divided between the two parties and that politicians signing on to anti-gay platforms get handily elected, the elation of Democratic inclusion needs to be tempered with the heartbreak of Republican exclusion, not just in the platform—which was a veritable cornucopia of anti-gay animus—but in the bodies invited to speak, a model of heterosexual and white dominion: openly gay speakers were as hard to find as pro-choice feminists. This story is clear and sobering and gives a bit more weight to the glass-half-empty part of the equation.

But there is another story here too, one that is a bit more complicated and frustrating. Let's imagine for the moment that the "gays are gross" half (or quarter: let's be optimistic) of the country disappeared or moved to a colony on Mars with gated space pods and restricted Martian country clubs. And, of course, no Martian-human intermarriage. And left here on Earth, in the United States of America, were only those who wish us well. That slight majority who think we can get married, serve in the military, raise children. Who don't expressly detest us and, moreover, who are tolerant of our supposedly benign differences from heterosexual ways of life and love. Now, I can tell you, given that choice, I will most assuredly take a pass on the Martian express and double down on the tolerant tomorrow. What sane homosexual wouldn't? But would this be the rainbow nirvana? In a word, no. The *absence* of overt and legalized discrimination is not the *presence* of gay positivity. As I hope I've detailed throughout this book, we too often stop at these important but limited goals (access to institutions, repeal of biased laws), interpret those victories as stable indicators of the tolerant and accepting society we desire, and rarely look beyond or through that tolerance to a vision of a deeply changed America. What should the queer future look like? Is it a live-and-let-live libertarian land of still-hated homos and the straights who bravely tolerate them? A "we are the world" Benetton ad of glossy togetherness where difference is only fashion deep? Or might it be something else altogether?

Surely removing structural barriers and challenging legalized discrimination are necessary, but not sufficient, conditions for full civic inclusion. As discussed in earlier chapters, the limitations of this narrow focus are legion. But more importantly, when gay rights are framed this way—as discrete rights that are offered up by an increasingly "tolerant" society—real and robust integration is avoided and ignored. By framing these gains in a discourse of tolerance, we set the bar too low. Thornier and more contentious and challenging questions persist: How might full inclusion undermine the sexist masculinity at the heart of military culture? What can queer kinship say to nuclear families? How can we detach acts from identities and still embrace egalitarian struggles? These challenging questions also enrich the "mainstream" culture, so it's not just a matter here of *reducing* homophobia but rather *producing* a more inclusive, flexible, interesting, happy society in general. By avoiding these questions, we allow animus new tributaries and byways through our cultural waterways. In other words, the difference that difference makes—for society writ large—can never be fully addressed when the endgame is tolerance and acceptance. Heterosexual tolerance—of gay marriage, gay soldiers, gay workers, gay sitcom characters—does both gays and straights a disservice in not engaging head-on with the challenges offered by sexual and gender difference.

Now this is not to say that all—or even most—gays think of themselves as possessing that difference. Most, I think, would claim a resolute sameness to heterosexuals and argue instead that sexual preference is largely irrelevant to who they are. Many would agree wholeheartedly with *New York Times* writer Frank Bruni that "the goal is for talking about homosexuality to be largely unnecessary" and for sexual orientation to be "irrelevant."[4] Our political discourse is filled with these voices, voices that proclaim not the battle cry of yesterday, "We're here, we're queer, get used to it," but rather, "We're here, we're not really queer but vaguely gayish, be nice to us." Most just want, I would guess, to be left alone to live their lives in openness and free of discriminatory laws. As Jerry Seinfeld would say, not that there's anything wrong with that. But that should be the baseline, not the end line. Deep and abiding integration implies real change, on both a structural level and on a more personal and intimate one.

Mainstream heterosexual culture (albeit the liberal part) is largely responsible for promoting the tolerance trap. But gays should not overlook our own complicity in this project. The amicus briefs for the successful *Lawrence* case, overturning anti-sodomy laws, illustrates just such a missed opportunity. On the one hand, the scholars who worked on the case and were brought in to testify did deepen the discourse on gay identity and gave real insight into our collective understanding of how anti-gay hatred develops and justifies itself. But on the other hand, many of the scholars were eager to assure the Court that gays are no "deviant subculture" but rather "live with long-term domestic partners in committed relationships," "serve their country," and are "raising children who are as emotionally well adjusted as children raised in heterosexual households."[5] The default zone of heterosexual nuclear family life goes unquestioned here, and in the process, possibilities for thinking outside the hetero box get narrowed even further.

## Deep Integration

In thinking through what the alternatives to tolerance are, I find myself returning again and again to the question of integration. It seems curious to me that for gays, integration as a framework has had little traction, and we seem instead to vacillate between debates around assimilation versus liberationism and leave integration out in the cold. In some ways, this is not surprising since gays—given the historical realities of the closet—have always been integrated into mainstream culture, even as we simultaneously formed gay ghettos and gayborhoods. Or perhaps integration has gotten a bad rap. Pilloried by the Left as a smoke screen for assimilation and parodied by the Right as melting-pot multiculturalism run amok, integration as both the sign of social progress and its best strategy seems decidedly retro. As law professor Michelle Adams notes, "Integration no longer captivates the progressive imagination."[6] While integration was largely the framework for the civil rights struggles of the 1950s and '60s (even though it was also in profound dispute, as evidenced by the seminal debate between Martin Luther King's commitment to integration and Malcolm X's separatist nationalism), it has held little appeal for many in the gay movement. For many queer radicals, in particular, the present moment—with its display of gay identity as fashion accessory, its commodification, its cleaning up and dumbing down—represents both the logical conclusion of bankrupt politics of assimilation and the death knell of a more vibrant queer way of life. Integration, then, has been seen as synonymous with weak assimilation, a political project of the past that is largely irrelevant to the problems facing gays.

There is much truth to this perspective, and I myself have added to the fears of what this kind of liberal inclusion excludes. But perhaps we are working with a weak—a too weak—notion of inclusion or integration that doesn't distinguish it substantively enough from assimilation. There is a difference, however, between substantive integration and thoughtless and tolerant assimilation. For many gays, these are often confused. We so fear/reject the relentless project of commodified assimilation that the integrationist project gets tossed out in the process of resisting assimilation. We mistake, in other words, integration for assimilation. And we get stuck with acceptance and tolerance.

Integration always implies an unfinished project or a project always in the making. Truly, if full integration exists, the very term loses its meaning. And, as Adams argues, "radical integration . . .

champions a forward-looking, aspirational vision of equality."[7] To be just a *little* integrated implies a kind of failure of political will and ethical depth. Full integration is always a radical and utopian project because it insists that the human project is made better through that lofty aspiration. How different this is from the goal of tolerance. Tolerance is dangerously figured as an endpoint in itself—not process or project but a benevolent act of dominance toward its other. With robust integration, there is no "we" that deigns to integrate the "other," in the way we imagine heterosexuals bravely becoming more tolerant of sexual minorities. Integration is a process both deeply social and inevitably intimate but one that can only succeed with a recognition of the absolute gains for *everyone* that robust integration brings. Integration implies a positivity at the heart of deep inclusion, while tolerance is inevitably reluctant forbearance.

Tolerance can't offer up robust integration on any level. Robust integration and inclusion of gays and lesbians operates on several levels simultaneously. Let's take an example of, say, school curricula. What tolerance offers is a wagging finger to outright bullying or, in some cases, gay-straight alliances to soften the blow of entrenched teenage homophobia. What real inclusion argues, instead, is that real change operates not just on gays but on straights as well. So a curriculum that didn't *assume* a heterosexual norm (for every classroom example, for every reading, for every essay assignment) would have the dual effect of recognizing gay students and simultaneously challenging and changing straight ones. This is as true for other realms as it is for our schools: robust inclusion articulates the deeper benefits of full integration for *all* concerned. It's not just that gays will be more welcome, less likely to suffer from self-hatred and fear, but that the ground of what is "normal" will itself begin to shift.

Cultural theorist Paul Gilroy cuts to the heart of it when he wonders "how we might invent conceptions of humanity that allow for the presumption of equal value and go beyond the issue of tolerance into a more active engagement with the irreducible value of diversity within sameness."[8] That model—of diversity within sameness, of a presumption of equal value—implicitly undermines the tolerance trap, for it pushes us all to reckon deeply (an "active engagement," as Gilroy puts it) with the ways in which different lifeways do in fact alter our most cherished national and sexual verities. To insist on the same rights as majority identities does not mean—or necessitate—that you are the same as them.

Let's think for a moment of that phrase so often used by the gay movement, particularly in its most "act-up" moments: "we are everywhere." The tolerance trap cannot abide by this insinuating gay presence. Tolerance is by definition circumscribed and doled out. One of the things that is clear from both the gay-marriage debates and, forcefully, the attempts to find an origin and an immutability for (gay) sexual orientation is that tolerance moves by marking gays out, tolerance wants to be able to pick "the other" out in a crowd, to identify (and what better way to do this than to marry gays off?). The discourse of passing as well as the common phrase uttered so often by astonished heterosexual friends ("He's gay? I would have never known!") or its corollary ("Yep, my gaydar was working! I *knew* she was a lesbian") indicates a deep discomfort with the very fact of a kind of viral gayness, a gayness that could putatively be anywhere, creeping along undetected. As critic Michael Warner put it a number of years ago, we may be reckoning here with the "fear of a queer planet," a fear that cannot be shunted aside in the march toward tolerance, or harsher intolerance will surely follow.[9]

This is one of the places where the usual analogies do fall apart. For, unlike our most handy comparative identity categories, we are both everywhere and largely invisible unless we deliberately mark ourselves or are marked by others. Not bound by geography, parentage, lines of kinship, or nationality, gays are potentially unmarked and simultaneously everywhere. The traditional link between theories of integration and theories of acculturation don't quite fit when it comes to gays. Because gays are almost always spies in the house of heterosexuality and thus intimately knowledgeable about heterosexual culture, the idea of gay *acculturation* doesn't quite jibe in the way that it can for, say, immigrant populations. Yet the same core tensions often emerge: can or should gays be somehow "less gay" in order to acquire the full mantle of citizenship applied without thought to their heterosexual brothers and sisters?

In fact, gays *have* been asked or even required to be "less gay" in a manner similar to "requests" made of other minority groups. As historian Thaddeus Russell notes, speaking of comparisons between blacks and gays, "There is, however, one way in which the two movements have been strikingly similar: both have demanded that in order to gain acceptance as full citizens, their constituents adopt the cultural norms of what they believe to be the idealized American citizen—productivity, selflessness, responsibility, sexual restraint, and the restraint of homosexuality in particular."[10] For legal theorist Kenji Yoshino, Jews too have reckoned with the demand to "tone it down," especially in more recent years, when, as he points out, "the question has shifted from whether they should convert or pass to whether they are 'Too Jewish?'—the title of a museum exhibit that traveled the nation in 1997."[11] And like all minority groups, a certain amount of internal policing is de rigueur: mainstream gay groups highlight their married male standard-bearers and downplay their dykes on bikes.

In fact, Yoshino has made a compelling argument that asks us to shift our national attention to this process of covering, in which a member of a minority group "tone[s] down a disfavored identity to fit into the mainstream."[12] It is this covering—this assimilationist mandate—that is for him what can link multiple communities together in common cause, ushering in a new paradigm for civil rights that champions authenticity over conformity, self-expression over both institutional and internal policing. And to resist covering is to resist the tolerance trap, for the mandate to cover is the price paid for tolerance since tolerance can always be doled out selectively or even revoked if those who are being tolerated make the rest too uncomfortable.

So if tolerance is too timid and superficial a goal, then what *is* the goal? If rights are the necessary but not sufficient condition for true liberation, then what are those other conditions that must be met? First, we must understand that no single right is the brass ring. To shift metaphors for a moment, putting all our eggs in the basket of marriage (or any single "right" for that matter) is a mistake both practically and ethically. We know this from history, from the story of women, of African Americans, of Jews, of Latinos. We know— even though we too often avoid the discussion—that individual civil rights are core to integration but are not the whole of it. We know that gaining those rights can provide safety and the imprimatur of legitimacy and can also change hearts and minds. But we also know and have learned the hard way that, for example, "the civil rights movement ended legal segregation in America, . . . but it simply couldn't build an integrated America."[13] Sadly, we remain a deeply segregated society. Ending racial segregation and inequity in a meaningful way means wrestling meaningfully with racism: its structural aspects, its personal investments, its insinuation into every nook and cranny of American life. Dealing deeply with racial inequity means thinking seriously about racism: how it works, where it comes from, how it changes shape but still finds welcome home. Tolerance has nothing to do with that project.

Similarly, ending inequity on the basis of sexual preference means wrestling meaningfully with homophobia: how it works, where it comes from, how it shifts about but still and always spreads its tentacles. Tolerance has nothing to do with that either. It is curious to me that the discourse on *homophobia* has decreased as the discourse on *tolerance* increases; we'd rather talk about happy gay married couples than the motivations of anti-gay bigots. Tolerance as a goal deflects that deeper probe into the heart of anti-gay animus because it asks little of those who are doing the tolerating. Tolerance is a mode that empowers those who are already empowered, pushing for a more open heart or a more generous spirit but not an altered body politic.

Tolerance, I am convinced, cannot ask more and will never push heterosexuals to deeply interrogate their abiding animus. But tolerance also cannot provide the framework for *integrating* queer difference. For the flip side of wrestling deeply with homophobia is opening all of us up to the exhilarating challenge that sexual and gender difference offers.

As many scholars of the family have persuasively argued, gay navigations of kinship and sexuality are not only pioneering models but have much to teach all of us, gay and straight alike. We cannot integrate the pioneering ways of doing kinship, the exhilarating embrace of sexual freedom, the utopian gestures to a gender-blurred world as long as tolerance is both means and end. Sexual and gender identities are formed interactively, that is, always in relation to others, dancing a curious pas de deux between straight and gay sensibilities and all those in-between and outside them. But this interaction can never achieve, to continue the ballet metaphor, the grand jeté if one partner so dominates the dance. Tolerance is a form of domination, perhaps one that caresses instead of grips tenaciously but domination nonetheless.

As longtime gay activist David Mixner persuasively argues,

One of the things we have to get over as a community is wanting to be liked. Or proving to others that we're just like them. These ads where we have, "This is my straight daughter, this is my lesbian daughter. We're just like you, and they're just like each other." First of all, nobody's gonna buy it, not in a million years. We can try to sell them the Brooklyn Bridge before we tell them a homosexual is just like them. But second of all, we're not. In some ways we bring remarkable gifts to this table of society. How can I be like them when I've lost 300 friends to AIDS? When my best friend, Freddie Davis, killed himself at 16? When I know people who had forced lobotomies in the '50s? When people were rounded up in parks and had their names printed in newspapers and their careers destroyed? When police raided the bars and lined people up outside? How can we be like them? Our experience is so different from them. But what we did in all of that, we triumphed because we had a different, unique journey. When our friends got sick with AIDS we created new health care systems; we created dental clinics for everybody. And we can show society we know how to do this. If they will embrace us and our gifts and talents because we're not like them. They need us.[14]

The persistent fact of the closet gives the lie to the fantasy of both the end of discrimination and the meaninglessness of sexuality.

When Anderson Cooper finally came out, for example, his insistence that he was never really closeted but rather "private" put him in a conflicted position. After Cooper's revelation, critic Daniel Mendelsohn noted that "the simple fact of being gay should be no more a 'privacy' issue than being straight is for straight people," and making that claim does mean you're "buying . . . into the notion that there is, at some level, something wrong with it."[15] Becoming a more tolerant society in and of itself says nothing about how values and beliefs may be altered by substantive gay inclusion and integration. As I have shown throughout this book, the toleration thesis finds strange common ground with the naturalization or biologization of homosexuality. We are to be tolerated because we can't help ourselves, because we are made this way. So gays react negatively to the assertion of our "lifestyle" (e.g., it is not a lifestyle but a life, it is in the core of who we are) and instead offer up insistence that it is not our culture/style that must be "tolerated" but rather our life, our nature.

Let's take an example. A young child, born male, prefers to wear brightly colored dresses to school and plays a dizzying array of make-believe games in which he is a princess and a queen and a fashion designer. The school he attends has conducted lectures and training on tolerance and does not send him home with a demand for more "appropriate" clothes. The teachers quickly step in to stop any teasing or bullying. That's far better than the tacit acceptance of jeers that typified earlier eras and that still permeate much of our school culture. So far so good. But imagine a bit more broadly and brashly. How might this boy's way of being prompt new ways of organizing school life? Perhaps his ease with gender might encourage teachers to think twice about dividing groups up so easily into boys and girls. Maybe they will mix up pronouns a bit more, stop the default of "he" as the automatic place of humanness. Maybe one could walk into a toy store and not see the world divided into gender aisles and read storybooks that didn't begin and end with heterosexual romance. Or, as Richard Kim writes in the *Nation*, "Imagine saying I really wish my son turns out to be gay. . . . Imagine hoping that your 2-year-old daughter grows up to be transgendered. Imagine not assuming the gender of your child's future prom date or spouse, . . . imagine petitioning your local school board of education to hire *more* gay elementary school teachers."[16]

Maybe some of the potential of old-style gay liberation can be realized in the new-style gender play of queer kids. Blithely taking many of the gains for granted, these kids may seem naively unaware of the persistence of structural impediments and moral revulsion. But they also challenge the oppositions (gay/straight, male/female) that are at the core of heterosexual dominion. If the alphabet-soup proliferation of identifiers (LGBTQ and on and on) appears ready-made for mockery, it also pushes beyond a tolerance that is dependent on readable, recognizable gender oppositions and hierarchies. How do you tolerate that which you cannot pin down?

Or let's imagine another scenario. Denise and Valerie are raising two kids. One child is produced through alternative insemination with an anonymous donor, and the other is through a male friend who wants to be a part of parenting. Denise has an old lover, Carol, whom she is intimately connected with and who has been involved in raising her daughter, along with Carol's new partner, Rosa. Like the dress-wearing boy, these kids go to schools where there is a new emphasis on tolerance of different sorts of families and where they can bring all the players into the parent-teacher meetings and school pageants. They feel different but accepted. So far so good. But what happens if parenting strategies and skills are separated from gender roles and expectations? When an expansive sense of kinship and collective responsibility replaces "mommy and daddy and baby makes three"? When biology is not only *not* destiny but assuredly not what makes a family? Might heterosexuals—many of whom have been chipping away at this framework themselves—begin to think even more outside the box, to begin to see creative connections and new opportunities where formerly they imagined only deficit and failure? What might happen to these "family values" debates if we didn't just tolerate or add in gay and lesbian families but actually embraced the different ways of constructing kinship? Is it possible, for example, that we might move away from the idea that kids growing up in these households don't suffer and wonder if just maybe they actually *flourish* when gender is not so tied to identity and complicated networks of care replace the narrowness of the nuclear? Because gays have been and still are excluded, estranged, and alienated from their families of origin, the networks of care and conviviality, of friendship and sexual intimacy, have been deliberately and creatively forged, perhaps rendering many freer, as Stacey puts it, to "express a full palette of gender options."[17] Isn't it important information that the only longitudinal study of children raised in lesbian households finds 0 percent incidents of sexual abuse, compared to the 26 percent of other American teens who report abuse by parents or caregivers?[18] How different is this way of looking at it than the ones promulgated by tolerance advocates, who look at an unmarried gay couple with children and see only the absence of rights and status and not the integrity of the unit itself?

For example, *New York Times* writer Frank Bruni describes a wedding in New York with "2 dads, 2 daughters." The dads marry in part because, as Bruni acknowledges, "having two dads is different." He recounts the wedding in heartwarming prose but also explicitly confirms that the absence of a marriage assured both the children and the larger culture that there was something "second-class about [the] family."[19] What is "second class," on the contrary, is a culture that insists marriage (gay or straight) is the marker of family love! What a missed opportunity here to educate both children and society that family integrity is not marked by state legitimacy but by how you love and nurture the people you care for.

So tolerance of gay families can short-circuit the potential of those same families to transform kinship as we know it. But what about our larger political world and culture? The problem of tolerance as the defining framework can be illustrated by an interview that Republican House leader Eric Cantor had with *BuzzFeed*, the all-you-can-eat Web news source. Here, Cantor tries to buck his party's image as anti-gay by arguing, "At some point we're all here as Americans and we all have to be appreciative of other people's views. . . . I think that . . . that tolerance is something that enables people to be passionate about their positions. And if you're for gay marriage, this country allows you to express your views. Some states support it and allow it, and others don't. But it's ok to have that difference of opinion in that."[20] But, of course, he has steadfastly supported legislation that undermines gay rights in every possible way. So the language of tolerance allows just such duplicity. It allows for an illusion of change under the rubric of supposedly benign "differences of opinion."

## The Same, Only Different

Difference is dangerous territory, to be sure. Gays—and many other minority groups—have far too often staked their gains on a rhetoric of sameness. We fear threatening the straight mainstream, fear they will see the difference and back away, fear they will think of our bodies and what we do with them. We fear they will think of sex, our sex. So we tidy up and yell as politely as we can that we are only as different as the left-handed person is from the right-handed one, the blonde from the brunette. Of course, there is a truth to this both in a practical and a more philosophical sense, and I don't want to dismiss those who feel deeply that their queerness is incidental and irrelevant. And surely social movements have their own life course; radical elements are so often squeezed out in the move to mainstream. We've seen this time and time again: radical and socialist feminism gives way to more liberal and acquiescent moves for gender equality, Black Power cedes to black capitalism. It's not that these radical tendencies disappear altogether (they are often very present but relegated to media invisibility), but they are often muted by the clarion call of legitimacy.

So some of what I'm feeling, I suppose, could be called assimilation blues, in which the radical gate smashing for sexual freedom becomes the gentle knock at the wedding-chapel door. But those oppositions (between assimilation and the ghetto, between radicalism and the tepid embrace) always miss out on something, always tell a story that is just too simplistic to capture the complexity of how minorities move through majority populations. Queer studies scholars such as Lisa Duggan and Michael Warner have been particularly pointed in their critique of what they call "homonormativity"—the assimilationist trend that threatens to engulf gay difference.[21] Some, like legal scholar and trans activist Dean Spade, claim that "the compromises made in lesbian and gay rights efforts to win formal legal equality gains have come with enormous costs: opportunities for coalition have been missed, large sectors of people affected by homophobia have been alienated, and the actual impact of the 'victories' has been so limited as to neutralize their effect on the populations most vulnerable to the worst harms of homophobia."[22] A sharp critique has risen throughout the academic Left bemoaning the state of gay politics as it becomes mired in liberal, accommodationist strategies. I have much sympathy for these critiques, even as I remain more optimistic about what appear to be some substantive moments of progress.

Truly, though, some of the earlier manifestos and gay rights broadsides appear both more radical and anachronistic in this time of the tolerance trap. The British Gay Liberation Front published a manifesto in 1971 that explicitly argued not for tolerance but for "a revolutionary change in our whole society" that would challenge gender norms and the male-dominant family. The group declared that "gay shows the way" to this new world order, not that it is a minor "difference" that meekly asks for civil rights and tolerant attitudes.[23] This radical agenda was part of the early gay rights groups in the US too and developed in (sometimes contentious) dialogue with the newly active feminist movement of the time. So there are models out there of paradigms and frameworks that eschew tolerance in favor of a more utopian vision of a sexually free future.

I agree: the political stance of sameness can only get you tolerance and can never get you comprehensive inclusion. I'm concerned about gays becoming stripped of their vivacious difference too, but even more concerned about the tolerance trap that both contains and exceeds that assimilationist homosexual. Too often, I think, the baby is tossed out with the bathwater. Or maybe it's just that we need to think beyond both babies and bathwater, past the tired old oppositions of righteous liberationism and assimilationist acceptance.

Not only can tolerance be invoked and then undermined by intolerant actions; it hides behind a veneer of civility to perpetuate inequality. Look at the insistence of the proponents of California's Proposition 8 who contended that it is not an attack on the "gay lifestyle." In their promotional materials, these activists claimed that "Proposition 8 does not take any rights away from gays and lesbians in domestic partnerships. Under California law, 'domestic partners shall have the same rights, protections, and benefits' as married spouses. There are no exceptions. Proposition 8 will not change this."[24] In reality, of course, Prop 8 was explicitly designed to amend existing marriage laws to restrict the institution to different-sex couples. Our new language of civility (by some people at least) mandates a nod to "tolerance" while simultaneously undermining gay rights. As law professor and EEOC commissioner Chai Feldblum notes,

> Whether it was Sarah Palin falling over herself in the vice presidential debate to proclaim her support for gay couples visiting each other in the hospital, or Mormon leaders proclaiming throughout their vigorous pro-8 campaign that their church does not object to equal rights for same-sex couples in hospitalization, housing, or employment, something had changed in terms of what it is legitimate to say about gay couples in polite company.[25]

This seems to be an updated version of "speak softly but carry a big stick": invoke tolerance and provoke animus. A neat trick. Or take another headline from an op-ed written after the 2012 Republican convention, a headline that sounds like yet another *Onion* jab: "Is the GOP deeply anti-gay?" Hardly. Though there are such sentiments in the Republican Party, polling data show large, overlooked pockets of tolerance among its rank and file."[26] What is a pocket of tolerance? Is it bigger than a breadbox?

No doubt, sometimes tolerance seems like manna from heaven when the norm has been hate-filled discrimination. And, as I hope I've made clear, the shifts in public attitudes and the uneven moves toward ending legalized discrimination are to be celebrated. I'd rather live in this world than in one in which that old norm isn't even on the table for contestation. Tolerance may bring us a modicum of justice for sure. Ending legalized discrimination (whether in marriage, the military, employment, or immigration) is a crucial stage in the justice project. But justice is not the same as freedom, just as acceptance is not the same as recognition. As philosopher Charles Taylor puts it, "Due recognition is not just a courtesy we owe people. It is a vital human need."[27] Freedom speaks to utopian visions of a better world; freedom *from* discrimination but also freedom *for* the exploration of human flourishing. In a inadvertently revealing *New York Times* op-ed, David Brooks actually celebrates how gay marriage (which signifies the restriction of pleasures) signals the death knell of the "freedom project," a project he associates with all the "excesses" of liberation movements of the 1960s, including early gay rights.[28]

The trick, perhaps, is both to avoid the fantasy of completion that tolerance perpetuates while at the same time refusing that old space of "otherness" and failure. People mocked Obama's campaign slogan of "hope and change," and truth be told, I too found it vague, albeit inspiring. But hope for substantive—and not surface—change must be the higher bar we set. For real and deep integration would imply that the whole issue of tolerance would seem a bit silly, right? My argument is not only that tolerance is too weak or too mild a goal, although by now that should be obvious. Rather, my argument is that the framework of tolerance actively *prevents* the development of a more inclusive and powerful sexual and gender freedom. It stands in the way.

For some people, this historical moment is so tolerant, so accepting, so hip and fluid with gender and sexuality that we have actually entered a "post-gay" period in which gayness as separate identity (signaled by cultural signs and practices, ghettos or gayborhoods, gay-only friends, etc.) has rapidly given way to an erosion of the distinction between gay and straight. A collective national shrug. A poll by the Human Rights Campaign in 2011 found that 58 percent of respondents said they could be close friends with a gay man. However, in response to whether they felt they had things in common with gay people, 48 percent stated they had nothing in common, versus 42 percent who felt they did. Interestingly, the same poll also found that 52 percent of respondents contended that their feelings toward LGBTQ people have not changed over the past five to ten years, 40 percent said they have become much more or somewhat more accepting, and 6 percent stated they have become less so.[29]

It's hard not to paraphrase the feminist response to the similar statement that we are living in a post-feminist age: I'll be post-feminist when you're post-patriarchy. As queer theorist Heather Love writes, "Given the new opportunities available to *some* gays and lesbians, the temptation to forget—to forget the outrage and humiliations of gay and lesbian history and to ignore the ongoing suffering of those not borne up by the rising tide of gay normalization—is stronger than ever."[30] I couldn't agree more.

But that future can't be imagined when tolerance is the objective. And that future is most assuredly further out of reach when we foolishly buy into the progress narrative that claims for our present a homo friendliness that just isn't there. Change takes time, and most cultures are riven with contradictions, particularly when it comes to matters sexual. But the dominant frameworks we are working with today—immutability, acceptance, tolerance, sameness—may get us some traction but inevitably fall short. This is, as Wendy Brown argues, "the way tolerance has operated for most of its history in the modern West: it is always a kind of substitute for equality." It lulls us into a type of complacency, so that we imagine equality is on offer when it is something else altogether. I share Brown's concern that "our tendency to just get sleepy and happy when we hear the world 'tolerance' is a problem."[31]

Things are better, but not better enough. Even in our pop culture, we insistently imagine the fantasy of full inclusion, or as *New York Times* TV critic Alessandra Stanley glibly puts it, "Gay marriage may not be the law of the land, but it has become a cornerstone of network television. . . . There is nothing particularly new about gay characters on sitcoms. This season they are not only normal, they seem de rigueur."[32] Really? A few queer characters may seem, as she puts it, like "gay is the new straight," but only in a world where hetero dominance still reigns unabated. As David Halperin argues, watching a few queers on TV may contribute to the "destigmatization of homosexuality. But a culture that places less stigma on homosexuality is not the same thing as a gay culture. And adding gay characters to mainstream culture forms does not make those forms themselves queer."[33] To claim we are living in a brave new world bubbling over with queer images is to willfully not see the hetero forest for the few lavender trees.

Halperin takes the gay movement to task in another, interesting way in arguing that the gays ourselves have downplayed the *feeling* of homosexuality—its subjective and cultural dimensions—in the move to make sure we are established as a social and political category, an identity, an orientation. And because the underlying goal of this "political category" is so often simple tolerance or acceptance, we are configured "not as subjects of a distinctive way of being and feeling but as members of a generic identity-based group" who are therefore "pressured to mask their queerness, rein in their sensibilities, and play down their differences from regular folks."[34] It's not just the "sex" that is taken out of homosexuality when we are politely assimilated "gays" but also—and this is what Halperin is getting at—the distinctive "structures of feeling" that have been part of queer life. As he writes, crushingly, "we are witnessing the rise of a new and vehement cult of gay ordinariness," which not only denies our own specificity but also denies our "ability to contribute anything of value to the world we live in."[35]

As long as tolerance is our reigning ethos, these contradictions will continue to rage unabated. As long as we deny our difference in the service of misplaced allegiance to gender and sexual norms, we deny "the unique genius in being queer."[36] We cannot find our way through the thicket of current contradictions within that framework. Repeal, enjoin, sign up, and pledge your troth to God and country and legally wedded spouse. But do not imagine that this is all that we can imagine.

# ACKNOWLEDGMENTS

This book took so long to write that I feel like I might as well thank my good friend Oscar Wilde for his witty asides and ready supply of absinthe. But seriously, since Oscar has denied it all, I thank my other absinthe-providing friends and colleagues who have aided and abetted but are in no way responsible for any of this.

Versions of this argument have been trotted out, debated, fine-tuned at many venues over the years, including the Centre for Narrative Research in London, the American Studies Institute at the University of Warsaw, the Humanities Center at Northeastern University, the University of Oregon women's studies program, and the Center for Law, Society, and Culture and the Kinsey Institute at Indiana University. Thanks to all who heard versions of this and provided vital feedback. I'd also like to thank the College Arts and Humanities Institute at Indiana University for a semester fellowship that allowed me crucial time to work on this project. Portions of this book have been published, in altered form, in the following places: *Chronicle of Higher Education*, *Sexualities*, and *William & Mary Journal of Women and the Law*.

A shout-out to my wonderful graduate students at Indiana University, especially Laura Harrison and Jenna Basiliere, who pitched in at various times (sometimes with brain, sometimes with brawn) and were generally righteous feminists who give me hope for the academic future. And this book would, literally, not have been possible without the able research assistance of Brett Nava-Coulter, grad student in sociology at Northeastern. Brett came in toward the end of this project and is, quite simply, a crackerjack research assistant. Really. The. Best. Ever. Thank you so much, Brett.

The wonderful tribe at the Ptown compound/kibbutz, where we all quaff the rainbow Kool-Aid: Melanie Braverman, Michael Cunningham, and Molly Perdue—you've all been a home away from home for me even though you cautiously vetted me when I first entered that hallowed space. I'm glad I made the grade. You can throw away the FBI report now. Thanks especially to the warm sisterhood of Melanie and the amazing generosity of Michael: you both have listened to my kvetching over many glasses of wine, read bits and pieces, brainstormed titles, and have helped in ways both ineffable and editorial.

My new colleagues at Northeastern University are stupendous, especially Lori Lefkovitz (my sister from another shtetl), Uta Poiger, Steve Vallas, Laura Green, and all the women of the WGSS program. A more welcome home for this refugee from the Midwest couldn't be found. Thank you all. I hope we have many years together.

I've always had an inordinate fondness for feminist literary theorists (and nurses, but that's another story). Two in particular have given generously of their time: Susan Gubar and Carla Kaplan have both read versions of this work, provided tough but terribly on-target notes, and have modeled a feminist solidarity that I can only hope to replicate. I may not be an English professor, but I do think I play one on the high-end cable show of my imagination (okay, an English professor who doubles as a dashing detective in her spare time).

I'd like to thank my cheerleader of an editor, Ilene Kalish, and the rest of the team at NYU Press, who have been a pleasure to work with. Thanks also to Judith Levine for her enormously attentive and sharp editorial ministrations—never one to mince words, she helped make this a significantly better book.

Many friends, family, and colleagues over the years have provided insight, edits, or just good old comradely conviviality. I thank especially Lisa Walters, Verta Taylor, Mary Gray, Catherine Guthrie, Lisa Henderson, Kathy Sreedhar, Valerie Grim, Mary Bernstein, Julia Heiman (righteously tall leader of the Kinsey Institute), Michael

Kimmel (my dear comrade-in-arms and all-around co-conspirator), Josh Gamson, Lynn Chancer, Larry Levner, Molly Andrews (who helped me have the best—and most debauched—sabbatical in London), Ken Plummer, Arlene Stein, Leila Rupp, Nancy Naples, and Dennis Altman. And I do want to thank my colleagues—past and present—who work in gay and lesbian and queer and feminist studies: while this book veers away from the academic marketplace, it would not have been possible without the energizing and paradigm-shifting work of the various pink and lavender menaces (meni?) of academia. A tip of the bent hat to you all.

I would be remiss if I didn't thank my sisterhood of the traveling martini: Annie Gibeau, Diane Lopez, Marcia Kuntz, Amy Horowitz, and Deborah Shore. We go way back (and lo, the waters parted), and there are so many dead bodies that I don't think any of us can remember where they are buried. I love you all, and I am really so grateful that none of you are academics. And Emma, my beloved daughter now entering adulthood, I promise to always watch insipid but inspiring, show-tuney, gay-ish television with you until they cart me off. I adore you beyond all rationality. I love that you decided early on that you are GBA (gay by association): I hope it gives you the queer cred that you curiously imagine it can. But really, enough already: read your mother's books.

Finding heady romance in (let's be honest here) middle age is always surprising yet rarely so gratifying and sustaining. And to "meet cute" sharing a table on a queer studies panel is either really creepy or just very, very gay. Either way, I am so thrilled to have met Laurie Essig—my notwife, partner, paramour, love, consigliere, and all-around sexy, smart, wonderful woman. She is the mint in my mojito, the olive in my martini, the maraschino in my Manhattan. Lest you think all we do is mix cocktails together, I should add that her help on this book was of the Olympian variety—she snipped, moved, reimagined, gave pep talks when needed and stern "finish it already" orders when I got (all too often) whiney and pathetic. What a delicious delight to have her in my life.

# NOTES

## NOTES TO THE INTRODUCTION

1. Throughout the book I generally use the term "gay," partly to avoid the clumsy, if more accurate, alphabet soup of LGBTQ and so on. Sometimes, the broader designation of "queer" will slip in, both to signify an edgier relationship to sex and identity and partly to hint at a more encompassing designation.

2. Interesting enough, LGBTQ voters really do constitute a reliably Democratic voting bloc and, in addition, are extremely active participants in the political process, perhaps even to a greater degree than the "general population." See especially Gates and Newport, "LGBT Americans Skew Democratic, Largely Support Obama."

3. Barabak, "Gays May Have the Fastest of All Civil Rights Movements."

4. Weeks, *World We Have Won*, 9.

5. I use the term "homophobia" throughout this book with no small amount of trepidation. As many commentators have pointed out, homophobia as a concept implies a sort of psychological and individual aversion or, more specifically and literally, an "irrational fear" of homosexuals. I think anti-gay animus works in much more complex ways—through institutions, laws, prejudicial ways of thinking, discriminatory acts, and so on. It is sometimes "irrational" and phobic in that literal sense, but it is also sometimes quite deliberate and thought out, shoring up normative ideas about gender and sex. But it is our culture's shorthand term for speaking of anti-gay acts and feelings, so I will be using it here.

6. Gendar, Sandoval, and McShange, "Rutgers Freshman Kills Self after Classmates Use Hidden Camera."

7. Wilson and Baker, "Lured into a Trap, Then Tortured for Being Gay."

8. Kann et al., "Sexual Identity, Sex of Sexual Contacts, and Health-Risk Behaviors."

9. Williams, *Marxism and Literature*.

10. Coates, "Good, Racist People."
11. Žižek, "Tolerance as an Ideological Category," 660.
12. Brown, *Regulating Aversion*, 89.
13. Zembylas, "Pedagogy of Unknowing."
14. Southern Poverty Law Center, "Teaching Tolerance," available at http://www.splcenter.org/what-we-do/teaching-tolerance.
15. D'Emilio, *Making Trouble*.

### NOTES TO CHAPTER 1

1. Didion, *White Album*.
2. Cory, *Homosexual in America*, 36.
3. Chauncey, *Gay New York*.
4. Seidman, "Beyond the Closet?," 15.
5. See especially Butler, "Imitation and Gender Insubordination."
6. Ibid.
7. Diamond, "Careful What You Ask For," 477.

### NOTES TO CHAPTER 2

1. Numerous studies still bear this out. For example, one study notes only 48 percent of gay people claiming to be out at work and another reports 56 percent of gay youth out to their immediate family. Hewlett and Sumberg, "For LGBT Workers, Being 'Out' Brings Advantages"; Human Rights Campaign, "National Coming Out Day Youth Report."
2. "Gay Witch Hunt," *The Office*, Season 3, Episode 1, September 21, 2006.
3. Lobron, "Easy Out."
4. Savin-Williams, *New Gay Teenager*, ix.
5. Quoted in Cloud, "Battle over Gay Teens."
6. Savin-Williams, *New Gay Teenager*, 1.
7. Halberstam, *Gaga Feminism*.
8. Lobron, "Easy Out."
9. Savin-Williams, *New Gay Teenager*, 1.
10. See especially the report by Russell, Clarke, and Clary, "Are Teens 'Post-Gay'?"
11. Alexiou, "Gay Youth Discover There's a Safe Place to Be Themselves."
12. Ibid. The percentage of homeless youth who are gay, lesbian, bisexual, or transgendered has been hotly contested, and firm numbers are hard to come by. Nonetheless, most researchers agree that a disproportionate number of homeless youth are LGBTQ, and furthermore, homelessness is

often caused by youth coming out to parents who then reject them and kick them out of the house. In addition, there is no doubt that this is doubly disproportionate when race and ethnicity are factored into the equation. See especially Gibson, "Street Kids"; Tucker et al., "Running Away from Home"; and Kann et al., "Sexual Identity, Sex of Sexual Contacts, and Health-Related Risk Behaviors."

13. GLSEN, "Playgrounds and Prejudice."
14. Ibid.
15. Lobron, "Easy Out."
16. Ibid.
17. Setoodeh, "Young, Gay and Murdered."
18. Hunter, "'Real L Word' Girls Exclusive."
19. Kann et al., "Sexual Identity, Sex of Sexual Contacts, and Health-Risk Behaviors."
20. Petrow, "Coming Out Online."
21. "Randy Phillips, Gay U.S. Airman, on Why He Came Out on YouTube."
22. The Jason Collins story was interesting on any number of levels. Of course, he was hailed as a hero and a role model, and most commentators took this as an opportunity to note how very far we have come. But others, notably and surprisingly the *New York Times* editorial for May 10, 2013, made the much more important point that the Employment Non-Discrimination Act (ENDA) still languishes in Congress, so that Collins can come out and be celebrated but gays are still unprotected in the workplace.
23. Fraser, "Queer Closets and Rainbow Hyperlinks," 30.
24. Ibid., 31.
25. Eight states ban the "promotion of homosexuality" in schools: Alabama, Arizona, Louisiana, Mississippi, Oklahoma, South Carolina, Texas, and Utah. GLSEN, "States with Safe Schools Laws."
26. Fraser, "Queer Closets and Rainbow Hyperlinks," 31.
27. Hillier and Harrison, "Building Realities Less Limited than Their Own," 91.
28. Ibid.
29. M. Ross, "Typing, Doing, and Being," 348.
30. C. Brooks, "How to Come Out on Facebook."
31. Munt, "Virtually Belonging," 131.
32. Foster, "Jodie Foster's Golden Globe Speech."
33. Nakamura, "After/Images of Identity," 325.
34. J. Egan, "Lonely Gay Teen Seeks Same."
35. Ibid.

36. Ibid.

37. M. Ross, "Typing, Doing, and Being," 348.

38. Gray, *Out in the Country*, 122.

39. Ibid., 124.

40. Boyd, "Why Youth (Heart) Social Network Sites."

## NOTES TO CHAPTER 3

1. Seidman, "Beyond the Closet?," 21.

2. Williams, Giuffre, and Dellinger, "The Gay-Friendly Closet," 36.

3. Ibid., 36.

4. Yoshino, "The Pressure to Cover."

5. Samuels, "My Body, My Closet," 241.

6. Herman, "I'm Gay," 19.

7. "Shirtless Surrogate Stealer," *The New Normal*, January 9, 2013.

8. Tony Kushner, *Angels in America* (1993).

9. Chauncey, *Gay New York*, 7.

10. Seidman, "Beyond the Closet?," 9–10.

11. Crowder, "Anna Paquin, Ricky Martin."

12. Zukerman, "Meredith Baxter 'I'm a Lesbian Mom.'"

13. Holson, "Ricky Martin's Personal Spin on His Own 'News.'"

14. Laudadio, "Ricky Martin: Proud to Be Gay," 80.

15. Tyler Clementi, a Rutgers University freshman, jumped to his death from the George Washington Bridge in 2010, apparently distraught after his roommate and another student used a webcam in his dorm room to surreptitiously film him kissing another man. Whether this was a direct cause of his suicide is of course contestable; the roommate, Dharun Ravi, was eventually convicted of various charges such as invasion of privacy (but was not implicated in the suicide itself) and served a brief jail time.

16. Mendelsohn, "Closet by Any Other Name."

17. Harris, "New Art of Coming Out."

18. Stelter, "Revelation Signals a Shift in Views of Homosexuality."

19. Mendelsohn, "Closet by Any Other Name."

20. Healy, "How Celebrities Come Out Now."

21. Ibid.

22. Harris, "New Art of Coming Out."

23. Victory Fund, "Out Leaders."

24. Chely Wright on *The Ellen Show*, May 28, 2010.

25. Connelly, "Rupert Everett."

26. Herman, "I'm Gay," 22.

1. Gallup, "Gay and Lesbian Rights": 47 percent in May of 2013, up from 31 percent in 1996 and 35 percent in 2009.
2. Goodman, "Vatican Retreat on Homosexuality."
3. J. Jones, "Support for Legal Gay Relations Hits New High." In this poll, 42 percent believe people are gay due to "factors such as environment and upbringing," 40 percent believe being gay is something "a person is born with." Of those who believe it is not inborn, 54 percent are against legalizing same-sex marriage.
4. Truth Wins Out, "History."
5. Jordan-Young, *Brain Storm*, 5.
6. O'Riordan, "Life of the Gay Gene."
7. Wilcox, "Cutural Context and the Conventions of Science Journalism," 231; Lancaster, *Life Is Hard*.
8. D'Emilio, *World Turned*, 163.
9. See especially the work of Jennifer Terry, Anne Fausto-Sterling, Roger Lancaster, Edward Stein.
10. See especially Hirschfeld, *Sex in Human Relationships*; Ulrichs, *The Riddle of "Man-Manly" Love*; Krafft-Ebing, *Psychopathia Sexualis*; Ellis, *Sex in Relation to Society*.
11. D'Emilio, *World Turned*, 155.
12. Radicalesbians, "The Woman Identified Woman."
13. Ibid.
14. UC Davis Department of Psychology, "Facts about Homosexuality and Mental Health."
15. Essentialism is a highly debated concept, but here I am using it to refer to a notion that something (say, gender or sexual desire) has a fixed "essence" or nature that is basically unchanging and not the product of social and historical forces. So essentialism is contrasted with various versions of constructionism, which understands bodies, desires, identities as existing in specific places and times and not expressing some underlying and unchanging "given."
16. Rich, "Compulsory Heterosexuality and Lesbian Existence."
17. Radner, "Compulsory Sexuality and the Desiring Woman," 96.
18. Ordover, *American Eugenics*, 64.
19. These include Jiang-Ning Zhou, Michel Hofman, Louis Gooren, and Dick Swaab's "A Sex Difference in the Human Brain and Its Relation to Transsexuality," which discovered "a region in the hypothalamus that is 60% larger in men than in male-to-female transsexuals" (69), and Cheryl McCormick and Sandra Witelson's 1994 study, which argued that "the

communication conduit between parts of the brain used for understanding speech and perceiving objects is bigger in gay men than straight men." McCormick and Witelson, "Functional Cerebral Asymmetry and Sexual Orientation in Men and Women," 528.

20. Bailey and Pillard, "Genetic Study of Male Sexual Orientation," 1093.
21. For examples, see Carey, "Criticism of a Gender Theory"; Burt and Jorgensen, "NU Panel to Investigate Prof's Research Tactics"; R. Wilson, "Transsexual 'Subjects' Complain about Professor's Research Methods."
22. Bering, "Sneaky F*cker Theory."
23. Barber, "Could Homosexual Genes Be Naturally Selected?"
24. Jordan-Young, *Brain Storm*, 168.
25. Lippa, "Are 2D:4D Finger-Length Ratios Related?"
26. Quoted in Bode, "Sexuality at Hand."
27. O'Riordan, "Life of the Gay Gene," 364.
28. Barash, "Evolutionary Mystery of Homosexuality."
29. O'Riordan, "Life of the Gay Gene," 364.
30. Terry, "'Unnatural Acts' in Nature," 153.
31. Abrams, "Real Story on Gay Genes."
32. Ibid.
33. Terry, *American Obsession*, 240.
34. Conrad, "Public Eyes and Private Genes," 146.
35. Lancaster, *Trouble with Nature*, 12.
36. McCaughy, "Perverting Evolutionary Narratives of Heterosexual Masculinity," 273.
37. Quoted in Kunzig, "Finding the Switch."
38. Kelly, "Daughter's Friendship with Effeminate Boy Isn't Hazardous."
39. Adriaens and de Block, "Evolution of a Social Construction," 573.
40. Ibid, 574.
41. Ibid., 576.
42. Ibid., 583.
43. Kunzig, "Finding the Switch."

**NOTES TO CHAPTER 5**

1. LeVay, *Gay, Straight, and the Reason Why*, 17.
2. LeVay, "Difference in Hypothalamic Structure between Homosexual and Heterosexual Men," 1036.
3. Wade, "Pas De Deux of Sexuality Is Written in the Genes."
4. Hamer and LeVay, "Evidence for a Biological Influence in Male Homosexuality."

5. Lemonick, "Behavior: The Scent of a Man."
6. Ibid.
7. Quoted in Wade, "Pas De Deux of Sexuality Is Written in the Genes."
8. Kunzig, "Finding the Switch."
9. Brookey, *Reinventing the Male Homosexual*, 19.
10. Kunzig, "Finding the Switch."
11. Quoted in Alice Park, "What the Gay Brain Looks Like."
12. Kunzig, "Finding the Switch."
13. Wade, "Pas De Deux of Sexuality Is Written in the Genes."
14. Quoted in ibid.
15. Irvine, *Disorders of Desire*, 194.
16. Wade, "Pas De Deux of Sexuality Is Written in the Genes."
17. "Is My Baby Gay?," 20/20, March 28, 2008.
18. Ibid.
19. Ibid.
20. Ibid.
21. Lancaster, *Trouble with Nature*, 17.
22. Barber, "Could Homosexual Genes Be Naturally Selected?"
23. Cloud, "Why Some Animals Are Gay."
24. Zuk, *Sexual Selections*, 178. Bonobos—a type of great ape—have a reputation as a polymorphously perverse animal, seemingly engaging in recreational sex with an indiscriminate array of other bonobos.
25. Smith, "Love That Dare Not Squeak Its Name."
26. Ibid.
27. Epstein, "Am I Anti-Gay?"
28. Barber, "Gay Animals."
29. Quoted in Wilcox, "Cutural Context and the Conventions of Science Journalism," 232.
30. Lowe, "Introduction."
31. Lowe, "Letter to Louise."
32. Ibid.
33. Ibid.
34. Ibid.
35. Kristof, "Gay at Birth."
36. Myerson, "God and His Gays."
37. Mohler, "Is Your Baby Gay?"
38. Myerson, "God and His Gays."
39. Brookey, *Reinventing the Male Homosexual*, 2.
40. Nicolosi, *Reparative Therapy of Male Homosexuality*, 141.
41. Quoted in Lindenberger, "Evangelical's Concession on Gays."

1. Whisman, *Queer by Choice*, 3.
2. "Democratic Presidential Primary Debate," Logo, August 9, 2007.
3. "2004 Presidential Election Debates," CBS, October 14, 2004.
4. Witchel, "Life after 'Sex.'"
5. Grindley, "Cynthia Nixon: Being Bisexual 'Is Not a Choice.'"
6. Fausto-Sterling, "Frameworks of Desire," 51.
7. Jakobsen and Pellegrini, *Love the Sin*, 77.
8. Robert Lopez and Jeff Marx, "If You Were Gay," *Avenue Q* (2003).
9. Truth Wins Out, "History."
10. Lancaster, *Trouble with Nature*, 22.
11. Ibid.
12. Ibid.
13. Marcus, *Is It a Choice?*
14. Quoted in Kabbany, "Scientific Studies Fail to Corroborate 'Gay Gene' Theory."
15. E. Wilson, "Neurological Preference," 24.
16. Stein, "Evidence for Queer Genes," 100.
17. Hamer and LeVay, "Evidence for a Biological Influence in Male Homosexuality," 44.
18. Allen, "Double-Edged Sword of Genetic Determinism," 263.
19. Stein, "Evidence for Queer Genes," 98.
20. Quoted in Lovett, "After 37 Years of Trying to Change People's Sexual Orientation, Group Is to Disband."
21. Truth Wins Out, "History."
22. Murphy, "Brief History of the 'Gay Gene.'"
23. "The Things That Matter," *The Oprah Winfrey Show*, February 10, 2013.
24. Katz, *Invention of Heterosexuality*.
25. Jordan-Young, *Brain Storm*, 49.
26. Certainly there is a lot of anecdotal evidence to confirm this, as referenced in blogs and websites such as Jezebel, Lesbilicious, and the Daily Beast. But a few studies also seem to confirm this: one by M. L. Chivers, M. C. Seto, and R. Blanchard ("Gender and Sexual Orientation Differences in Sexual Response to Sexual Activities versus Gender of Actors in Sexual Films") shows that, for women, action or activity is more arousing than the sex of the actors. For both gay and straight women, the sex of actors was less significant to their arousal than it was for men. Thus, many things may be physically arousing but may not incite action or affect one's sexual identity.

27. McCaughy, "Perverting Evolutionary Narratives of Heterosexual Masculinity," 278.
28. Jordan-Young, *Brain Storm*, 144.
29. "Gay Gene Isolated, Ostracized."
30. Chris Taylor, "Gay Scientists Isolate Christian Gene."
31. "Family Gay," *Family Guy*, Season 7, Episode 8, March 8, 2009.
32. Terry, *American Obsession*, 7.
33. Chinn, "Anatomizing Eugenics," 473.
34. Schwartz, "Genes, Hormones, and Sexuality."
35. Interestingly, in the original play, she aborts the fetus and is rendered sterile (and estranged from her gay brother). In the all-star movie, made a few years later and perhaps reflecting a changing social landscape, she actually gives birth to the child and loses her husband, who can't bear the idea of raising a gay child.
36. Brookey, *Reinventing the Male Homosexual*, 11.
37. Gallagher, "Fixing Sexual Direction."
38. Ramsey Colloquium, "Homosexual Movement," 145.
39. Quoted in Duke, "The Problem, in a Fundamental Nutshell."
40. Ibid.
41. Quoted in *London Sunday Telegraph*, February 17, 1997.
42. C. Burr, "Why Conservatives Should Embrace the Gay Gene."
43. Baram, "If There Was a Gay-Straight Switch, Would You Switch?"
44. Lancaster, *Trouble with Nature*, 18.
45. McCaughy, "Perverting Evolutionary Narratives of Heterosexual Masculinity," 281.
46. *Nightline*, August 31, 1991.
47. Romer v. Evans, 517 U.S. 620 (1996).
48. Quoted in Kabbany, "Scientific Studies Fail to Corroborate 'Gay Gene' Theory."
49. Brookey, *Reinventing the Male Homosexual*, 11.
50. Rohy, "On Homosexual Reproduction."
51. Hamer and Rosbash, "Genetics and Proposition 8."
52. D'Emilio, *World Turned*, 163.
53. Simpson, "Bored This Way."
54. Mooallem, "Love That Dare Not Squawk Its Name."
55. PFLAG, "Frequently Asked Questions."
56. Rohy, "On Homosexual Reproduction," 112.

1. Hay, *Radically Gay*, 79.
2. Quoted in Hirshman, *Victory*, 37.
3. Simmel, "Sociological Significance of the 'Stranger.'"
4. Roy Romer v. Richard Evans, No. 94-1039, 517 U.S. 620 (May 20, 1996).
5. Bernstein, "Nothing Ventured, Nothing Gained?," 354.
6. Naomi Klein has written extensively on this general topic of consumerism and capitalism (*No Logo*), and others have written more specifically about this in relation to gays, including my own book *All the Rage*, Katherine Sender's *Business, Not Politics*, and Alexandra Chasin's *Selling Out*.
7. Bankoff, "Joe Biden Is 'Absolutely Comfortable' with Gay Marriage."
8. Gross, "Gay Is the New Black?"
9. Cahill, "Disproportionate Impact of Anti-Gay Family Policies," 219.
10. M. Davis and Company, Inc., et al., "Estimate of Housing Discrimination against Same-Sex Couples."
11. Human Rights Campaign, "Corporate Equality Index 2013."
12. Ibid.
13. Cahill, "Disproportionate Impact of Anti-Gay Family Policies," 219.
14. King and Cortina, "Social and Economic Imperative of Lesbian, Gay, Bisexual, and Transgendered Supportive Organizational Policies."
15. Harris Interactive, "Out & Equal Workplace Culture Report."
16. King and Cortina, "Social and Economic Imperative of Lesbian, Gay, Bisexual, and Transgendered Supportive Organizational Policies," 71.
17. Walters, "The Proud, the Few, the Gays."
18. "'Gays Too Precious to Risk in Combat,' Says General."
19. "Repeal of 'Don't Ask, Don't Tell' Paves Way for Gay Sex Right on Battlefield, Opponents Fantasize."
20. "Mortal Combat—Dan Choi Is Gay," *The Daily Show with Jon Stewart*, Comedy Central television broadcast, May 14, 2009, available at http://www.thedailyshow.com/watch/thu-may-14-2009/dan-choi-is-gay.
21. Powell, in Hawaii State Bar Association, "Same Sex Marriage," 69.
22. Kruse, "'Don't Ask, Don't Tell' Repeal Urged at Congressional Black Caucus Conference."
23. One such positive effect will be the retention of Arabic and Farsi translators. Kesler, "Serving with Integrity." This is particularly important given our continued involvement in Middle Eastern conflicts. Open service and gay inclusion would stop the loss of translators necessary for such efforts.

24. Johnson and Ham, "Report of the Comprehensive Review of the Issues," 84.
25. Ibid., 85.
26. Powell later came out for repeal of DADT. Hawaii State Bar Association, "Same Sex Marriage," 69.
27. Johnson and Ham, "Report of the Comprehensive Review of the Issues," 13–14.
28. Ibid., 131. The DoD report notes that, in an effort not to make those who have particular religious beliefs feel rejected, "individual service members are *not* expected to change their personal . . . beliefs" upon repeal of DADT.
29. Ibid.
30. Quoted in B. Ross, "House Panel Votes to Ban Gay Weddings on Military Bases."
31. Johnson and Ham, "Report of the Comprehensive Review of the Issues," 82, 84.
32. Ibid., 86.
33. Somerville, "Queer Loving," 337.
34. See especially Hull, Scott, and Smith, *All the Women Are White.*
35. Mezey, *Queers in Court,* 137.
36. Pickhardt, "Choose or Lose," 921, 931, 932. The status/conduct distinction seems specific to the language of DADT but has larger, albeit vaguer, iterations across the political spectrum (e.g., in appeals to "normalcy": do not be too gay, too flamboyant, too gender nonnormative). DADT repeal efforts therefore illustrate well the limits of tolerance in the absolute refusal to address homophobia by positing an "acceptable" (just the same as you and me) gayness counterposed to the still available abject queer. The interviews excerpted in the recent DoD report put gay service members, unsurprisingly, on the side of discretion and fitting in. Like interviews with long-term couples desirous of the marriage option, interviews with gay service members largely mimic the hegemonic frame of "fitting in" and "discretion" that is often explicitly juxtaposed to those few flamboyant gays who give the rest of them a bad name. In the move to repeal DADT, both gay advocates and reluctant military personnel repeatedly assert that it is much ado about nothing: that after repeal, little will change because most gay service members "will continue to be discreet." Johnson and Ham, "Report of the Comprehensive Review of the Issues Associated with 'Don't Ask, Don't Tell,' " 85; Wood, "Pentagon Asks for Repeal of 'DADT.' "
37. Statement of Gregory M. Herek, Psychologist, American Psychological Association, *Policy Implications of Lifting the Ban on Homosexuals in*

the Military: Hearings before the Committee on Armed Services, 103rd Cong. (1993), 245.

38. See, e.g., *Testimony Relating to the "Don't Ask, Don't Tell" Policy: Hearing before the Committee on Armed Services*, 111th Cong. (2010), 1–41 (statement of General John J. Sheehan, Retired, United States Marine Corps).

39. McPeak, "Don't Ask, Don't Tell, Don't Change."

40. Brown and Ayres, "The Inclusive Command," 156 (quoting Able v. United States, 968 F. Supp. 850, 858 [E.D.N.Y. 1997]).

41. Madhani, "Don't Drop 'Don't Ask, Don't Tell,' Pace Says."

42. Statement of Sen. Carl Levin, Chairman, Senate Committee on Armed Services, *Testimony Relating to the "Don't Ask, Don't Tell" Policy: Hearing before the Committee on Armed Services*, 111th Cong. (2010), 45.

43. Stating that DADT promotes this view, see, e.g., Krygowski, "Homosexuality and the Military Mission," 919.

44. Correales, "Don't Ask, Don't Tell."

45. Describing LGBTQ internal debate over same-sex marriage, see Schacter, "Other Same-Sex Marriage Debate," 382.

46. Asserting that the DoD believes allowing homosexuals to serve would cause problems, see, e.g., *Policy Implications of Lifting the Ban of Homosexuals in the Military*, 255.

47. Lutz, "Who Joins the Military?," 36 (explaining overrepresentation of African Americans and working class in the military).

48. Rauch, "What We Learned from an Obama Win."

49. Rich, "40 Years Later, Still Second-Class Americans."

50. T. Egan, "Dismissed from Army as Lesbian, Colonel Will Fight Homosexual Ban."

51. Rich, "40 Years Later, Still Second-Class Americans."

### NOTES TO CHAPTER 8

1. Berkin, "Fashionable People Support Gay Marriage."

2. Testimony of Maggie Gallagher before the New Hampshire Legislature, February 17, 2011.

3. Talbot, "Wedding Bells."

4. Klarman, *From the Closet to the Altar*, 197.

5. CBS/*New York Times*, "Poll: Slim Majority Back Same Sex Marriage," May 2012.

6. "What Is the Most Pressing Issue Facing the LGBT Community?," *HuffPost Gay Voices*.

7. Waldman, "We've Already Won the Battle over Gay Marriage."

8. Talbot, "Risky Proposal."
9. Badgett, *When Gay People Get Married*, 1.
10. Quoted in Talbot, "Risky Proposal."
11. See especially the work of Nancy Polikoff, Suzanne Goldberg, and Jaye Cee Whitehead.
12. Altman, "Same-Sex Marriage Just a Sop to Convention."
13. Coontz, "Disestablishment of Marriage."
14. D'Emilio, "Marriage Fight Is Setting Us Back," 11.
15. Stacey, *Unhitched*, 199.
16. Polikoff, *Beyond (Gay and Straight) Marriage.*
17. Beyond Marriage, "New Strategic Vision for All Our Families & Relationships."
18. Pollitt, "No Presents, Please."
19. Conrad, *Against Equality.*
20. "Tracking the Money: Final Numbers"; Cover, "Millions Expected to Be Spent in Vote on Gay Marriage"; Nagourney and Barnes, "Evolving Donor Network in Gay Marriage Drive."
21. Haberman, "Gay Marriage Ruling Praised by Mega-Donor Paul Singer."
22. Eckholm, "Corporate Call for Change in Gay Marriage Case."
23. Blankenhorn, "How My View on Gay Marriage Changed."
24. Oppenheimer, "In Shift, an Activist Enlists Same-Sex Couples in a Pro-Marriage Coalition."
25. Bruni, "G.O.P.'s Gay Trajectory."
26. Quoted in ibid.
27. Quoted in "GOProud Puts Economics before Gay Marriage at 'Homocon' Dance Party in Tampa."
28. Speech to Conservative Party Conference, December 11, 2011.
29. Bruni, "To Know Us Is to Let Us Love."
30. Eckholm, "Push Expands for Legalizing Same-Sex Marriage."
31. American Academy of Pediatrics, Committee on Psychosocial Aspects of Child and Family Health, "Promoting the Well-Being of Children Whose Parents Are Gay or Lesbian."
32. Rauch, *Gay Marriage*, 1–2.
33. Ibid., 81.
34. Coontz, "How Straight Marriage's Evolution Led to Obama's Gay-Marriage Endorsement."
35. World Health Organization, "Responding to Intimate Partner Violence and Sexual Violence against Women."
36. Badgett, *When Gay People Get Married*, 202.
37. Ibid., 203.

38. Mundy, "Gay Guide to Wedded Bliss."
39. Quoted in ibid.
40. Wolfson, *Why Marriage Matters*, 87.
41. Charles Cooper, "Opening Arguments on Behalf of the Petitioners," Supreme Court Case 12-144, *Hollingsworth v. Perry* (March 26, 2013).
42. Eskridge and Spedale, *Gay Marriage*, 251.
43. Rollins, "Same-Sex Unions and the Spectacles of Recognition," 459.
44. Klarman, *From the Closet to the Altar*, xi.
45. This is no small matter. While the excessive focus on same-sex marriage has had, in my estimation, all kinds of negative effects, it had also had the salutary effect of pushing all kinds of constituencies to become more politically active and engaged.

## NOTES TO CHAPTER 9

1. Regnerus, "How Different Are the Adult Children of Parents Who Have Same-Sex Relationships?"
2. Garcia, "Professor Stands by Biased Gay Parenting Study."
3. Wahls, "Zach Wahls Speaks about Family."
4. Kentucky, Michigan, Mississippi, Nebraska, North Carolina, Ohio, and Utah all ban second-parent adoption.
5. Public Religion Research Institute, "Majority of Americans Say They Support Same-Sex Marriage."
6. Pew Research Center, "Decline of Marriage and Rise of New Families."
7. Fischer, "Why Same-Sex Marriage Is Bad for Children."
8. Bill Donahue, on *Lou Dobbs Tonight*, May 10, 2012.
9. Stacey, *Unhitched*, 4.
10. National Center for Lesbian Rights, "LGBTQ Youth in the Foster Care System."
11. Ibid.
12. Sarah Schulman has made just such an argument in her book *Ties That Bind*.
13. This is also known—by me at least—as the *Dick Cheney dilemma*, in reference to former US vice president Dick Cheney, a well-known conservative with an openly gay daughter. In other words, his gay progeny had little effect on his support of anti-gay legislation.
14. Pew Research Center, "In Gay Marriage Debate, Both Supporters and Opponents See Legal Recognition as 'Inevitable.' "
15. And its always two here: the single mother remains the specter that haunts Western civilization.

16. The literature here is vast, including the work of Kath Weston (*Families We Choose*); Stephanie Coontz (*The Way We Never Were*); Jeffrey Weeks, Catherine Donovan, and Brian Heaphy (*Same Sex Intimacies*); Hilde Lindemann Nelson (ed., *Feminism and Families*); Stephen Hicks (*Lesbian, Gay and Queer Parenting*); Valerie Lehr (*Queer Family Values*); and Yvette Taylor (*Lesbian and Gay Parenting*), to name just a few.

17. As an aside, why do lesbians in films and television programs always have androgynous or manly names, or just weird names like Calliope and Arizona, while the straight people are named, uh, Mark or Paul? Really, the names are not what make us lesbians. If they were, many proud lesbians would be litigious toward their normative-naming parents.

18. Indeed, one piece in the *Advocate* was both effusive in its praise and explicitly made the comparison with *Brokeback Mountain*, by deeming *Kids* "our" *Brokeback Mountain*. This piece focused on the significance of having major stars in both films (apparently making it more accessible to a non-gay audience) yet never once mentioned that these are *straight* actors!

19. Halberstam, "The Kids Aren't Alright!"

20. Edelstein, "New Normal."

21. Ebert, "The Kids Are All Right."

22. Scott, "Meet the Sperm Donor: Modern Family Ties."

23. T. Burr, "The Kids Are All Right."

24. Austerlitz, "Same-Sex, with the Same Family Issues."

25. E. Taylor, " 'The Kids Are All Right' Puts the 'Fun' in 'Dysfunction.' "

26. Like the word "liberal," the word "political" (and "partisan" even more!) has gotten a bad rap lately. I assume here that "political" would mean taking an overtly gay rights stance, while nonpolitical would therefore be associated with "human," which is somehow not gay. Quote from Austerlitz, "Same Sex—with the Same Family Issues."

27. Sharkey, "The Kids Are All Right."

28. Stevens, "The Kids Are All Right."

29. Quoted in Puente, "Hollywood Now Opening Arms to Gay Characters, Families."

30. Savage, "Truth about Gay Families."

31. The one scene in which Jules and Nic are out with another adult couple depicts that couple as heterosexual.

32. There was even a recent longitudinal study that found that kids of planned lesbian families actually are more empathetic, more open to negotiation instead of confrontation, more successful generally than their normative peers. See van Gelderen et al., "Quality of Life of Adolescents Raised from Birth by Lesbian Mothers."

33. Stacey and Biblarz, "How Does the Gender of Parents Matter?," 10.
34. Ibid., 12.
35. See especially Balsam et al., "Three-Year Follow-Up of Same-Sex Couples Who Had Civil Unions in Vermont, Same-Sex Couples Not in Civil Unions, and Heterosexual Married Couples."
36. Stacey, Unhitched, 83. See also Stacey and Biblarz, "(How) Does the Sexual Orientation of Parents Matter?" and "How Does the Gender of Parents Matter?"
37. *Glee* is a somewhat more complicated structure. Created by uber gay producer Ryan Murphy (of *Nip/Tuck* fame), *Glee* burst on the scene to become—somewhat improbably—one of those expansive cultural moments when marketing, entertainment, social commentary, fanaticism, and critical appeal converge. It is, in other words, not merely a success but a phenomenon.
38. In a wonderful scene, one of Coop's mothers has come in for an emergency operation and—as the other mother rushes in and the family configuration becomes apparent—Dr. O'Hara gazes at him with new respect: "Two mothers, Coop? Bravo." Here you get that unusual moment of marking the difference without fetishizing it or using it as a signifier for other more "important" universal "truths."
39. Halperin, *How to Be Gay*, 448.

### NOTES TO CHAPTER 10

1. T. Jones, "Gay-Friendly Countries Named Happiest in the World."
2. Brewer, "Shifting Foundations of Public Opinion about Gay Rights," 1208.
3. Blow, "Gay? Whatever, Dude."
4. In the 2012 election, voters in Maine legalized same-sex marriage, but earlier it had been passed by the legislature, only to be overturned by the courts. In 2011, the New Hampshire House Judiciary Committee did vote to repeal same-sex marriage. However, the governor threatened to veto the bill, and the House then voted to kill the bill. In Vermont, the bill was actually vetoed by the governor after being passed by both houses, but the veto was subsequently overridden in the state congress.
5. Peters, "Why the Gay Rights Movement Has No National Leader."
6. "Scott Brown Engaged in Culture Wars at Mass Poll."
7. In a speech given at the EdWatch.com National Education Conference, 2004.
8. In a campaign speech in Iowa City, IA, May 3, 2011.

9. Socarides, "Where's Our 'Fierce Advocate'?"

10. Socarides, "Way Forward on Gay Marriage."

11. Quoted in Eckholm, "Boy Scouts End Longtime Ban on Openly Gay Youth."

12. Saad, "U.S. Acceptance of Gay/Lesbian Relations Is the New Normal."

13. Quoted in Murdoch, *Courting Justice*, 57.

14. Rauch, "What We Learned from an Obama Win."

15. Ibid.

16. Ibid.

17. Rich, "Smoke the Bigots Out of the Closet."

18. Savan, "Without Anti-Gay Hysteria, Massa's a Dud for the GOP."

19. Rich, "Gay Bashing at the Smithsonian."

20. Ibid.

21. Nagourney, "Political Shifts on Gay Rights Lag behind Culture."

22. Rich, "Two Weddings, a Divorce and 'Glee.' "

23. Nagourney, "Political Shifts on Gay Rights Lag behind Culture."

24. Ibid.

25. Rich, "40 Years Later, Still Second-Class American."

26. Rich, "Smoke the Bigots Out of the Closet."

27. One such poll from CNN/ORC International shows a rise of twelve points from 2007 to 2013. CNN/ORC Poll (June 6, 2012), http://i2.cdn .turner.com/cnn/2012/images/06/06/rel5e.pdf.

28. "Jeffrey Fehr, Gay California Teen and Cheerleading Squad Captain, Commits Suicide on New Year's Day."

29. Hibbard, "Brandon Elizares, Gay Teen, Commits Suicide."

30. Martin, "Four Teens Attack Gay Chatham Elementary Student."

31. Savage and Miller, *It Gets Better*, 5.

### NOTES TO CHAPTER 11

1. Quoted in Nagourney, "Gay Democrats Celebrate a Newfound Visibility."

2. President Obama's Inaugural Address, delivered January 21, 2013.

3. Rauch, "What We Learned from the Obama Win"; Johnson and Ham, "Report of the Comprehensive Review of the Issues," 152–53.

4. Bruni, "Love among the Spuds."

5. Lawrence v. Texas (02-102), 539 U.S. 558 (2003), 41 S.W. 3d 349, reversed and remanded.

6. Adams, "Radical Integration," 263.

7. Ibid., 264.

8. Gilroy, *After Empire*, 67.

9. Warner, *Fear of a Queer Planet.*
10. Russell, "Color of Discipline," 101.
11. Yoshino, *Covering*, 169.
12. Ibid., xi.
13. Steinhorn and Diggs-Brown, *By the Color of Our Skin*, 91.
14. Garcia, "Activist Reflects."
15. Mendelsohn, "Closet by Any Other Name."
16. Kim, "Against 'Bullying' or on Loving Queer Kids."
17. Stacey, *Unhitched*, 82.
18. National Longitudinal Lesbian Family Study, 2012 results.
19. Bruni, "2 Dads, 2 Daughters, 1 Big Day."
20. Stanton, "Cantor Urges Tolerance on Gays, Muslims."
21. Duggan, *Twilight of Equality*; Warner, *Fear of a Queer Planet.*
22. Spade, *Normal Life*, 15.
23. Gay Liberation Front, *Manifesto.*
24. Prentice, Avila, and McKinney, "Argument in Favor of Proposition 8."
25. Feldblum, "Selling of Proposition 8."
26. Lampo, "Is the GOP Deeply Anti-Gay? Hardly."
27. Charles Taylor, *Multiculturalism and "The Politics of Recognition,"* 26.
28. D. Brooks, "Freedom Loses One."
29. Human Rights Campaign survey, July 2011, iPOLL Databank, Roper Center for Public Opinion Research, University of Connecticut, http://o-www.ropercenter.uconn.edu.ilsprod.lib.neu.edu/data_access/ipoll/ipoll.html (accessed August 25, 2012).
30. Love, *Feeling Backward*, 10.
31. Brown, "Problem with Tolerance."
32. Stanley, " 'New Normal' Fall Shows Feature Gay Characters or Not."
33. Halperin, *How to Be Gay*, 119.
34. Ibid., 173.
35. Ibid., 447.
36. Ibid., 74.

# BIBLIOGRAPHY

Abrams, Michael. "The Real Story on Gay Genes." *Discover*, June 5, 2007.

Adams, Michelle. "Radical Integration." *California Law Review* 94, no. 2 (2006): 261–311.

Adriaens, Pieter, and Andreas de Block. "The Evolution of a Social Construction: The Case of Male Homosexuality." *Perspectives in Biology and Medicine* 49, no. 4 (2006): 570–585.

Alexiou, Alice Sparberg. "Gay Youth Discover There's a Safe Place to Be Themselves." *New York Times*, April 2, 2000.

Allen, Garland E. "The Double-Edged Sword of Genetic Determinism: Social and Political Agendas in Genetic Studies of Homosexuality, 1940–1994." In *Science and Homosexualities*, edited by Vernon A. Rosario, 244–270. New York: Routledge, 1997.

Altman, Dennis. "Same-Sex Marriage Just a Sop to Convention." *Australian*, February 5, 2011.

American Academy of Pediatrics, Committee on Psychosocial Aspects of Child and Family Health. "Promoting the Well-Being of Children Whose Parents Are Gay or Lesbian." Policy statement. March 20, 2013.

Austerlitz, Saul. "Same Sex—with the Same Family Issues." *Boston Globe*, July 11, 2010.

Badgett, M. V. Lee. *When Gay People Get Married: What Happens When Societies Legalize Same-Sex Marriage*. New York: NYU Press, 2009.

Bailey, J. Michael, and Richard C. Pillard. "A Genetic Study of Male Sexual Orientation." *Archives of General Psychiatry* 48 (December 1991): 1089–1096.

Balsam, Kimberly F., Theodore P. Beauchaine, Esther D. Rothblum, and Sondra E. Solomon. "Three-Year Follow-Up of Same-Sex Couples Who Had Civil Unions in Vermont, Same-Sex Couples Not in Civil Unions, and Heterosexual Married Couples." *Developmental Psychology* 44, no. 1 (January 2008): 102–116.

Bankoff, Caroline. "Joe Biden Is 'Absolutely Comfortable' with Gay Marriage." *New York*, May 5, 2012. http://nymag.com/daily/intelligencer/2012/05/biden-absolutely-comfortable-with-gay-marriage.html.

Barabak, Mark. "Gays May Have the Fastest of All Civil Rights Movements." *Los Angeles Times*, May 20, 2012.

Baram, Marcus. "If There Was a Gay-Straight Switch, Would You Switch?" *ABCNews.com*, December 14, 2007. http://abcnews.go.com/Health/storynew?id=3997085&page=1#.UdPboT5oQ5U.

Barash, David P. "The Evolutionary Mystery of Homosexuality." *Chronicle of Higher Education*, November 19, 2012.

Barber, Nigel. "Could Homosexual Genes Be Naturally Selected?" *The Human Beast* (blog), *Psychology Today*, June 9, 2009. http://www.psychologytoday.com/blog/the-human-beast/200906/could-homosexual-genes-be-naturally-selected.

———. "Gay Animals." *The Human Beast* (blog), *Psychology Today*, June 17, 2009. http://www.psychologytoday.com/blog/the-human-beast/200906/gay-animals.

Bering, Jesse. "The Sneaky F*cker Theory (and Other Gay Ideas)." *Quirky Little Things* (blog), *Psychology Today*, May 15, 2008.

Berkin, George. "Fashionable People Support Gay Marriage." *NJ Voices* (blog), May 11, 2012. http://blog.nj.com/njv_george_berkin/2012/05/fashionable_people_support_gay.html.

Bernstein, Mary. "Nothing Ventured, Nothing Gained? Conceptualizing Social Movement 'Success' in the Lesbian and Gay Movement." *Sociological Perspectives* 46, no. 3 (2003): 353–379.

Besen, Wayne. "Rift Forms in Movement as Belief in Gay 'Cure' Is Renounced." *New York Times*, July 6, 2012.

Beyond Marriage. "Beyond Same-Sex Marriage: A New Strategic Vision for All Our Families & Relationships." July 26, 2006. http://www.beyondmarriage.org/full_statement.html.

Blankenhorn, David. "How My View on Gay Marriage Changed." *New York Times*, June 22, 2012.

Blow, C. M. "Gay? Whatever, Dude." *New York Times*, June 4, 2010.

Bode, Nicole. "Sexuality at Hand." *Psychology Today*, November 1, 2000. http://www.psychologytoday.com/articles/200011/sexuality-hand.

Boyd, Danah. "Why Youth (Heart) Social Network Sites: The Role of Networked Publics in Teenage Social Life." In *Youth, Identity, and Digital Media*, edited by David Buckingham, 119–142. Cambridge: MIT Press, 2007.

Brewer, Paul R. "The Shifting Foundations of Public Opinion about Gay Rights." *Journal of Politics* 65, no. 4 (2003): 1208–1220.

Bronski, Michael. "Positive Images & the Coming Out Film." *Cineaste* 26, no. 1 (2000): 20–26.

Brookey, Robert Alan. *Reinventing the Male Homosexual: The Rhetoric and Power of the Gay Gene, Race, Gender, and Science.* Bloomington: Indiana University Press, 2002.

Brooks, Caryn. "How to Come Out on Facebook." *Time*, June 2, 2009.

Brooks, David. "Freedom Loses One." *New York Times*, April 1, 2013.

Brown, Jennifer Gerarda, and Ian Ayres. "The Inclusive Command: Voluntary Integration of Sexual Minorities into the U.S. Military." *Michigan Law Review* 103, no. 21 (2004): 150–156.

Brown, Wendy. "The Problem with Tolerance." In *Philosophy Bites*, edited by David Edmonds and Nigel Warbuton, 88–96. New York: Oxford University Press, 2010.

———. *Regulating Aversion: Tolerance in the Age of Identity and Empire.* Princeton: Princeton University Press, 2006.

Bruni, Frank. "The G.O.P.'s Gay Trajectory." *New York Times*, June 9, 2012.

———. "Love among the Spuds." *New York Times*, July 10, 2012.

———. "To Know Us Is to Let Us Love." *New York Times*, June 10, 2012.

———. "2 Dads, 2 Daughters, 1 Big Day." *New York Times*, July 20, 2011.

Burr, Chandler. "Why Conservatives Should Embrace the Gay Gene." *Weekly Standard*, December 15, 1996.

Burr, Ty. "The Kids Are All Right." *Boston Globe*, July 16, 2010.

Burt, Sheila, and Laurel Jorgensen. "NU Panel to Investigate Prof's Research Tactics." *Daily Northwestern*, November 18, 2003.

Butler, Judith. "Imitation and Gender Insubordination." In *Inside/Out: Lesbian Theories, Gay Theories*, edited by Diana Fuss, 13–31. New York: Routledge, 1991.

Cahill, Sean. "The Disproportionate Impact of Anti-Gay Policies on Black and Latino Same-Sex Couple Households." *Journal of African American Studies* 13 (2009): 219–250.

Carey, Benedict. "Criticism of a Gender Theory, and a Scientist under Siege." *New York Times*, August 21, 2007.

Chasin, Alexandra. *Selling Out: The Gay and Lesbian Movement Goes to Market.* New York: Palgrave Macmillan, 2000.

Chauncey, George. *Gay New York: Gender, Urban Culture, and the Makings of the Gay Male World, 1890–1940.* New York: Basic Books, 1994.

———. *Why Marriage? The History Shaping Today's Debate over Gay Equality.* New York: Basic Books, 2004.

Chinn, Sarah. "Anatomizing Eugenics: Tracing the Legacy of Biology in Public Policy." *GLQ* 11, no. 3 (2005): 472–475.

Chivers, M. L., M. C. Seto, and R. Blanchard. "Gender and Sexual Orientation Differences in Sexual Response to Sexual Activities versus Gender of Actors in Sexual Films." *Journal of Personality and Social Psychology* 93, no. 6 (2007): 1108–1121.

Cloud, John. "The Battle over Gay Teens." *Time*, October 2, 2005.

———. "Why Some Animals Are Gay." *Time*, June 19, 2009.

Coates, Ta-Nehisi. "The Good, Racist People." *New York Times*, March 7, 2013.

Connelly, Sherryl. "Rupert Everett: Coming Out of the Closet Ruined My Career in Hollywood." *Daily News*, December 3, 2009.

Conrad, Peter. "Public Eyes and Private Genes: Historical Frames, News Constructions, and Social Problems." *Social Problems* 44, no. 2 (1997): 139–154.

Conrad, Ryan, ed. *Against Equality: Queer Critiques of Gay Marriage*. Lewiston, ME: Against Equality Press, 2010.

Coontz, Stephanie. "The Disestablishment of Marriage." *New York Times*, June 22, 2013.

———. "How Straight Marriage's Evolution Led to Obama's Gay-Marriage Endorsement." *Daily Beast*, May 14, 2012. http://www.thedailybeast .com/articles/2012/05/14/how-straight-marriage-s-evolution-led-to -obama-s-gay-marriage-endorsement.html.

———. *Marriage, a History: From Obedience to Intimacy or How Love Conquered Marriage*. New York: Viking, 2005.

———. *The Way We Never Were: American Families and the Nostalgia Trap*. New York: Basic Books, 2000.

Correales, Robert I. "Don't Ask, Don't Tell: A Dying Policy on the Precipice." *California Law Review* 44 (2008): 413–463.

Cory, Donald Webster. *The Homosexual in America: A Subjective Approach*. New York: Greenberg, 1951.

Cover, Susan M. "Millions Expected to Be Spent in Vote on Gay Marriage." *Kennebec Journal*, May 15, 2012.

Crowder, Courtney. "Anna Paquin, Ricky Martin: More Stars Coming Out Than Ever Before." *ABCNews.com*, April 2, 2010. http://abcnews.go.com/ Entertainment/coming-hollywood-ricky-martin-shows-hard/story?id= 10252987.

D'Emilio, John. *Making Trouble: Essays on Gay History, Politics, and the University*. New York: Routledge, 1992.

———. "The Marriage Fight Is Setting Us Back." *Gay and Lesbian Review* 13, no. 6 (November–December 2006): 10–11.

———. *The World Turned: Essays on Gay History, Politics, and Culture*. Durham: Duke University Press, 2002.

Diamond, Lisa. "Careful What You Ask For: Reconsidering Feminist Epistemology and Autobiographical Narrative in Research on Sexual Identity Development." *Signs* 31, no. 2 (2006): 471–491.

Didion, Joan. *The White Album: Essays.* New York: Farrar, Straus and Giroux, 1979.

Duggan, Lisa. *The Twilight of Equality? Neoliberalism, Cultural Politics, and the Attack on Democracy.* Boston: Beacon, 2003.

Duke, Lynne. "The Problem, in a Fundamental Nutshell: 'Is Your Baby Gay?'" *Washington Post,* March 18, 2007.

Ebert, Roger. "The Kids Are All Right." *Chicago Sun-Times,* July 7, 2010.

Eckholm, Erik. "Boy Scouts End Longtime Ban on Openly Gay Youth." *New York Times,* May 23, 2013.

———. "Corporate Call for Change in Gay Marriage Case." *New York Times,* February 27, 2013.

———. "Push Expands for Legalizing Same-Sex Marriage." *New York Times,* November 12, 2012.

Edelstein, David. "The New Normal." *New York,* July 4, 2010.

Egan, Jennifer. "Lonely Gay Teen Seeks Same." *New York Times,* December 10, 2000.

Egan, Timothy. "Dismissed from Army as Lesbian, Colonel Will Fight Homosexual Ban." *New York Times,* May 31, 1992.

Eisenstein, Zillah R. *The Radical Future of Liberal Feminism.* Boston: Northeastern University Press, 1993.

Ellis, Havelock. *Sex in Relation to Society.* Philadelphia: Philip Davis, 1910.

Epstein, Robert. "Am I Anti-Gay?" *Psychology Today,* January 1, 2003. http://www.psychologytoday.com/articles/200301/am-i-anti-gay.

Eskridge, William N., Jr., and Darren R. Spedale. *Gay Marriage: For Better or for Worse?* Oxford: Oxford University Press, 2006.

Fausto-Sterling, Anne. "Frameworks of Desire." *Daedalus,* Spring 2007, 47–57.

Feldblum, Chai. "The Selling of Proposition 8." *Gay and Lesbian Review Worldwide* 16, no. 1 (2009). https://www344.safesecureweb.com/glreview/article.php?articleid=140.

Fischer, Bryan. "Why Same-Sex Marriage Is Bad for Children." *RenewAmerica,* July 7, 2008. http://www.renewamerica.com/columns/fischer/080707.

Foster, Jodie. "Jodie Foster's Golden Globe Speech: Full Transcript." *ABC News.com,* January 14, 2013. http://abcnews.go.com/blogs/entertainment/2013/01/full-transcript-jodie-fosters-golden-globes-speech/.

Fraser, Vikki. "Queer Closets and Rainbow Hyperlinks: The Construction and Constraint of Queer Subjectivities Online." *Sexuality Research & Social Policy* 7, no. 1 (2010): 30–36.

Gallagher, Maggie. "Fixing Sexual Direction." *Washington Post*, May 12, 2001.

Gallup. "Gay and Lesbian Rights." May 2013. http://www.gallup.com/poll/1651/Gay-Lesbian-Rights.aspx.

Garcia, Michelle. "An Activist Reflects." *Advocate*, April 12, 2010.

———. "Professor Stands by Biased Gay Parenting Study." *Advocate*, June 18, 2012.

Gates, Gary J., and Frank Newport. "LGBT Americans Skew Democratic, Largely Support Obama." Gallup. October 18, 2012. http://www.gallup.com/poll/158102/lgbt-americans-skew-democratic-largely-support-obama.aspx.

"'Gays Too Precious to Risk in Combat,' Says General." *Onion*, August 13, 2007. Video. http://www.theonion.com/video/gays-too-precious-to-risk-in-combat-says-general,14158/.

"Gay Gene Isolated, Ostracized." *Onion* 44, no. 26 (April 9, 1997).

Gay Liberation Front. *Manifesto*. 1971. Accessed at Fordham University archives, http://www.fordham.edu/halsall/pwh/glf-london.asp.

Gendar, Alison, Edgar Sandoval, and Larry McShange. "Rutgers Freshman Kills Self after Classmates Use Hidden Camera to Watch His Sexual Activity." *Daily News*, September 29, 2010. http://www.nydailynews.com/news/crime/rutgers-freshman-kills-classmates-hidden-camera-watch-sexual-activity-sources-article-1.438225.

Gibson, Kristina. "Street Kids: Risk Factors for Homelessness among Lesbian, Gay, and Bisexual Youths: A Developmental Milestone Approach." *Child Youth Services Review* 34, no. 1 (2012): 186–193.

Gilroy, Paul. *After Empire: Melancholia or Convivial Culture?* New York: Taylor & Francis, 2004.

GLSEN. "Playgrounds and Prejudice: Elementary School Climate in the United States." 2012. http://glsen.org/sites/default/files/Playgrounds%20%26%20Prejudice.pdf.

———. "States with Safe Schools Laws." http://www.glsen.org/cgi-bin/iowa/all/library/record/2344.html (accessed January 2013).

Goldberg, Suzanne B. "Discrimination by Comparison." *Yale Law Journal* 120, no. 4 (January 2011): 728–812.

Goodman, Ellen. "A Vatican Retreat on Homosexuality." *Washington Post*, December 3, 2005.

"GOProud Puts Economics before Gay Marriage at 'Homocon' Dance Party in Tampa." *Washington Post*, August 29, 2012.

Gray, Mary L. *Out in the Country: Youth, Media, and Queer Visibility in Rural America*. New York: NYU Press, 2009.

Grindley, Lucas. "Cynthia Nixon: Being Bisexual 'Is Not a Choice.'" *Advocate*, January 30, 2012.

Gross, Michael Joseph. "Gay Is the New Black?" *Advocate*, November 16, 2008. http://www.advocate.com/news/2008/11/16/gay-new-black?page=full.

———."Pride and Prejudice." *Advocate*, November 19, 2008, 30–33.

Haberman, Maggie. "Gay Marriage Ruling Praised by Mega-Donor Paul Singer." *Politico*, June 27, 2013. http://www.politico.com/story/2013/06/paul-singer-gay-marriage-rulings-93457.html.

Halberstam, J. Jack. *Gaga Feminism: Sex, Gender, and the End of Normal*. Boston: Beacon, 2012.

———. "The Kids Aren't Alright!" *Bullybloggers*, July 15, 2010. http://www.bullybloggers.wordpress.com/2010/07/15/The-Kids-Aren't-Alright/.

Halperin, David. *How to Be Gay*. Cambridge: Harvard University Press, 2012.

Hamer, Dean H., Stella Hu, Victoria L. Magnuson, Nan Hu, and Angela M. L. Pattatucci. "A Linkage between DNA Markers on the X Chromosome and Male Sexual Orientation." *Science* 261, no. 5119 (July 16, 1993): 321–327.

Hamer, Dean H., and Simon LeVay. "Evidence for a Biological Influence in Male Homosexuality." *Scientific American* 270, no. 5 (1994): 44–49.

Hamer, Dean H., and Michael Rosbash. "Genetics and Proposition 8." *Los Angeles Times*, February 23, 2010.

Harris, Mark. "The New Art of Coming Out." *Entertainment Weekly*, June 29, 2012.

Harris Interactive. "Out & Equal Workplace Culture Report." 2008. http://outandequal.org/documents/OE_workplace_culture_report.pdf.

Hawaii State Bar Association. "Same Sex Marriage." *Hawaii Bar Journal*, February 1995.

Hay, Harry. *Radically Gay*. Boston: Beacon, 1997.

Healy, Patrick. "How Celebrities Come Out Now." *New York Times*, June 9, 2012.

Herman, Didi. "'I'm Gay': Declarations, Desire, and Coming Out on Prime-Time Television." *Sexualities* 8, no. 1 (2005): 7–29.

Hewlett, Sylvia Ann, and Karen Sumberg. "For LGBT Workers, Being 'Out' Brings Advantages." *Harvard Business Review Magazine*, July 2011.

Hibbard, Laura. "Brandon Elizares, Gay Teen, Commits Suicide, Writing 'I Couldn't Make It. I Love You Guys.'" *Huffington Post*, June 14, 2012. http://www.huffingtonpost.com/2012/06/14/brandon-elizares-gay-teen-commits-suicide-leaves-note_n_1598272.html.

Hicks, Stephen. *Lesbian, Gay and Queer Parenting: Families, Intimacies, Genealogies*. New York: Palgrave Macmillan, 2011.

Hillier, Lynne, and Lyn Harrison. "Building Realities Less Limited Than Their Own: Young People Practising Same-Sex Attraction on the Internet." *Sexualities* 10, no. 1 (2007): 82–100.

Hirschfeld, Magnus. *Sex in Human Relationships*. London: John Lane, 1935.

Hirshman, Linda. *Victory: The Triumphant Gay Revolution*. New York: HarperCollins, 2012.

Holson, Laura M. "Ricky Martin's Personal Spin on His Own 'News.'" *New York Times*, April 4, 2010.

Hull, Gloria T., Patricia Bell Scott, and Barbara Smith, eds. *All the Women Are White, All the Blacks Are Men, but Some of Us Are Brave: Black Women's Studies*. New York: CUNY Press, 1993.

Human Rights Campaign. "Corporate Equality Index 2013." January 8, 2013. http://www.hrc.org/corporate-equality-index/#.UQzKRkrBOaF.

———. "National Coming Out Day Youth Report." 2010. From *Growing Up Gay In America*, HRC's national survey of LGBT youth. http://www.hrc.org/files/assets/resources/NCOD-Youth-Report.pdf.

Hunter, Aina. "'Real L Word' Girls Exclusive: Coming Out Stories." *CBSNews.com*, June 28, 2010. http://www.cbsnews.com/8301-504763_162-20008976-10391704.html.

Irvine, Janice M. *Disorders of Desire: Sexuality and Gender in Modern American Sexology*. Rev. and exp. ed. Philadelphia: Temple University Press, 2005.

Jakobsen, Janet R., and Ann Pellegrini. *Love the Sin: Sexual Regulation and the Limits of Religious Tolerance*. New York: NYU Press, 2003.

"Jeffrey Fehr, Gay California Teen and Cheerleading Squad Captain, Commits Suicide on New Year's Day." *Huffington Post*, January 17, 2012. http://www.huffingtonpost.com/2012/01/17/jeffrey-fehr-gay-california-teen-cheerleader-suicide_n_1211623.html.

Johnson, Jeh Charles, and Carter Ham. "Report of the Comprehensive Review of the Issues Associated with 'Don't Ask, Don't Tell.'" US Department of Defense. November 30, 2012.

Jones, Jeffrey. "Support for Legal Gay Relations Hits New High." Gallup. May 25, 2011. http://www.gallup.com/poll/147785/Support-Legal-Gay-Relations-Hits-NewHigh.aspx.

Jones, Thomas. "Gay-Friendly Countries Named 'Happiest' in the World," *Gay Star News*, May 29, 2013. http://www.gaystarnews.com/article/gay-friendly-countries-named-happiest-world290513.

Jordan-Young, Rebecca. *Brain Storm: The Flaws in the Science of Sex Difference*. Cambridge: Harvard University Press, 2011.

Kabbany, Jennifer. "Scientific Studies Fail to Corroborate 'Gay Gene'

Theory: Homosexual Activists Split on Issue." *Washington Times*, August 1, 2000.

Kann, Laura, Emily O'Malley Olsen, Tim McManus, Steve Kinchen, David Chyen, William A. Harris, and Howell Wechsler. "Sexual Identity, Sex of Sexual Contacts, and Health-Risk Behaviors among Students in Grades 9–12—Youth Risk Behavior Surveillance, Selected Sites, United States, 2001–2009." *Morbidity and Mortality Weekly Report* 60 (June 2011): 1–133.

Katz, Jonathan Ned. *The Invention of Heterosexuality*. Chicago: University of Chicago Press, 2007.

Kelly, Marguerite. "Daughter's Friendship with Effeminate Boy Isn't Hazardous." *Washington Post*, July 30, 2004.

Kesler, Laura R. "Serving with Integrity: The Rationale for the Repeal of 'Don't Ask, Don't Tell' and Its Ban on Acknowledged Homosexuals in the Armed Forces." *Military Law Review* 203 (2010): 284–380.

*Kids Are All Right, The*. Directed by Lisa Cholodenko. Los Angeles: Focus Features, 2010. Film.

Kim, Richard. "Against 'Bullying' or on Loving Queer Kids." *Nation*, October 6, 2010.

King, E. B., and J. Cortina. "The Social and Economic Imperative of Lesbian, Gay, Bisexual, and Transgendered Supportive Organizational Policies." *Industrial and Organizational Psychology: Perspectives on Science and Practice* 3 (2010): 69–78.

Klarman, Michael. *From the Closet to the Altar: Courts, Backlash, and the Struggle for Same-Sex Marriage*. Oxford: Oxford University Press, 2012.

Klein, Naomi. *No Logo*. New York: Picador, 2009.

Krafft-Ebing, Richard. *Psychopathia Sexualis*. Charleston, SC: Nabu, 2010.

Kristof, Nicholas. "Gay at Birth." *New York Times*, October 25, 2003.

Kruse, Julie. " 'Don't Ask, Don't Tell' Repeal Urged at Congressional Black Caucus Conference." *Servicemembers Legal Defense Network Blog*, October 18, 2007. http://www.sldn.org/blog/archives/dont-ask-dont-tell-repeal -urged-at-congressional-black-caucus-conference/.

Krygowski, Walter John. "Homosexuality and the Military Mission: The Failure of the 'Don't Ask, Don't Tell' Policy." *University of Dayton Law Review* 20 (1995): 875–933.

Kunzig, Robert. "Finding the Switch." *Psychology Today*, May 1, 2008. http://www.psychologytoday.com/articles/200804/finding-the-switch.

Lampo, David. "Is the GOP Deeply Anti-Gay? Hardly." *Los Angeles Times*, July 16, 2012.

Lancaster, Roger N. *Life Is Hard: Machismo, Danger, and the Intimacy of Power in Nicaragua*. Berkeley: University of California Press, 1992.

———. *The Trouble with Nature: Sex in Science and Popular Culture*. Berkeley: University of California Press, 2003.

Laudadio, Marisa. "Ricky Martin: Proud to Be Gay." *People*, April 12, 2010.

Lehr, Valerie. *Queer Family Values: Rethinking the Myth of the Nuclear Family*. Philadelphia: Temple University Press, 1999.

Lemonick, Michael D. "Behavior: The Scent of a Man." *Time*, May 15, 2005.

LeVay, Simon. "A Difference in Hypothalamic Structure between Homosexual and Heterosexual Men." *Science* 253, no. 5023 (August 1991): 1034–1037.

———. *Gay, Straight, and the Reason Why*. New York: Oxford University Press, 2010.

Lindenberger, Michael. "An Evangelical's Concession on Gays." *Time*, March 16, 2007.

Lippa, Richard. "Are 2D:4D Finger-Length Ratios Related to Sexual Orientation? Yes for Men, No for Women." *Journal of Personality and Social Psychology* 85, no. 1 (2003): 179–188.

Lobron, Alison. "Easy Out." *Boston Globe*, November 11, 2007.

Love, Heather. *Feeling Backward: Loss and the Politics of Queer History*. Cambridge: Harvard University Press, 2009.

Lovett, Ian. "After 37 Years of Trying to Change People's Sexual Orientation, Group Is to Disband." *New York Times*, June 20, 2013.

Lowe, Bruce. "Introduction." *God Made Me Gay* (blog), January 2002. http://godmademegay.blogspot.com/p/introduction.html.

———. "Letter to Louise." *God Made Me Gay* (blog), January 2002. http://godmademegay.blogspot.com/p/letter-to-louise.html.

Lutz, Amy. "Who Joins the Military? A Look at Race, Class, and Immigration Status." *Journal of Political and Military Sociology* 36 (2008): 167–184.

Madhani, Aamer. "Don't Drop 'Don't Ask, Don't Tell,' Pace Says." *Chicago Tribune*, March 13, 2007. http://articles.chicagotribune.com/2007-03-13/news/0703130169_1_immoral-homosexual-acts-gay-behavior.

Marcus, Eric. *Is It a Choice?* New York: HarperCollins, 2009.

Martin, Diana. "Four Teens Attack Gay Chatham Elementary Student." *Chatham Daily News*, May 17, 2013. http://www.chathamdailynews.ca/2013/05/17/four-teens-attack-gay-elementary-student.

McCaughy, Martha. "Perverting Evolutionary Narratives of Heterosexual Masculinity or Getting Rid of the Heterosexual Bug." *GLQ* 3 (1996): 261–287.

McCormick, Cheryl M., and Sandra F. Witelson. "Functional Cerebral Asymmetry and Sexual Orientation in Men and Women." *Behavioral Neuroscience* 108, no. 3 (1994): 525–531.

McPeak, Merrill A. "Don't Ask, Don't Tell, Don't Change." *New York Times*, March 5, 2010.

M. Davis and Company, Inc., et al. "An Estimate of Housing Discrimination against Same-Sex Couples." U.S. Department of Housing and Urban Development, June 2013.

Meeker, Martin. "A Queer and Contested Medium: The Emergence of Representational Politics in the 'Golden Age' of Lesbian Paperbacks, 1955–1963." *Journal of Women's History* 17, no. 1 (2005): 165–188.

Mendelsohn, Daniel. "A Closet by Any Other Name." *New York Times*, July 4, 2012.

Mezey, Susan G. *Queers In Court: Gay Rights Law and Public Policy.* Lanham, MD: Rowman & Littlefield, 2007.

Mohler, Albert. "Is Your Baby Gay? What If You Could Know? What If You Could Do Something about It?" *AlbertMohler.com*, March 2, 2007. http://www.albertmohler.com/2007/03/02/is-your-baby-gay-what-if-you-could-know-what-if-you-could-do-something-about-it-2/.

Mooallem, Jon. "The Love That Dare Not Squawk Its Name." *New York Times Magazine*, April 4, 2010.

Mundy, Liza. "The Gay Guide to Wedded Bliss." *Atlantic*, May 22, 2013.

Munt, Sally. "Virtually Belonging: Risk, Connectivity, and Coming Out On-Line." *International Journal of Sexuality and Gender Studies* 7, nos. 2–3 (2002): 125–137.

Murdoch, Joyce. *Courting Justice.* New York: Basic Books, 2002.

Murphy, Timothy F. "A Brief History of the 'Gay Gene.'" *GeneWatch* 24, no. 6 (2011). http://www.councilforresponsiblegenetics.org/genewatch/GeneWatchPage.aspx?pageId=386.

Myerson, Harold. "God and His Gays." *Washington Post*, March 21, 2007.

Nagourney, Adam. "Gay Democrats Celebrate a Newfound Visibility." *New York Times*, September 6, 2012.

———. "Political Shifts on Gay Rights Lag behind Culture." *New York Times*, June 28, 2009.

Nagourney, Adam, and Brooks Barnes. "Evolving Donor Network in Gay Marriage Drive." *New York Times*, March 24, 2012.

Nakamura, Lisa. "After/Images of Identity: Gender, Technology and Identity Politics." In *Reload: Rethinking Women and Cyberculture*, edited by Mary Flanagan and Austin Booth, 321–331. Cambridge: MIT Press, 2002.

National Center for Lesbian Rights. "LGBTQ Youth in the Foster Care System." June 2006.

Nelson, Hilde Lindemann, ed. *Feminism and Families*. New York: Rout-ledge, 1997.

Nicolosi, Joseph. *Reparative Therapy of Male Homosexuality: A New Clinical Approach*. Lanham, MD: Jason Aronson, 1997.

"Obama Calls for 'Don't Ask, Don't Tell' Repeal." *CNN.com*, January 27, 2010. http://www.cnn.com/2010/POLITICS/01/27/obama.gays.military/index.html.

Oppenheimer, Mark. "In Shift, an Activist Enlists Same-Sex Couples in a Pro-Marriage Coalition." *New York Times*, January 29, 2013.

Ordover, Nancy. *American Eugenics: Race, Queer Anatomy, and the Science of Nationalism*. Minneapolis: University of Minnesota Press, 2003.

O'Riordan, Kate. "The Life of the Gay Gene: From Hypothetical Genetic Marker to Social Reality." *Journal of Sex Research* 49, no. 4 (2012): 362–368.

Padva, Gilad. "Edge of Seventeen: Melodramatic Coming-Out in New Queer Adolescence Films." *Communication and Critical/Cultural Studies* 1, no. 4 (2004): 355–372.

Park, Alice. "What the Gay Brain Looks Like." *Time*, June 17, 2008. http://www.time.com/time/health/article/0%2C8599%2C1815538%2C00.html.

Peters, Jeremy W. "Why the Gay Rights Movement Has No National Leader." *New York Times*, June 21, 2009.

Petrow, Stephen. "Coming Out Online." *Advocate*, October 10, 2011.

Pew Research Center. "The Decline of Marriage and Rise of New Fam-ilies." Social and Demographic Trends report. November 18, 2010. http://pewsocialtrends.org/files/2010/11/pew-social-trends-2010-families.pdf.

———. "In Gay Marriage Debate, Both Supporters and Opponents See Legal Recognition as 'Inevitable.'" Center for the People & the Press. June 6, 2013. http://www.people-press.org/files/legacy-pdf/06-06-13%20LGBT%20General%20Public%20FINAL%20Release.pdf.

PFLAG. "Frequently Asked Questions." http://community.pflag.org/page.aspx?pid=290 (accessed January 29, 2013).

Pickhardt, Jonathan E. "Choose or Lose: Embracing Theories of Choice in Gay Rights Litigation Strategies." *NYU Law Review* 73 (1998): 928–952.

Polikoff, Nancy. *Beyond (Gay and Straight) Marriage: Valuing All Families under the Law*. Boston: Beacon Press, 2009.

Pollitt, Katha. "No Presents, Please." *Nation*, July 27, 2006.

Prentice, Ron, Rosemarie Avila, and George McKinney. "Argument in Favor of Proposition 8." In *California General Election Guide*, 2008.

Public Religion Research Institute. "Majority of Americans Say They Support Same-Sex Marriage, Adoption by Gay and Lesbian Couples." May 19, 2011. http://publicreligion.org/research/2011/05/majority-of-americans-say-they-support-same-sex-marriage-adoption-by-gay-and-lesbian-couples/.

Puente, Maria. "Hollywood Now Opening Arms to Gay Characters, Families." *USA Today*, August 24, 2010.

Radicalesbians. "The Woman Identified Woman." Pittsburgh: Know, 1970. Available online at http://library.duke.edu/rubenstein/scriptorium/wlm/womid/ (accessed June 17, 2013).

Radner, Hilary. "Compulsory Sexuality and the Desiring Woman." *Sexualities* 11, nos. 1–2 (2008): 94–99.

Ramsey Colloquium. "The Homosexual Movement: A Response by the Ramsey Colloquium." In *The Columbia Reader on Lesbians and Gay Men in Media, Society, Politics*, edited by Larry Gross and James D. Woods, 141–46. New York: Columbia University Press, 1999.

"Randy Phillips, Gay U.S. Airman, on Why He Came Out on YouTube." *Huffington Post*, February 4, 2012. http://www.huffingtonpost.com/2012/02/04/randy-phillips-gay-us-airman-youtube_n_1254454.html.

Rauch, Jonathan. *Gay Marriage: Why It Is Good for Gay, Good for Straights, and Good for America*. New York: Times Books, 2004.

———. "What We Learned from an Obama Win." *Advocate*, December 2008, 27–28.

Regnerus, Mark. "How Different Are the Adult Children of Parents Who Have Same-Sex Relationships? Findings from the New Family Structures Study." *Social Science Research* 41, no. 4 (July 2012): 752–770.

"Repeal of 'Don't Ask, Don't Tell' Paves Way for Gay Sex Right on Battlefield, Opponents Fantasize." *Onion*, July 12, 2010. http://www.theonion.com/articles/repeal-of-dont-ask-dont-tell-paves-way-for-gay-sex,17698/.

Rich, Adrienne. "Compulsory Heterosexuality and Lesbian Existence." *Signs: Journal of Women in Culture and Society* 5, no. 4 (summer 1980): 631–660.

Rich, Frank. "40 Years Later, Still Second-Class Americans." *New York Times*, June 28, 2009.

———. "Gay Bashing at the Smithsonian." *New York Times*, December 12, 2010.

———. "Smoke the Bigots Out of the Closet." *New York Times*, February 6, 2010.

Rich, Frank. "Two Weddings, a Divorce and 'Glee.'" *New York Times*, June 12, 2010.

Rohy, Valerie. "On Homosexual Reproduction." *Differences* 25, no. 1 (2012): 101–130.

Rollins, Joe. "Same-Sex Unions and the Spectacles of Recognition." *Law & Society Review* 39, no. 2 (June 2005): 457–483.

Ross, Beth Ford. "House Panel Votes to Ban Gay Weddings on Military Bases." *KPBS.org*, May 10, 2012. http://www.kpbs.org/news/2012/may/10/house-panel-votes-ban-gay-weddings-military-bases/.

Ross, Michael. "Typing, Doing, and Being: Sexuality and the Internet." *Journal of Sex Research* 42, no. 4 (2005): 342–352.

Russell, Stephen T., Thomas J. Clarke, and Justin Clary. "Are Teens 'Post-Gay'? Contemporary Adolescents' Sexual Identity Labels." *Journal of Youth and Adolescence* 38 (2009): 884–890.

Russell, Thaddeus. "The Color of Discipline: Civil Rights and Black Sexuality." *American Quarterly* 60, no. 1 (2008): 101–128.

Saad, Lydia. "U.S. Acceptance of Gay/Lesbian Relations Is the New Normal." Gallup. May 14, 2012. http://www.gallup.com/poll/154634/Acceptance-Gay-Lesbian-Relations-New-Normal.aspx.

Samuels, Ellen. "My Body, My Closet: Invisible Disability and the Limites of Coming-Out Discourse." *GLQ* 9, nos. 1–2 (2003): 233–55.

Savage, Dan. "The Truth about Gay Families." *New York Times*, July 27, 2010.

Savage, Dan, and Terry Miller. Introduction to *It Gets Better: Coming Out, Overcoming Bullying, and Creating a Life Worth Living*, edited by Dan Savage and Terry Miller, 1–11. New York: Dutton, 2011.

Savan, Leslie. "Without Anti-Gay Hysteria, Massa's a Dud for the GOP." *Nation*, March 11, 2010.

Savin-Williams, Ritch. *The New Gay Teenager*. Cambridge: Harvard University Press, 2006.

Schacter, Jane S. "The Other Same-Sex Marriage Debate." *Chicago-Kent Law Review* 84 (2009): 379–402.

Schmalz, Jeffrey. "Poll Finds an Even Split on Homosexuality's Cause." *New York Times*, March 5, 1993.

Schulman, Sarah. *Ties That Bind: Familial Homophobia and Its Consequences*. New York: New Press, 2009.

Schwartz, Neena. "Genes, Hormones, and Sexuality." *Gay & Lesbian Review Worldwide*, 2008.

Scott, A. O. "Meet the Sperm Donor: Modern Family Ties." *New York Times*, July 8, 2010.

"Scott Brown Engaged in Culture Wars at Mass Poll." *Huffington Post*, March 3, 2010. http://www.huffingtonpost.com/2010/01/15/scott-brown -engaged-in-cu_n_425385.html.

Seidman, Steven. "Beyond the Closet? The Changing Social Meaning of Homosexuality in the United States." *Sexualities* 2, no. 9 (1999): 9–34.

Sender, Katherine. *Business, Not Politics: The Making of the Gay Market*. New York: Columbia University Press, 2004.

Setoodeh, Ramin. "Young, Gay and Murdered: Kids Are Coming Out Younger, but Are Schools Ready to Handle the Complex Issues of Identity and Sexuality? For Larry King, the Question Had Tragic Implications." *Newsweek*, July 28, 2008.

Sharkey, Betsy. "The Kids Are All Right." *Los Angeles Times*, July 8, 2010.

Simmel, Georg. "The Sociological Significance of the 'Stranger.'" In *Introduction to the Science of Sociology*, edited by Robert Park and Ernest Burgess, 322–327. Chicago: University of Chicago Press, 1921.

Simpson, Mark. "Bored This Way." *Mark Simpson Blog*, February 16, 2011. http://www.marksimpson.com/blog/2011/02/16/bored-this-way/.

Smith, Dinitia. "Love That Dare Not Squeak Its Name." *New York Times*, February 7, 2004.

Socarides, Richard. "A Way Forward on Gay Marriage." *Politico*, August 18, 2010.

———. "Where's Our 'Fierce Advocate'?" *Washington Post*, May 2, 2009.

Somerville, Siobhan B. "Queer Loving." *GLQ: A Journal of Lesbian and Gay Studies* 11, no. 3 (2005): 335–370.

Spade, Dean. *Normal Life: Administrative Violence, Critical Trans Politics, and the Limits of Law*. Brooklyn, NY: South End, 2009.

Stacey, Judith. *Unhitched: Love Marriage, and Family Values*. New York: NYU Press, 2011.

Stacey, Judith, and Timothy Biblarz. "How Does the Gender of Parents Matter?" *Journal of Marriage and Family Therapy* 72 (February 2010): 3–22.

———. "(How) Does the Sexual Orientation of Parents Matter?" *American Sociological Review* 66, no. 2 (April 2001): 159–183.

Stanley, Alessandra. "'New Normal' Fall Shows Feature Gay Characters or Not." *New York Times*, September 6, 2012.

Stanton, John. "Cantor Urges Tolerance on Gays, Muslims." *BuzzFeed*, July 19, 2012. http://www.buzzfeed.com/johnstanton/cantor-urges-tolerance -on-gays-muslims.

Stein, Edward. "Evidence for Queer Genes: An Interview with Richard Pillard." *GLQ* 1 (1993): 93–110.

Steinhorn, Leonard, and Barbara Diggs-Brown. *By the Color of Our Skin: The Illusion of Integration and the Reality of Race.* New York: Dutton, 1999.

Stelter, Brian. "Revelation Signals a Shift in Views of Homosexuality." *Media Decoder* (blog), *New York Times*, July 3, 2012. http://mediadecoder.blogs .nytimes.com/2012/07/02/anderson-cooper-says-the-fact-is-im-gay/.

Stevens, Dana. "The Kids Are All Right." *Slate*, July 8, 2010. http://www .slate.com/articles/arts/movies/2010/07/the_kids_are_all_right.html.

Sullivan, Andrew. *Same-Sex Marriage: Pro and Con.* New York: Vintage Books, 1997.

Talbot, Margaret. "A Risky Proposal." *New Yorker*, January 18, 2010.

———. "Wedding Bells." *New Yorker*, May 21, 2012.

Taylor, Charles. *Multiculturalism and "The Politics of Recognition."* Princeton: Princeton University Press, 1994.

Taylor, Chris. "Gay Scientists Isolate Christian Gene." CNNNN video. YouTube, May 3, 2007. http://www.youtube.com/watch?v=qCzbNkyXO5o.

Taylor, Ella. " 'The Kids Are All Right' Puts the 'Fun' in 'Dysfunction.' " *NPR.com*, July 6, 2010. http://www.npr.org/templates/story/story.php?storyId=128266739.

Taylor, Yvette. *Lesbian and Gay Parenting: Securing Social and Educational Capital.* New York: Palgrave Macmillan, 2009.

Terry, Jennifer. *An American Obsession: Science, Medicine, and Homosexuality in Modern Society.* Chicago: University of Chicago Press, 1999.

———. " 'Unnatural Acts' in Nature: The Scientific Fascination with Queer Animals." *GLQ* 6, no. 2 (2000): 151–193.

"Tracking the Money: Final Numbers." *Los Angeles Times*, February 3, 2009. http://www.latimes.com/news/local/la-moneymap,0,2198220.htmlstory.

Truth Wins Out. "The History." http://www.truthwinsout.org/the-history/ (accessed October 14, 2012).

Tucker, Joan S., Maria Orlando Edelen, Phyllis L. Ellickson, and David J. Klein. "Running Away from Home: A Longitudinal Study of Adolescent Risk Factors and Young Adult Outcomes." *Journal Youth and Adolescence* 40, no. 5 (2011): 507–518.

UC Davis Department of Psychology. "Facts about Homosexuality and Mental Health." 2012. http://psychology.ucdavis.edu/rainbow/html/facts _mental_health.html.

Ulrichs, Heinrich. *The Riddle of "Man-Manly" Love: The Pioneering Work on Male Homosexuality.* Translated by Michael A. Lombardi-Nash. Buffalo, NY: Prometheus Books, 1994.

van Gelderen, Loes, Henny M. W. Bos, Nanette Gartrell, Jo Hermanns, and Ellen C. Perrin. "Quality of Life of Adolescents Raised from Birth by Lesbian Mothers: The US National Longitudinal Family Study." *Journal of Developmental & Behavioral Pediatrics* 33, no. 1 (June 2012): 1–7.

Victory Fund. "Out Leaders: Find an Official." 2013. http://www.victory institute.org/out_officials/view_all.

Wade, Nicholas. "Pas De Deux of Sexuality Is Written in the Genes." *New York Times*, April 10, 2007.

Wahls, Zach. "Zach Wahls Speaks about Family." YouTube. February 1, 2011. http://www.youtube.com/watch?v=FSQQK2Vuf9Q.

Waldman, Paul. "We've Already Won the Battle over Gay Marriage." *American Prospect*, April 14, 2009.

Walters, Suzanna Danuta. *All the Rage: The Story of Gay Visibility in America*. Chicago: University of Chicago Press, 2001.

———. "The Few, the Proud, the Gays: Don't Ask, Don't Tell and the Trap of Tolerance." *William & Mary Journal of Women & Law* 18 (2011): 87–114.

———. "The Kids Are All Right but the Lesbians Aren't: Queer Kinship in US Culture." *Sexualities* 15, no. 8 (December 2012): 917–933.

———. "Threat Level Lavender: The Truthiness of Gay Marriage." *Chronicle of Higher Education* 53, no. 20 (January 19, 2007): B12–B14.

Warner, Michael. *Fear of a Queer Planet*. Minneapolis: University of Minnesota Press, 1993.

Weeks, Jeffrey. *The World We Have Won*. London: Routledge, 2006.

Weeks, Jeffrey, Catherine Donovan, and Brian Heaphy. *Same Sex Intimacies: Families of Choice and Other Life Experiments*. New York: Routledge, 2001.

Weston, Kath. *Families We Choose: Lesbians, Gays, Kinship*. New York: Columbia University Press, 1997.

"What Is the Most Pressing Issue Facing the LGBT Community? Vote Now! (Poll)." *HuffPost Gay Voices*, May 11, 2012. http://www.huffington post.com/2012/05/11/what-is-the-lgbt-community-pressing-issue_n_1507136.html.

Whisman, Vera. *Queer by Choice: Lesbians, Gay Men, and the Politics of Identity*. New York: Routledge, 1996.

Whitehead, Jaye Cee. *The Nuptial Deal: Same-Sex Marriage and Neo-liberal Governance*. Chicago: University of Chicago Press, 2011.

Wilcox, Sarah. "Cutural Context and the Conventions of Science Journalism: Drama and Contradiction in Media Coverage of Biological Ideas about Sexuality." *Critical Studies in Media Communication* 20, no. 3 (2003): 225–247.

Williams, Christine, Patti A. Giuffre, and Kirsten Dellinger. "The Gay-Friendly Closet." *Journal of Sexuality Research & Social Policy* 6, no. 1 (2009): 29–45.

Williams, Raymond. *Marxism and Literature*. Oxford: Oxford University Press, 1978.

Wilson, Elizabeth A. "Neurological Preference: LeVay's Study of Sexual Orientation." *SubStance* 91 (2000): 23–38.

Wilson, Glenn D., and Qazi Rahman. *Born Gay: The Psychobiology of Sex Orientation*. Chester Springs, PA: Peter Owen, 2005.

Wilson, Michael, and Al Baker. "Lured into a Trap, Then Tortured for Being Gay." *New York Times*, October 8, 2010.

Wilson, Robin. "Transsexual 'Subjects' Complain about Professor's Research Methods." *Chronicle of Higher Education* 49, no. 46 (2003): A10.

Witchel, Alex. "Life after 'Sex.'" *New York Times Magazine*, January 19, 2012.

Wolfson, Evan. *Why Marriage Matters*. New York: Simon & Schuster, 2005.

Wood, David. "Pentagon Asks for Repeal of 'DADT': Most Troops OK with Gays in Service." *Huffpost Politics Daily*, November 30, 2010. http://www.politicsdaily.com/2010/11/30/pentagon-says-troops-ok-with-dont-ask-repeal-gates-urges-qui/.

World Health Organization. "Responding to Intimate Partner Violence and Sexual Violence against Women." 2013.

Yoshino, Kenji. *Covering: The Hidden Assault on Our Civil Rights*. New York: Random House, 2007.

———. "The Pressure to Cover." *New York Times Magazine*, January 15, 2006.

Zembylas, Michalinos. "A Pedagogy of Unknowing: Witnessing Unknowability in Teaching and Learning." *Studies in Philosophy and Education* 24 (2005): 139–160.

Zhou, Jiang-Ning, Michel A. Hofman, Louis J. G. Gooren, and Dick F. Swaab. "A Sex Difference in the Human Brain and Its Relation to Transsexuality." *International Journal of Transgenderism* 1, no. 1 (July 1997): 68–70.

Žižek, Slavoj. "Tolerance as an Ideological Category." *Critical Inquiry* 34, no. 4 (2008): 660–682.

Zuk, Marlene. *Sexual Selections: What We Can and Can't Learn about Sex from Animals*. Berkeley: University of California Press, 2003.

Zukerman, Blaine. "Meredith Baxter 'I'm a Lesbian Mom.'" *People*, December 14, 2009. http://www.people.com/people/archive/article/o,20325687,00.html.

# INDEX

Apple, Inc., 178, 189
Arizona, 52, 246
Arizona (*Grey's Anatomy* character), 235
Arkansas, 246
arousal, 288n26
artificial insemination, 210–211
assimilation: acceptance, 220, 271; covering, 264; debates about, 260; gay parenting, 203; gay visibility, 8, 220; "homonormativity," 271; integration, 13–14, 16, 261; liberals, 220; politics of, 261; sameness, 158; same-sex marriage, 188; tolerance, 220, 261
assimilation blues, 270
*Avenue Q* (musical show), 118

Bachmann, Michele, 244–245
Badgett, Lee, 194
Bailey, J. Michael, 90, 99, 120–121
Baker, Jack, 199
Baldwin, Tammy, 242–243
Barash, David, 92
Barbie dolls, 103–104
Baxter, Meredith, 71
Behar, Joy, 124
Belgium, 179
Bening, Annette, 222, 223
Berkus, Nate, 123–124
Bernstein, Mary, 150–151
Besen, Wayne, 118, 123
*Beyond the Closet* (Seidman), 32
beyondmarriage.org, 187, 188
Biblarz, Tim, 230
Biden, Joe, 156
*Big Bang Theory, The* (television series), 73
biological determination, 92–93, 111
bisexuality, 38, 121
Blanchard, Ray, 90, 288n26
Blankenhorn, David, 189–190
Boies, David, 184
"born that way" argument, 81–141; abortion, 133–134; Americans' belief in, 81–85; anti-gay activism, 113, 132–133; anti-gay animus, 131; celebrities, 122–123; consequences, 130–135; contagion premise, 135, 142; critics of, 120–121; "Don't Ask, Don't Tell"

(DADT), 168; equal rights, 101–102; feminists, 131; Fischer on, Bryan, 79; gap between biological factors and biological determination, 92–93, 118; gay rights, support for, 82, 152; gender differences, essentialism notions of, 97–105; godmademegay.com, 110–111; Hamer, Dean, 89; heterosexuality, 134; historical and cross-cultural studies, 125–126; inevitable failure of, 274; internal self-loathing, combating, 118; *Lawrence v. Texas,* 140; legal/constitutional protections, 136–138; lesbian approach to, 131; LeVay, Simon, 89–90; media, 115; medicalization of sexual identity, 84–86; myths dispelled by, 121–122; naturalistic fallacy, 140–141; "nature *vs.* nurture" dichotomy, 83–84, 94; normalcy of the norm as natural law, 134; *Onion* (magazine), 129–130; pain of homophobia as evidence for, 124; political uses of, 140; progressive gays, 204; progressives, 85; Proposition 8 (California), 140; "proving," 131; religious revisionism, 109–114; reparative therapy, 113–114; reporting about, 92, 93–94, 95; risk of linking rights to scientific theory, 139; same-sex marriage, 107, 168; scientific evidence, 88–91; sexual identity, 137; sodomy laws, 107, 168; Supreme Court, 136; tolerance, 84, 117; twins, studies of, 90, 120–121; weapon against harsh family treatment, 117–118
Botwin, Nancy (*Weeds* character), 21
*Bowers v. Hardwick,* 149–150
Boy Scouts, 247
Boyd, Danah, 62
boys with Barbies, 103
*Brady Bunch, The* (television series), 211
Bragman, Howard, 227
Breedlove, Marc, 101
Brewer, Paul, 241
Brock, Wayne, 247
*Brokeback Mountain* (film), 4, 39, 225
Bronx, 6
Brookey, Robert, 132, 139

"spread" of, 135; sterilization, 95;
Williams on, Karen, 79
Honey Boo Boo (Alana Thompson), 1
*House* (television series), 81
Huckabee, Mike, 246
Hugh Grant Theory, 106
Hull, Gloria, 167
Human Genome Project, 88
Human Rights Campaign, 115, 205,
273–274
*Hunger, The* (film), 26

Ian, Janis, 23
immigration, 146, 153, 156–157, 273
Immigration and Nationality Act
(McCarran-Walter Act) (1952), 156–157
immutability. *See* "born that way"
argument
"inclusion" (the term), 14
inclusion: integration, 262; liberals, 14,
204, 261; marriage, 175; sameness as
path to, 271; same-sex marriage, 197.
*See also* gay inclusion
income disparities, 158
*Incredibly True Adventures of Two Girls in
Love, The* (film), 234
independent films, 234
integration: assimilation, 13–14, 16,
261; civil rights, 265; gay integration,
260–270; inclusion, 262; progressives,
261–262; tolerance, 12–13
Intel Corporation, 247
"internal aliens," 147–148
Internet, 49–62; anonymity, 60; artificial
insemination, 210–211; coming out
on, 49–57; coming-out stories, 57–58;
coming-out videos, 56; gay bars, 55, 59;
gay identity, 59–61; gay youth, 52–54,
59–61; information about homosexuality, 53–55; porn, 59; as respite or
"release valve," 61–62
"Internet disconnects," 61–62
interracial marriage, 195–196
invisibility: Jews, 68
IRS (Internal Revenue Service), 178–179
Isherwood, Christopher, 237
"It Gets Better" project, 253–255

Jacques, Cheryl, 244
Jakobsen, Janet, 117
Jay (*Modern Family* character), 206
Jews: anti-Jewish analogy to anti-gay
activism, 155; biological arguments,
131; forced conversion of, 162; immigration, 13; invisibility, 68, 155; job
discrimination, 159; as sperm donors,
212; as strangers, 147; "tone it down,"
264; Weimar Germany, 9; yellow stars
for, 201
Jimmy Choo shoes, 29
Joni (*Kids Are All Right* character), 222,
230
Jordan-Young, Rebecca, 83, 91, 127, 129
Jules (*Kids Are All Right* character), 222,
224, 225, 228
justice, social, 148
justice, tolerance and, 11
Justin (*Ugly Betty* character), 41

Kameny, Frank, 248–249
Katz, Jonathan Ned, 125, 126
Keith (*Six Feet Under* character), 37
Kelly, Marguerite, 95
Kerry, John, 116, 189
*Kids Are All Right, The* (film), 221–230;
*Advocate* (magazine), 295n18; "already
gay" characters, 39; ball-transfer
scene, 224; "de-gaying" gays, 225,
229; failed-lesbian romance, 223–224;
gay male porn, 223; hetero affair, 223;
heterosexual-revelation scene, 224–225;
Joni (character), 222, 230; Jules (character), 222, 224, 225, 228; Laser (character), 222, 224, 230; lesbianism, lesbians,
236; mainstream entertainment, 4; Nic
(character), 222, 224, 225, Paul (character), 222, 224, 225, 228; politics of,
223–224; reviews, 226–228; stars, 222;
story line, 222; universalist discourse of
"family," 225–229
Kim, Richard, 267–268
King, Eden, 158
King, Larry (a California youth), 47–48
King, Martin Luther, Jr., 261
Kinsey, Alfred, 106, 108, 139, 216

kinship, transformation of, 268–269
Klarman, Michael, 180, 204
Koch, David, 190
Krafft-Ebing, Richard von, 85
Kristof, Nicholas, 111–112
Kunzig, Robert, 99–100
Kurt (*Glee* character), 41, 206–207, 232–233, 255
Kushner, Tony, 143

*L Word* (television series), 37, 235
Lady Gaga, 79, 254
LaLumiere, Martin, 91–92
Lancaster, Roger, 95, 104, 119, 134
Landers, Ann, 109
Larry (Quaker teacher), 26
Laser (*Kids Are All Right* character), 222, 224, 230
Latin America, 125
Lawrence, John, 149
*Lawrence v. Texas*: amicus briefs, 260; anti-sodomy laws, 140; "born that way" argument, 140; gay rights, 149–150; Obama, Barack, 160; post-decision era, 153; public attitudes toward homosexuals, 241
lesbianism, lesbians: "born that way" argument, 131; children raised in lesbian households, 269, 295n32; as a choice, 87; Employment Non-Discrimination Act (ENDA), 196; environmental influences, 94; failed-lesbian romance, 223–224; gay male porn, 127, 228; *Kids Are All Right, The* (film), 236; media, contemporary, 230–231; names of lesbians in films and television programs, 295n17; physical characteristics of lesbians, 91; "political lesbianism," 87–88
LeVay, Simon: "born that way" argument, 89–90, 91; equating male (female) homosexuality with femininity (masculinity), 94; gay rights litigation, 136; gender stereotypes, 97; sample size, 120; use of categories "heterosexual" and "homosexual," 120
liberal citizenship, 151
liberal cultural analysts, 193

liberal societies, 8
liberals: assimilation, 220; being "too out," 78; egalitarianism, 257; gender equality, 270; inclusion, 14, 204, 261; same-sex marriage, 182–184, 194, 205, 249–250; tolerance, 182; universalism, 229
Liddy, G. Gordon, 210
"Linkage between DNA Markers on the X Chromosome and Male Sexual Orientation" (Hamer), 89
Logo cable network, 58, 115
Long Island, New York, 44–45
Love, Heather, 274
*Loving v. Virginia,* 195–196
Lowe, Bruce, 110–111
Lynch, Jane, 207

macaques, 105
*Mad Men* (television series), 38
Maddow, Rachel, 4
Maine, 191, 242, 296n4
"Make It Better" campaign, 255
*Making Love* (film), 39
Marcus, Eric, 119–120, 257
Mark (*Grey's Anatomy* character), 235
Marmor, Judd, 136
marriage, 192–200; changes to, 192–194; Christian Right, 203; citizenship, 153, 154, 196; contradictions about, 194; crisis in, 193; Europe, 199–200, 203; family love, as marker of, 269; as a "fundamental right," 202; gay rights, 2; inclusion, 175; liberal cultural analysts, 193; pull of as a meta-institution, 199–200; rate of, 180–181; as a right, 201, 203, 205; same-sex marriage's effects on, 180–181, 194–195; social-welfare provisions, 203; as timeless, 194. *See also* same-sex marriage
*Marriage, a History* (Coontz), 192–193
"marriage equality" (the term), 205
marriage equality, 190–192, 194
Martin, Ricky, 71, 75, 207
Martinez, Oscar (*The Office* character), 39–40
Maryland, 7

race: coming out, 31–32; "Don't Ask, Don't Tell" (DADT), 161–167, 169; interracial marriage, 195–196; visibility of, 68

racism, 9

*Radical Future of Liberal Feminism, The* (Eisenstein), 204

Rahman, Qazi, 95

Ramsey Colloquium, 133

Rauch, Jonathan, 190, 192, 194, 197, 250

Raven-Symoné, 50

Ravi, Dharun, 284n15

Regnerus, Mark, 206, 208

*Regulating Aversion* (Brown), 11

religious conservatives, 111–113, 119

religious progressives, 113

religious revisionism, 109–114

*Rent* (musical show), 256

reparative therapy, 82–83, 113–114, 122–124

*Reparative Therapy of Male Homosexuality* (Nicolosi), 113–114

reproductive rights, 194, 199

reproductive success, 95–96

Republican Party: 2004 elections, 179; 2012 platform, 258, 272; anti-gay activism, 218, 258, 272; gay rights, 250; same-sex marriage, 179, 186, 189; Singer, Paul, 190; tolerance, 272

respect, tolerance and, 12

Rich, Adrienne, 87–88

Rich, Frank, 250–251, 252

Richardson, Bill, 115–116

Rohy, Valerie, 139, 142

Rollins, Joe, 201–202

*Romer v. Evans,* 150

Romney, Mitt, 189, 190

Rosbash, Michael, 140

Ruffalo, Mark, 222

Russell, Thaddeus, 26 4

sameness to heterosexuals: assimilation, 158; being respected for, 147; diversity within sameness, 262–263; gay claims to, 259, 270; inevitable failure of, 274; political stance of, 271; same-sex marriage, 184, 196; tolerance, 66, 172, 271

sameness to one's own sex, 114

same-sex marriage, 173–205; African Americans, 184; assimilation, 188; bans on, 246; "born that way" argument, 107, 168; celebrities, 184; children, 198; Christian Right, 182–183; civic inclusion, 197; civil rights, 174, 190, 195, 196, 202; crisis in marriage, 193; Democratic Party, 257–258; family values, traditional, 196; focus on, 196; gay rights movement's, 181–182, 183, 186–189, 201–205, 294n44; funding for, 188; gay critics of, 203–204; gay inclusion, 153; gay rights, 181, 190, 203; gender, 198–199; gender equality, 196–197; homophobia, 201; interracial marriage, analogies to, 196; legalization, support for, 242, 296n4; liberals, 182–184, 194, 205, 249–250; marriage, effect on, 180–181, 194–195; media, mainstream, 182; miscegenation laws, analogies to, 182; name changes, 200–201; Obama, Barack, 245; opponents, 178–179; progressives, 197–198; public announcement of love, 177; repeal of, 296n4; reproductive rights, 199; Republican Party, 179, 186, 189; sameness to heterosexuals, 184, 196; sexual and gender liberation, 187; as suburban humdrum, 185; support for, 177–182, 189–190, 193, 197–198, 203, 249; Supreme Court, 5, 153, 173–174; taxes, 179; tolerance, 182, 201, 203; as tolerance trap, 177, 204; "trickle down" effect of legalizing, 204; West Coast, 183–184; workplace issues, 199

*Same-Sex Marriage* (Sullivan), 192

Santana (*Glee* character), 233

Santorum, Kate, 199

Santorum, Rick, 199, 245

Saunders, Dave, 251–252

Savage, Dan, 227–228, 254, 255

Savan, Leslie, 250

Savin-Williams, Ritch, 42, 43–44

Sayles, John, 65

Scalia, Antonin, 174

*Scandal* (television series), 207

Schulman, Sarah, 217
Schwartz, Neena, 131
Schwarzenegger, Arnold, 191
science: "born that way" argument, 88–91;
    conservative scientists, 83–84; gap
    between biological factors and biological
    determination, 92–93, 118; politics,
    139–140; progressive scientists, 138;
    sexology, 86; sexuality, 85–86, 285n18
*Science* (journal), 89
Scientific Humanitarian Committee, 85
Scott, A. O., 226
Scott, Michael (*The Office* character), 39–40
Scott, Patricia, 167
Seidman, Steven, 32, 65–66, 70, 75
Seinfeld, Jerry, 260
"self-policing," 154, 264
Seto, M. C., 288n26
Setoodah, Ramin, 47–48
sexology, 86
sexual behavior, 137–138
sexual freedom as a won battle, 233
sexual identity, 32–34, 84–86, 157–159;
    aging, 127–128; anti-gay activists, 113;
    "born that way" argument, 137; brain
    organization research, 129; compared
    to hair, 124; development of, 33–34;
    disclosure of, 57; employment discrim-
    ination, 157–159; evolutionary social
    constructivism, 96; geography, 125;
    God's love, 112; historical and cross-
    cultural studies, 125–126; homosexu-
    ality and heterosexuality as categories
    of, 125; medical records of post-mortem
    individuals, 120; medicalization of,
    84–86; passing, 32–33; penal arousal,
    90; Savin-Williams, Ritch, 42; secular
    progressives, 113; self-understandings
    of, 137; sexual behavior, 138; stories of,
    128. *See also* gay identity
"sexual orientation" (the term), 115
sexual orientation, biological explanations
    of, 84
"sexual preference" (the term), 115
*Sexual Selections* (Zuk), 106, 287n24
sexuality: arousal, 288n26; biological
    discourse about, 83; gay sexuality as

a "medical mystery," 103–104; het-
    erosexuality as the standard, 14; male
    profligacy, 98; ownership of one's own,
    119; predetermined (*see* "born that way"
    argument); religious progressives, 113;
    science, 85–86, 285n18. *See also* gayness;
    heterosexuality; homosexuality
sheep, 105, 108
Shelley, Martha, 237
Shepard, Matthew, 241
Simmel, Georg, 147–148
Simpson, Mark, 140
"Sing If You're Glad to Be Gay" (song), 23
Singer, Paul, 189, 190, 205
*Sissy Boy Syndrome, The* (Green), 136
*Six Feet Under* (television series), 37
Smith, Barbara, 167
Socarides, Richard, 245–246
social activism, 66
social constructionists, 95–96
social justice, 148
social recognition, 12, 15
sociobiology, 95
sodomy laws, 107, 150, 168. See also
    *Lawrence v. Texas*
Solomon, Marc, 185
Somerville, Siobhan, 166
South Africa, 179
South Asia, 125
*South Park* (television series), 17
Southern Policy Law Center, 12
Spade, Dean, 271
Spain, 179
Spedale, Darren R., 199
sperm banks, 210–212
Stacey, Judith, 187, 216, 230, 269
Stanley, Alessandra, 274
Starbucks, 178, 189
status/conduct distinction, 167–172,
    291n36
Stein, Ed, 120–121, 139
Steinem, Gloria, 176
*Stella Dallas* (film), 209
Stevens, Robert, 190
Stewart, Jon, 7, 161
Stonewall Riots: as archaic, 7; coming out,
    252; gay bars, 55; Obama, Barack, 3–4,

257; post-Stonewall America, 30–31, 55, 70, 87; pre-Stonewall America, 29, 55, 147

"strangers," 147–148

suicide: biological determination, 111; gay youth, 7, 48, 244, 284n15; homophobia, 111

Sullivan, Andrew: coming-out story, 50; Cooper, Anderson, 72; marriage-as-citizenship, 196; same-sex marriage, 194; *Same-Sex Marriage*, 192

Supreme Court: American Academy of Pediatrics report, 191; "born that way" argument, 136; Defense of Marriage Act (DOMA), 7, 153, 189; interracial marriage, 195–196; Kameny petition to, 248–249; Proposition 8 (California), 174, 184–185, 198; same-sex marriage, 5, 153, 173–174

Swaab, Dick F., 94

Talbot, Margaret, 180, 184–185

Tavistock Clinic for Psychotherapy, 20

Taylor, Charles, 273

*Tea and Sympathy* (film), 30

Teaching Tolerance, 12

Teddy (*90210* character), 232

Terry, Jennifer, 87, 130

Thailand, 125

"third sex" theory, 85

*Ties That Bind* (Schulman), 217

*Time* (magazine), 177–178

tolerance, 10–15, 260–274; acceptance, 3, 10, 12, 151; alternatives to, 260–261, 264–265; as an end, 10; as an endpoint, 262; anti-gay activism, 256, 265; anti-gay animus, 265, 272; assimilation, 220, 261, avoidance and disgust, 2; bigotry, 10; "born that way" argument, 84, 117; civil rights, 247–248; coming out, 28; conservatives, 12; covering, 264; Declaration of Principles on Tolerance (UNESCO), 12; definitions, 1–2; "de-gaying" gays, 229; as domination, 266; duplicity, 269–270; equal rights, 274; forbearance, 11–12, 262; freedom, 16, 273; gay inclusion, 8, 273;

gay rights, as a path to, 2, 12–15, 256; gay youth, 49; for gays dying, 160; gender differences, 259–260; gender essentialism, 102; homophobia, 28; homosexuality, "gay-positive" version of, 3; homosexuality, naturalization or biologization of, 11; inevitable failure of, 274; integration, 12–13; justice, 11; liberal societies, 8; liberals, 182; limits to, 10–11, 12, 67; within the military, 162; multiculturalism, 11; pockets of, 272; progressive revolutions, aftereffect of failed, 11; radical homosexuals, 237; reparative therapy, 123; Republican Party, 272; respect, 12; sameness to heterosexuals as underlying feature, 66, 172, 271; same-sex marriage, 177, 182, 201, 203; social recognition, 12; "tone it down," 264; transience of, 12

tolerance trap: anti-gay animus unaddressed, 189; being open to charges of being intolerant of others, 246; being trapped in a different closet, 78; diversity within sameness, 262–263; early gay rights manifestos, 271; fallacy of familiarity, 218–219, 252–253; gay youth in Boy Scouts, 247; gays being stripped of their vivacious difference, 271; heterosexuality accepted as the standard, 14; history dethroned by myth, 11; inevitability of setbacks on road to gay inclusion, 251; keeping liberal societies from becoming more liberal, 8; legitimacy of gayness being dependent on acceptance by heterosexuals, 248; mainstream heterosexual culture, 260; marriage rights as pinnacle of gay liberation, 201, 203, 205; measuring gays by their similarity to heterosexuals, 218–219; post-gay discourse, 43; promotion of, 260; resistance to covering, 264; same-sex marriage as a, 177, 204; social justice, equal rights framed as "gifts," 148; universality, reliance on, 229; at work, 189

tomboyishness, 103

"tone it down," 264

# ABOUT THE AUTHOR

Suzanna Danuta Walters is Professor of Sociology and Director of the Women's, Gender, and Sexuality Studies program at Northeastern University. She is the author of several books, including *All the Rage: The Story of Gay Visibility in America* and *Material Girls: Making Sense of Feminist Cultural Theory*, and coeditor of the book series "Intersections: Transdisciplinary Perspectives on Genders and Sexualities" for NYU Press.

# INTERSECTIONS

*Transdisciplinary Perspectives on Genders and Sexualities*

General Editors: Michael Kimmel and Suzanna Walters

Printed and bound by CPI Group (UK) Ltd, Croydon, CR0 4YY

09/06/2025

14685815-0001